尾田栄一郎

Brown is the warm color of Mother Earth. But I don't think it would be a good color for toilet paper. Right? 'Cause you wouldn't be able to see stuff, y'know? But enough of this disgusting subject! Stop talking about it, okay?!
All right, get ready... Vol. 19 of *One Piece* is about to begin!!

-Eiichiro Oda, 2001

Eiichiro Oda began his manga career at the age of 17, when his one-shot cowboy manga **Wanted!** won second place in the coveted Tezuka manga awards. Oda went on to work as an assistant to some of the biggest manga artists in the industry, including Nobuhiro Watsuki, before winning the Hop Step Award for new artists. His pirate adventure **One Piece**, which debuted in **Weekly Shonen Jump** in 1997, quickly became one of the most popular manga in Japan.

# ONE PIECE VOL. 19
# BAROQUE WORKS PART 8

## SHONEN JUMP Manga Edition

This graphic novel contains material that was originally published in English in
**SHONEN JUMP** #66–69. Artwork in the magazine may have been
slightly altered from that presented here.

## STORY AND ART BY EIICHIRO ODA

English Adaptation/Lance Caselman
Translation/JN Productions
Touch-up Art & Lettering/Vanessa Satone
Additional Touch-up/Rachel Lightfoot
Design/Sean Lee
Editor/ Yuki Murashige

ONE PIECE © 1997 by Eiichiro Oda. All rights reserved.
First published in Japan in 1997 by SHUEISHA Inc., Tokyo.
English translation rights arranged by SHUEISHA Inc.

The rights of the author(s) of the work(s) in this publication to be so
identified have been asserted in accordance with the Copyright, Designs
and Patents Act 1988. A CIP catalogue record for this book is available
from the British Library.

Printed in the U.S.A.

Published by VIZ Media, LLC
P.O. Box 77010
San Francisco, CA 94107

10 9 8 7 6 5 4
First printing, October 2008
Fourth printing, June 2011

www.viz.com

# •BAROQUE WORKS•

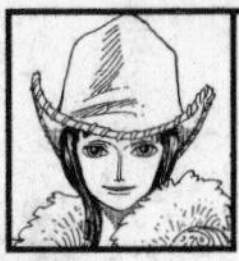

**Ms. All Sunday**

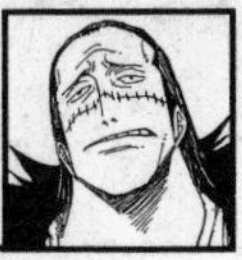

**Mr. Zero**
(Sir Crocodile)

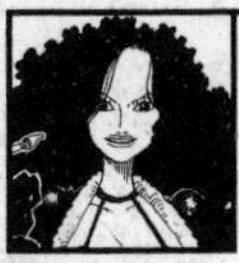

**Ms. Doublefinger**

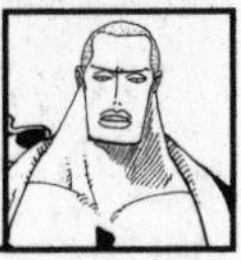

**Mr. 1**

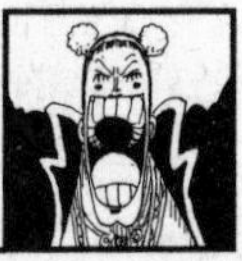

**Mr. 2 Bon Clay**

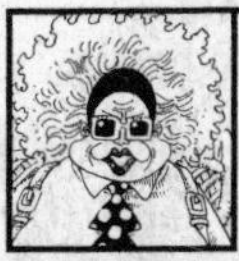

**Ms. Merry Christmas**

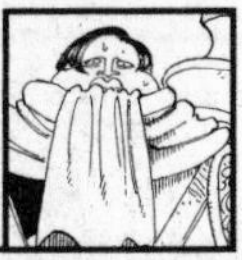

**Mr. 4**

Monkey D. Luffy started out as just a kid with a dream—and that dream was to become the greatest pirate in history! Stirred by the tales of pirate "Red-Haired" Shanks, Luffy vowed to become a pirate himself. That was before the enchanted Devil Fruit gave Luffy the power to stretch like rubber, at the cost of being unable to swim—a serious handicap for an aspiring sea dog. Undeterred, Luffy set out to sea and recruited some crewmates: master swordsman Zolo, treasure-hunting thief Nami, lying sharpshooter Usopp, the high-kicking chef Sanji, and the latest addition Chopper—the walkin' talkin' reindeer doctor.

In the beleaguered Kingdom of Alabasta on the Grand Line, Luffy and crew struggle to help Princess Vivi save her country, a drought-ravaged land descending into civil war. Hoping to prevent a wholesale slaughter, they head for the rebel stronghold of Yuba, and along the way pass the ruins of Erumalu, a once thriving city destroyed by drought. At Yuba they find a sandstorm-blasted, waterless ghost town inhabited only by Toh-Toh, father of the rebel leader Koza, Vivi's childhood friend. Angered by what they have seen, Luffy resolves to find the man responsible for all the misery, Sir Crocodile, and kick his butt. But even as they set out to find him, the forces of Baroque Works prepare to launch their final offensive—which could mean the total destruction of Alabasta!

BAROQUE WORKS

# ONE PIECE

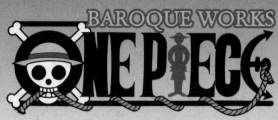

## Vol. 19

## Rebellion

## CONTENTS

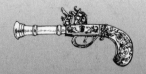

# Chapter 167:
# BATTLEFRONT

TEXT ON FAN: OBJECTION

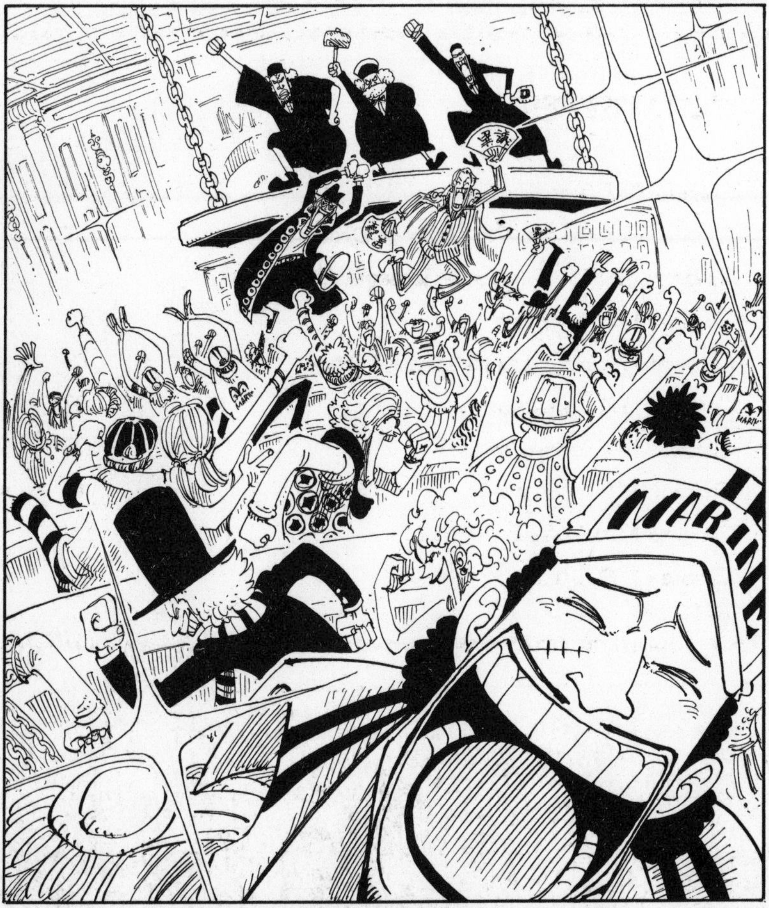

DJANGO'S DANCE PARADISE, VOL. 32:
"COURTROOM BOOGIE!!"

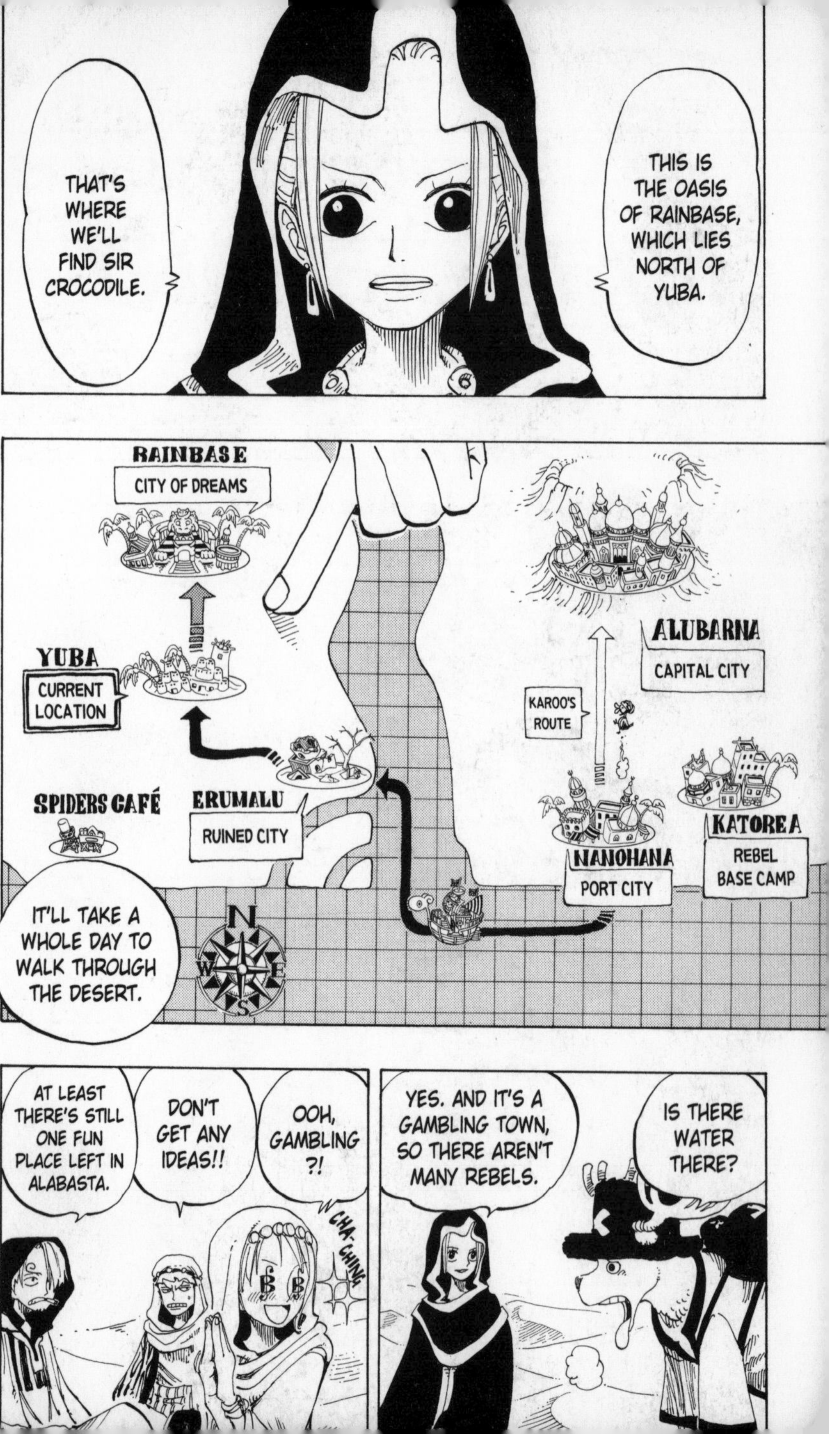
THIS IS THE OASIS OF RAINBASE, WHICH LIES NORTH OF YUBA.
THAT'S WHERE WE'LL FIND SIR CROCODILE.
RAINBASE
CITY OF DREAMS
ALUBARNA
CAPITAL CITY
KAROO'S ROUTE
YUBA
CURRENT LOCATION
KATOREA
REBEL BASE CAMP
NANOHANA
PORT CITY
ERUMALU
RUINED CITY
SPIDERS CAFÉ
IT'LL TAKE A WHOLE DAY TO WALK THROUGH THE DESERT.
N
W
E
S
IS THERE WATER THERE?
YES. AND IT'S A GAMBLING TOWN, SO THERE AREN'T MANY REBELS.
OOH, GAMBLING ?!
CHA-CHING
DON'T GET ANY IDEAS!!
AT LEAST THERE'S STILL ONE FUN PLACE LEFT IN ALABASTA.

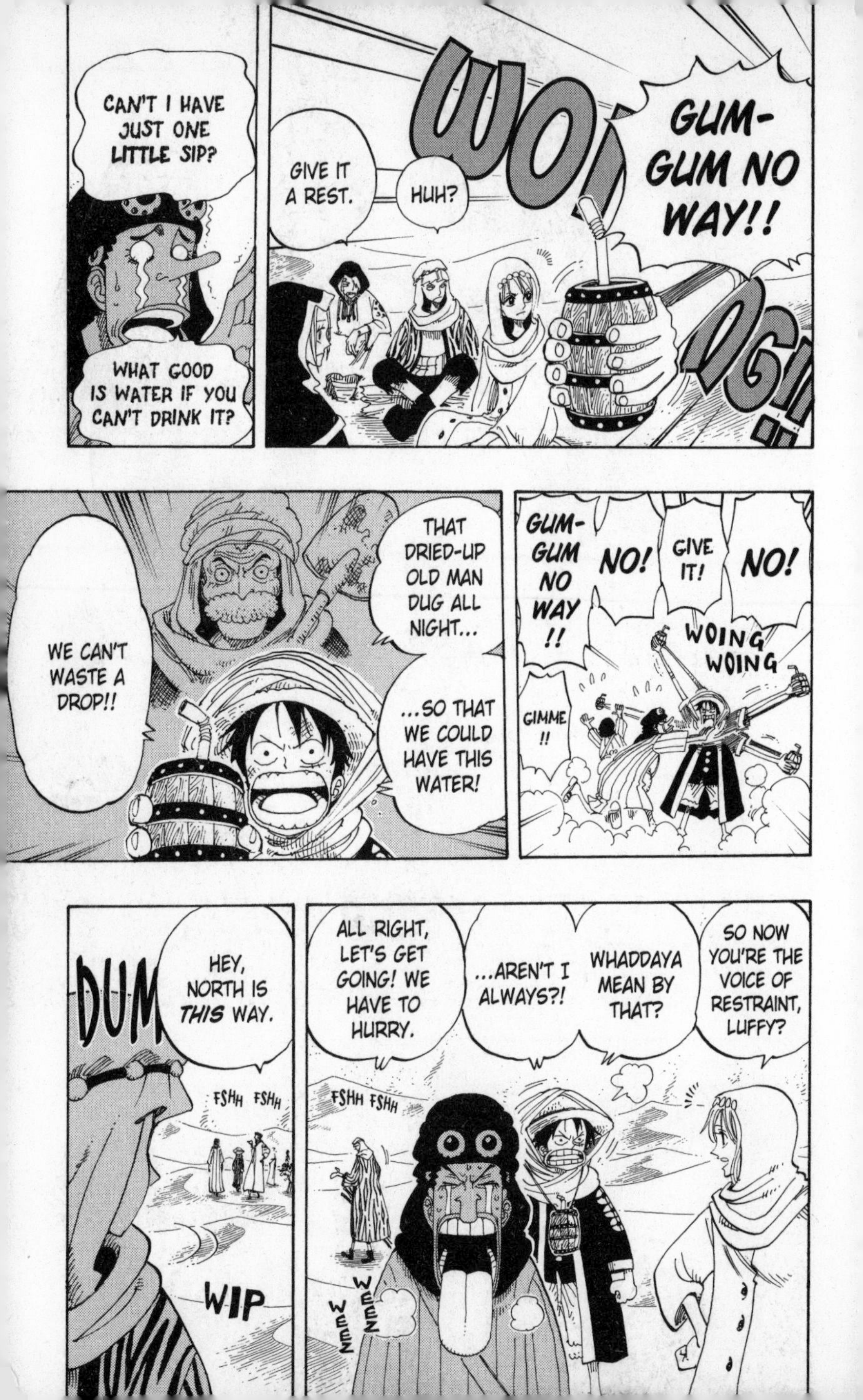
GUM-GUM NO WAY!!
HUH?
GIVE IT A REST.
CAN'T I HAVE JUST ONE LITTLE SIP?
WHAT GOOD IS WATER IF YOU CAN'T DRINK IT?
NO!
GIVE IT!
NO!
GUM-GUM NO WAY!!
WOING WOING
GIMME!!
THAT DRIED-UP OLD MAN DUG ALL NIGHT...
...SO THAT WE COULD HAVE THIS WATER!
WE CAN'T WASTE A DROP!!
SO NOW YOU'RE THE VOICE OF RESTRAINT, LUFFY?
WHADDAYA MEAN BY THAT?
...AREN'T I ALWAYS?!
ALL RIGHT, LET'S GET GOING! WE HAVE TO HURRY.
FSHH FSHH
WEEN WEEN
HEY, NORTH IS *THIS* WAY.
DUM
FSHH FSHH
WIP

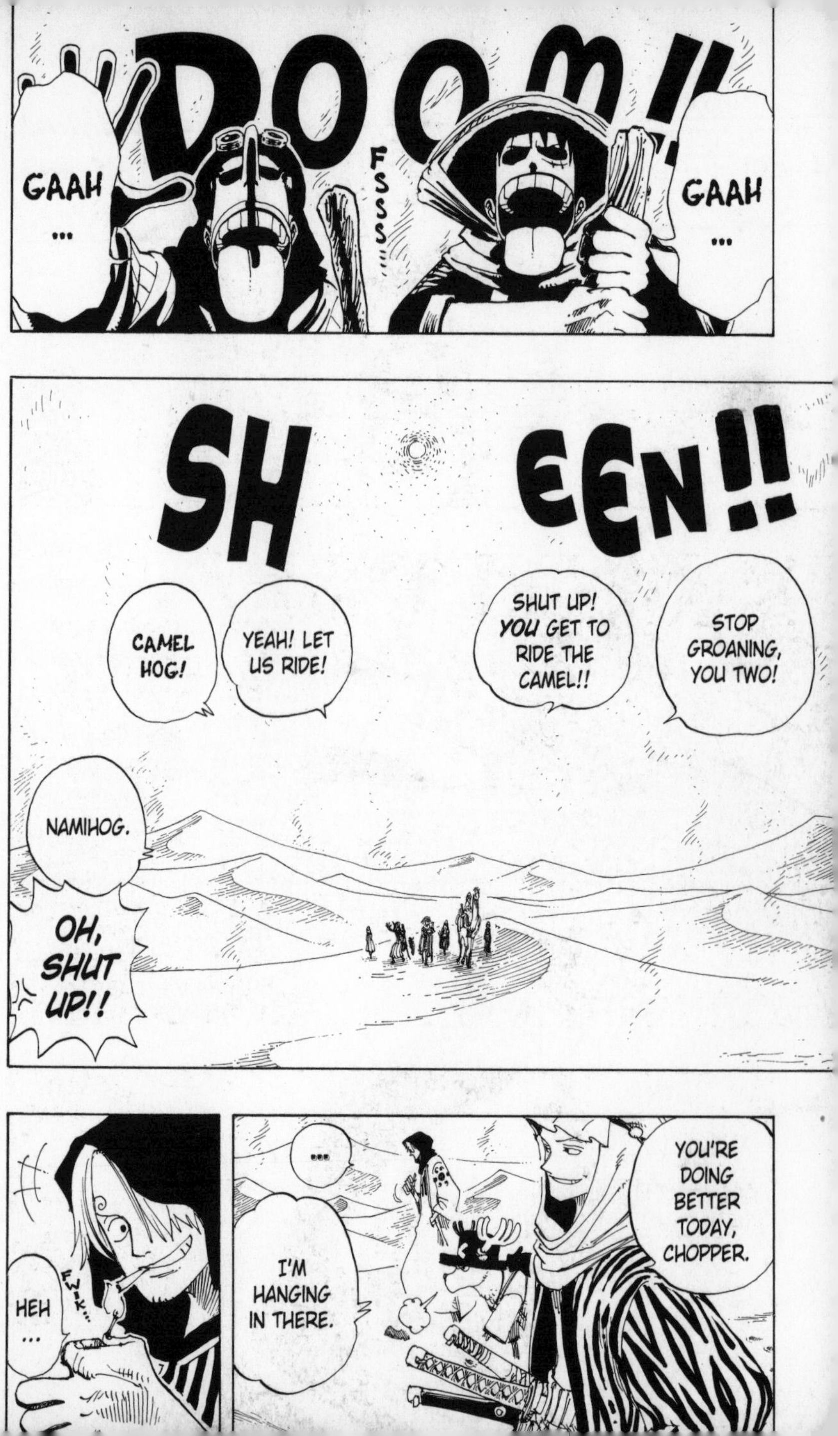
DOOM!!
GAAH ...
FSSS...
GAAH ...
SH EEN!!
STOP GROANING, YOU TWO!
SHUT UP! YOU GET TO RIDE THE CAMEL!!
YEAH! LET US RIDE!
CAMEL HOG!
NAMIHOG.
OH, SHUT UP!!
YOU'RE DOING BETTER TODAY, CHOPPER.
...
I'M HANGING IN THERE.
FWIK...
HEH ...

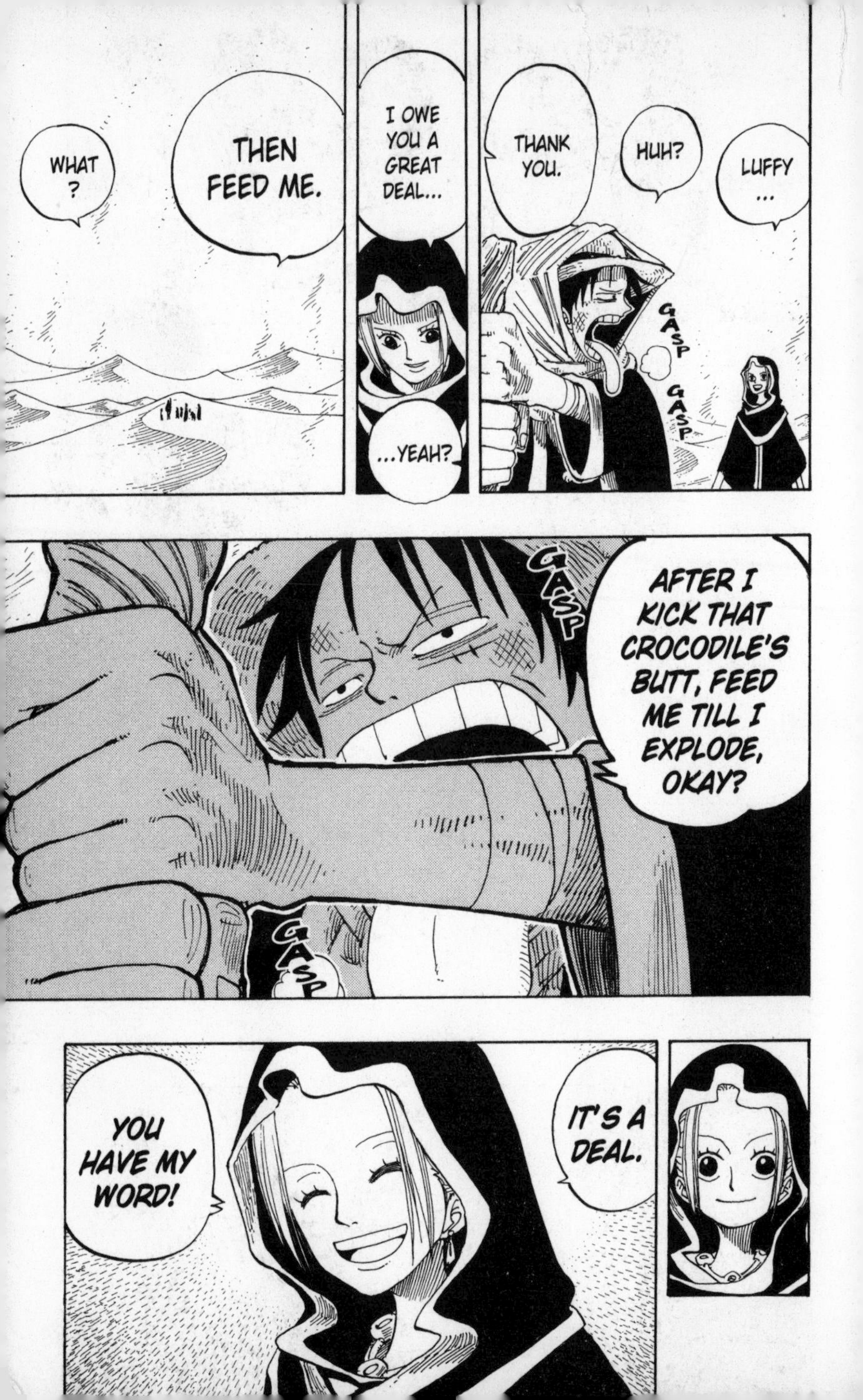
LUFFY ...
HUH?
THANK YOU.
GASP
GASP
I OWE YOU A GREAT DEAL...
...YEAH?
THEN FEED ME.
WHAT ?
GASP
AFTER I KICK THAT CROCODILE'S BUTT, FEED ME TILL I EXPLODE, OKAY?
GASP
IT'S A DEAL.
YOU HAVE MY WORD!

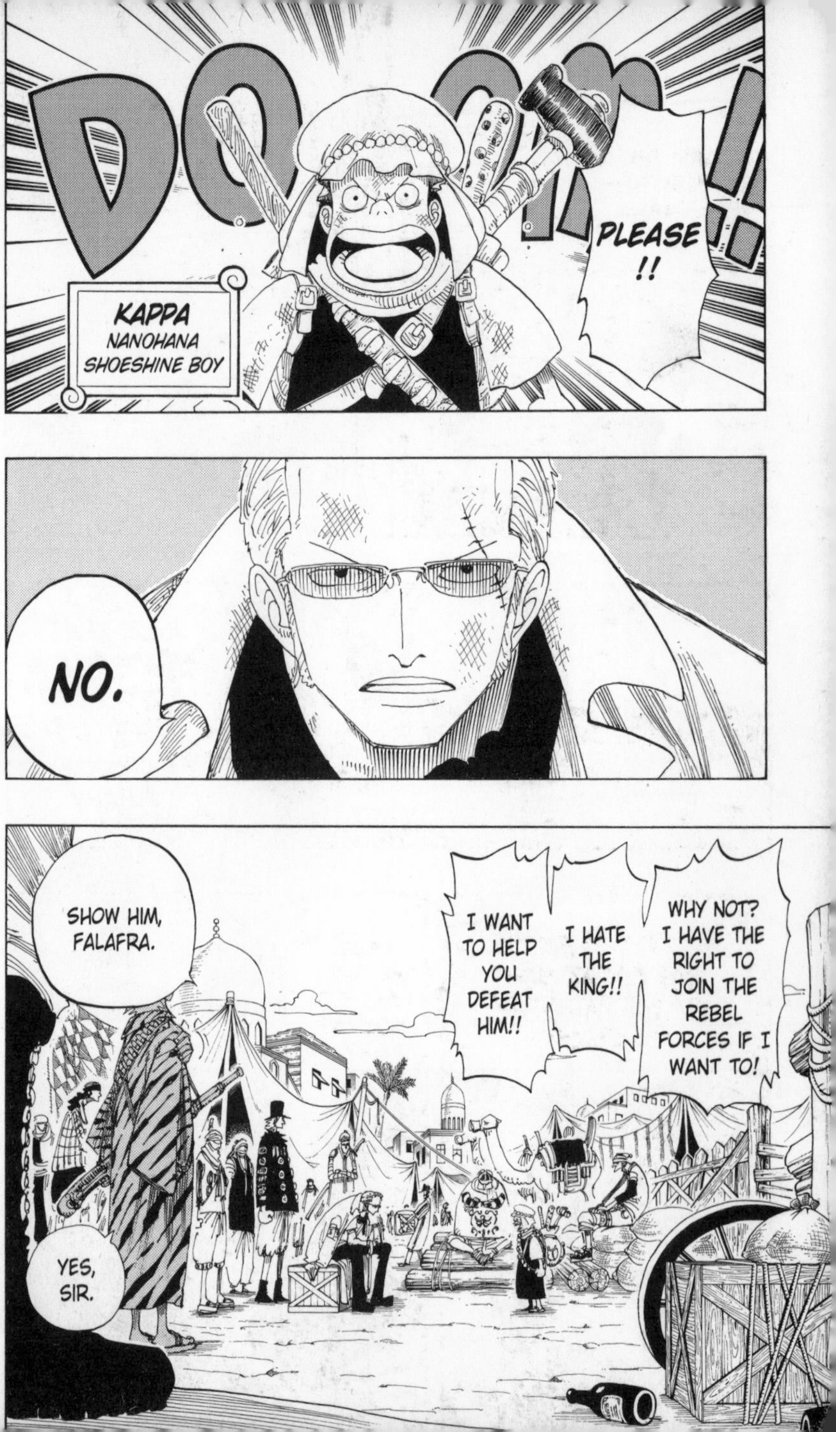
DO
PLEASE!!
KAPPA
NANOHANA SHOESHINE BOY
NO.
WHY NOT? I HAVE THE RIGHT TO JOIN THE REBEL FORCES IF I WANT TO!
I HATE THE KING!!
I WANT TO HELP YOU DEFEAT HIM!!
SHOW HIM, FALAFRA.
YES, SIR.

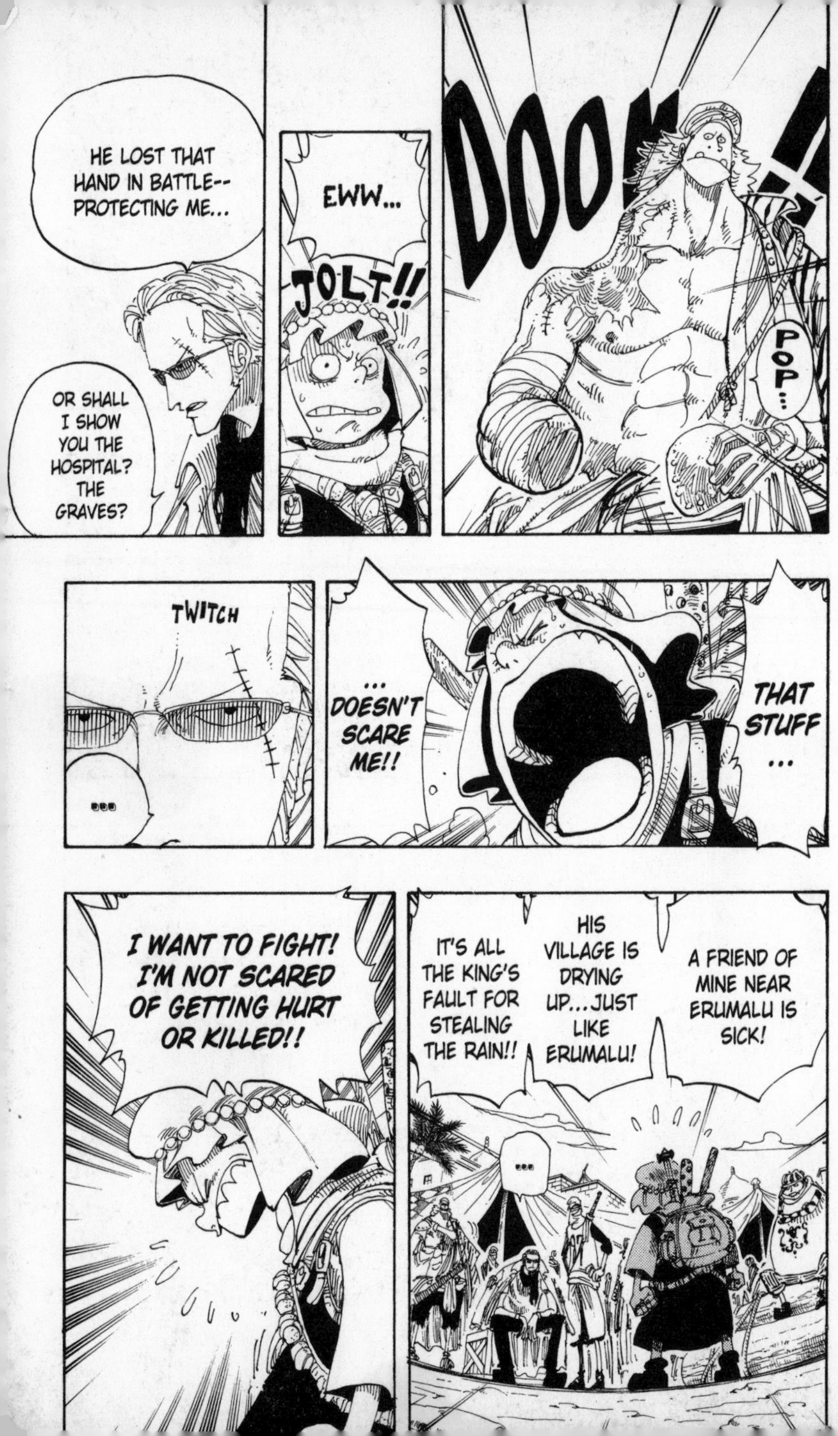
DOOM
POP...
EWW...
JOLT!!
HE LOST THAT HAND IN BATTLE--PROTECTING ME...
OR SHALL I SHOW YOU THE HOSPITAL? THE GRAVES?
THAT STUFF...
...DOESN'T SCARE ME!!
TWITCH
...
A FRIEND OF MINE NEAR ERUMALU IS SICK!
HIS VILLAGE IS DRYING UP...JUST LIKE ERUMALU!
IT'S ALL THE KING'S FAULT FOR STEALING THE RAIN!!
...
I WANT TO FIGHT! I'M NOT SCARED OF GETTING HURT OR KILLED!!

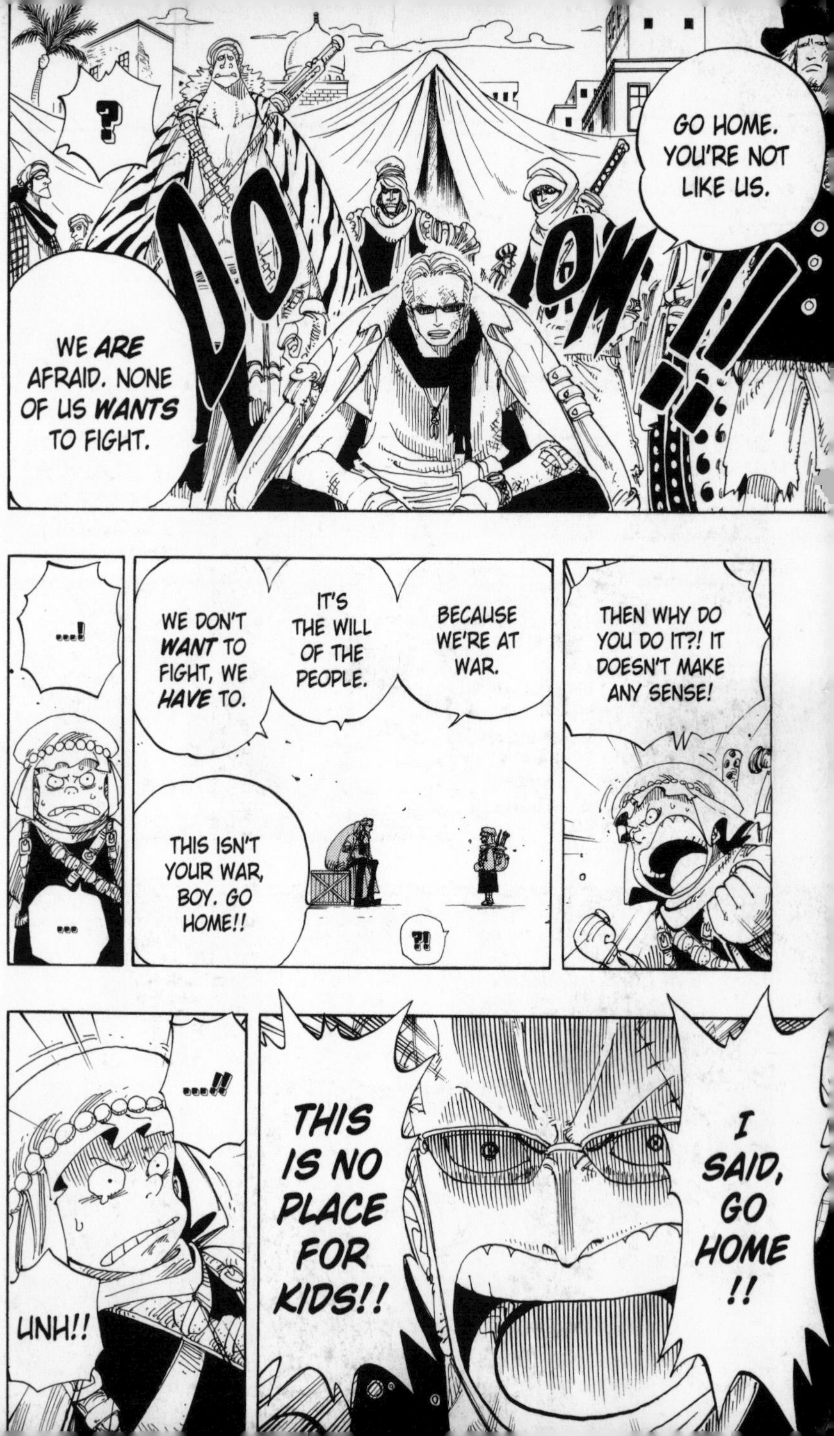
GO HOME. YOU'RE NOT LIKE US.
?
DOOM!!
WE ARE AFRAID. NONE OF US WANTS TO FIGHT.
THEN WHY DO YOU DO IT?! IT DOESN'T MAKE ANY SENSE!
BECAUSE WE'RE AT WAR.
IT'S THE WILL OF THE PEOPLE.
WE DON'T WANT TO FIGHT, WE HAVE TO.
?!
THIS ISN'T YOUR WAR, BOY. GO HOME!!
...!
...
I SAID, GO HOME!!
THIS IS NO PLACE FOR KIDS!!
...!!
UNH!!

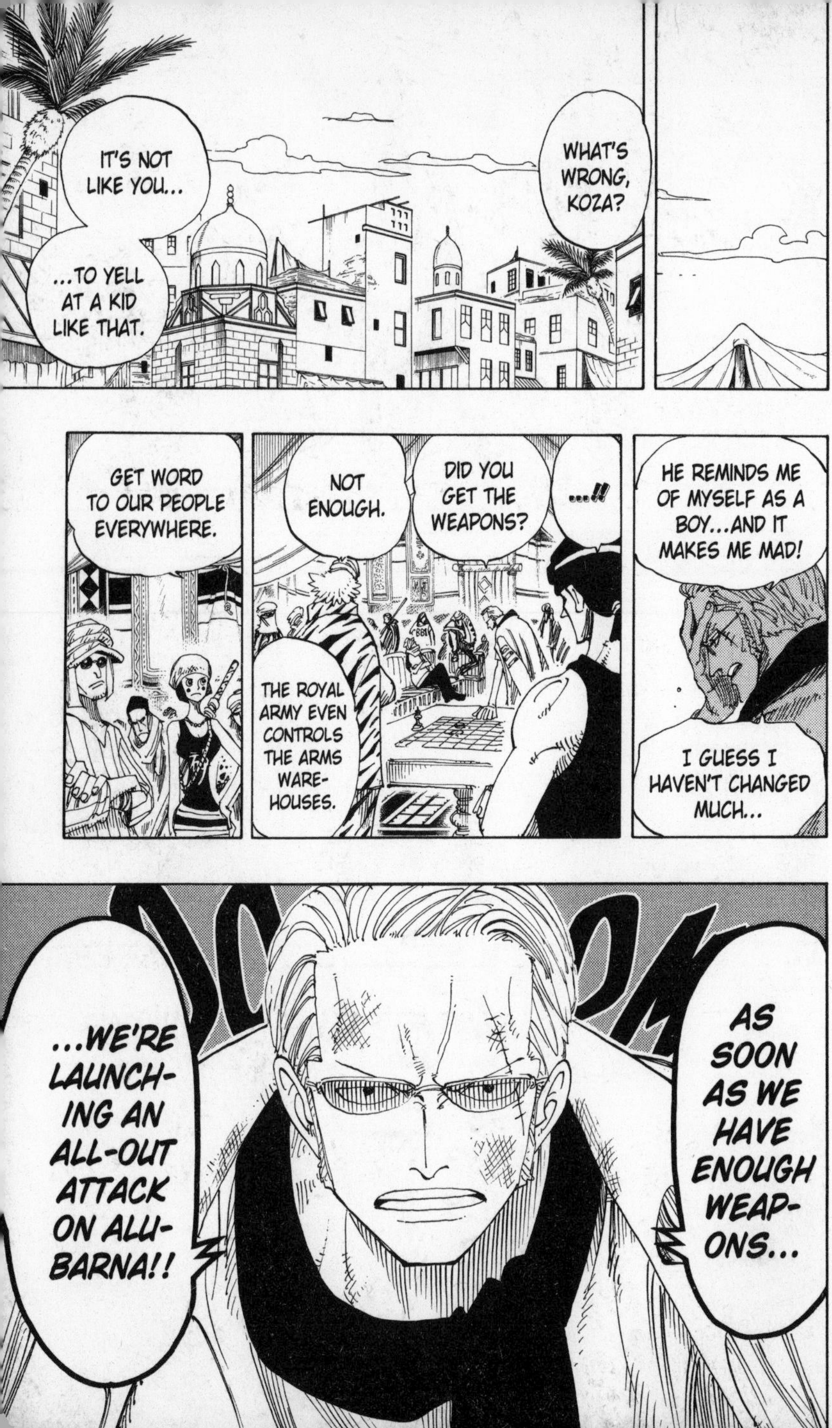
WHAT'S WRONG, KOZA?
IT'S NOT LIKE YOU...
...TO YELL AT A KID LIKE THAT.
HE REMINDS ME OF MYSELF AS A BOY...AND IT MAKES ME MAD!
I GUESS I HAVEN'T CHANGED MUCH...
...!!
DID YOU GET THE WEAPONS?
NOT ENOUGH.
THE ROYAL ARMY EVEN CONTROLS THE ARMS WAREHOUSES.
GET WORD TO OUR PEOPLE EVERYWHERE.
AS SOON AS WE HAVE ENOUGH WEAPONS...
...WE'RE LAUNCHING AN ALL-OUT ATTACK ON ALUBARNA!!

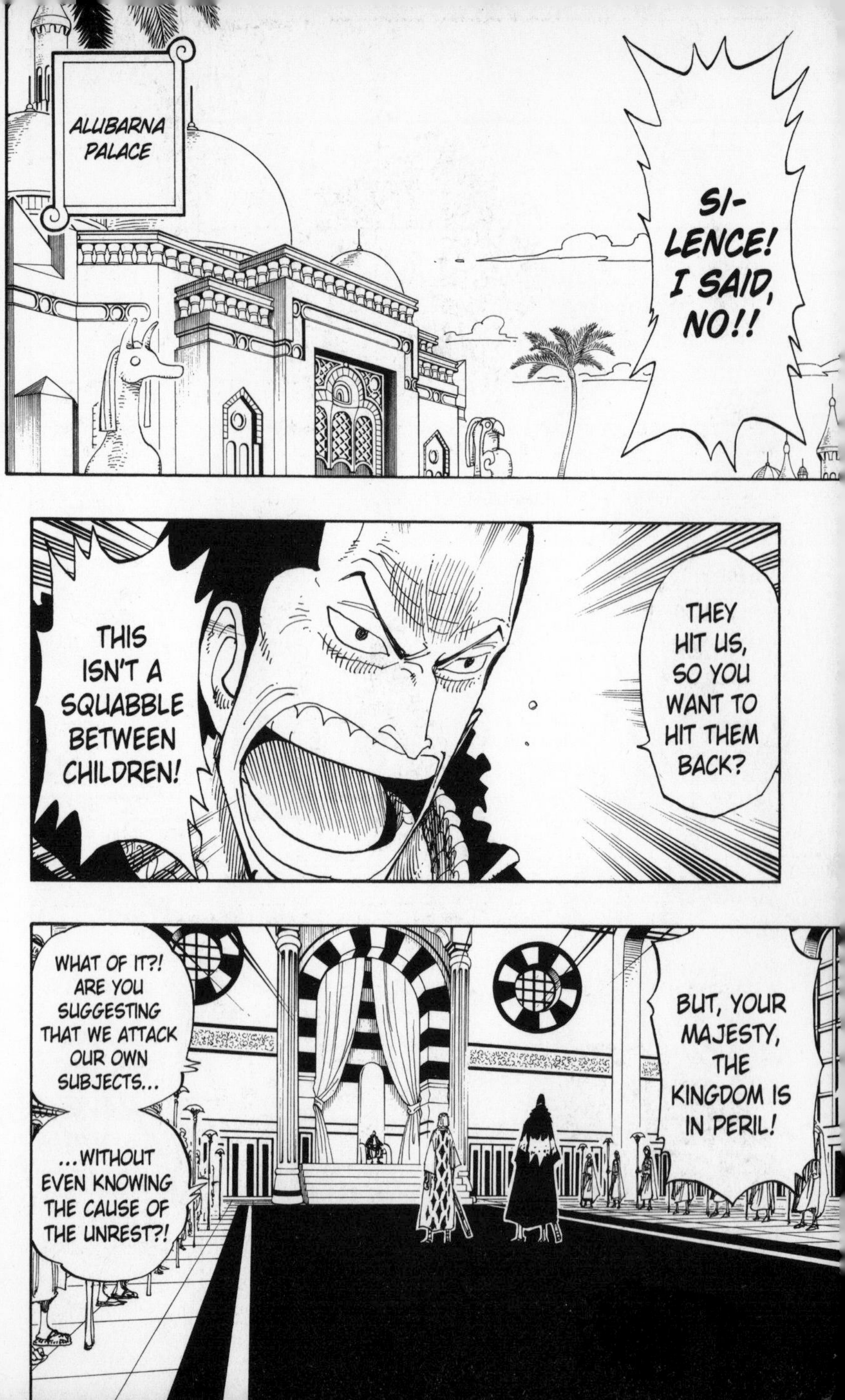
SI-LENCE! I SAID, NO!!
ALUBARNA PALACE
THEY HIT US, SO YOU WANT TO HIT THEM BACK?
THIS ISN'T A SQUABBLE BETWEEN CHILDREN!
BUT, YOUR MAJESTY, THE KINGDOM IS IN PERIL!
WHAT OF IT?! ARE YOU SUGGESTING THAT WE ATTACK OUR OWN SUBJECTS...
...WITHOUT EVEN KNOWING THE CAUSE OF THE UNREST?!

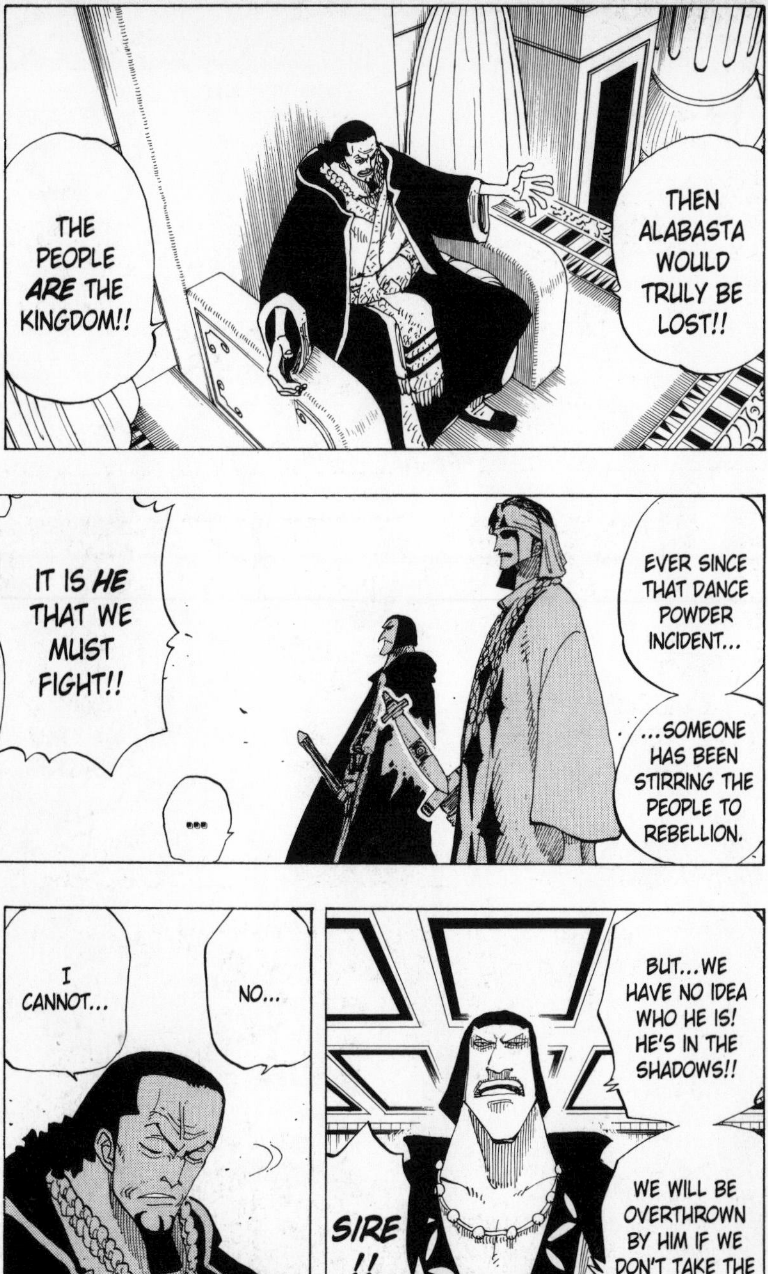
THEN ALABASTA WOULD TRULY BE LOST!!
THE PEOPLE *ARE* THE KINGDOM!!
EVER SINCE THAT DANCE POWDER INCIDENT...
...SOMEONE HAS BEEN STIRRING THE PEOPLE TO REBELLION.
IT IS *HE* THAT WE MUST FIGHT!!
...
BUT...WE HAVE NO IDEA WHO HE IS! HE'S IN THE SHADOWS!!
WE WILL BE OVERTHROWN BY HIM IF WE DON'T TAKE THE OFFENSIVE!!
*SIRE!!*
NO...
I CANNOT...

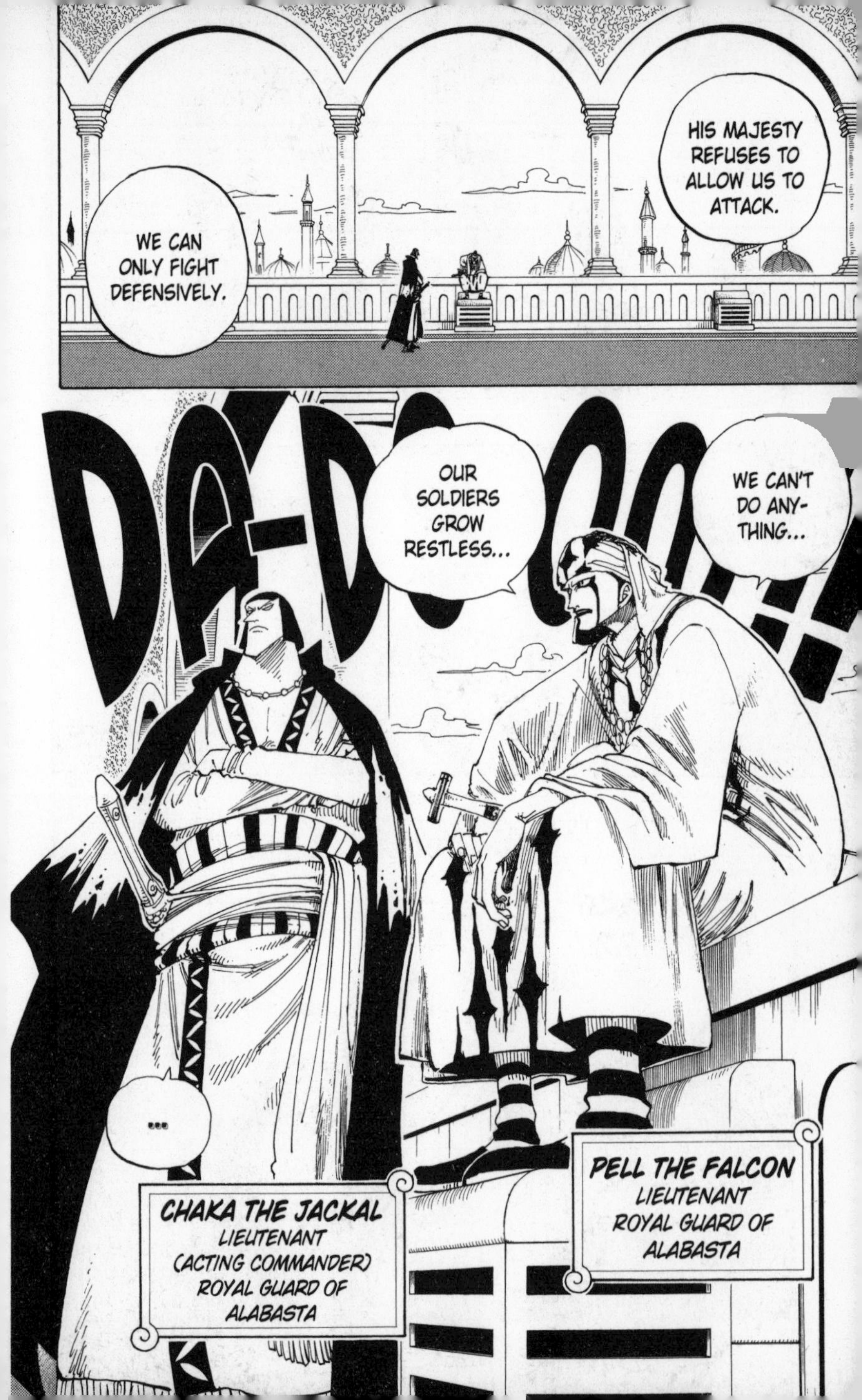
HIS MAJESTY REFUSES TO ALLOW US TO ATTACK.
WE CAN ONLY FIGHT DEFENSIVELY.
WE CAN'T DO ANY-THING...
OUR SOLDIERS GROW RESTLESS...
PELL THE FALCON LIEUTENANT ROYAL GUARD OF ALABASTA
...
CHAKA THE JACKAL LIEUTENANT (ACTING COMMANDER) ROYAL GUARD OF ALABASTA

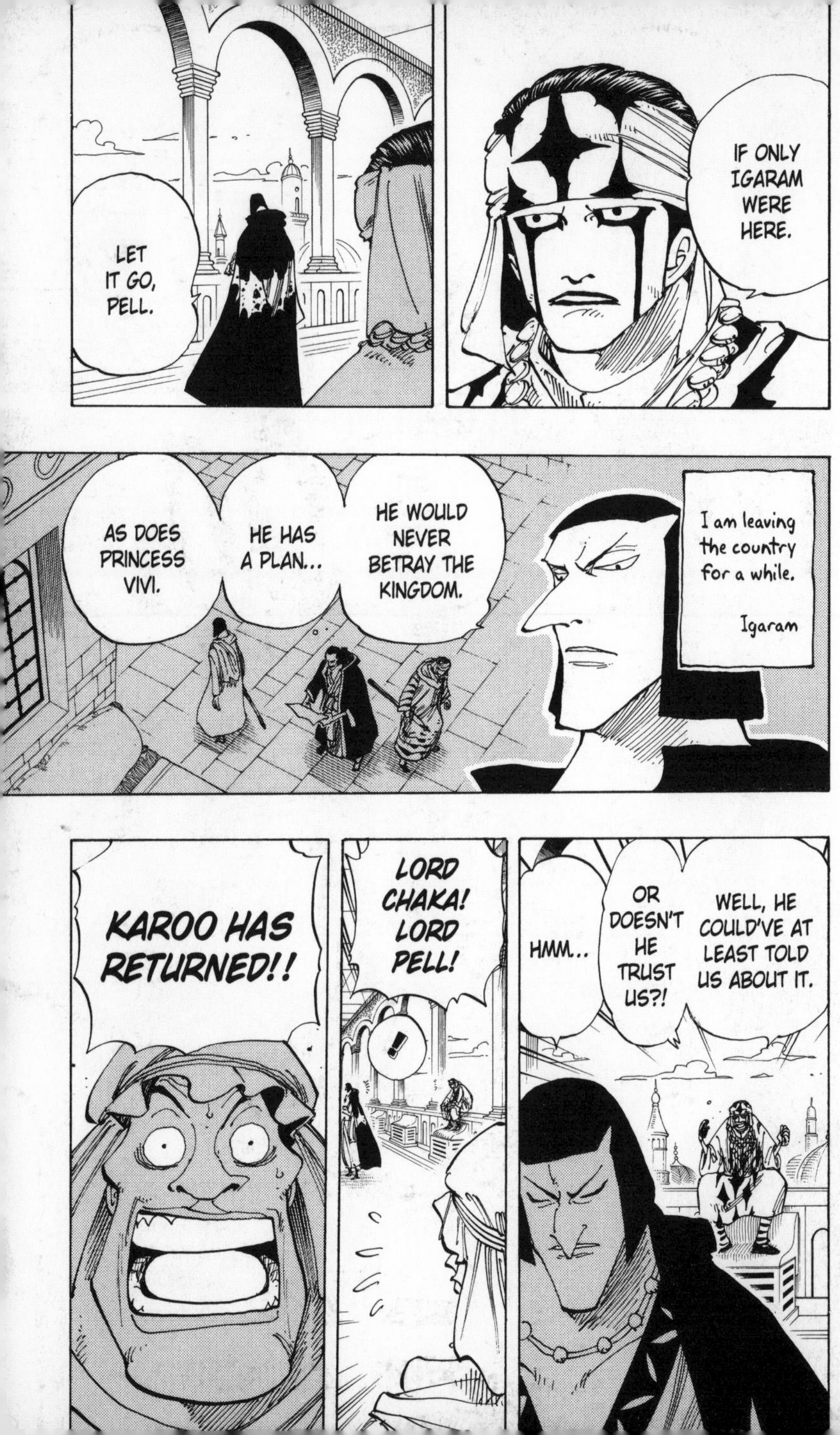
IF ONLY IGARAM WERE HERE.
LET IT GO, PELL.
I am leaving the country for a while.
Igaram
HE WOULD NEVER BETRAY THE KINGDOM.
HE HAS A PLAN...
AS DOES PRINCESS VIVI.
WELL, HE COULD'VE AT LEAST TOLD US ABOUT IT.
OR DOESN'T HE TRUST US?!
HMM...
LORD CHAKA! LORD PELL!
!
KAROO HAS RETURNED!!

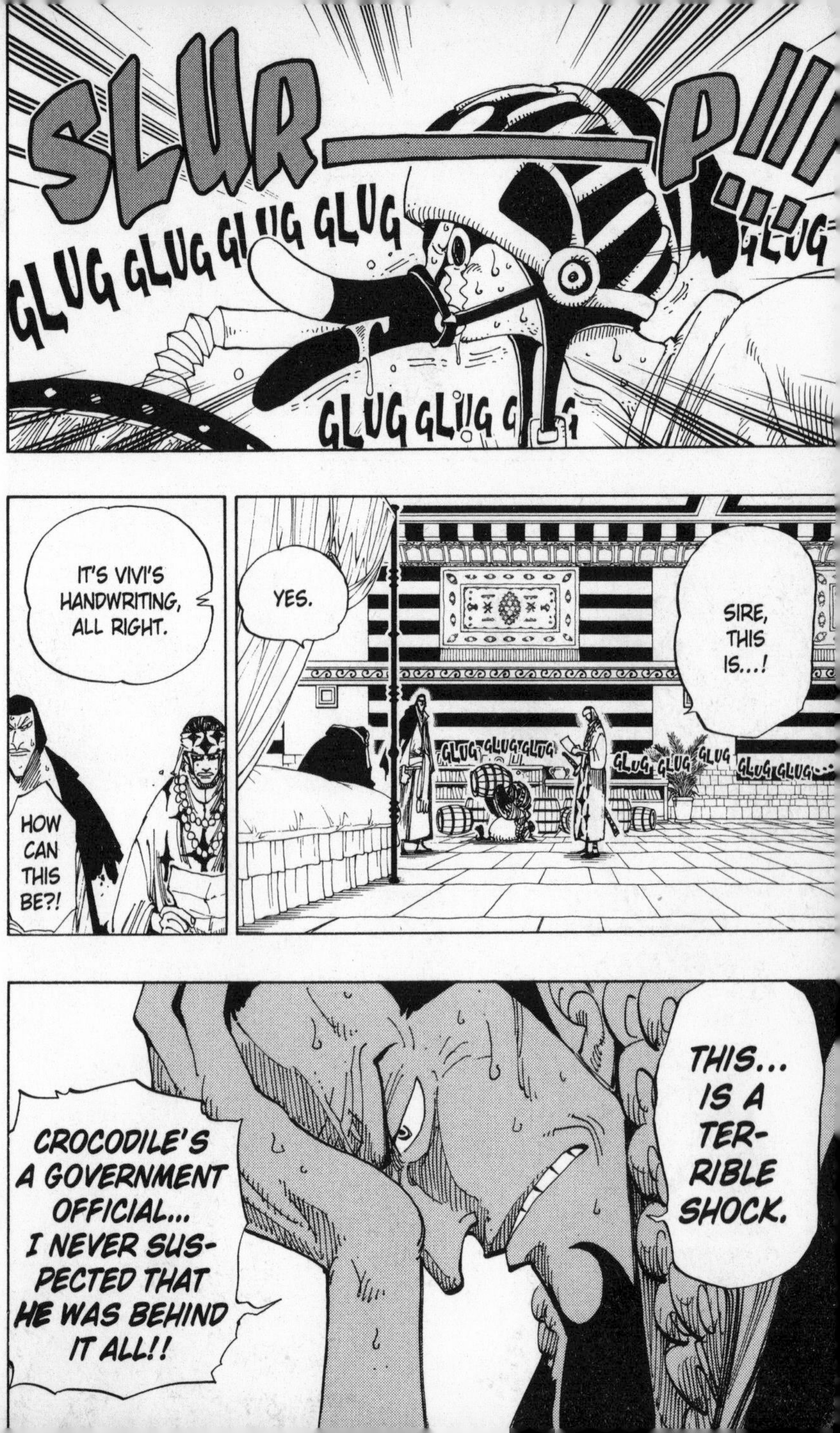
SLUR—P!!!
GLUG
GLUG GLUG GLUG GLUG
GLUG GLUG
SIRE, THIS IS...!
GLUG GLUG GLUG
GLUG GLUG GLUG
GLUG GLUG...
YES.
IT'S VIVI'S HANDWRITING, ALL RIGHT.
HOW CAN THIS BE?!
THIS... IS A TERRIBLE SHOCK.
CROCODILE'S A GOVERNMENT OFFICIAL... I NEVER SUSPECTED THAT HE WAS BEHIND IT ALL!!

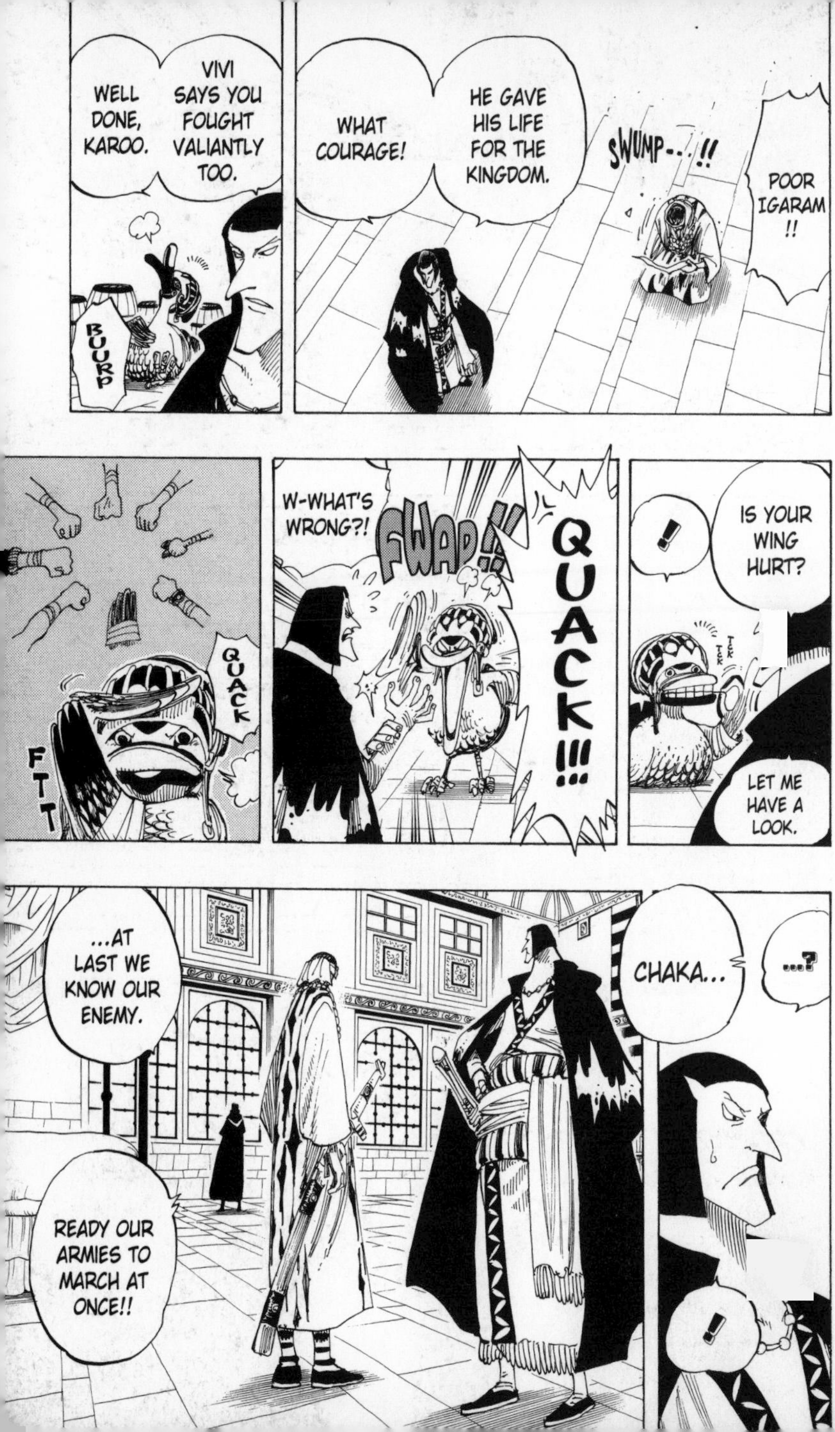
SWUMP...!!
POOR IGARAM!!
HE GAVE HIS LIFE FOR THE KINGDOM.
WHAT COURAGE!
VIVI SAYS YOU FOUGHT VALIANTLY TOO.
WELL DONE, KAROO.
BUURP
IS YOUR WING HURT?
!
TCK TCK
LET ME HAVE A LOOK.
QUACK!!!
FWAP!!
W-WHAT'S WRONG?!
QUACK
FTT
...?
CHAKA...
!
...AT LAST WE KNOW OUR ENEMY.
READY OUR ARMIES TO MARCH AT ONCE!!

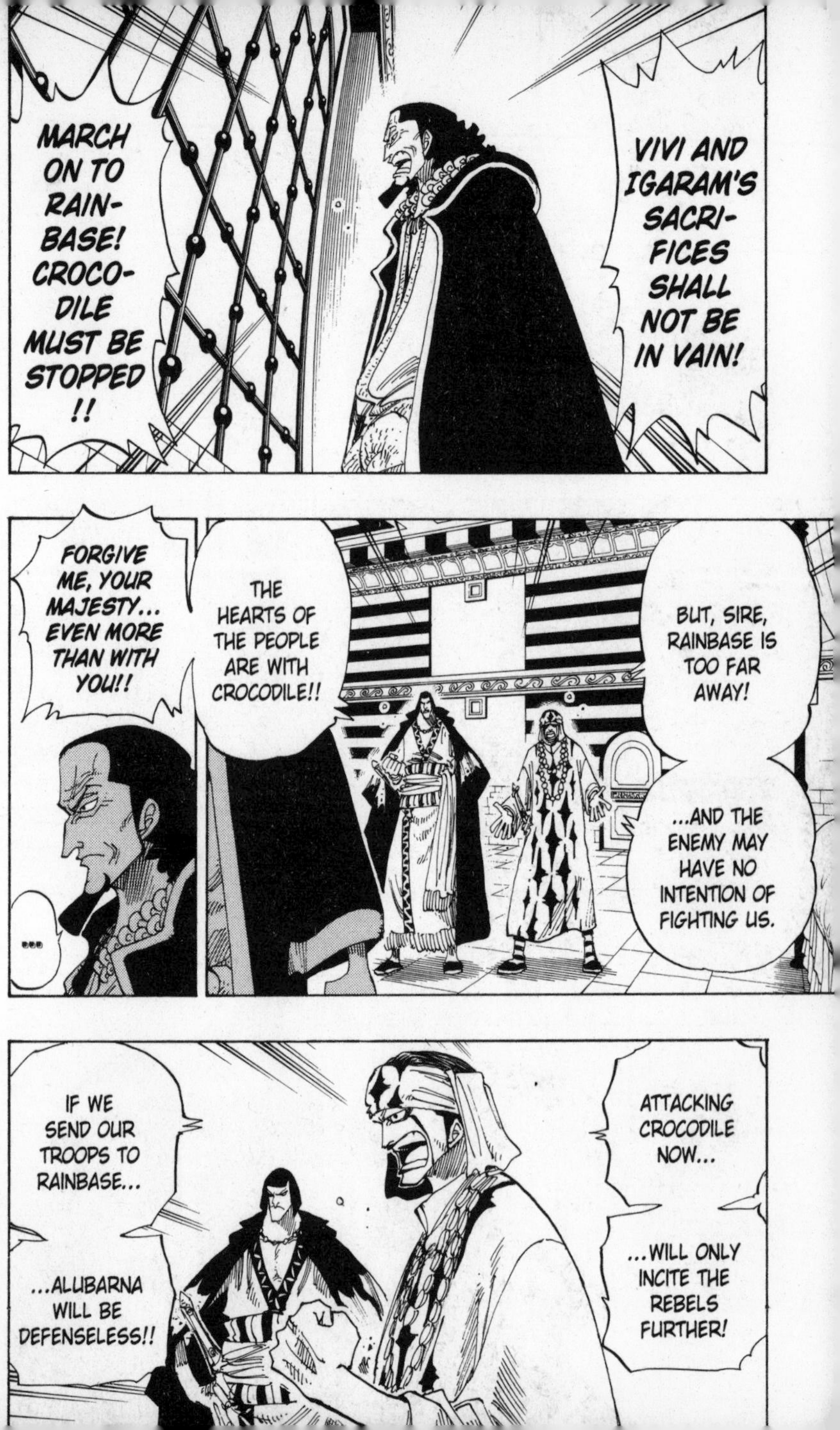

VIVI AND IGARAM'S SACRIFICES SHALL NOT BE IN VAIN!
MARCH ON TO RAINBASE! CROCODILE MUST BE STOPPED!!
BUT, SIRE, RAINBASE IS TOO FAR AWAY!
...AND THE ENEMY MAY HAVE NO INTENTION OF FIGHTING US.
THE HEARTS OF THE PEOPLE ARE WITH CROCODILE!!
FORGIVE ME, YOUR MAJESTY... EVEN MORE THAN WITH YOU!!
...
ATTACKING CROCODILE NOW...
...WILL ONLY INCITE THE REBELS FURTHER!
IF WE SEND OUR TROOPS TO RAINBASE...
...ALUBARNA WILL BE DEFENSELESS!!

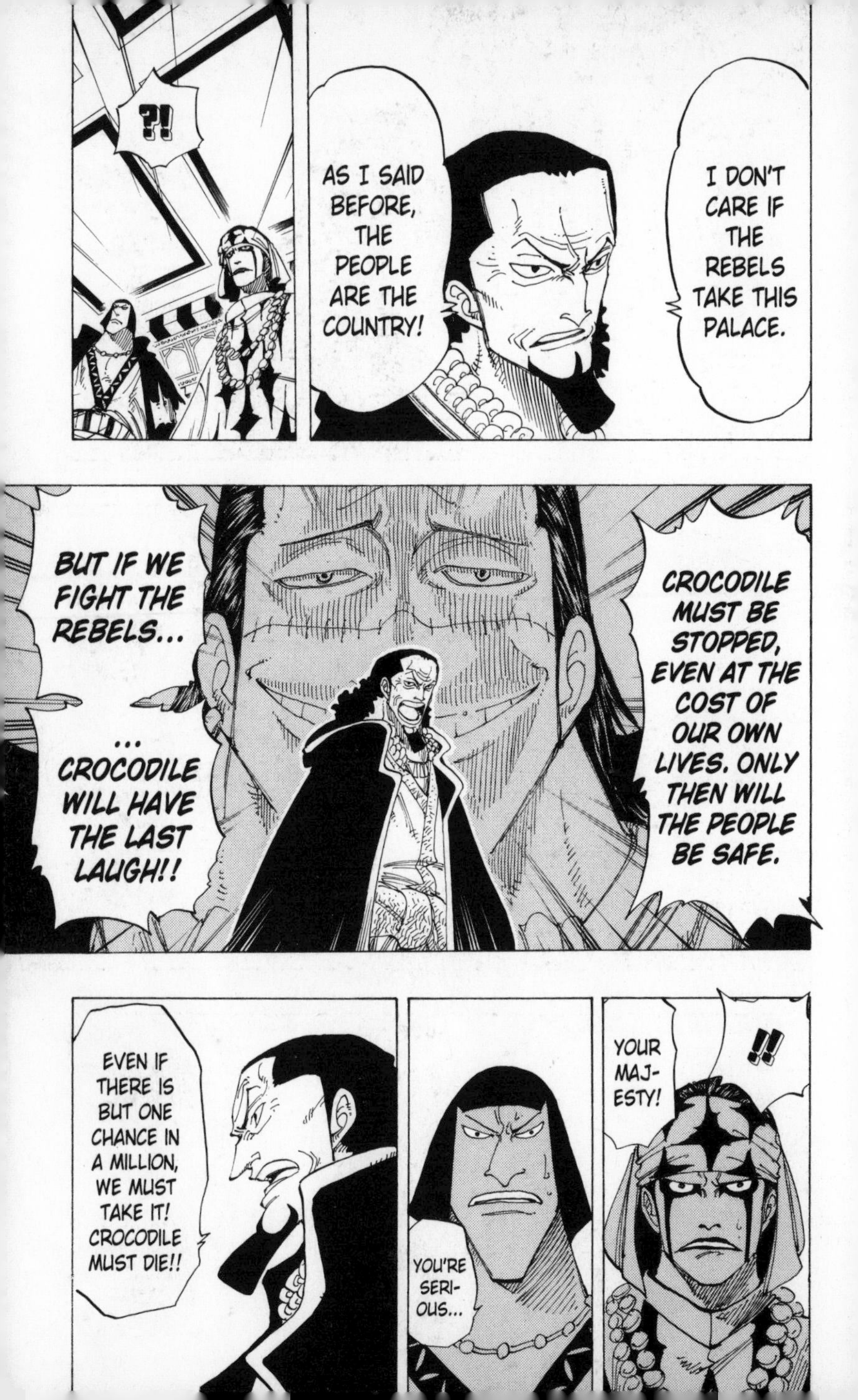
I DON'T CARE IF THE REBELS TAKE THIS PALACE.
AS I SAID BEFORE, THE PEOPLE ARE THE COUNTRY!
?!
CROCODILE MUST BE STOPPED, EVEN AT THE COST OF OUR OWN LIVES. ONLY THEN WILL THE PEOPLE BE SAFE.
BUT IF WE FIGHT THE REBELS...
...CROCODILE WILL HAVE THE LAST LAUGH!!
!!
YOUR MAJ- ESTY!
YOU'RE SERI- OUS...
EVEN IF THERE IS BUT ONE CHANCE IN A MILLION, WE MUST TAKE IT! CROCODILE MUST DIE!!

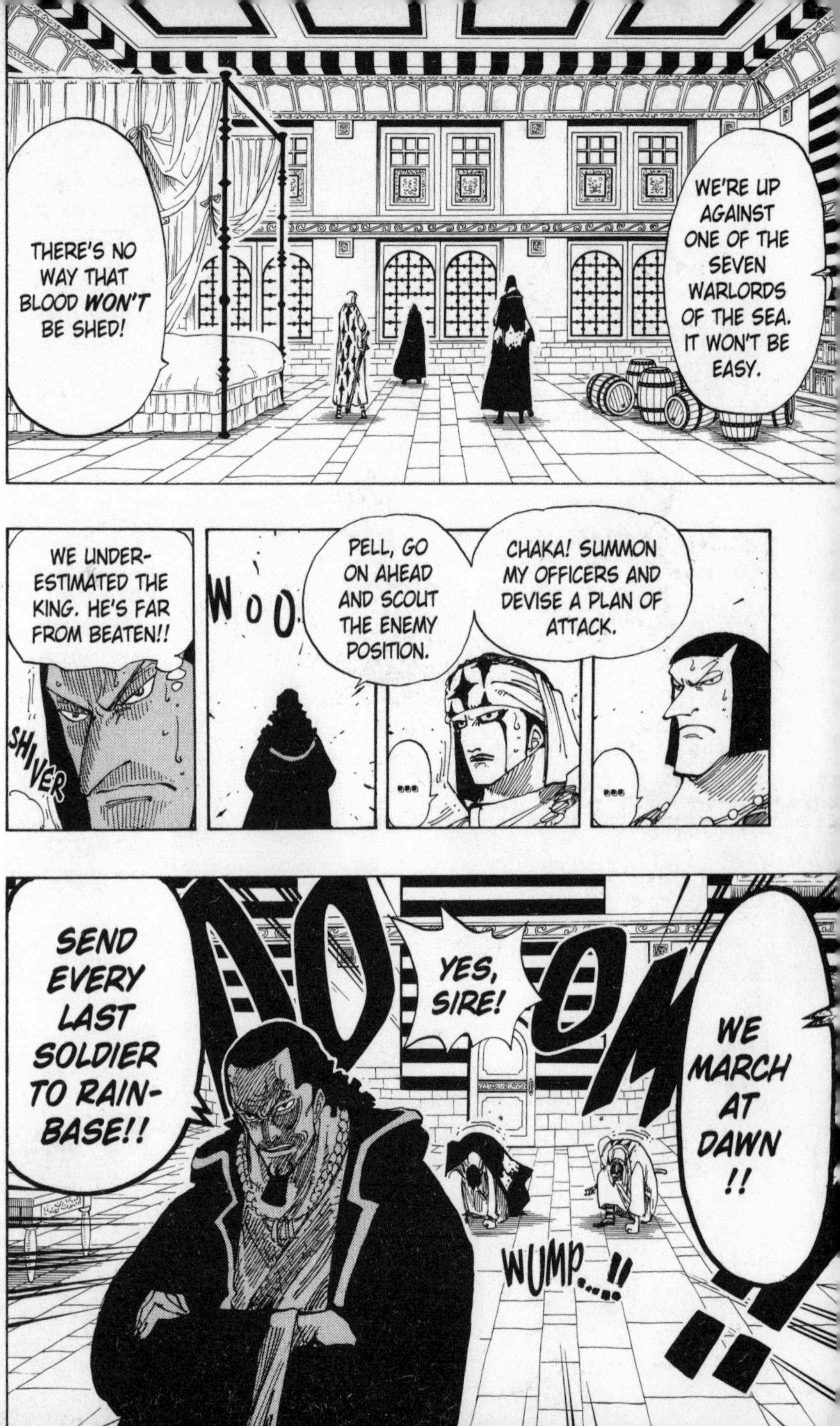
WE'RE UP AGAINST ONE OF THE SEVEN WARLORDS OF THE SEA. IT WON'T BE EASY.
THERE'S NO WAY THAT BLOOD *WON'T* BE SHED!
CHAKA! SUMMON MY OFFICERS AND DEVISE A PLAN OF ATTACK.
...
PELL, GO ON AHEAD AND SCOUT THE ENEMY POSITION.
...
WOO
WE UNDER-ESTIMATED THE KING. HE'S FAR FROM BEATEN!!
SHIVER
WE MARCH AT DAWN!!
YES, SIRE!
SEND EVERY LAST SOLDIER TO RAIN-BASE!!
WUMP...!!

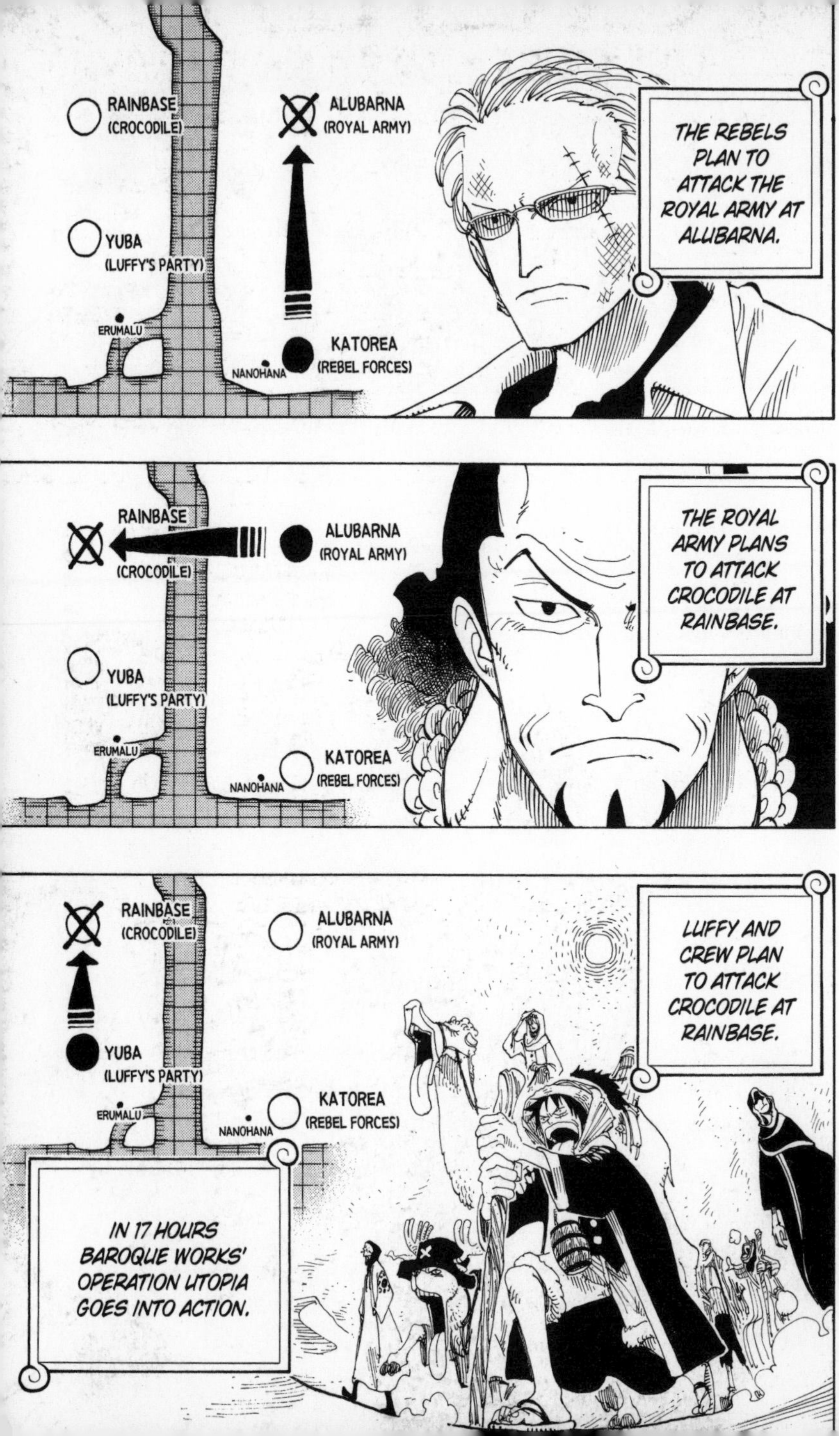
THE REBELS PLAN TO ATTACK THE ROYAL ARMY AT ALUBARNA.
ALUBARNA
(ROYAL ARMY)
RAINBASE
(CROCODILE)
YUBA
(LUFFY'S PARTY)
KATOREA
(REBEL FORCES)
ERUMALU
NANOHANA
THE ROYAL ARMY PLANS TO ATTACK CROCODILE AT RAINBASE.
ALUBARNA
(ROYAL ARMY)
RAINBASE
(CROCODILE)
YUBA
(LUFFY'S PARTY)
KATOREA
(REBEL FORCES)
ERUMALU
NANOHANA
LUFFY AND CREW PLAN TO ATTACK CROCODILE AT RAINBASE.
ALUBARNA
(ROYAL ARMY)
RAINBASE
(CROCODILE)
YUBA
(LUFFY'S PARTY)
KATOREA
(REBEL FORCES)
ERUMALU
NANOHANA
IN 17 HOURS BAROQUE WORKS' OPERATION UTOPIA GOES INTO ACTION.

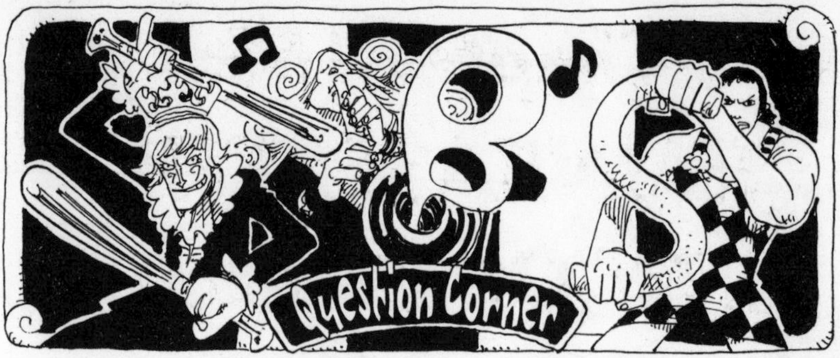
SBS
Question Corner

Reader: Hello, Mr. Oda. I fell in love with the outrageous way you portrayed Ms. Merry Christmas! So now I'm going to do something equally outrageous.

Eh!! (Let the Question Corner begin!)

Oda: Whaaat?!

Reader: Oda-sensei! Please draw the six main characters with your left hand!

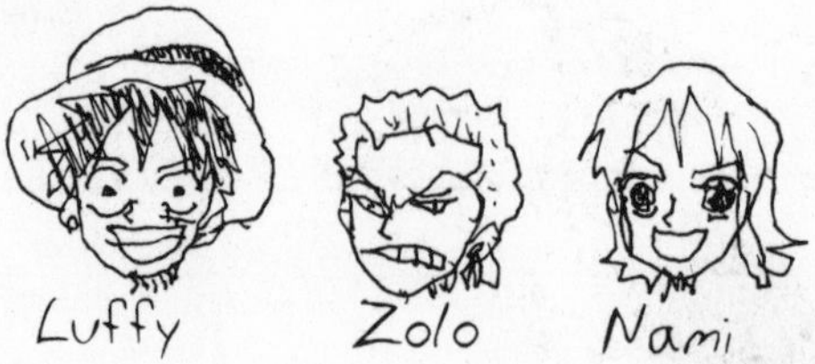
Luffy
Zolo
Nami

Oda: For the sake of space, can I stop at three?

Reader: For some time now I've been wondering how old Vivi and Chopper are. Vivi looks like she's about the same age as Luffy and gang, but Chopper looks like a little kid! Tell me!

Oda: Vivi is 16 years old. Chopper is a man-reindeer, and he's about 15 in human years. So there you go.

Reader: What happens at a Chinese restaurant if you say, "I'll have fried rice, but hold the rice"?

Oda: What happens--? Don't order like that! And don't say, "I'd like boiled tofu, but hold the tofu" either. 'Kay? But what does any of this have to do with *One Piece*?

# Chapter 168:
# RAINBASE, THE CITY OF DREAMS

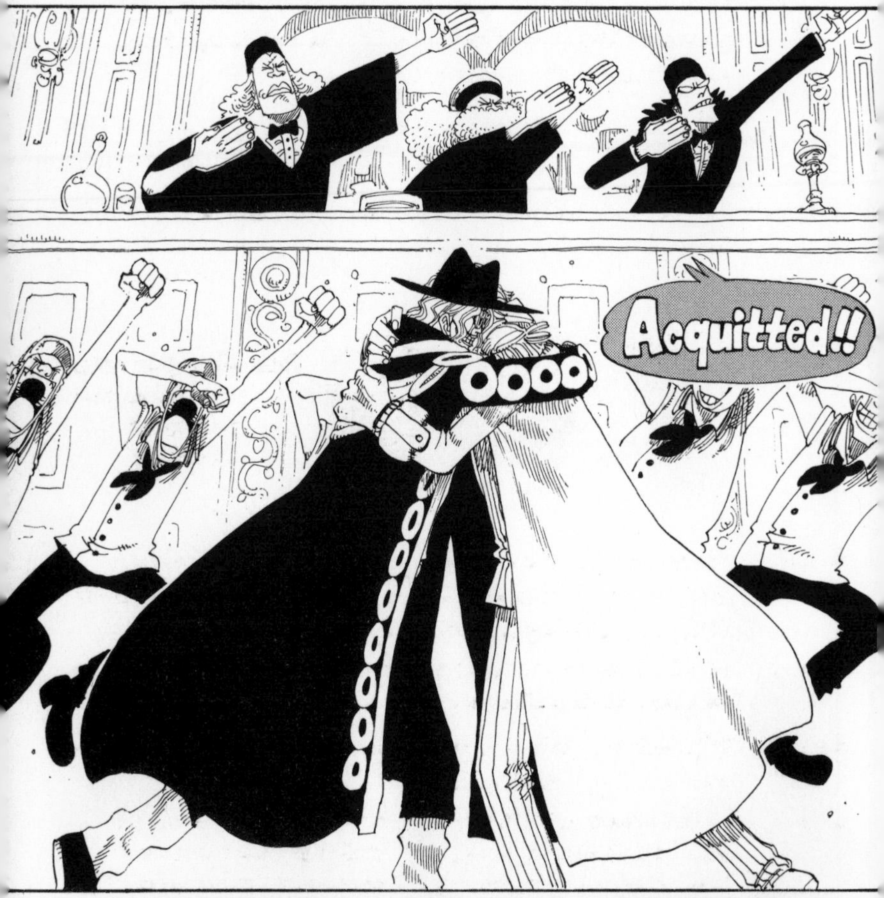
Acquitted!!

DJANGO'S DANCE PARADISE, VOL. 33: "ACQUITTAL BY FEELING THE BEAT!! FULLBODY DEMOTED."

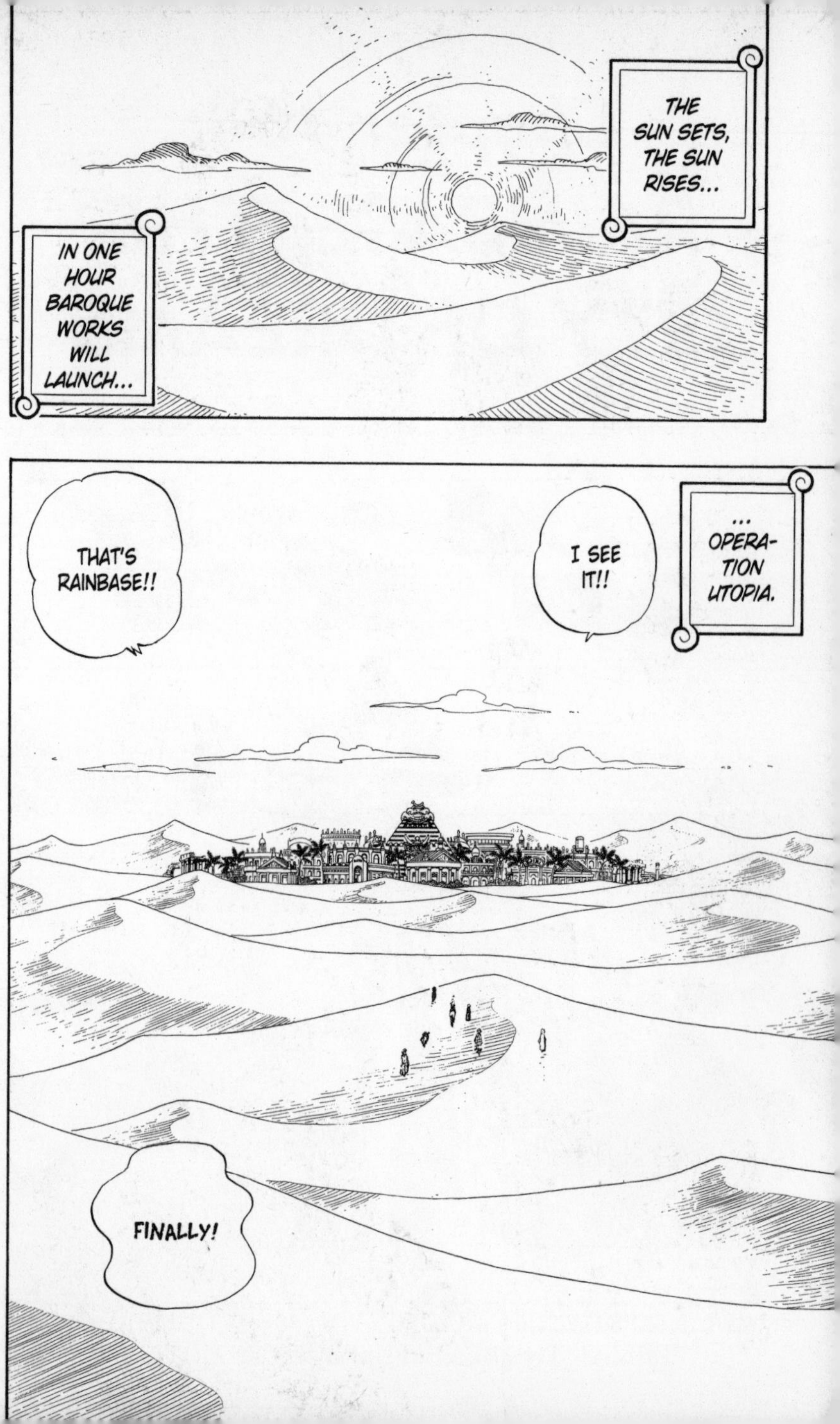
THE SUN SETS, THE SUN RISES...
IN ONE HOUR BAROQUE WORKS WILL LAUNCH...
...OPERATION UTOPIA.
I SEE IT!!
THAT'S RAINBASE!!
FINALLY!

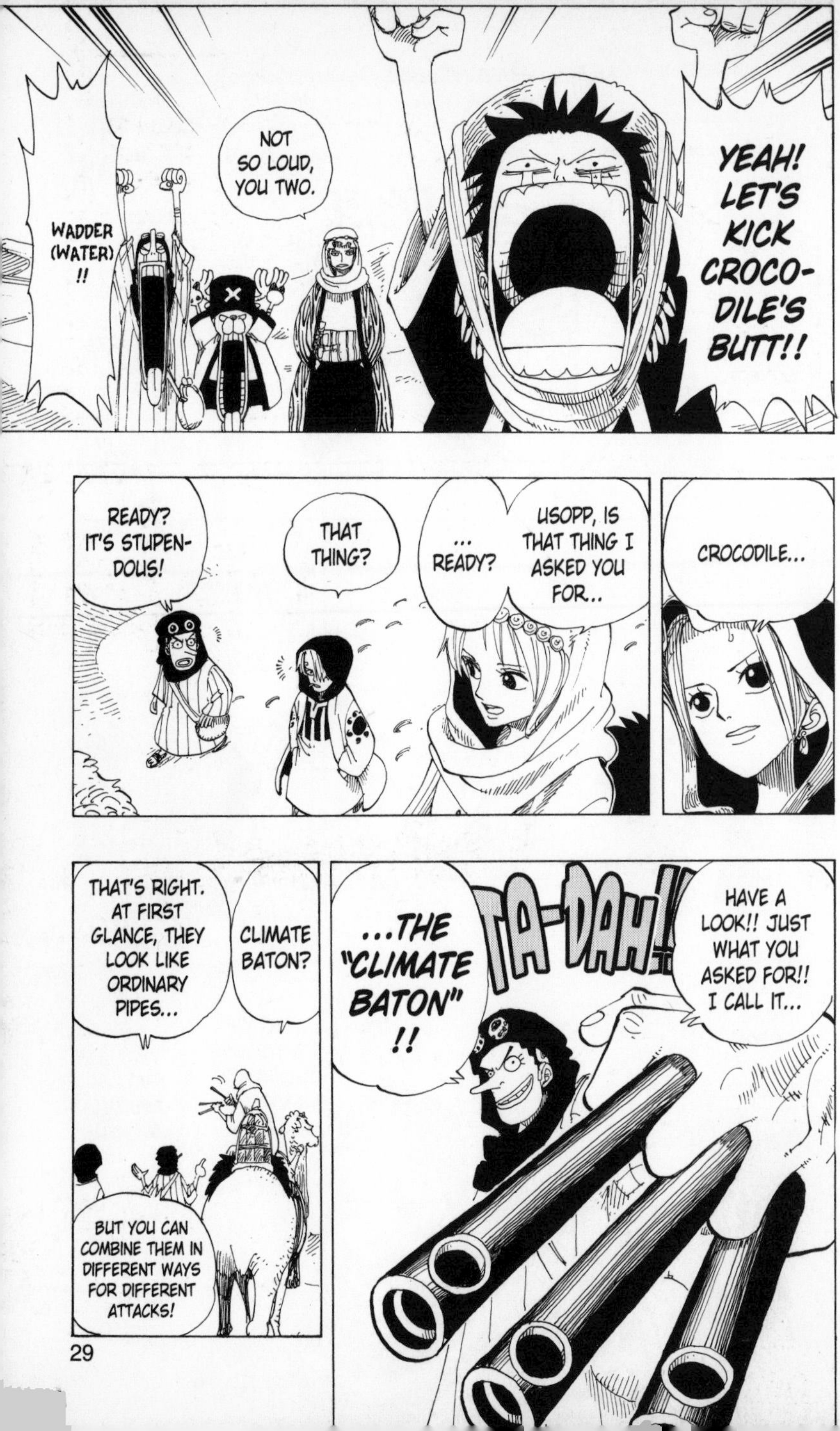
YEAH! LET'S KICK CROCO-DILE'S BUTT!!
NOT SO LOUD, YOU TWO.
WADDER (WATER) !!
CROCODILE...
USOPP, IS THAT THING I ASKED YOU FOR...
... READY?
THAT THING?
READY? IT'S STUPEN-DOUS!
HAVE A LOOK!! JUST WHAT YOU ASKED FOR!! I CALL IT...
TA-DAH!!
...THE "CLIMATE BATON" !!
CLIMATE BATON?
THAT'S RIGHT. AT FIRST GLANCE, THEY LOOK LIKE ORDINARY PIPES...
BUT YOU CAN COMBINE THEM IN DIFFERENT WAYS FOR DIFFERENT ATTACKS!

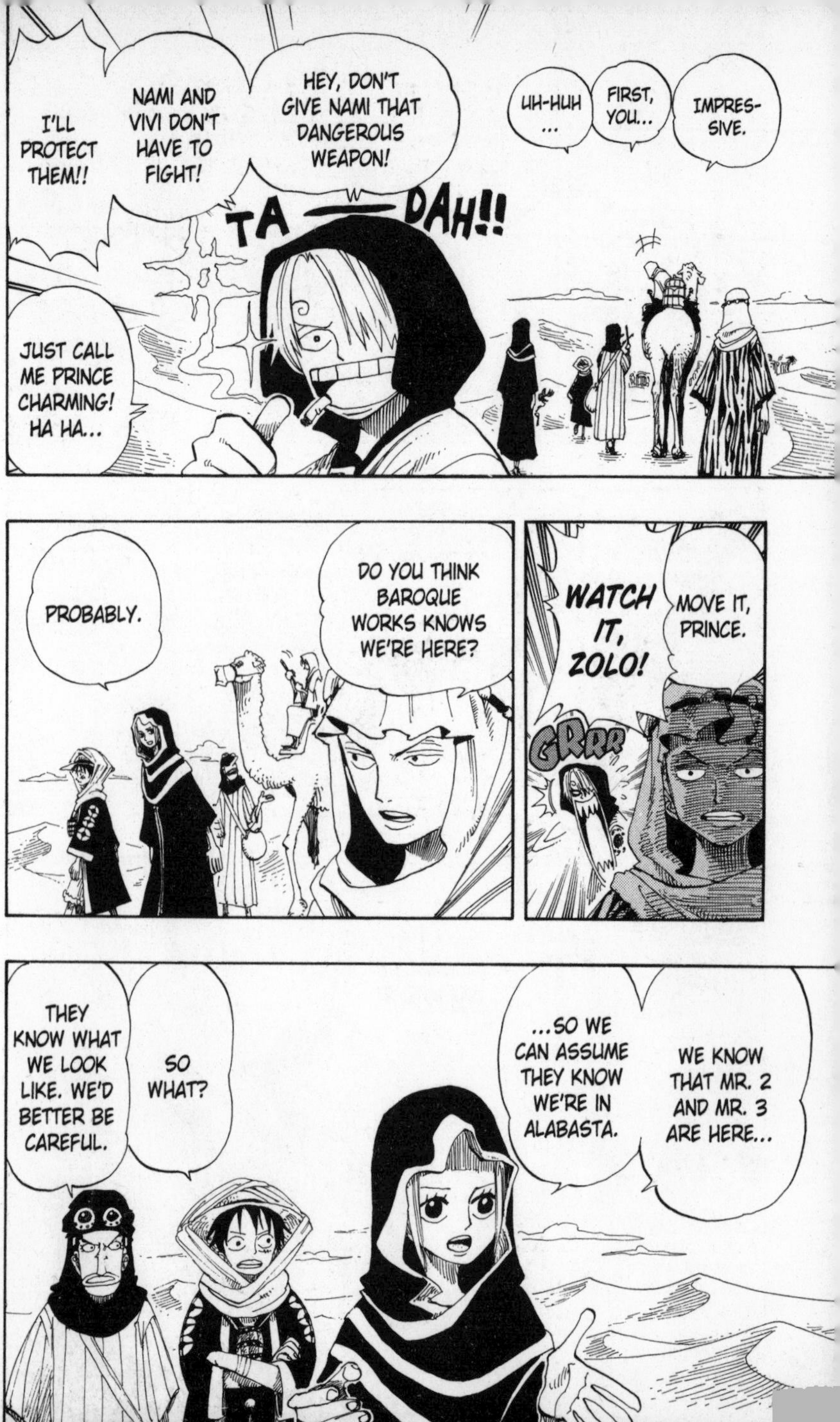
IMPRES-SIVE.
FIRST, YOU...
UH-HUH ...
HEY, DON'T GIVE NAMI THAT DANGEROUS WEAPON!
NAMI AND VIVI DON'T HAVE TO FIGHT!
I'LL PROTECT THEM!!
TA—DAH!!
JUST CALL ME PRINCE CHARMING! HA HA...
MOVE IT, PRINCE.
WATCH IT, ZOLO!
GRRR
DO YOU THINK BAROQUE WORKS KNOWS WE'RE HERE?
PROBABLY.
WE KNOW THAT MR. 2 AND MR. 3 ARE HERE...
...SO WE CAN ASSUME THEY KNOW WE'RE IN ALABASTA.
SO WHAT?
THEY KNOW WHAT WE LOOK LIKE. WE'D BETTER BE CAREFUL.

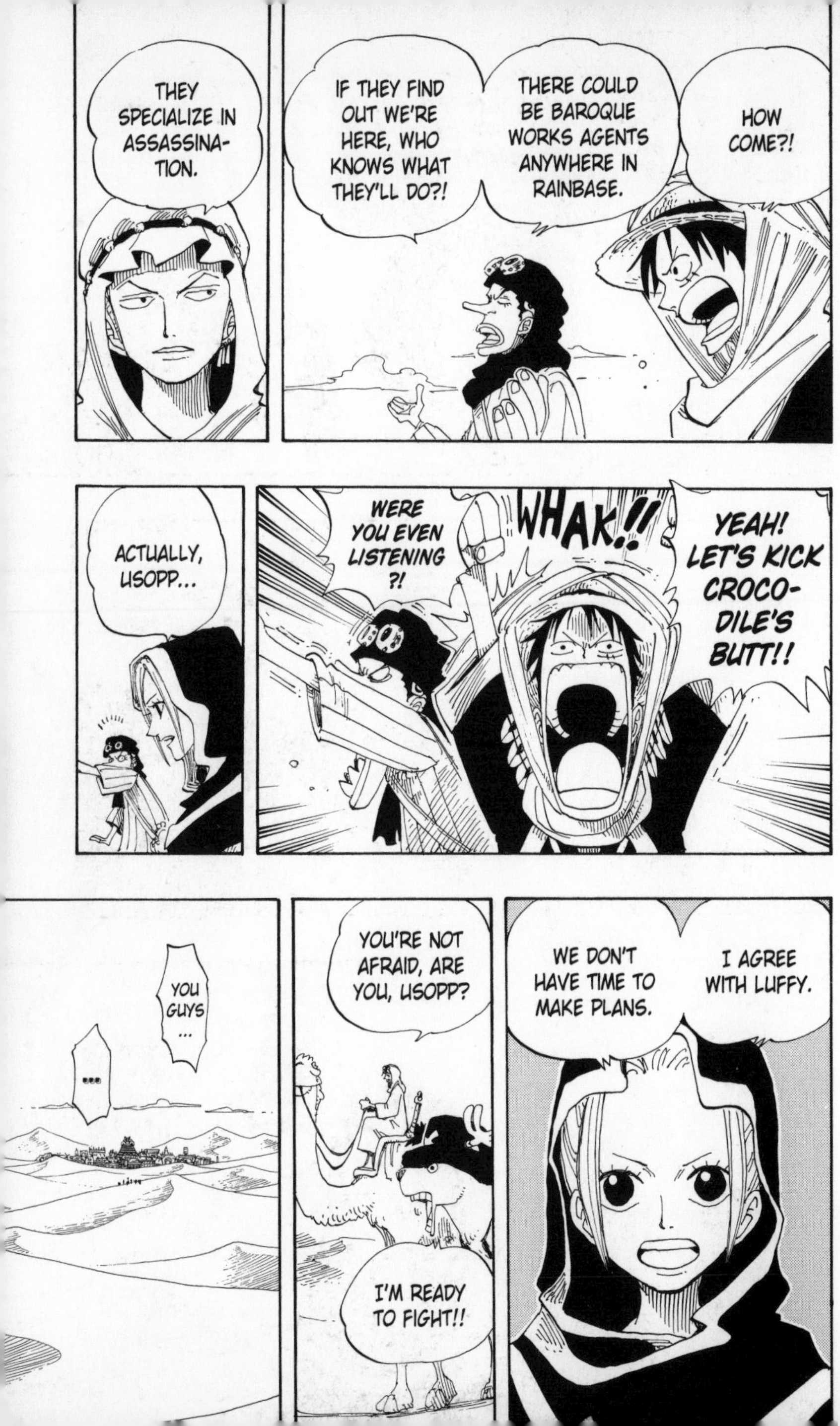
HOW COME?!
THERE COULD BE BAROQUE WORKS AGENTS ANYWHERE IN RAINBASE.
IF THEY FIND OUT WE'RE HERE, WHO KNOWS WHAT THEY'LL DO?!
THEY SPECIALIZE IN ASSASSINATION.
YEAH! LET'S KICK CROCODILE'S BUTT!!
WHAK!!
WERE YOU EVEN LISTENING?!
ACTUALLY, USOPP...
I AGREE WITH LUFFY.
WE DON'T HAVE TIME TO MAKE PLANS.
YOU'RE NOT AFRAID, ARE YOU, USOPP?
I'M READY TO FIGHT!!
YOU GUYS ...
...

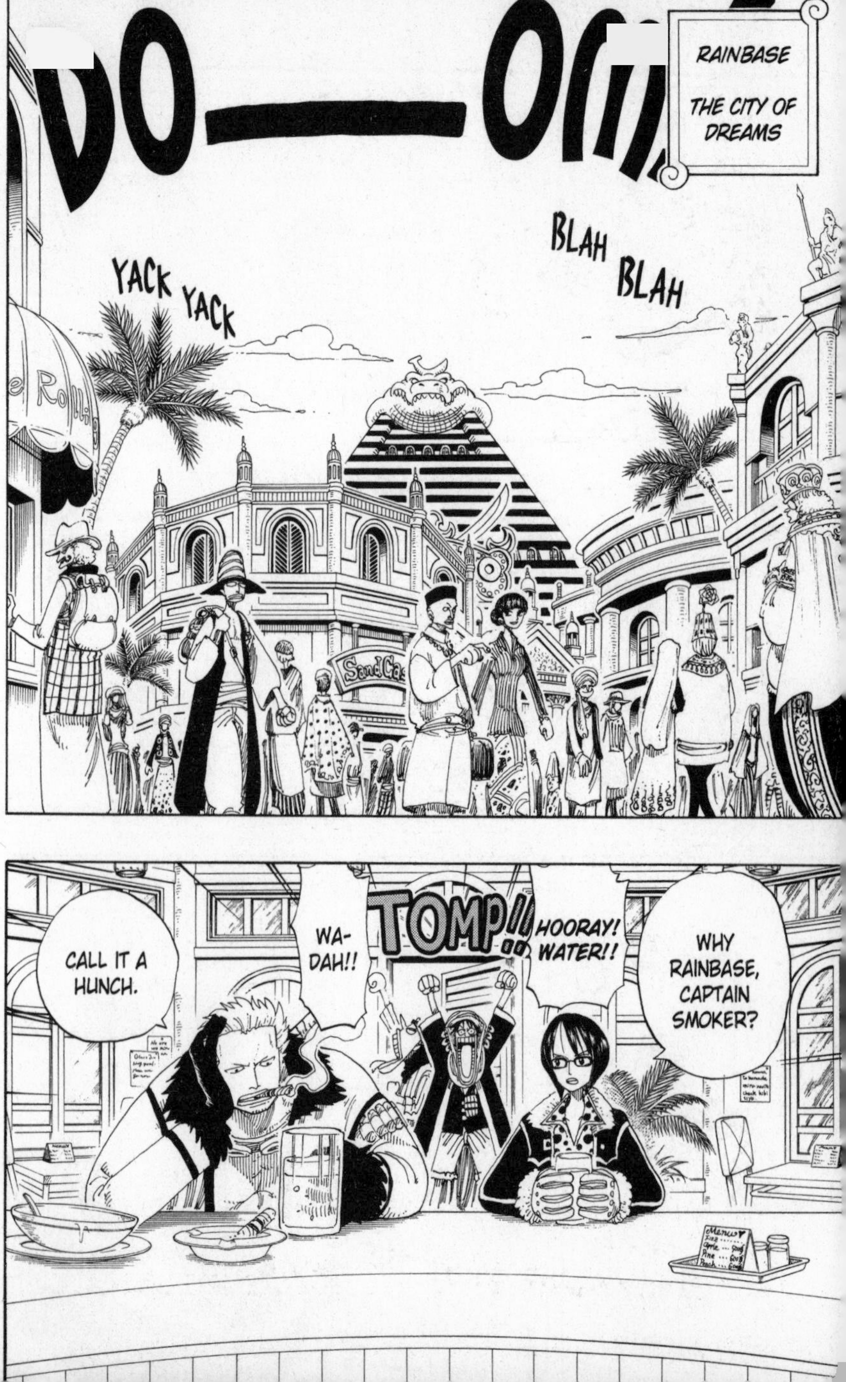
RAINBASE
THE CITY OF DREAMS
DO—OM
BLAH BLAH
YACK YACK
WHY RAINBASE, CAPTAIN SMOKER?
HOORAY! WATER!!
TOMP!!
WA-DAH!!
CALL IT A HUNCH.

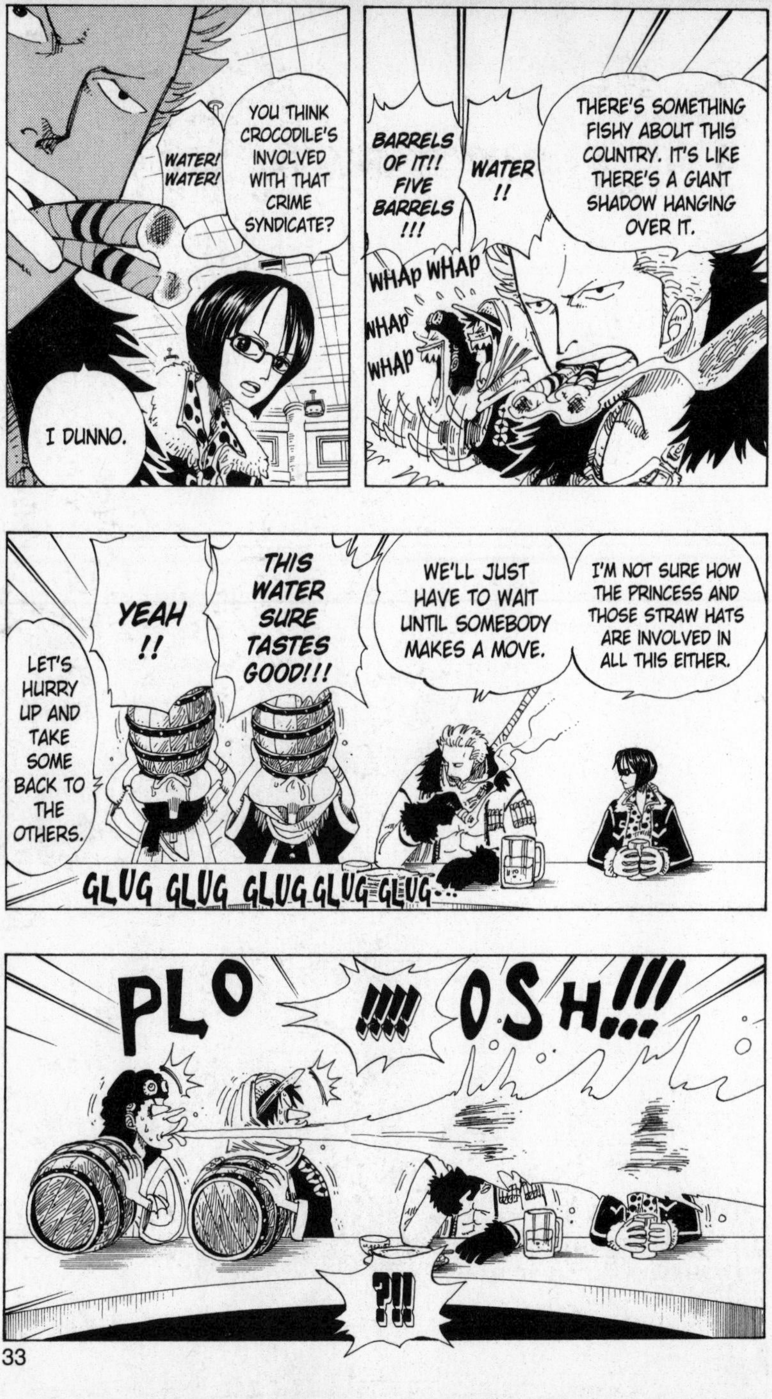
THERE'S SOMETHING FISHY ABOUT THIS COUNTRY. IT'S LIKE THERE'S A GIANT SHADOW HANGING OVER IT.
WATER !!
BARRELS OF IT!! FIVE BARRELS !!!
WHAp WHAP WHAp WHAp
YOU THINK CROCODILE'S INVOLVED WITH THAT CRIME SYNDICATE?
WATER! WATER!
I DUNNO.
I'M NOT SURE HOW THE PRINCESS AND THOSE STRAW HATS ARE INVOLVED IN ALL THIS EITHER.
WE'LL JUST HAVE TO WAIT UNTIL SOMEBODY MAKES A MOVE.
THIS WATER SURE TASTES GOOD!!!
YEAH !!
LET'S HURRY UP AND TAKE SOME BACK TO THE OTHERS.
GLUG GLUG GLUG GLUG GLUG...
PLO!!!! OSH!!!
?!!

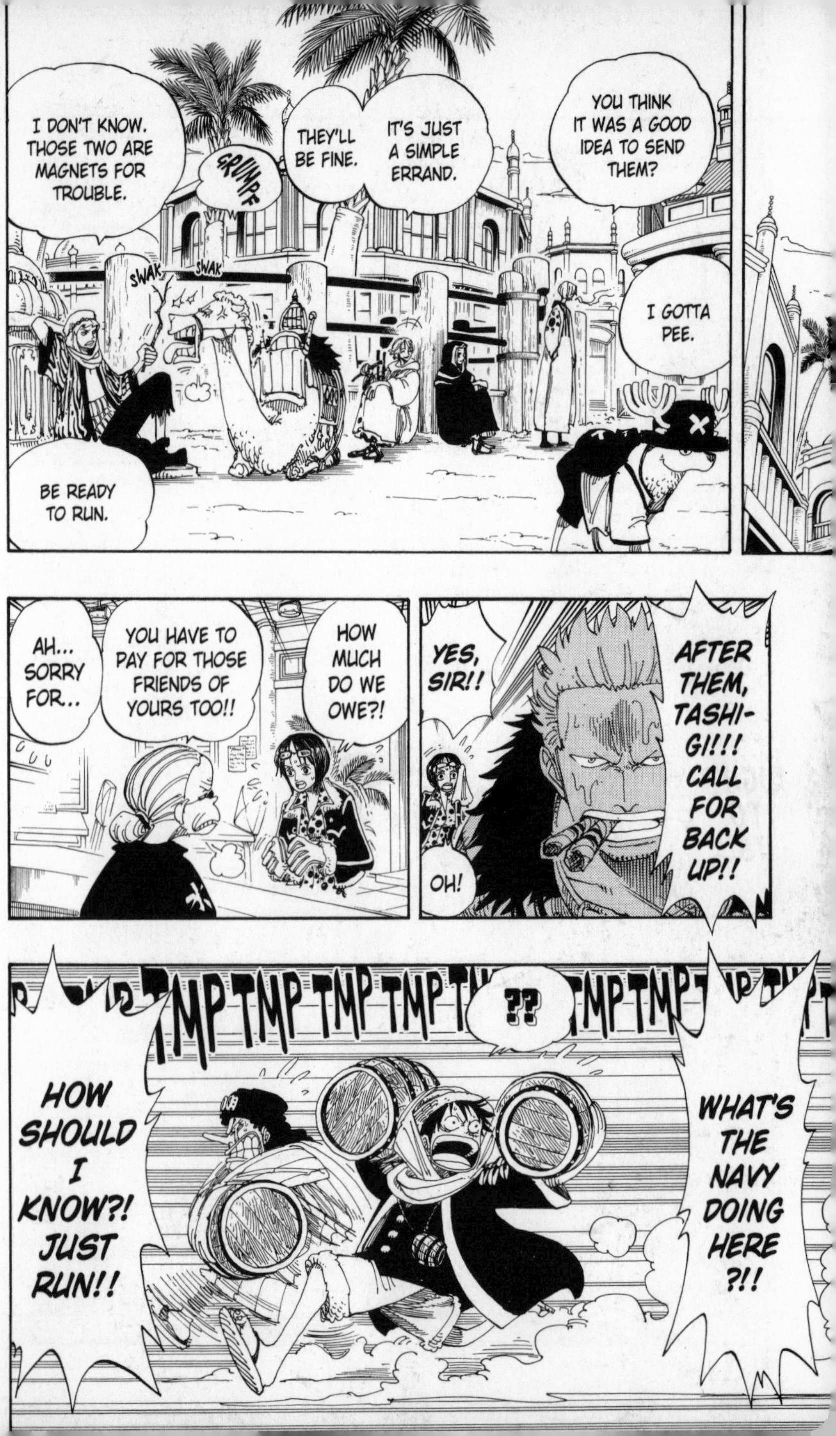
YOU THINK IT WAS A GOOD IDEA TO SEND THEM?
IT'S JUST A SIMPLE ERRAND.
THEY'LL BE FINE.
GRUMPF
I DON'T KNOW. THOSE TWO ARE MAGNETS FOR TROUBLE.
I GOTTA PEE.
SWAK
SWAK
BE READY TO RUN.
AFTER THEM, TASHIGI!!! CALL FOR BACK UP!!
YES, SIR!!
OH!
HOW MUCH DO WE OWE?!
YOU HAVE TO PAY FOR THOSE FRIENDS OF YOURS TOO!!
AH... SORRY FOR...
TMP TMP TMP TMP TMP TMP TMP
WHAT'S THE NAVY DOING HERE?!!
??
HOW SHOULD I KNOW?! JUST RUN!!

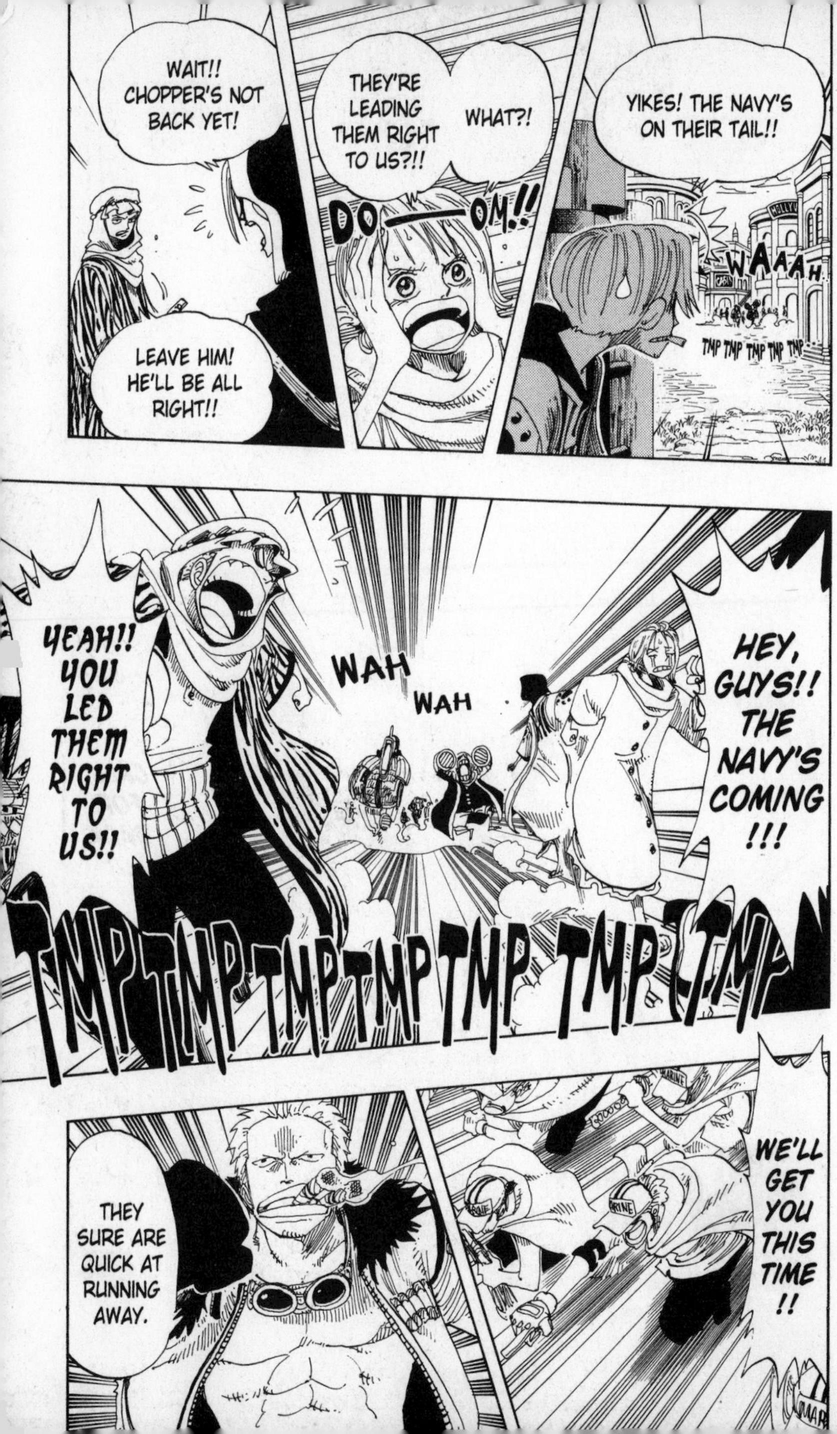
YIKES! THE NAVY'S ON THEIR TAIL!!
WAAAAH
TMP TMP TMP TMP TMP
WHAT?!
THEY'RE LEADING THEM RIGHT TO US?!!
DO——OM!!
WAIT!! CHOPPER'S NOT BACK YET!
LEAVE HIM! HE'LL BE ALL RIGHT!!
HEY, GUYS!! THE NAVY'S COMING!!!
WAH
WAH
YEAH!! YOU LED THEM RIGHT TO US!!
TMP TMP TMP TMP TMP TMP TMP
WE'LL GET YOU THIS TIME!!
THEY SURE ARE QUICK AT RUNNING AWAY.

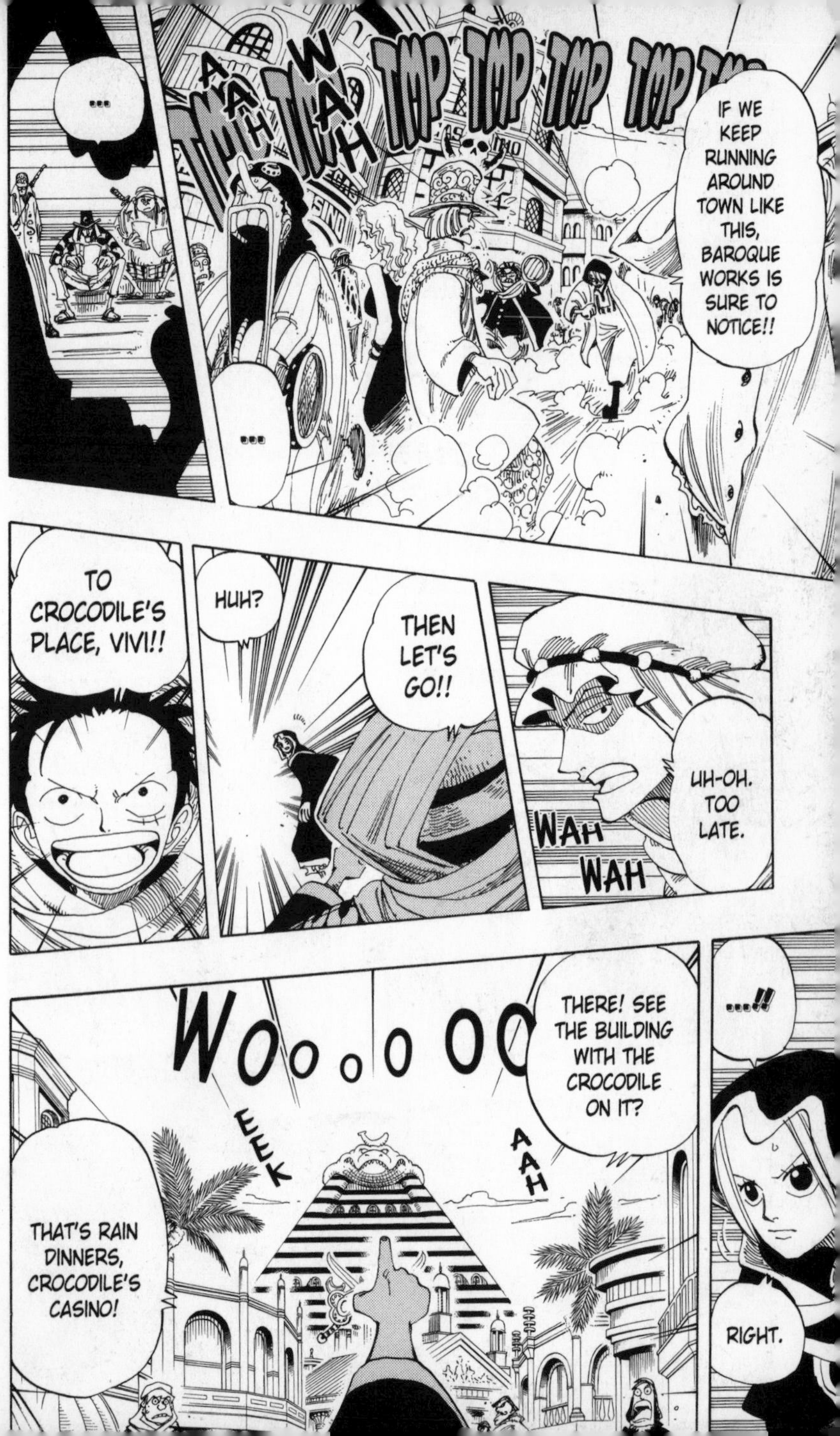
IF WE KEEP RUNNING AROUND TOWN LIKE THIS, BAROQUE WORKS IS SURE TO NOTICE!!
TMP TMP TMP TMP
WAAH
AAAH
...
...
UH-OH. TOO LATE.
WAH WAH
THEN LET'S GO!!
HUH?
TO CROCODILE'S PLACE, VIVI!!
...!!
RIGHT.
THERE! SEE THE BUILDING WITH THE CROCODILE ON IT?
AAH
WOooOO
EEEK
THAT'S RAIN DINNERS, CROCODILE'S CASINO!

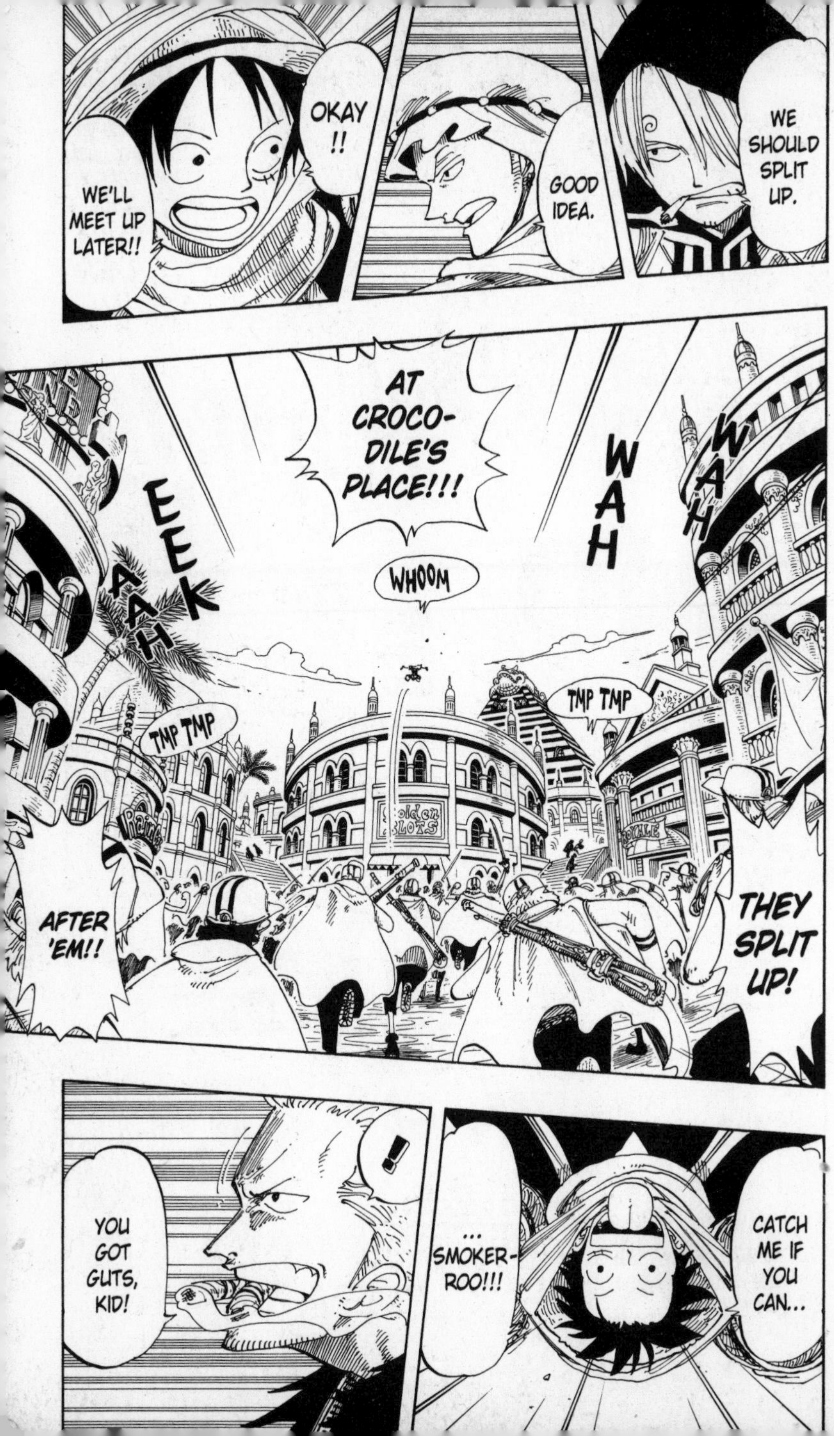
WE SHOULD SPLIT UP.
GOOD IDEA.
OKAY !!
WE'LL MEET UP LATER!!
WAH
WAH
AT CROCO-DILE'S PLACE!!!
EEEK
AAH
WHOOM
TMP TMP
TMP TMP
Golden SLOTS
ROYALE
THEY SPLIT UP!
AFTER 'EM!!
CATCH ME IF YOU CAN...
... SMOKER-ROO!!!
!
YOU GOT GUTS, KID!

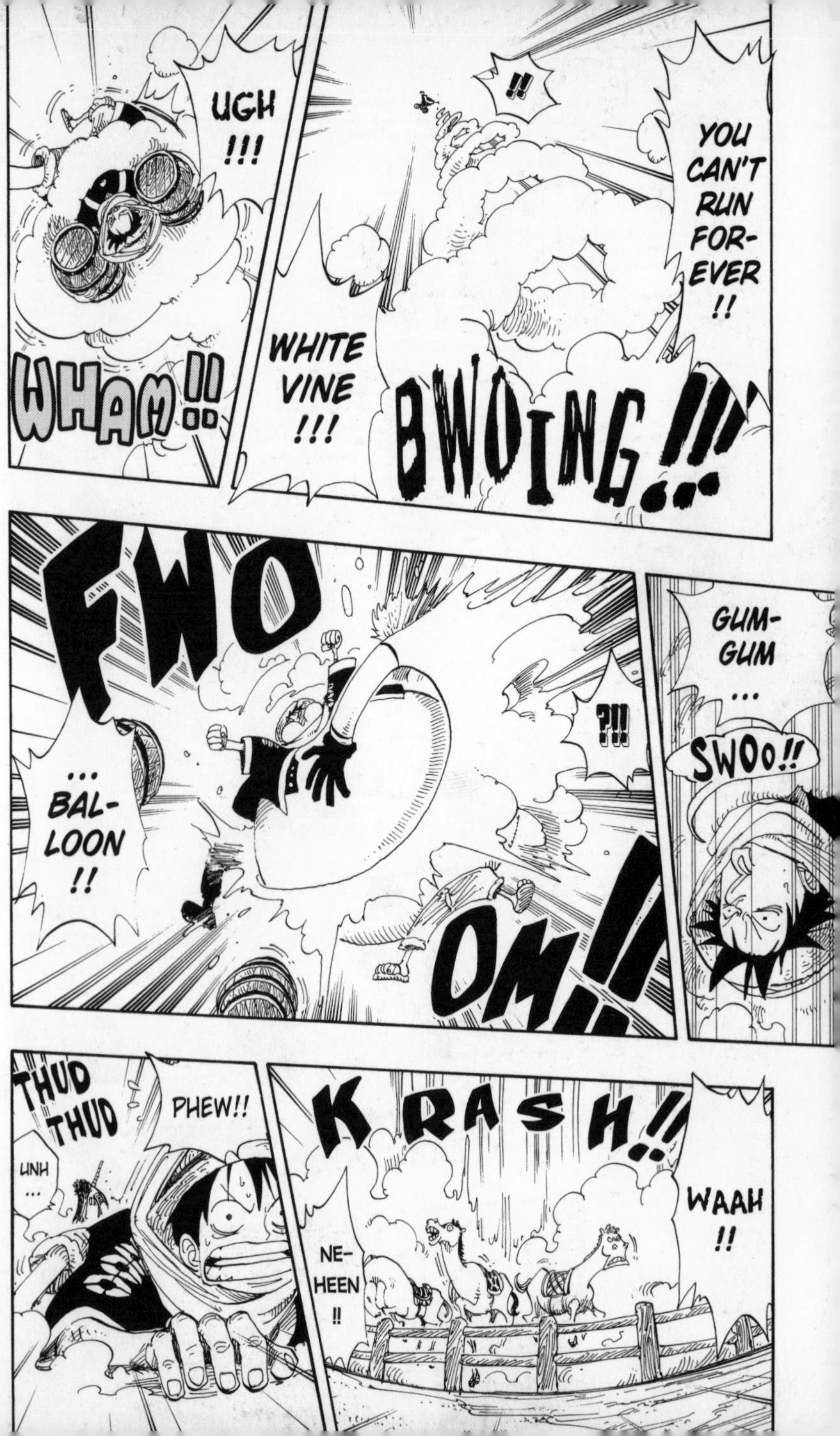
!!
YOU CAN'T RUN FOR-EVER !!
WHITE VINE !!!
BWOING!!
UGH !!!
WHAM!!
GUM-GUM ...
SWOO!!
?!!
FWOOM!!
... BAL-LOON !!
KRASH!!
WAAH !!
NE-HEEN !!
PHEW!!
THUD THUD
UNH ...

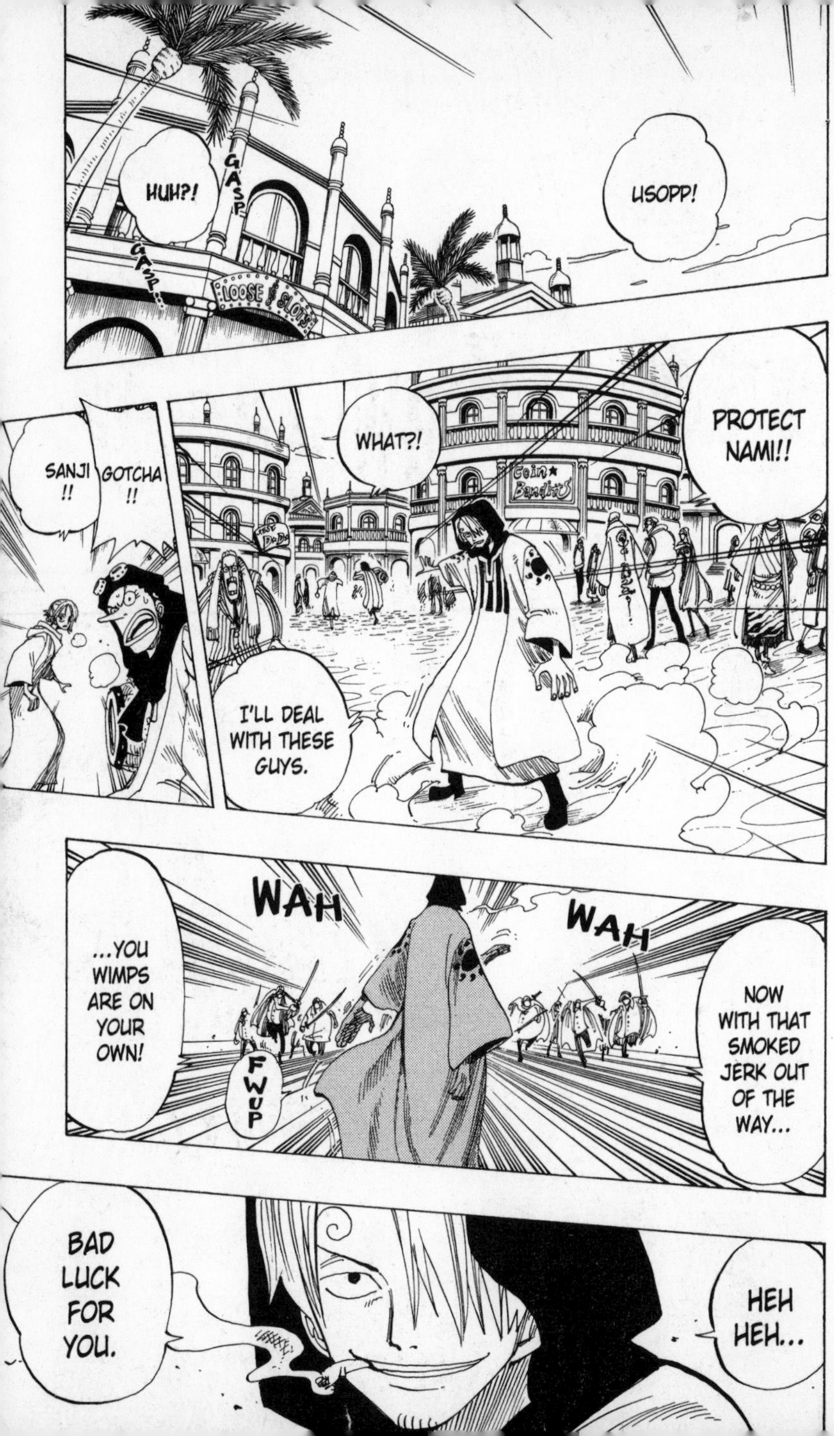
USOPP!
HUH?!
GASP
GASP...
LOOSE SLOTS
PROTECT NAMI!!
WHAT?!
Coin★Bandits
I'LL DEAL WITH THESE GUYS.
GOTCHA!!
SANJI!!
NOW WITH THAT SMOKED JERK OUT OF THE WAY...
WAH
WAH
...YOU WIMPS ARE ON YOUR OWN!
FWUP
HEH HEH...
BAD LUCK FOR YOU.

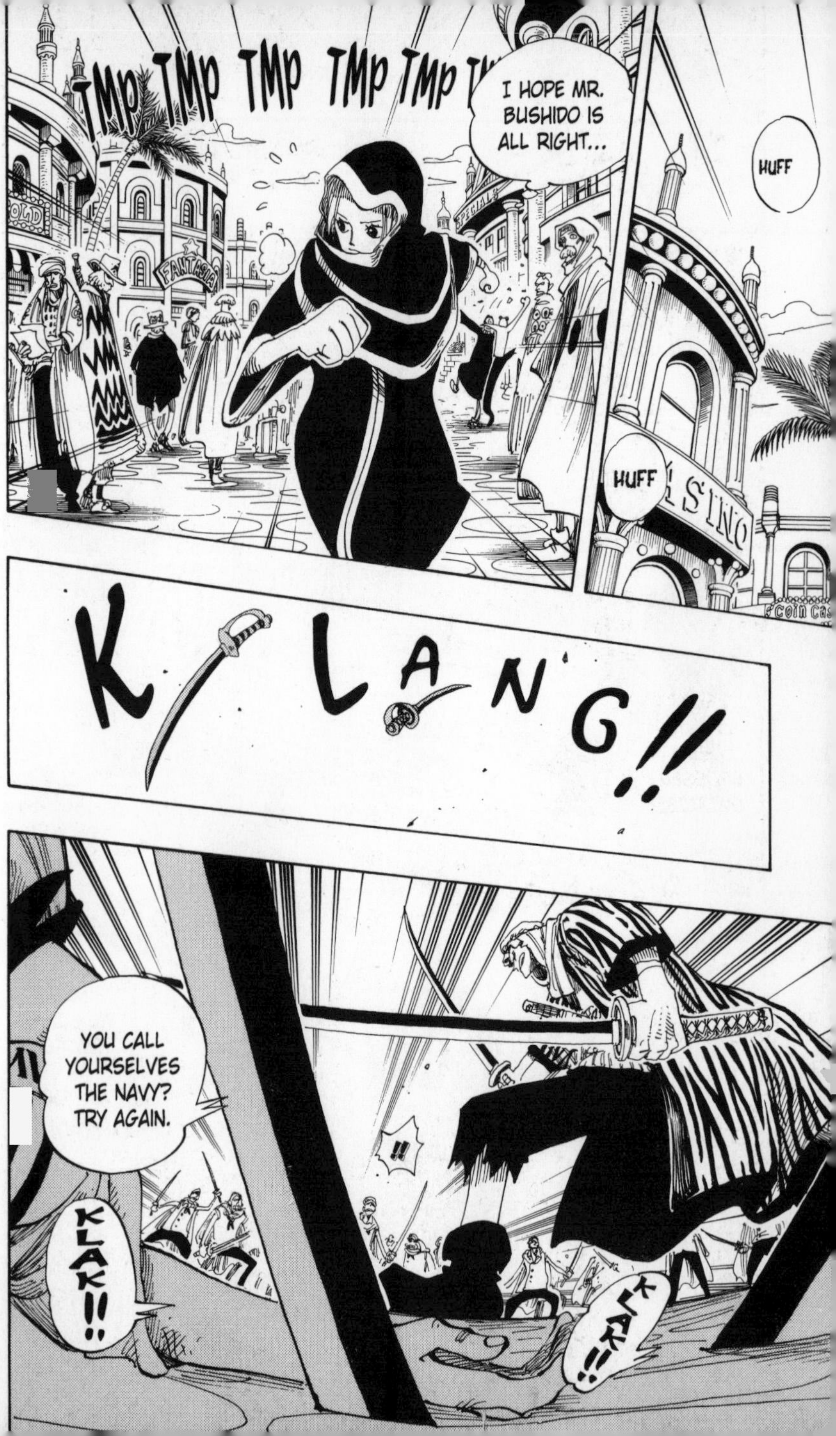
HUFF
I HOPE MR. BUSHIDO IS ALL RIGHT...
TMP TMP TMP TMP TMP
HUFF
CASINO
KLANG!!
!!
YOU CALL YOURSELVES THE NAVY? TRY AGAIN.
KLAK!!
KLAK!!

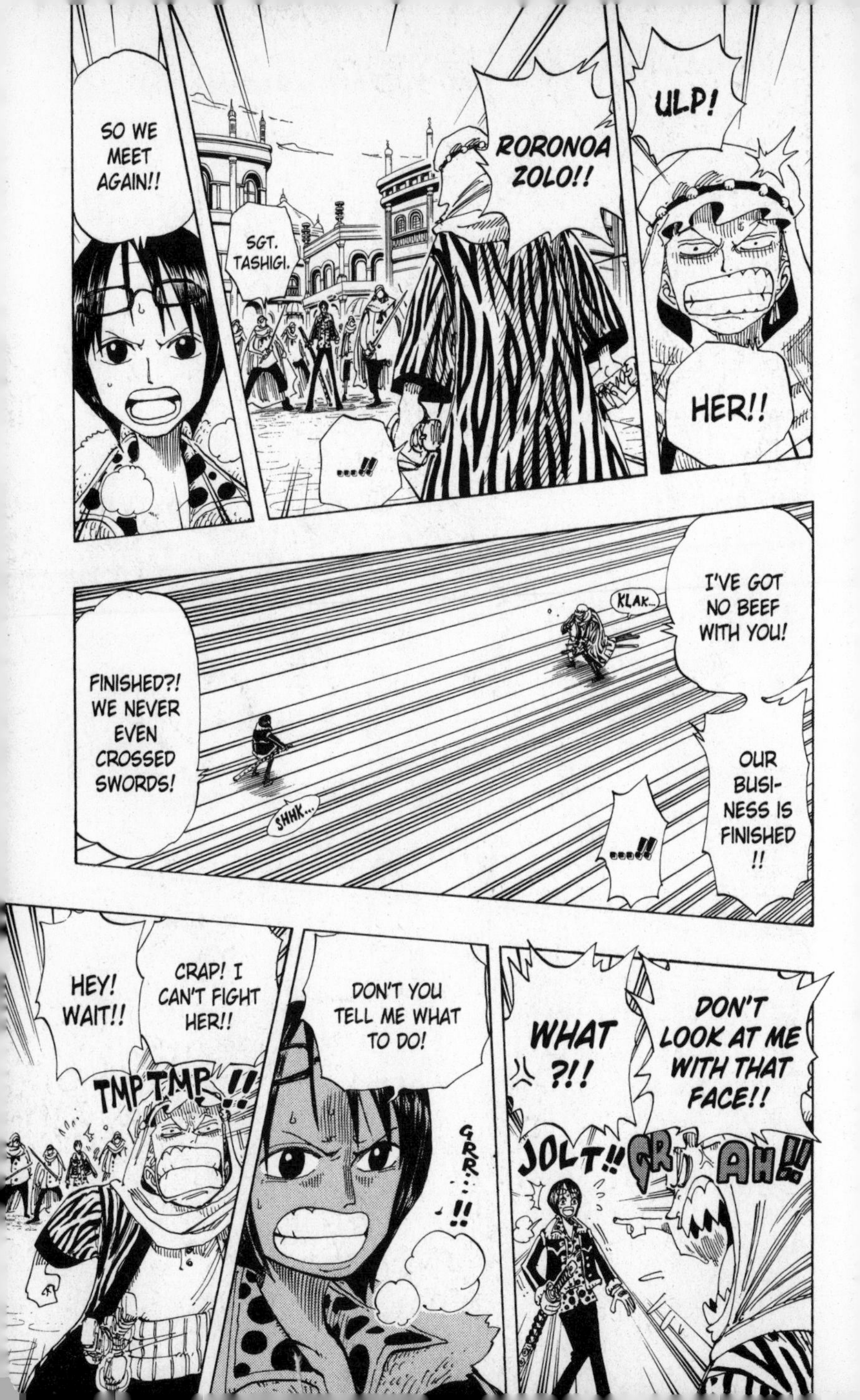
ULP!
HER!!
RORONOA ZOLO!!
SGT. TASHIGI.
...!!
SO WE MEET AGAIN!!
I'VE GOT NO BEEF WITH YOU!
KLAK...
OUR BUSI-NESS IS FINISHED!!
...!!
FINISHED?! WE NEVER EVEN CROSSED SWORDS!
SHHK...
DON'T LOOK AT ME WITH THAT FACE!!
WHAT?!!
JOLT!!
GR AH!!
DON'T YOU TELL ME WHAT TO DO!
GRR...!!
CRAP! I CAN'T FIGHT HER!!
HEY! WAIT!!
TMP TMP!!

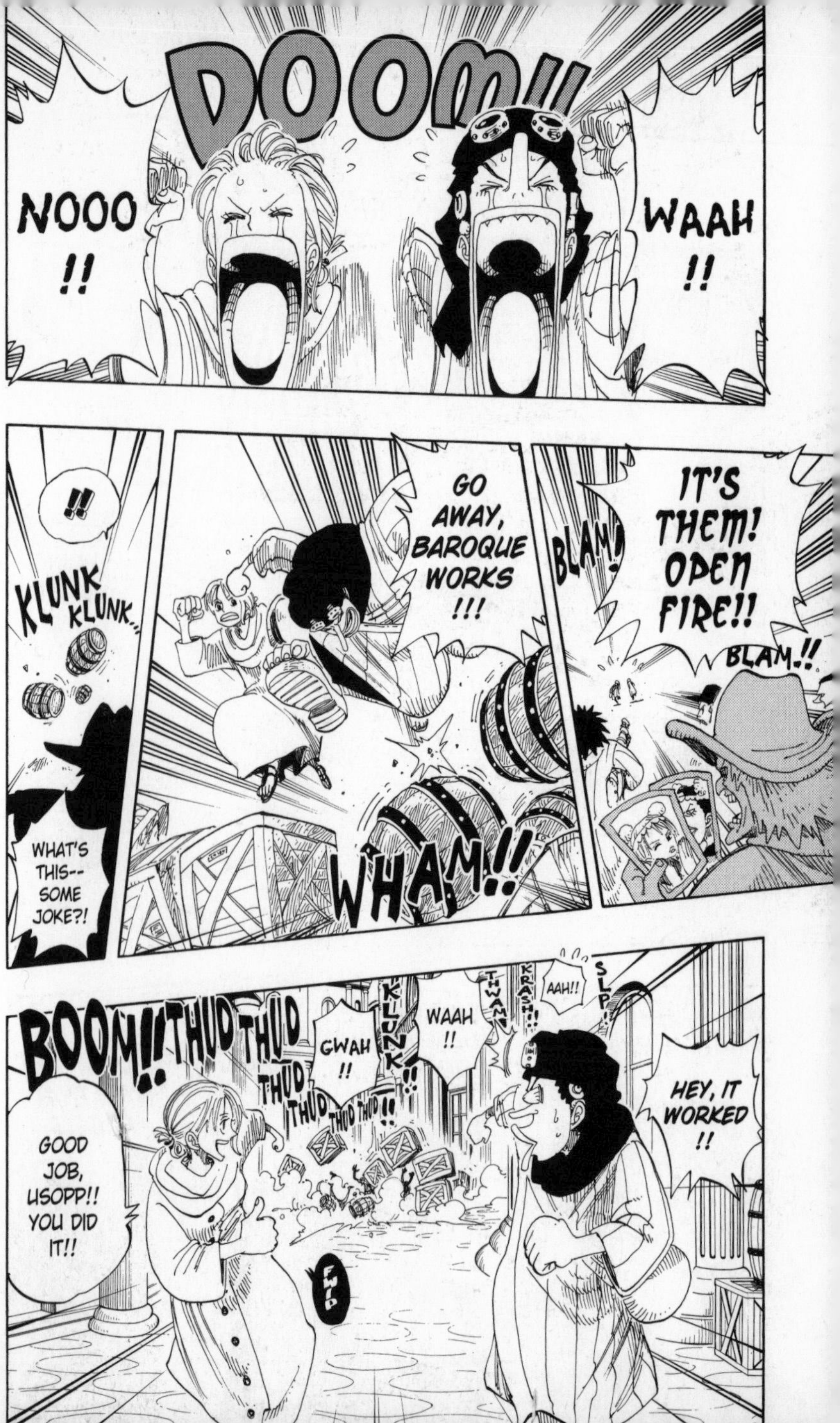
DOOM!!
WAAH!!
NOOO!!
IT'S THEM! OPEN FIRE!!
BLAM!
BLAM!!
GO AWAY, BAROQUE WORKS!!!
WHAM!!
!!
KLUNK KLUNK...
WHAT'S THIS-- SOME JOKE?!
SLP!
AAH!!
KRASH!!
THWAM
WAAH!!
KLUNK!!
HEY, IT WORKED!!
GWAH!!
BOOM!!
THUD THUD THUD THUD THUD THUD!!
GOOD JOB, USOPP!! YOU DID IT!!
FWIP

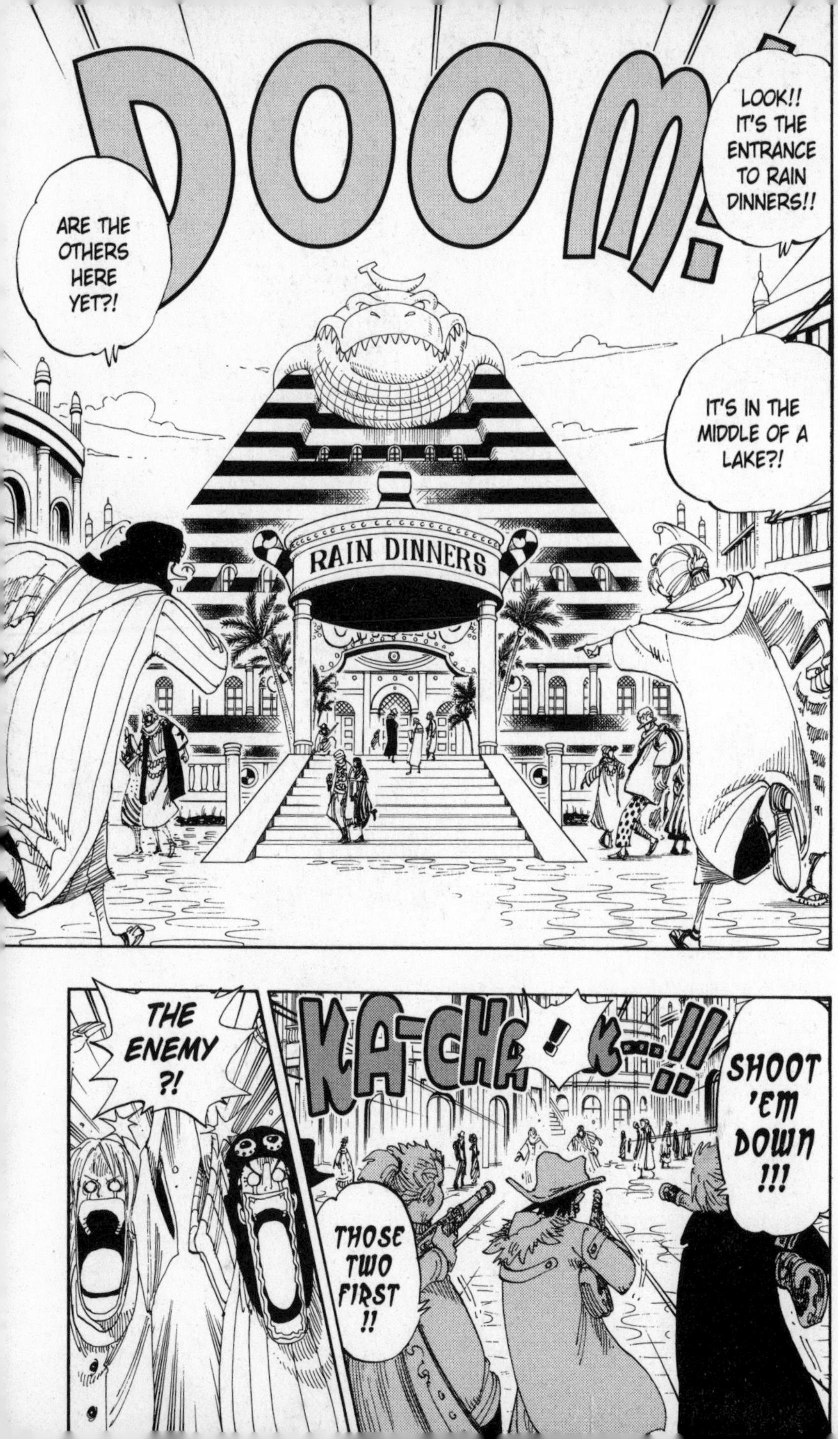
DOOM!
LOOK!! IT'S THE ENTRANCE TO RAIN DINNERS!!
ARE THE OTHERS HERE YET?!
IT'S IN THE MIDDLE OF A LAKE?!
RAIN DINNERS
SHOOT 'EM DOWN!!!
KA-CHAK...!!
THE ENEMY?!
THOSE TWO FIRST!!

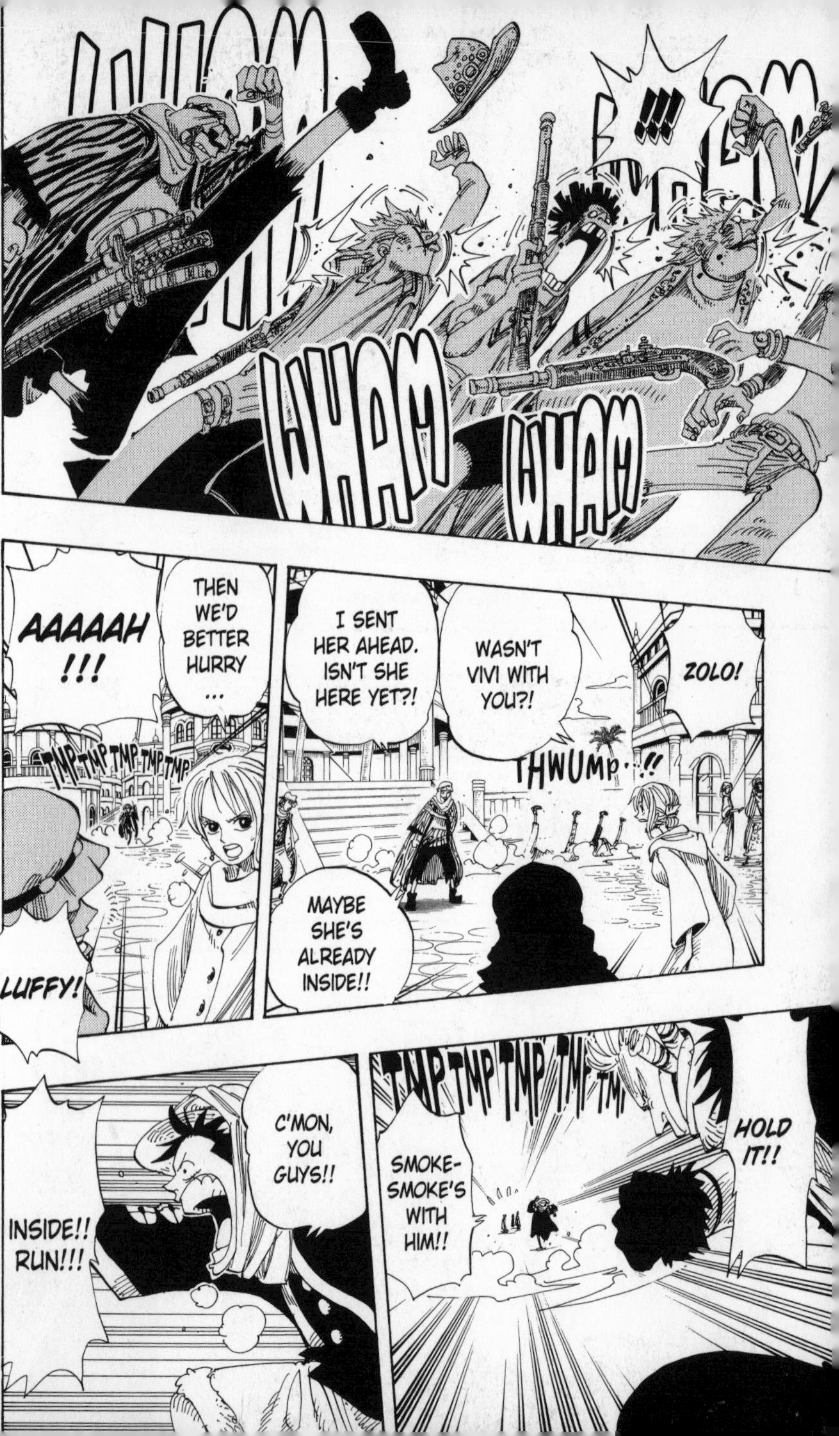
WHAM
WHAM
ZOLO!
WASN'T VIVI WITH YOU?!
I SENT HER AHEAD. ISN'T SHE HERE YET?!
THWUMP...!!
MAYBE SHE'S ALREADY INSIDE!!
THEN WE'D BETTER HURRY...
AAAAAH!!!
TMP TMP TMP TMP TMP
LUFFY!
TMP TMP TMP TMP TM
HOLD IT!!
SMOKE-SMOKE'S WITH HIM!!
C'MON, YOU GUYS!!
INSIDE!! RUN!!!

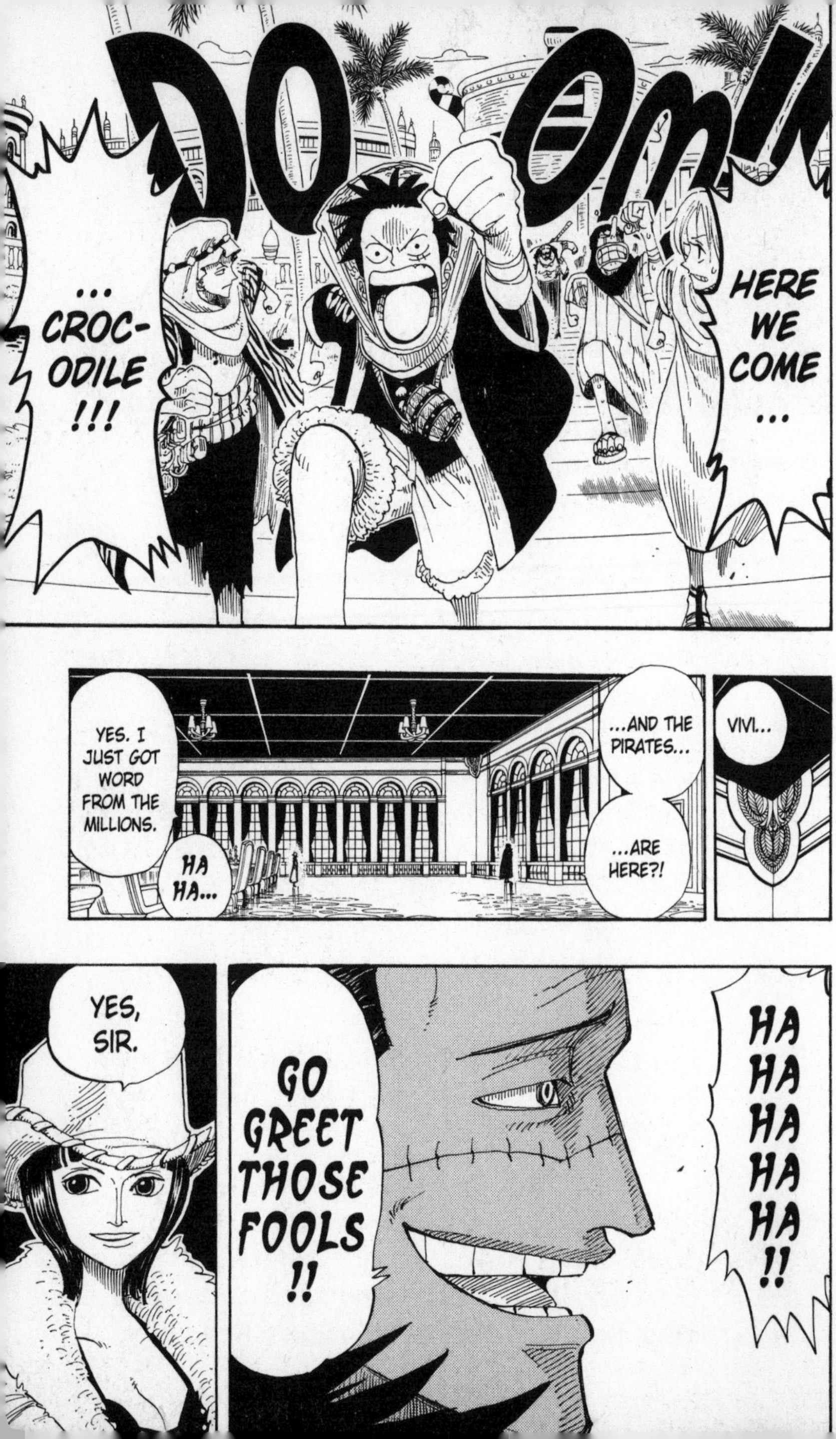
DOOM!!
HERE WE COME...
...CROCODILE!!!
VIVI...
...AND THE PIRATES...
...ARE HERE?!
YES. I JUST GOT WORD FROM THE MILLIONS.
HA HA...
HA HA HA HA HA!!
GO GREET THOSE FOOLS!!
YES, SIR.

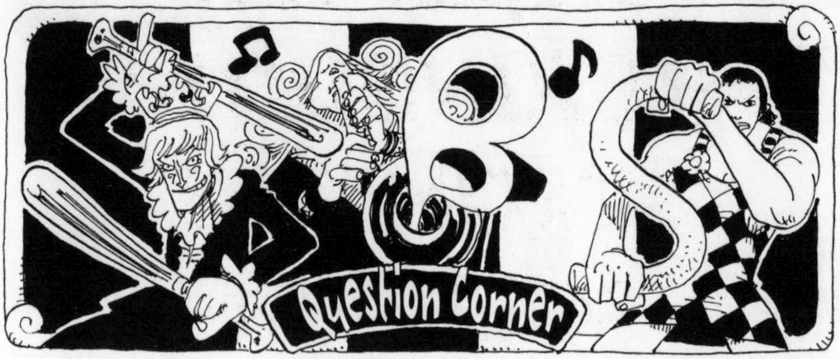
Question Corner

Reader: Oda Sensei, how old are Dorry and Broggy?

Oda: Well, giants can live to be 300 years old and they mature at about half the rate of normal humans. That means they reach adulthood at the age of 40. Dorry and Broggy were both 58 years old (the equivalent of 29 for humans) when they first began fighting on Little Garden. They went on fighting for 100 years, so that makes them 158 years old. Since they can live for 300 years, they're still in their fighting prime. But they're a little older than Dr. Kureha.

Reader: Hi! My nose won't stop running. Oh, it finally stopped. Mr. Oda, I've been wondering about Chopper, the blue-nosed reindeer. Why is there an "X" on Chopper's hat? Uh-oh, my nose is running again…

Oda: Oh, I see. So, about the snot… Whoops! I mean…the "X" on Chopper's hat is the cross symbol from the hospital, only it's crooked. Not too many people noticed this, but it's also on Hiriluk's head.

# Chapter 169:
# THE KINGDOM'S STRONGEST WARRIOR

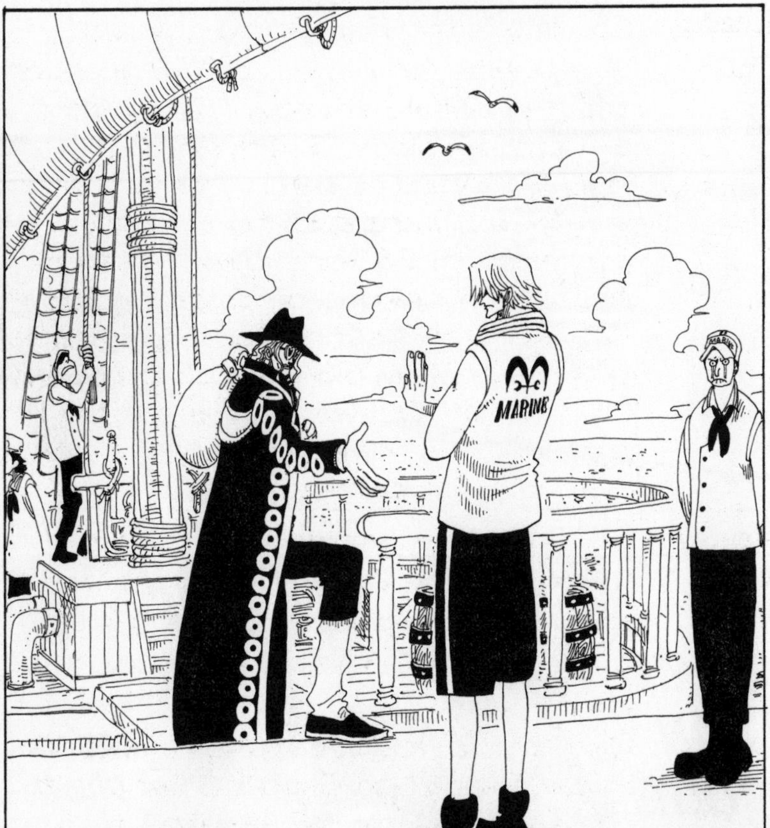
MARINE
MARINE
DJANGO'S DANCE PARADISE, VOL. 34:
"AN IMPOSSIBLE FRIENDSHIP"

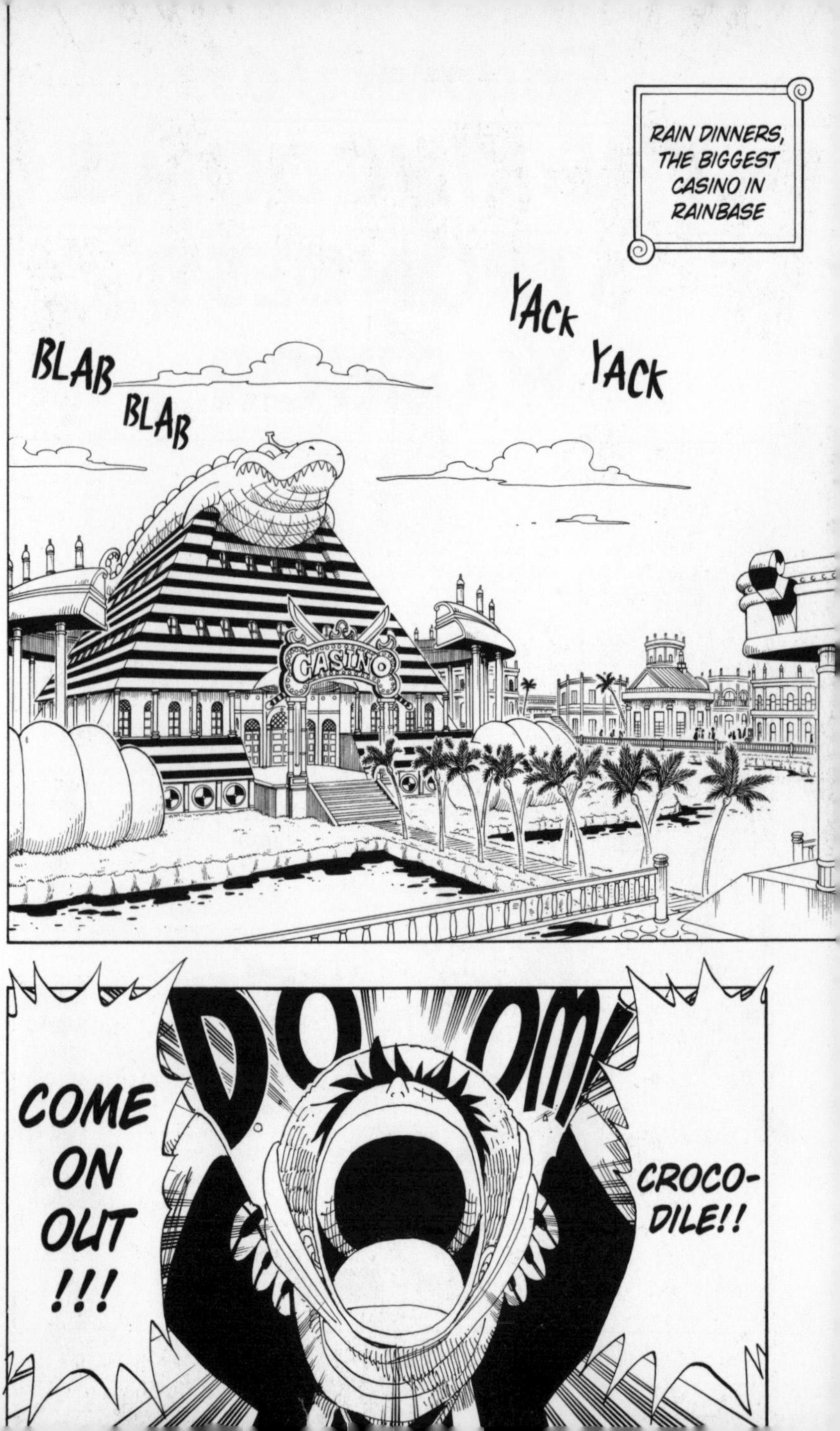
RAIN DINNERS, THE BIGGEST CASINO IN RAINBASE
YACK YACK
BLAB BLAB
CASINO
DOOM
CROCO-DILE!!
COME ON OUT!!!

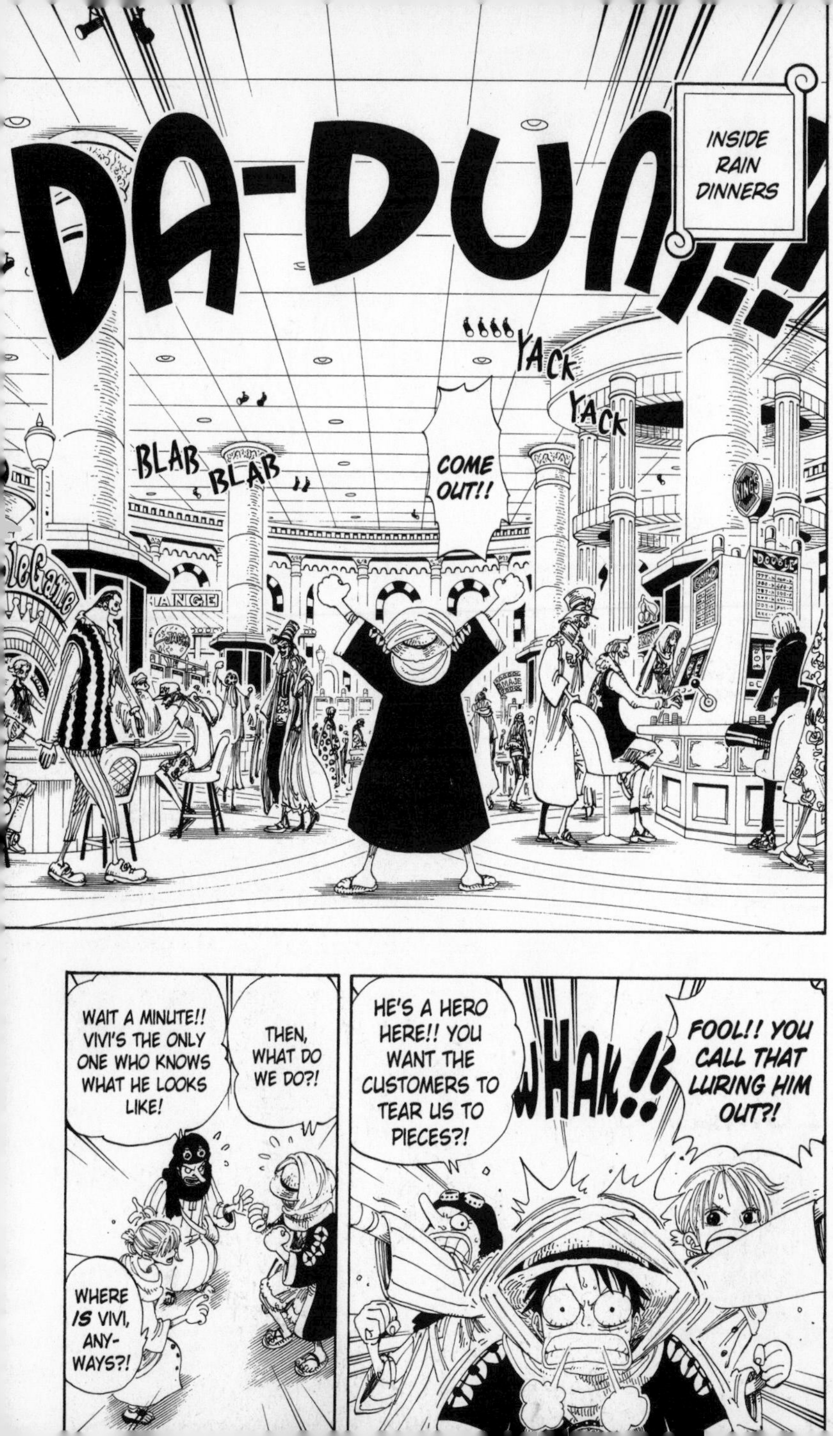
INSIDE RAIN DINNERS
DA-DUN!!!
YACK YACK
COME OUT!!
BLAB BLAB
FOOL!! YOU CALL THAT LURING HIM OUT?!
WHAK!!
HE'S A HERO HERE!! YOU WANT THE CUSTOMERS TO TEAR US TO PIECES?!
THEN, WHAT DO WE DO?!
WAIT A MINUTE!! VIVI'S THE ONLY ONE WHO KNOWS WHAT HE LOOKS LIKE!
WHERE IS VIVI, ANY-WAYS?!

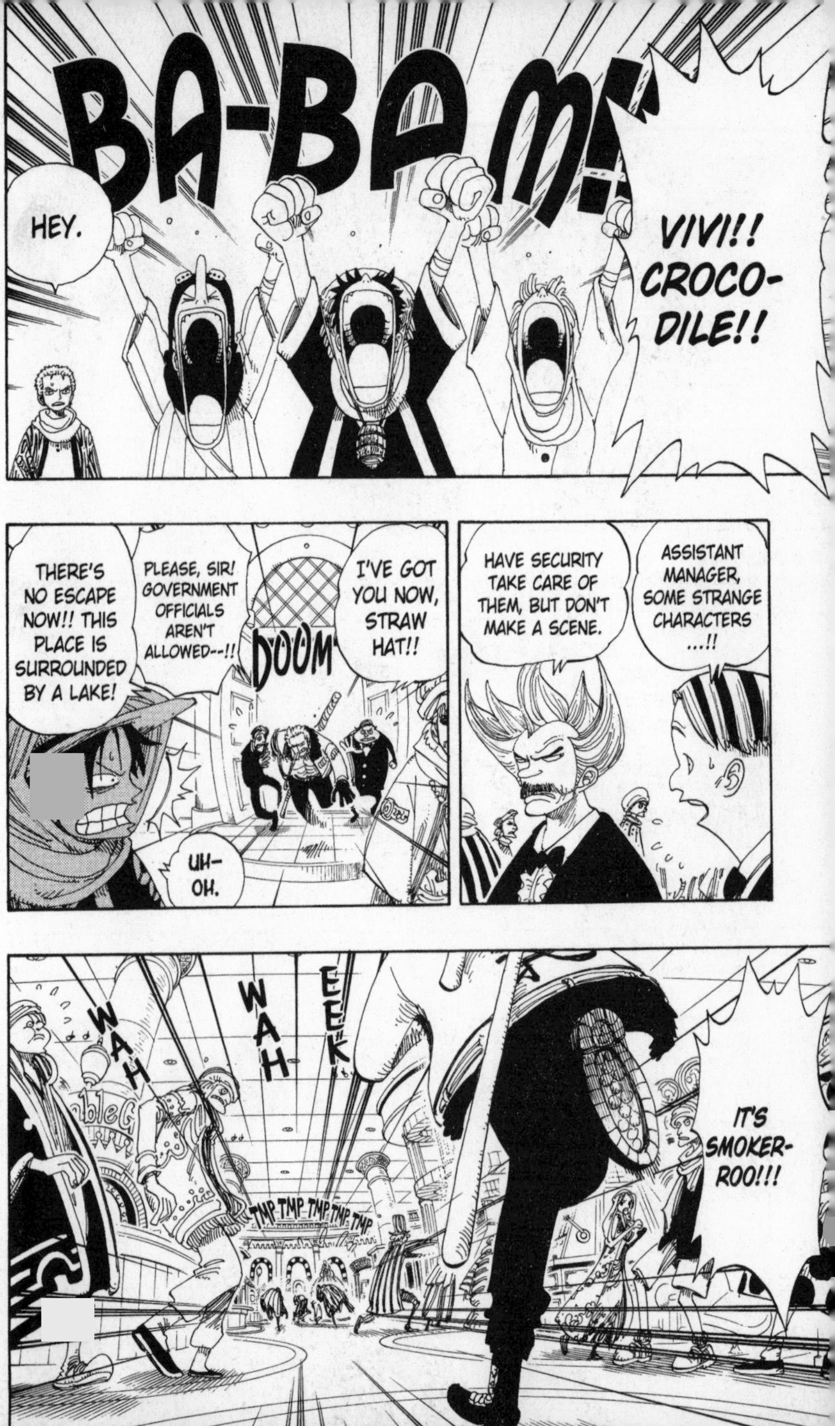
VIVI!! CROCO-DILE!!
BA-BAM
HEY.
ASSISTANT MANAGER, SOME STRANGE CHARACTERS ...!!
HAVE SECURITY TAKE CARE OF THEM, BUT DON'T MAKE A SCENE.
I'VE GOT YOU NOW, STRAW HAT!!
DOOM
PLEASE, SIR! GOVERNMENT OFFICIALS AREN'T ALLOWED--!!
THERE'S NO ESCAPE NOW!! THIS PLACE IS SURROUNDED BY A LAKE!
UH-OH.
IT'S SMOKER-ROO!!!
EEK
WAH
WAH
TMP TMP TMP TMP TMP

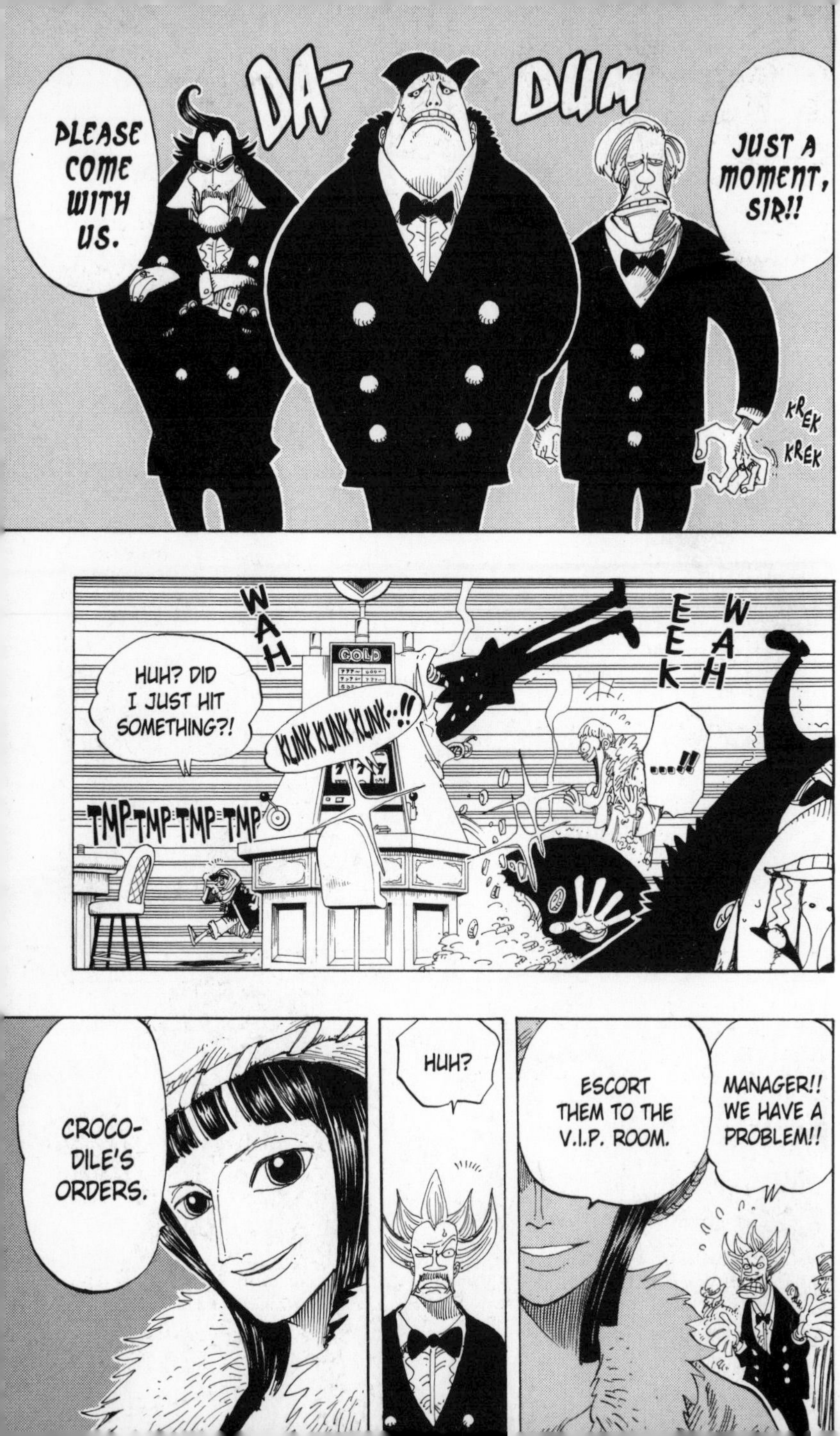
JUST A MOMENT, SIR!!
DA-DUM
PLEASE COME WITH US.
KREK KREK
WAH
WEEK
...!!
KLUNK KLUNK KLUNK..!!
HUH? DID I JUST HIT SOMETHING?!
WAH
TMP TMP TMP TMP
MANAGER!! WE HAVE A PROBLEM!!
ESCORT THEM TO THE V.I.P. ROOM.
HUH?
CROCO-DILE'S ORDERS.

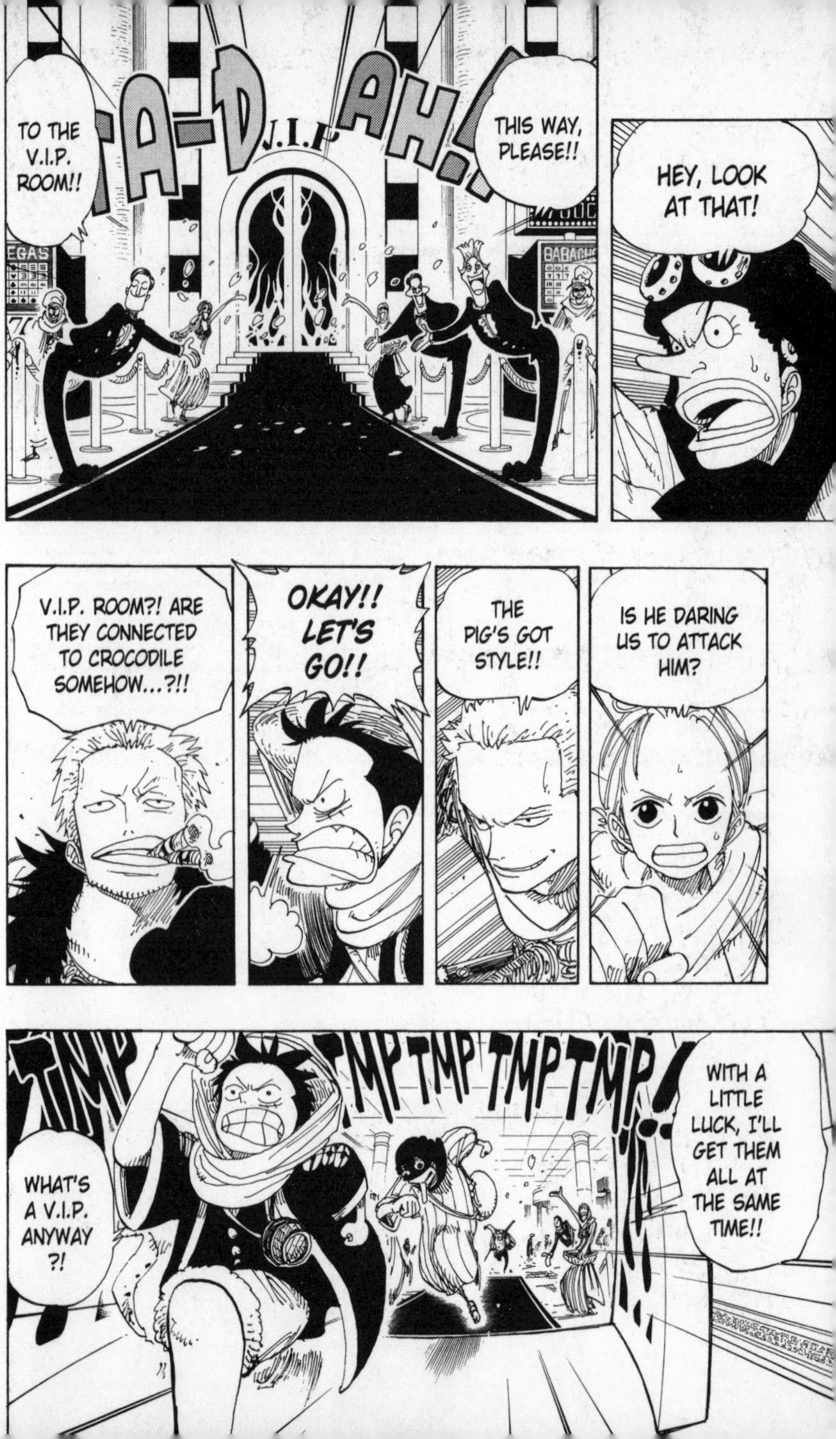
HEY, LOOK AT THAT!
THIS WAY, PLEASE!!
TA-DAH!!
TO THE V.I.P. ROOM!!
IS HE DARING US TO ATTACK HIM?
THE PIG'S GOT STYLE!!
OKAY!! LET'S GO!!
V.I.P. ROOM?! ARE THEY CONNECTED TO CROCODILE SOMEHOW...?!!
WITH A LITTLE LUCK, I'LL GET THEM ALL AT THE SAME TIME!!
TMP TMP TMP TMP TMP!
WHAT'S A V.I.P. ANYWAY?!

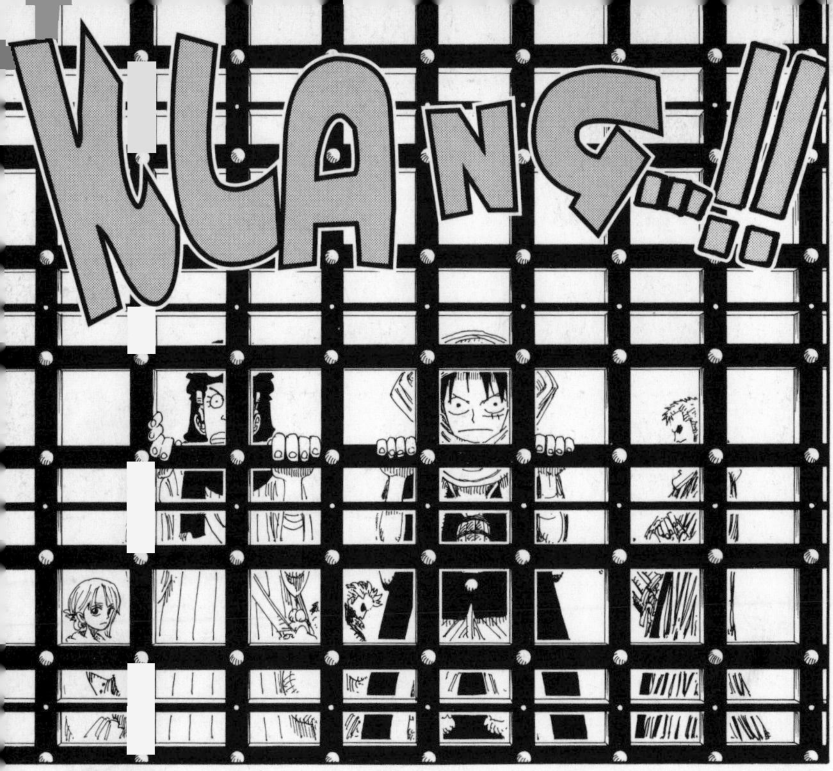
KLANG...!!
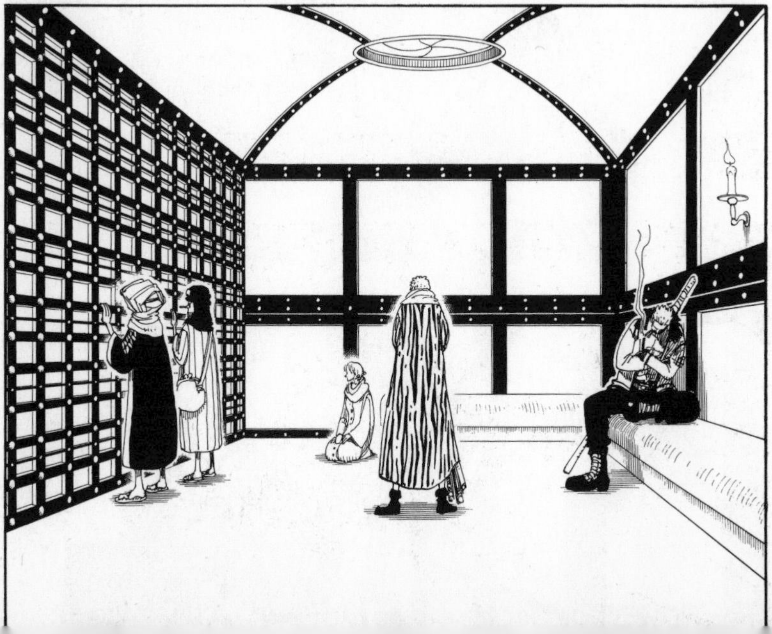

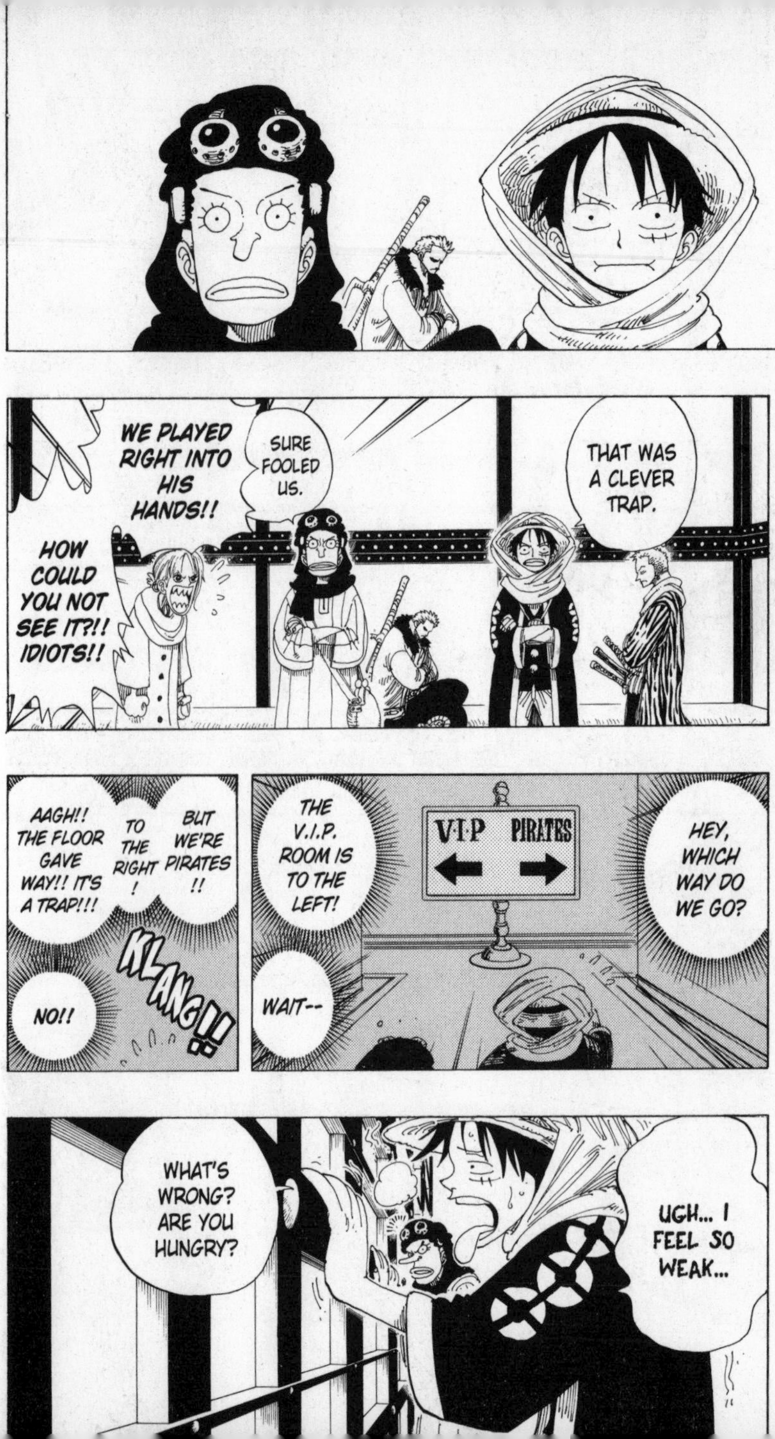
THAT WAS A CLEVER TRAP.
SURE FOOLED US.
WE PLAYED RIGHT INTO HIS HANDS!!
HOW COULD YOU NOT SEE IT?!! IDIOTS!!
HEY, WHICH WAY DO WE GO?
V.I.P
PIRATES
THE V.I.P. ROOM IS TO THE LEFT!
WAIT--
BUT WE'RE PIRATES!!
TO THE RIGHT!
AAGH!! THE FLOOR GAVE WAY!! IT'S A TRAP!!!
KLANG!!
NO!!
UGH... I FEEL SO WEAK...
WHAT'S WRONG? ARE YOU HUNGRY?

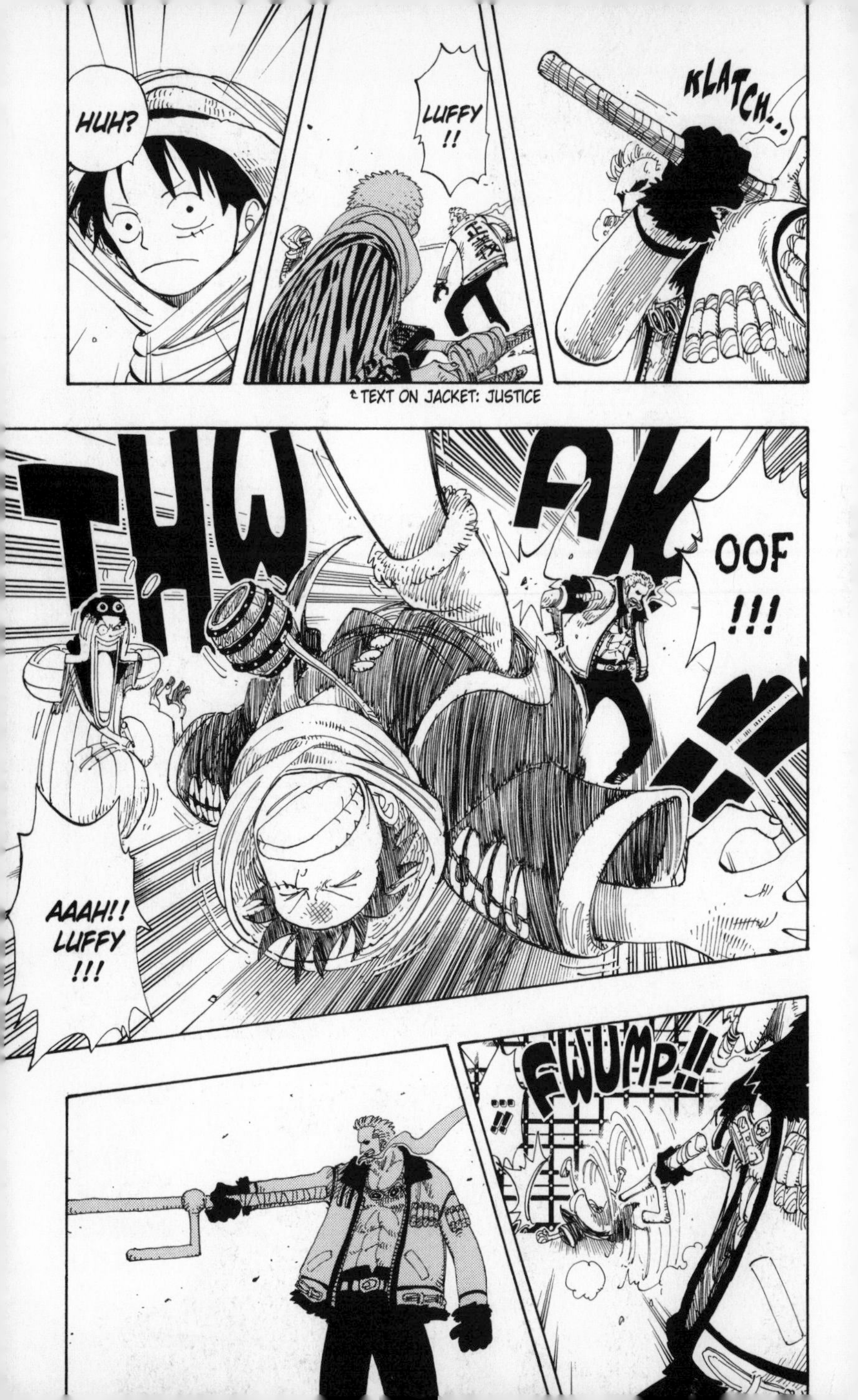
KLATCH...
LUFFY !!
HUH?
TEXT ON JACKET: JUSTICE
THWAK
OOF !!!
AAAH!! LUFFY !!!
FWUMP!!
...!!

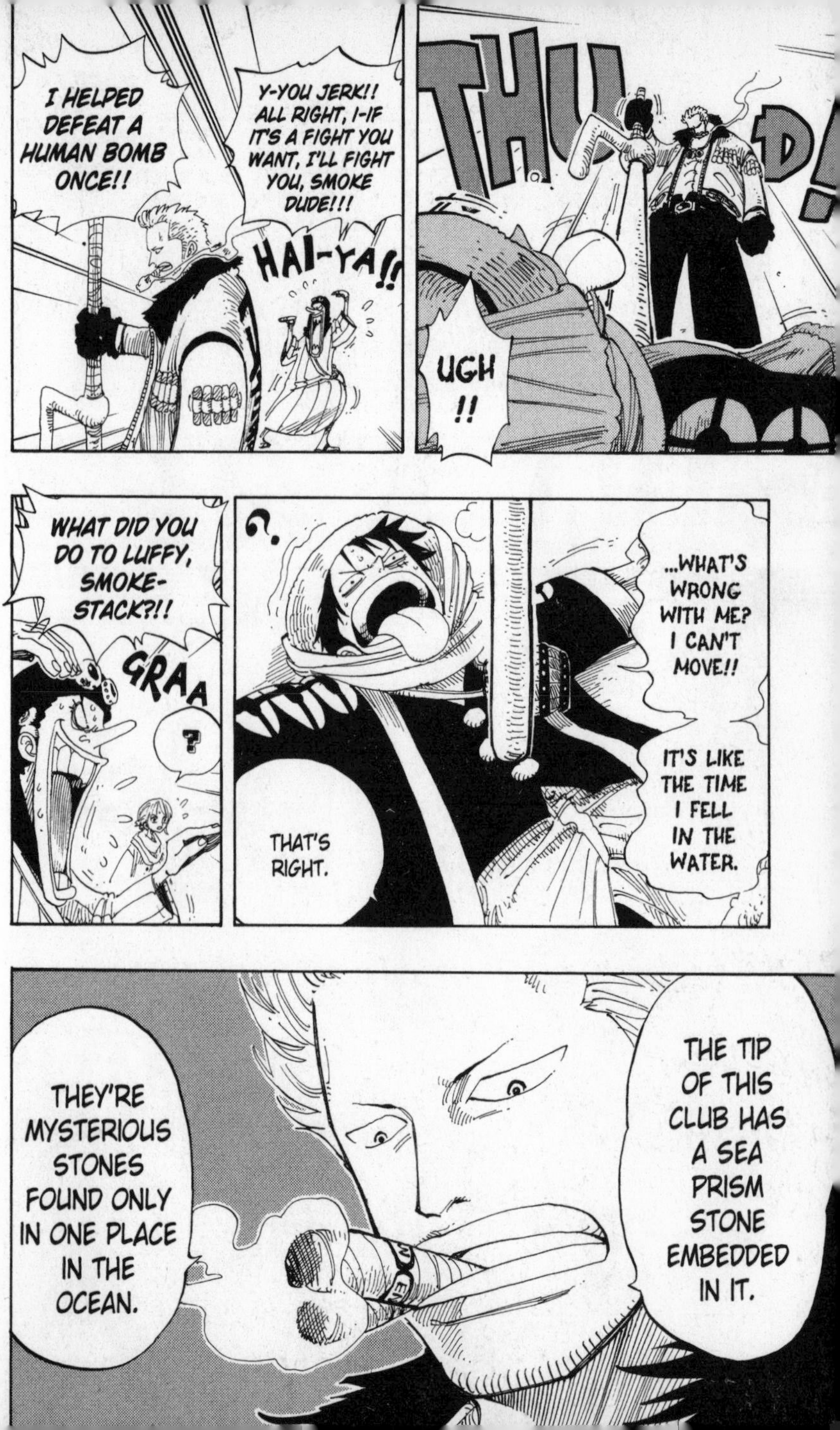
THUD!!
UGH!!
I HELPED DEFEAT A HUMAN BOMB ONCE!!
Y-YOU JERK!! ALL RIGHT, I-IF IT'S A FIGHT YOU WANT, I'LL FIGHT YOU, SMOKE DUDE!!!
HAI-YA!!
...WHAT'S WRONG WITH ME? I CAN'T MOVE!!
IT'S LIKE THE TIME I FELL IN THE WATER.
?
THAT'S RIGHT.
WHAT DID YOU DO TO LUFFY, SMOKE-STACK?!!
GRAA
?
THE TIP OF THIS CLUB HAS A SEA PRISM STONE EMBEDDED IN IT.
THEY'RE MYSTERIOUS STONES FOUND ONLY IN ONE PLACE IN THE OCEAN.

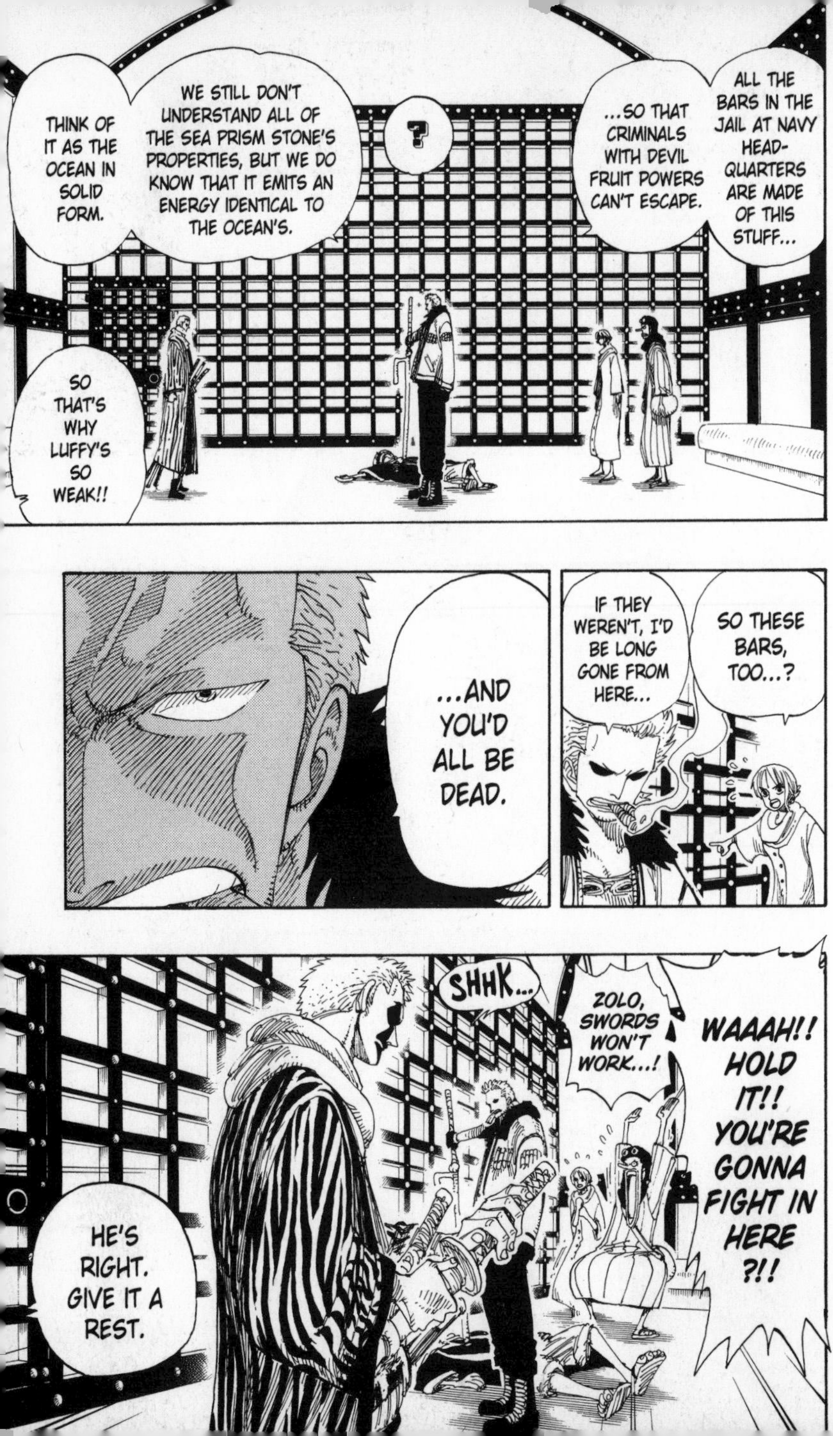
ALL THE BARS IN THE JAIL AT NAVY HEAD-QUARTERS ARE MADE OF THIS STUFF...
...SO THAT CRIMINALS WITH DEVIL FRUIT POWERS CAN'T ESCAPE.
?
WE STILL DON'T UNDERSTAND ALL OF THE SEA PRISM STONE'S PROPERTIES, BUT WE DO KNOW THAT IT EMITS AN ENERGY IDENTICAL TO THE OCEAN'S.
THINK OF IT AS THE OCEAN IN SOLID FORM.
SO THAT'S WHY LUFFY'S SO WEAK!!
SO THESE BARS, TOO...?
IF THEY WEREN'T, I'D BE LONG GONE FROM HERE...
...AND YOU'D ALL BE DEAD.
WAAAH!! HOLD IT!! YOU'RE GONNA FIGHT IN HERE?!!
ZOLO, SWORDS WON'T WORK...!
SHHK...
HE'S RIGHT. GIVE IT A REST.

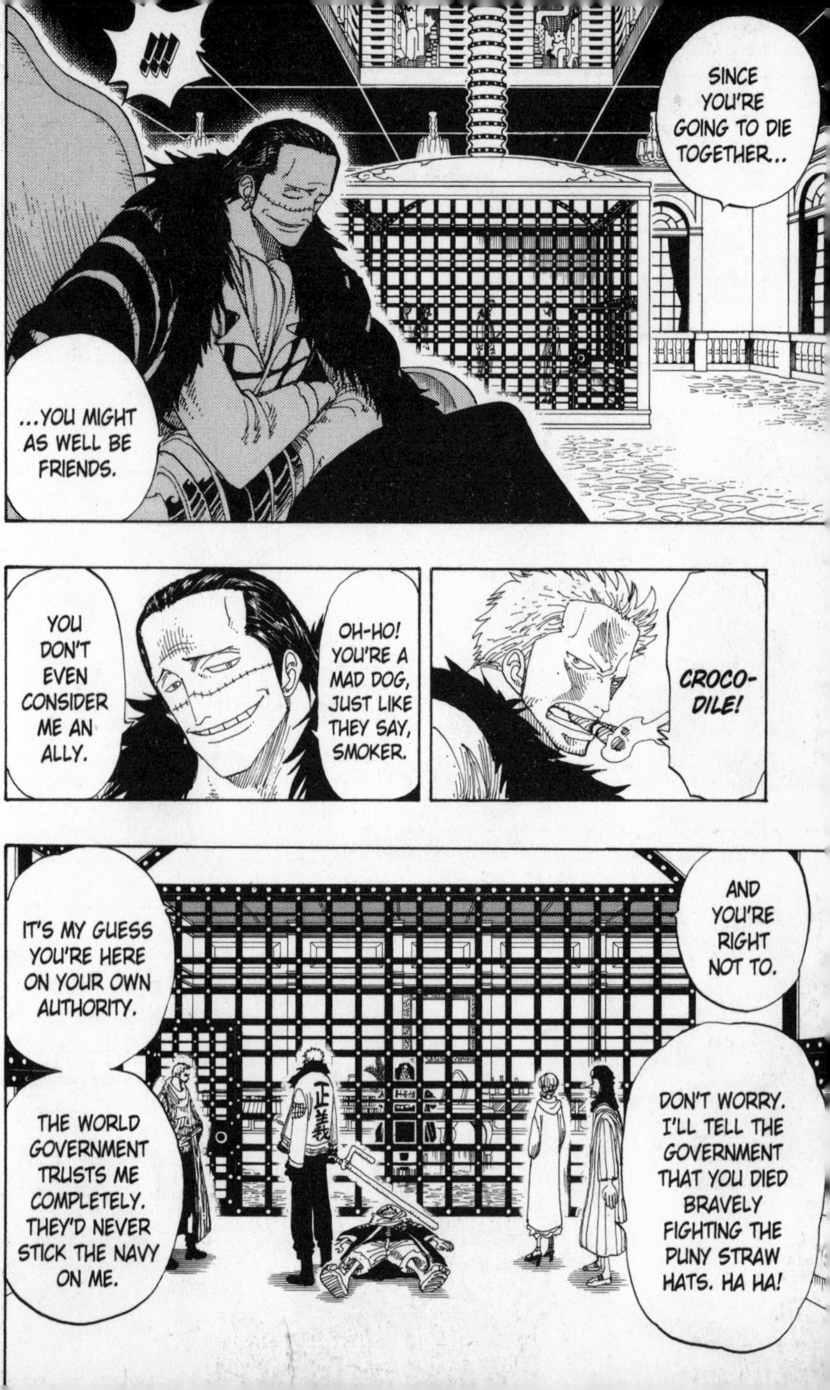
SINCE YOU'RE GOING TO DIE TOGETHER...
!!!
...YOU MIGHT AS WELL BE FRIENDS.
CROCO-DILE!
OH-HO! YOU'RE A MAD DOG, JUST LIKE THEY SAY, SMOKER.
YOU DON'T EVEN CONSIDER ME AN ALLY.
AND YOU'RE RIGHT NOT TO.
IT'S MY GUESS YOU'RE HERE ON YOUR OWN AUTHORITY.
THE WORLD GOVERNMENT TRUSTS ME COMPLETELY. THEY'D NEVER STICK THE NAVY ON ME.
DON'T WORRY. I'LL TELL THE GOVERNMENT THAT YOU DIED BRAVELY FIGHTING THE PUNY STRAW HATS. HA HA!

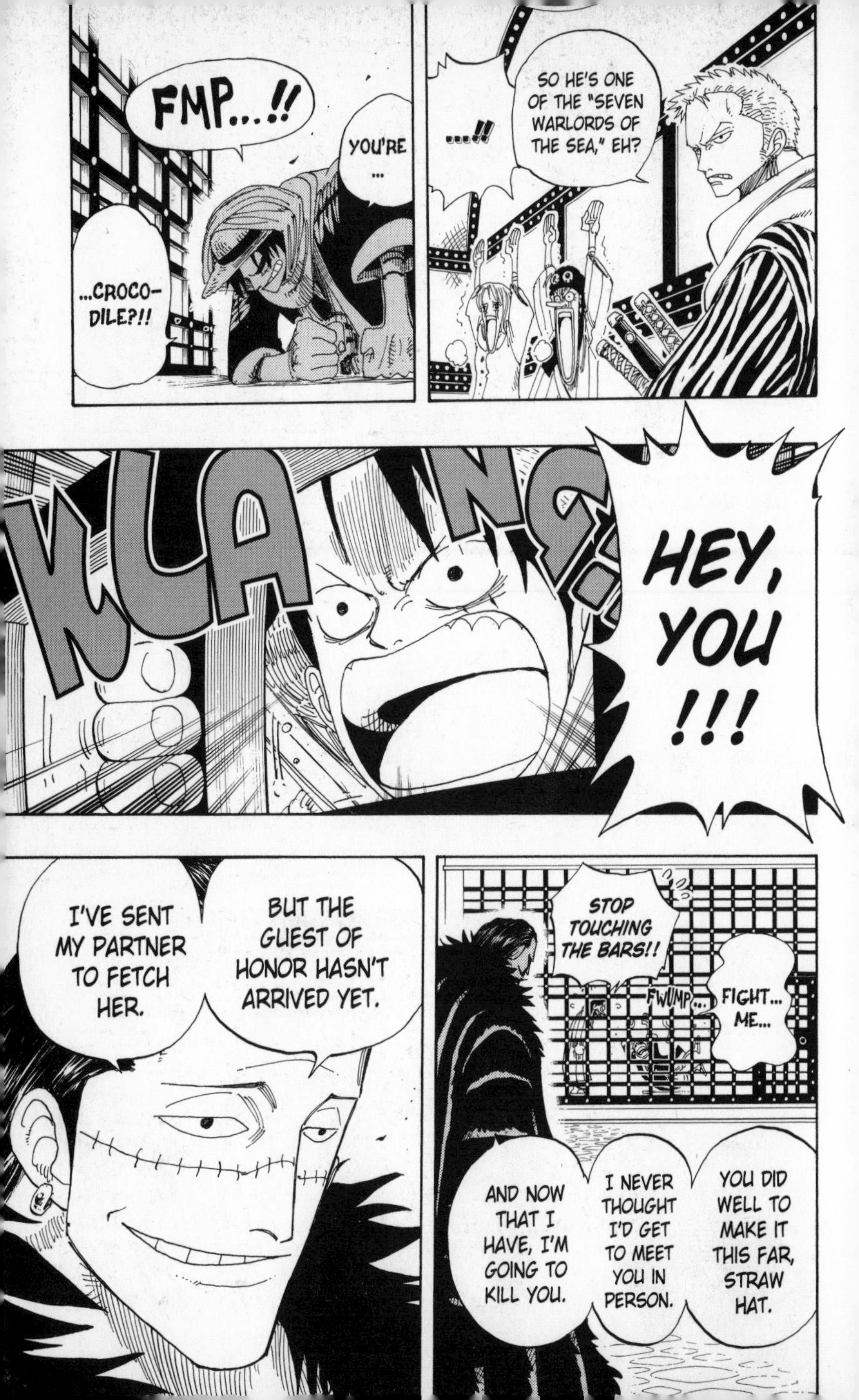
SO HE'S ONE OF THE "SEVEN WARLORDS OF THE SEA," EH?
...!!
FMP...!!
YOU'RE ...
...CROCO-DILE?!!
HEY, YOU!!!
KLANG
STOP TOUCHING THE BARS!!
FWUMP...
FIGHT... ME...
YOU DID WELL TO MAKE IT THIS FAR, STRAW HAT.
I NEVER THOUGHT I'D GET TO MEET YOU IN PERSON.
AND NOW THAT I HAVE, I'M GOING TO KILL YOU.
BUT THE GUEST OF HONOR HASN'T ARRIVED YET.
I'VE SENT MY PARTNER TO FETCH HER.

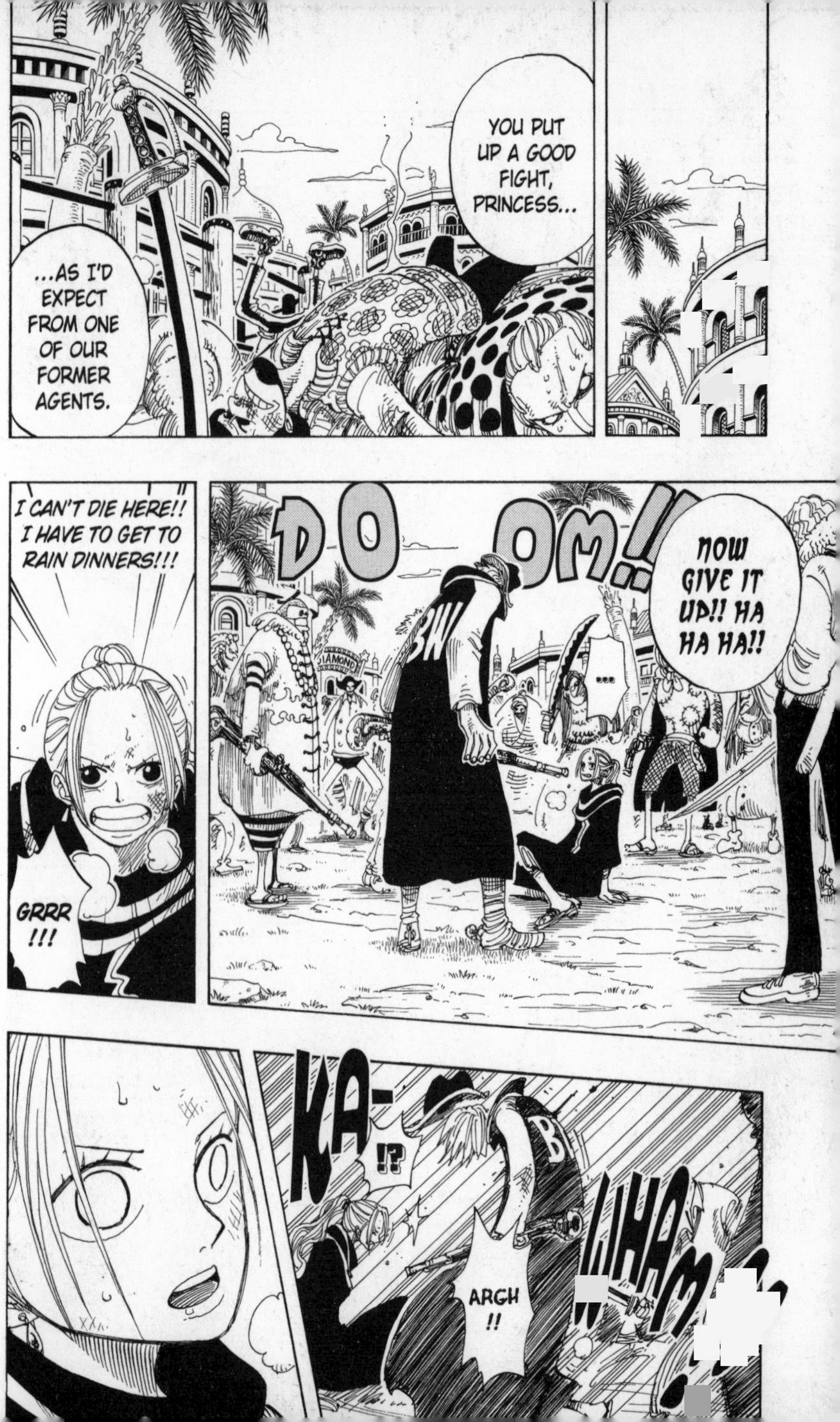
YOU PUT UP A GOOD FIGHT, PRINCESS...
...AS I'D EXPECT FROM ONE OF OUR FORMER AGENTS.
DOOM!!
NOW GIVE IT UP!! HA HA HA!!
...
I CAN'T DIE HERE!! I HAVE TO GET TO RAIN DINNERS!!!
GRRR !!!
KA-
!?
WHAM
ARGH !!

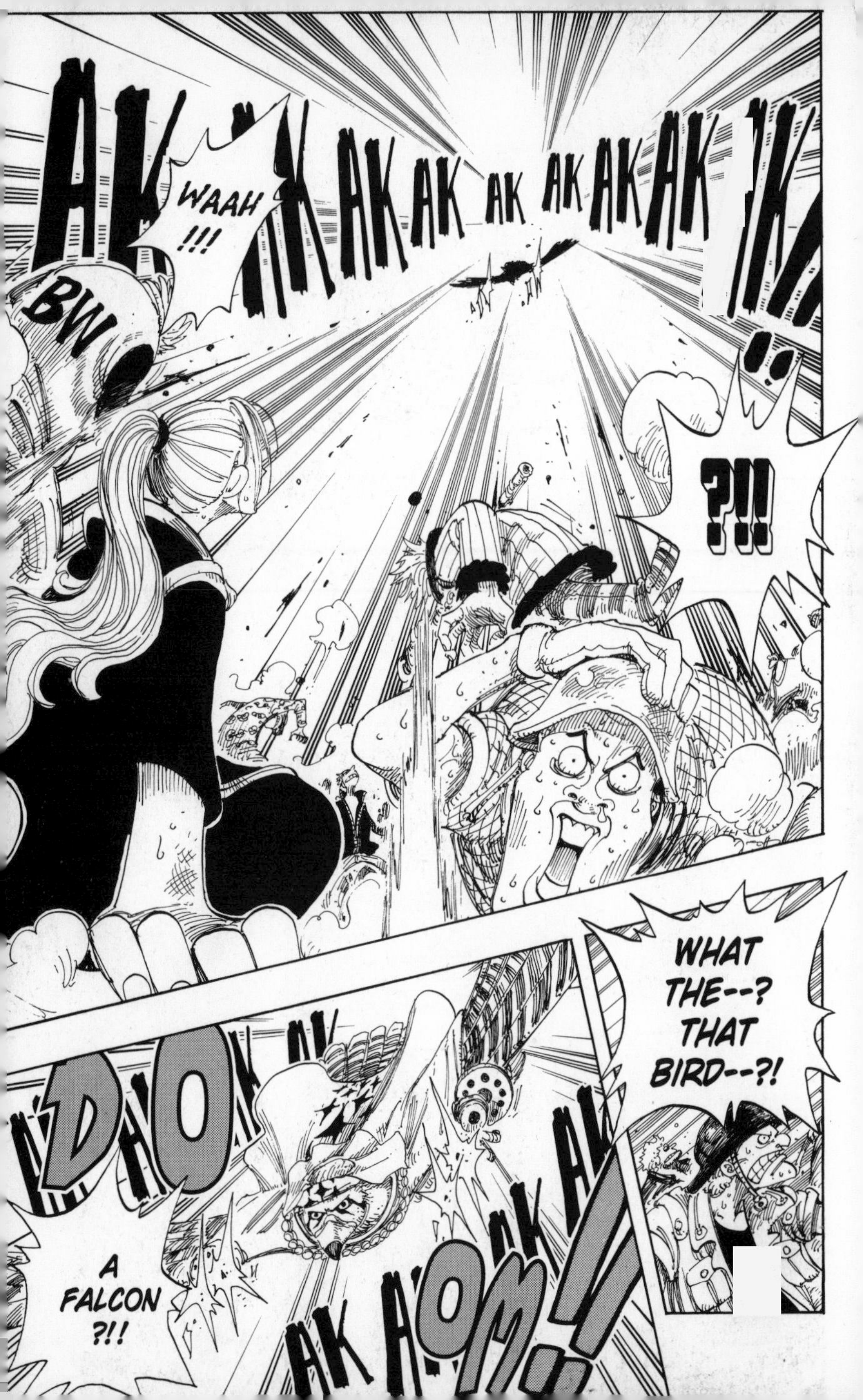
AK AK AK AK AK AK
?!!
WAAH !!!
BW
WHAT THE--? THAT BIRD--?!
AK AK AK AK
A FALCON ?!!

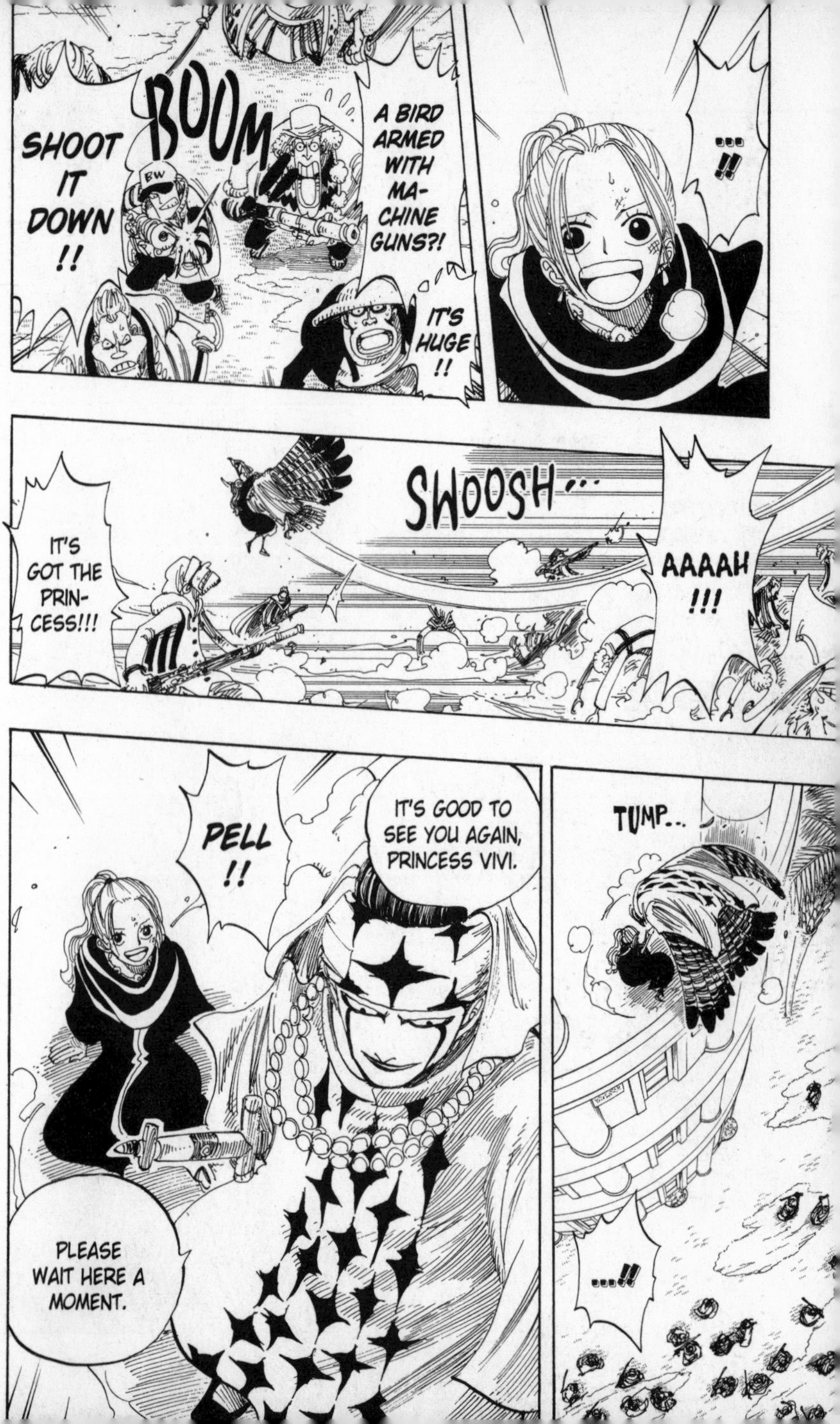
...!!
A BIRD ARMED WITH MA-CHINE GUNS?!
BOOM
IT'S HUGE!!
SHOOT IT DOWN!!
AAAAH!!!
SWOOSH...
IT'S GOT THE PRIN-CESS!!!
TUMP...
...!!
IT'S GOOD TO SEE YOU AGAIN, PRINCESS VIVI.
PELL!!
PLEASE WAIT HERE A MOMENT.

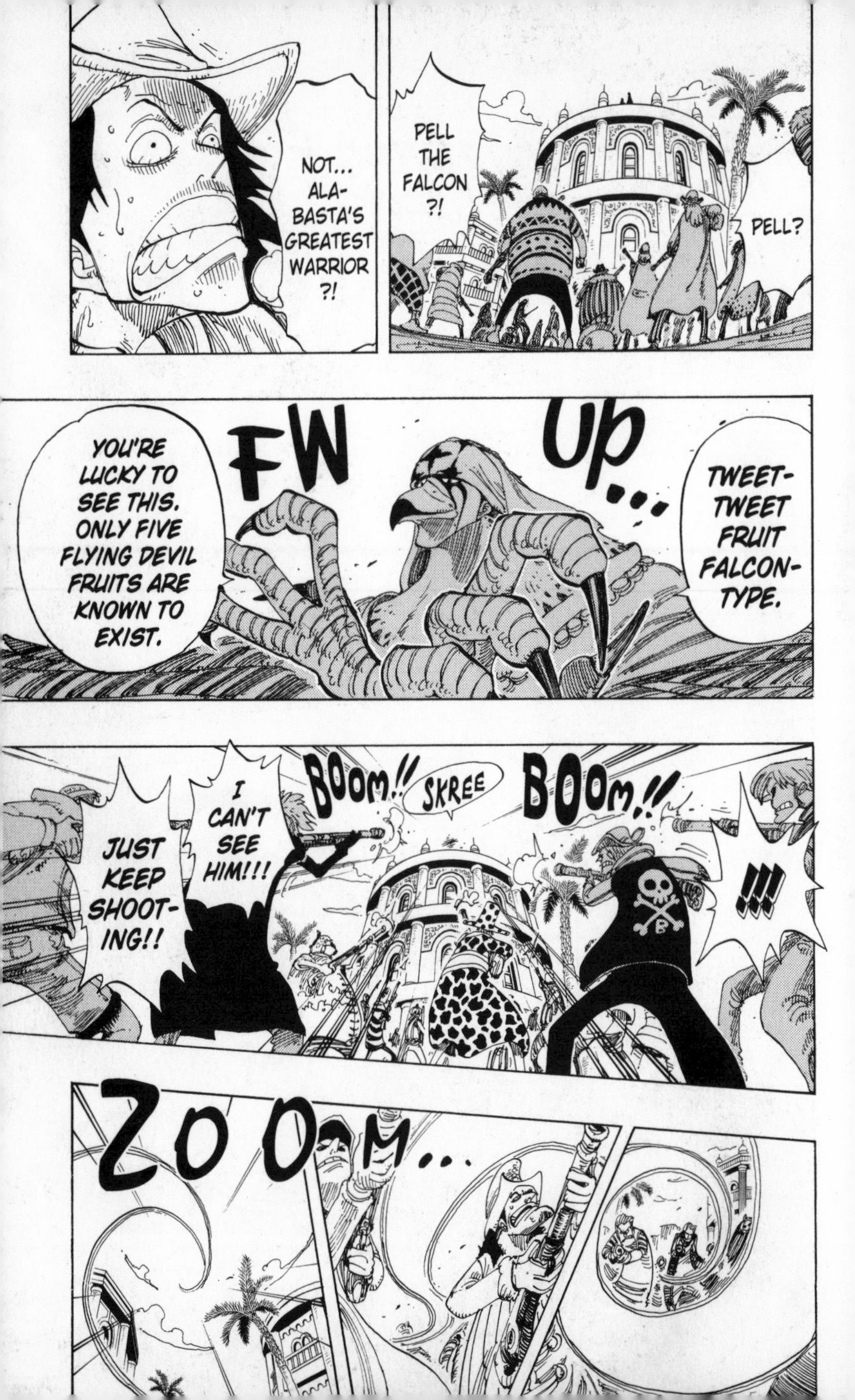
PELL?
PELL THE FALCON ?!
NOT... ALA-BASTA'S GREATEST WARRIOR ?!
TWEET-TWEET FRUIT FALCON-TYPE.
FWUP...
YOU'RE LUCKY TO SEE THIS. ONLY FIVE FLYING DEVIL FRUITS ARE KNOWN TO EXIST.
!!!
BOOM!!
SKREE
BOOM!!
I CAN'T SEE HIM!!!
JUST KEEP SHOOTING!!
ZOOOM...

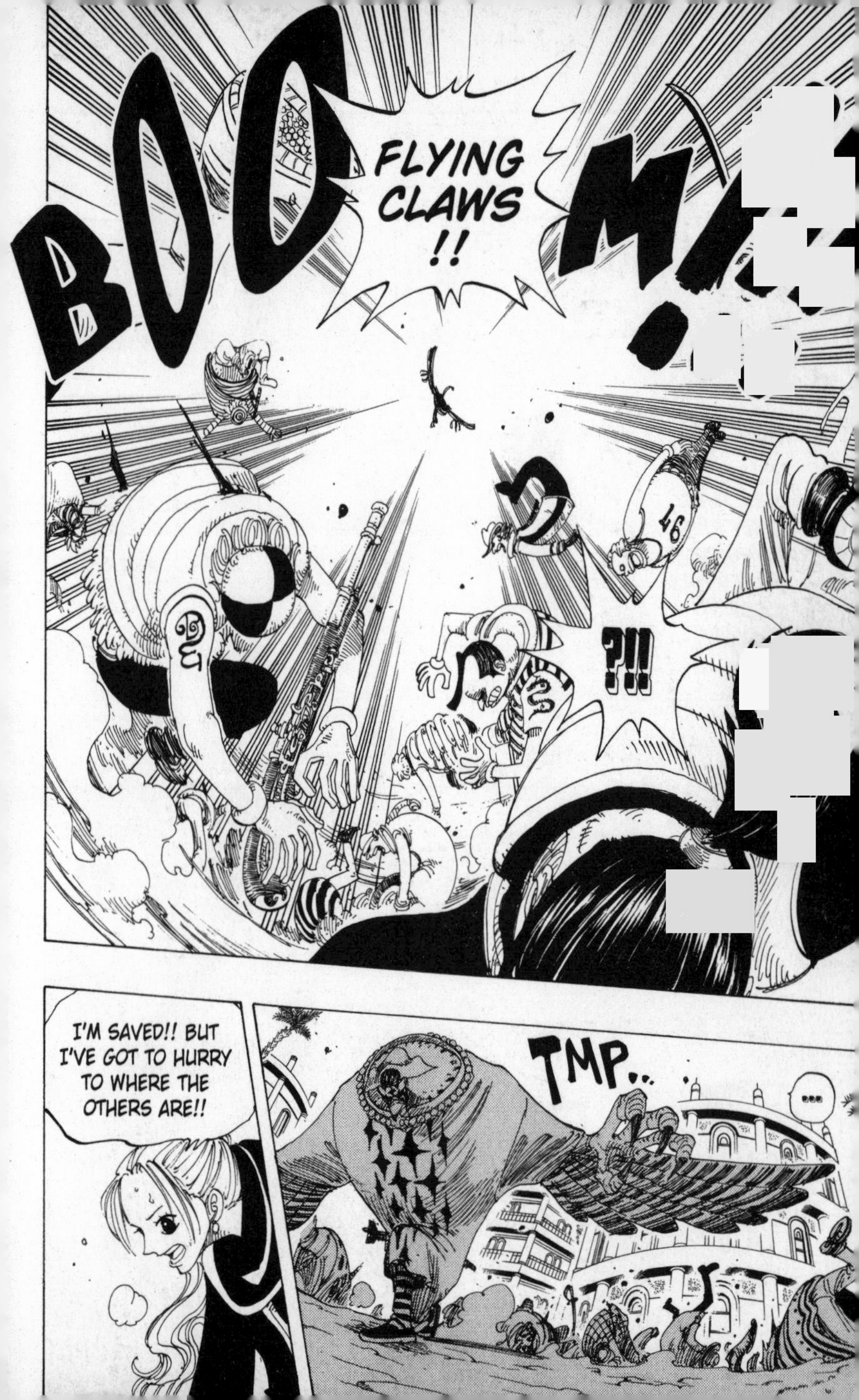
BOO
FLYING CLAWS !!
M
?!!
TMP...
...
I'M SAVED!! BUT I'VE GOT TO HURRY TO WHERE THE OTHERS ARE!!

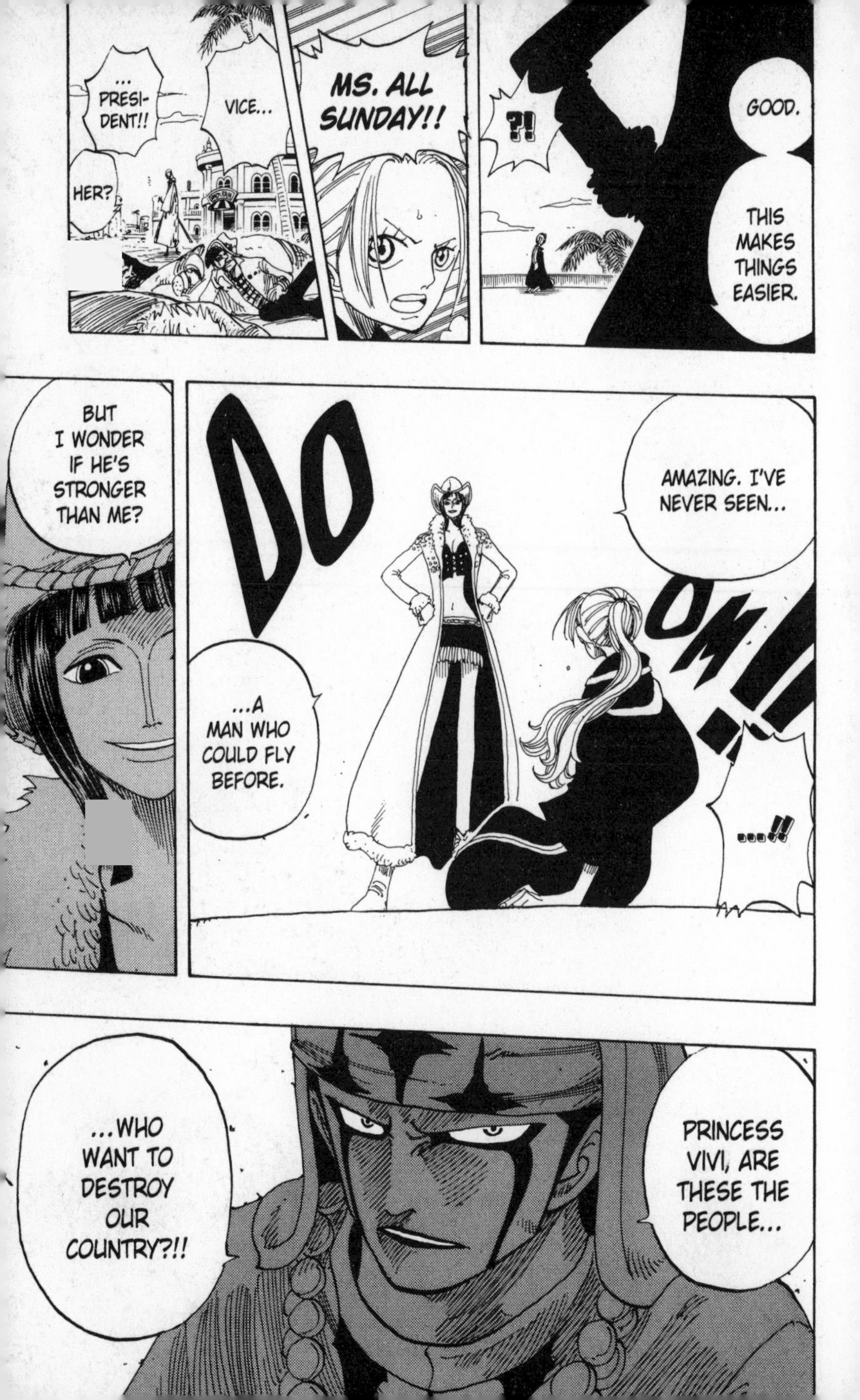
GOOD.
THIS MAKES THINGS EASIER.
?!
MS. ALL SUNDAY!!
VICE...
...PRESIDENT!!
HER?
AMAZING. I'VE NEVER SEEN...
DOOM!!
...A MAN WHO COULD FLY BEFORE.
...!!
BUT I WONDER IF HE'S STRONGER THAN ME?
PRINCESS VIVI, ARE THESE THE PEOPLE...
...WHO WANT TO DESTROY OUR COUNTRY?!!

# Chapter 170:
# BEGINNING

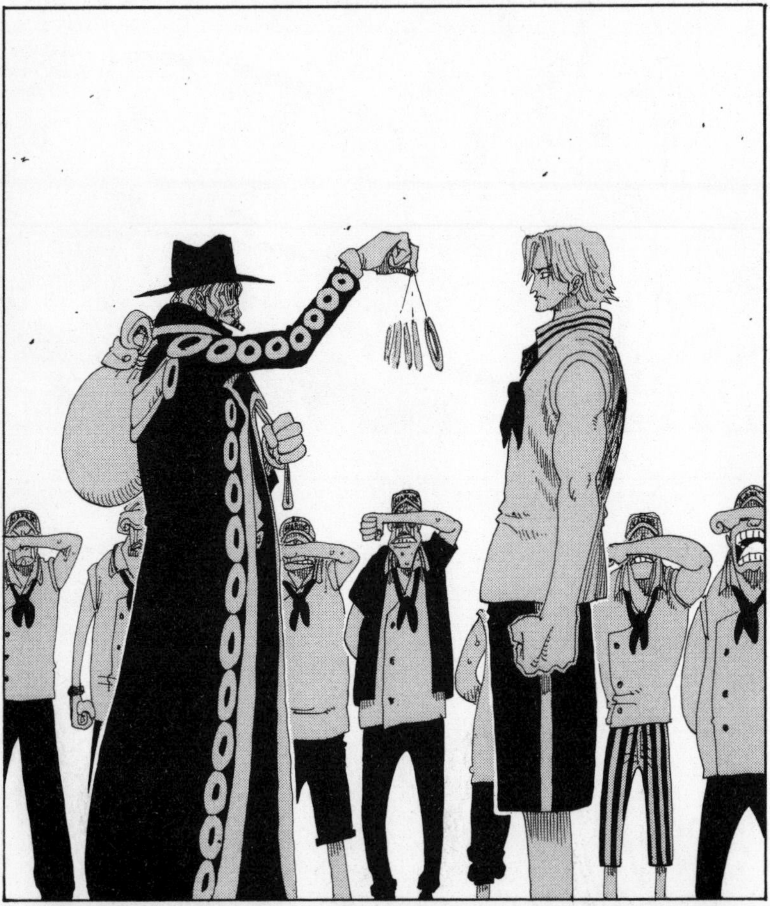

DJANGO'S DANCE PARADISE, VOL. 35: "HYPNOSIS: 'JUST FORGET ABOUT THIS FRIENDSHIP.' ONE...TWO..."

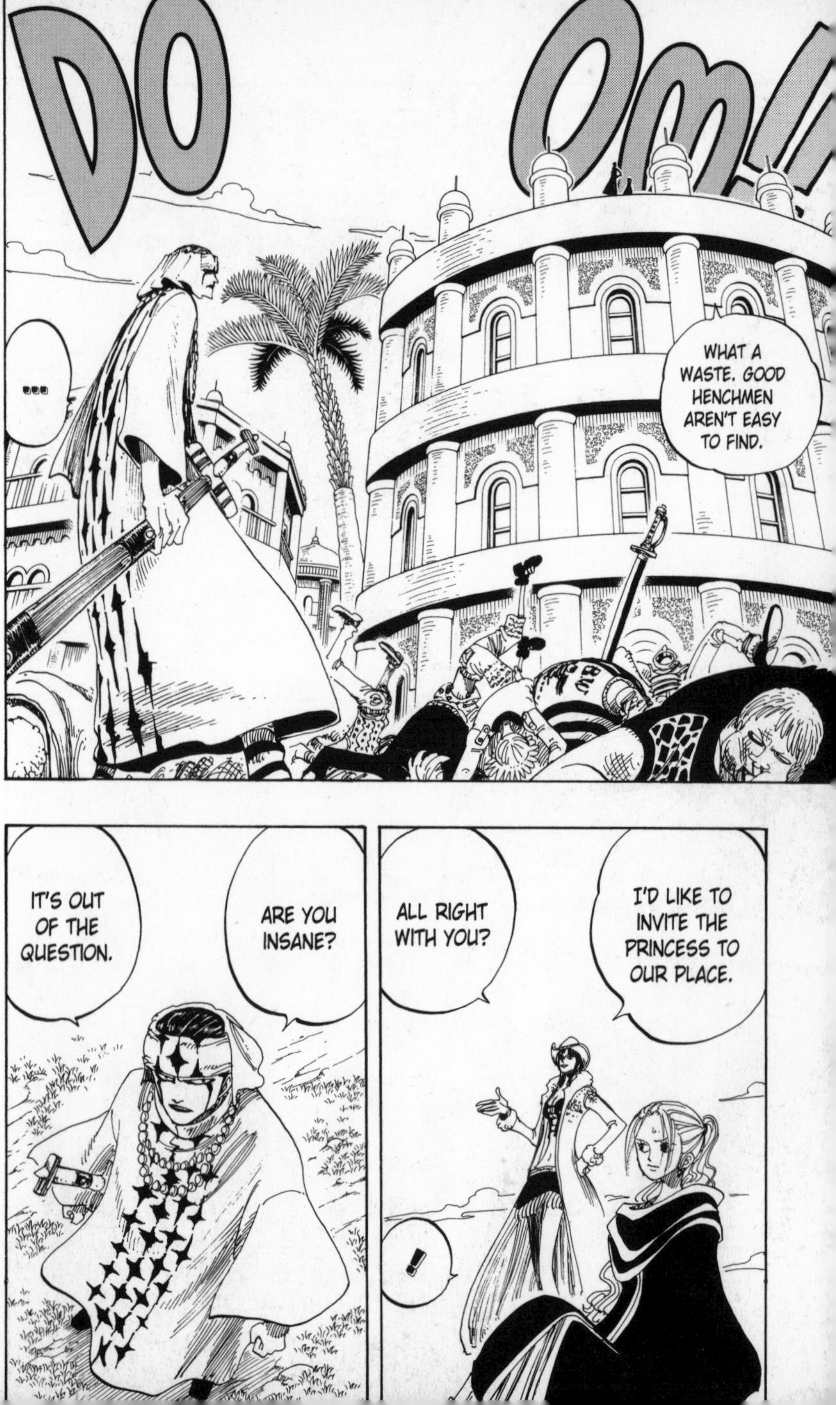
DO
OM
WHAT A WASTE. GOOD HENCHMEN AREN'T EASY TO FIND.
...
I'D LIKE TO INVITE THE PRINCESS TO OUR PLACE.
ALL RIGHT WITH YOU?
!
ARE YOU INSANE?
IT'S OUT OF THE QUESTION.

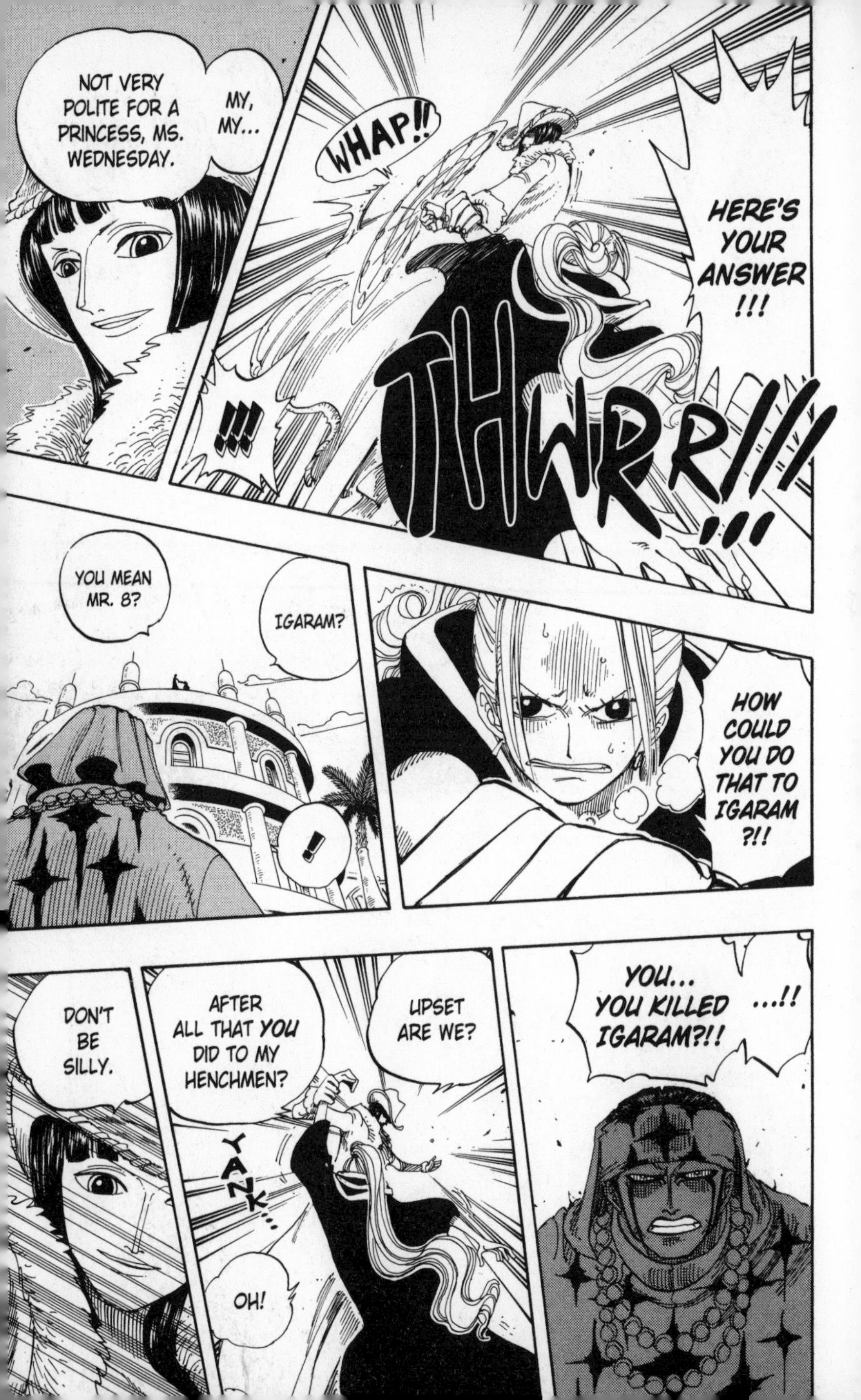
HERE'S YOUR ANSWER!!!
WHAP!!
THWRR!!!
!!!
MY, MY...
NOT VERY POLITE FOR A PRINCESS, MS. WEDNESDAY.
HOW COULD YOU DO THAT TO IGARAM?!!
!
IGARAM?
YOU MEAN MR. 8?
...!!
YOU... YOU KILLED IGARAM?!!
UPSET ARE WE?
AFTER ALL THAT YOU DID TO MY HENCHMEN?
YANK...
OH!
DON'T BE SILLY.

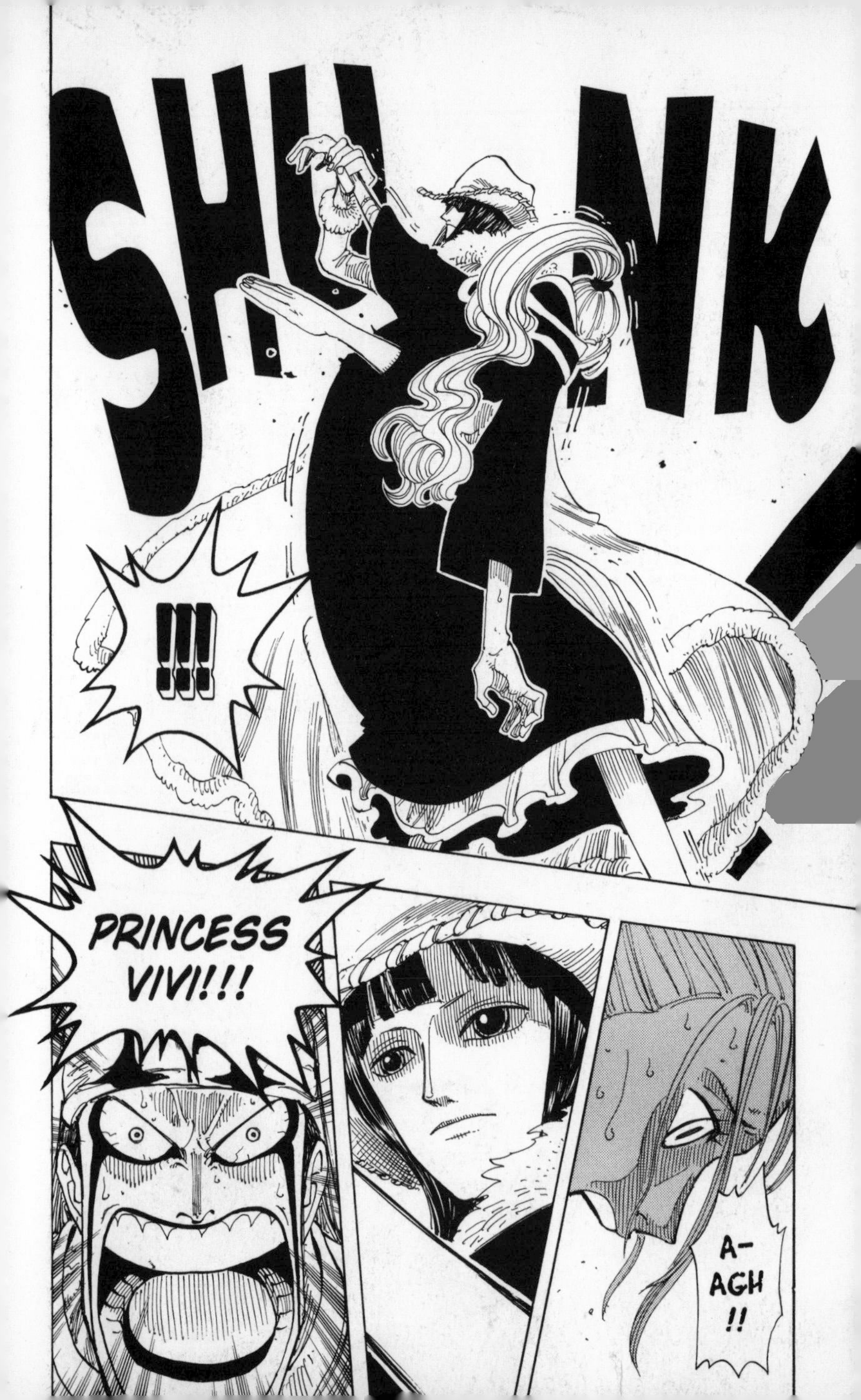
SHIIINK!
!!!
A-AGH!!
PRINCESS VIVI!!!

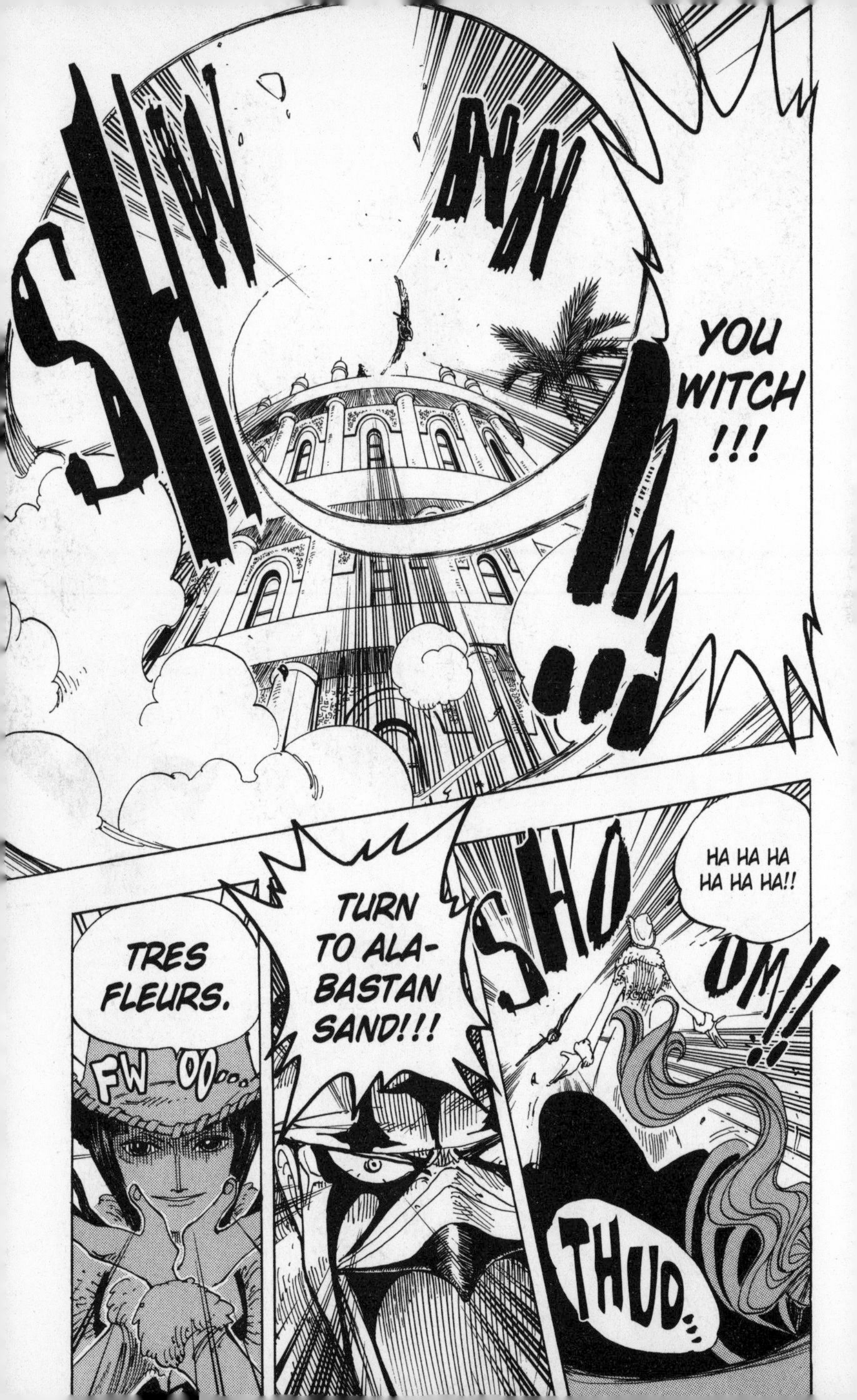
SHWNN!!
YOU WITCH!!!
HA HA HA HA HA HA!!
SHOOM!!
THUD...
TURN TO ALA-BASTAN SAND!!!
TRES FLEURS.
FWOO...

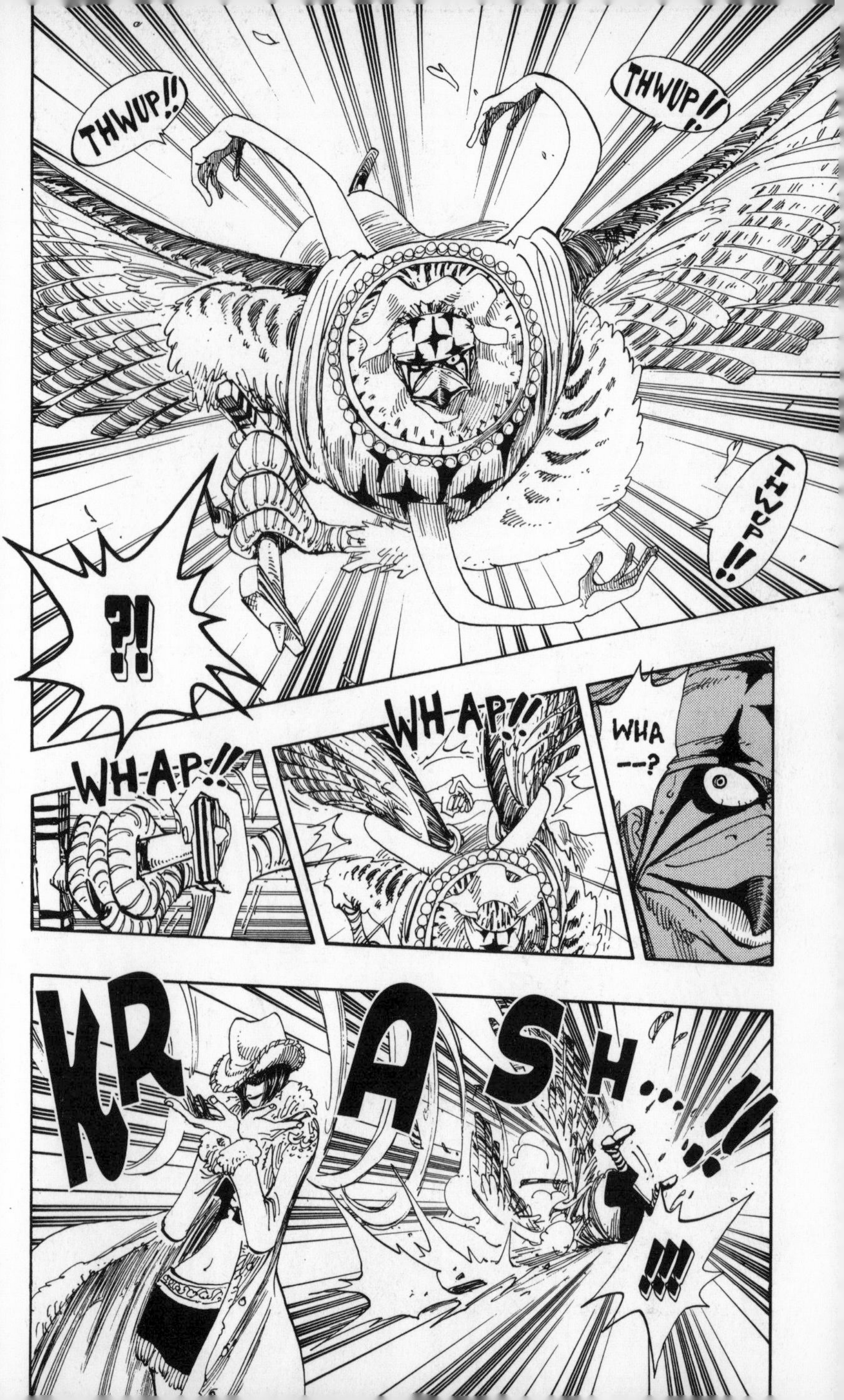
THWUP!!
THWUP!!
THWUP!!
?!
WHA--?
WHAP!!
WHAP!!
KRASH...!!
!!!

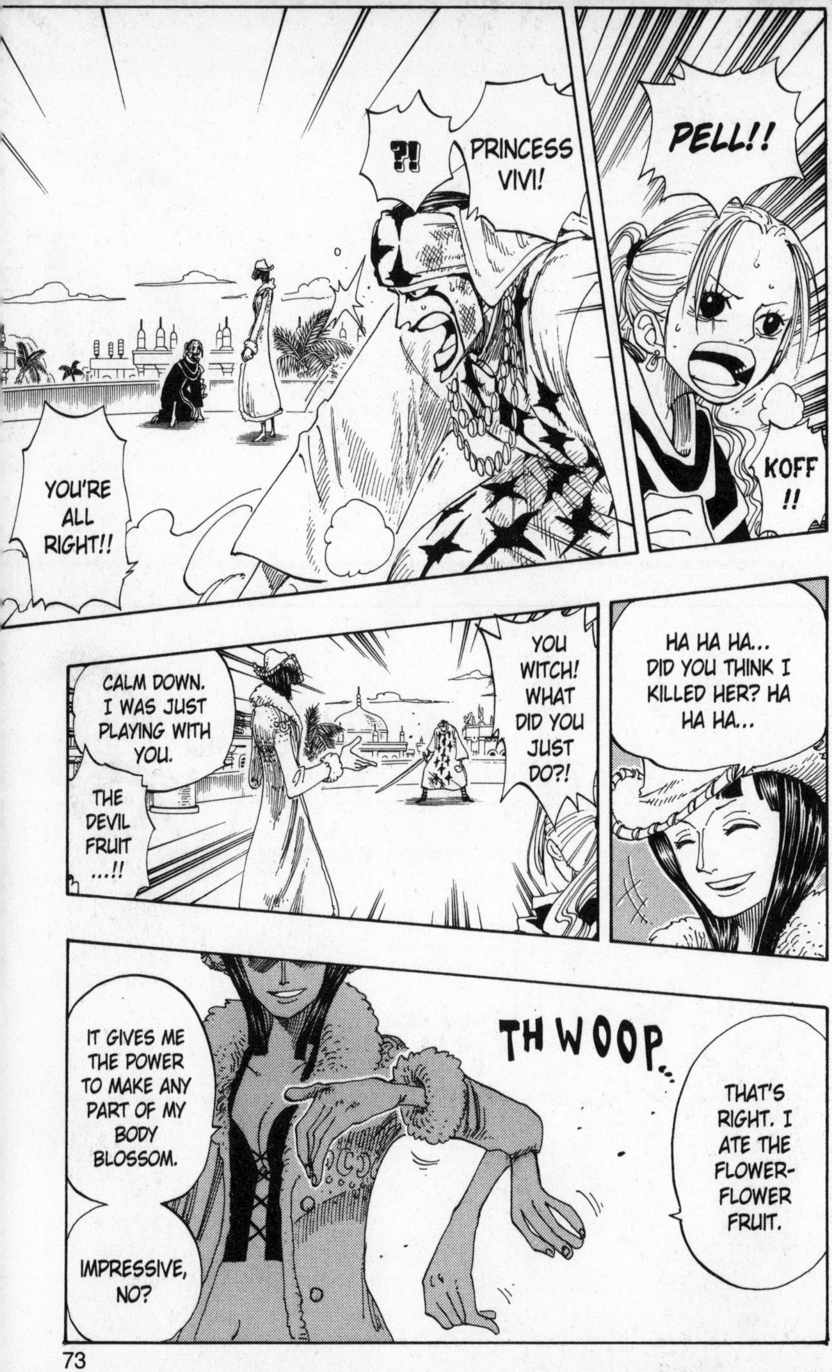
PELL!!
KOFF !!
PRINCESS VIVI!
?!
YOU'RE ALL RIGHT!!
HA HA HA... DID YOU THINK I KILLED HER? HA HA HA...
YOU WITCH! WHAT DID YOU JUST DO?!
CALM DOWN. I WAS JUST PLAYING WITH YOU.
THE DEVIL FRUIT ...!!
THAT'S RIGHT. I ATE THE FLOWER-FLOWER FRUIT.
THWOOP...
IT GIVES ME THE POWER TO MAKE ANY PART OF MY BODY BLOSSOM.
IMPRESSIVE, NO?

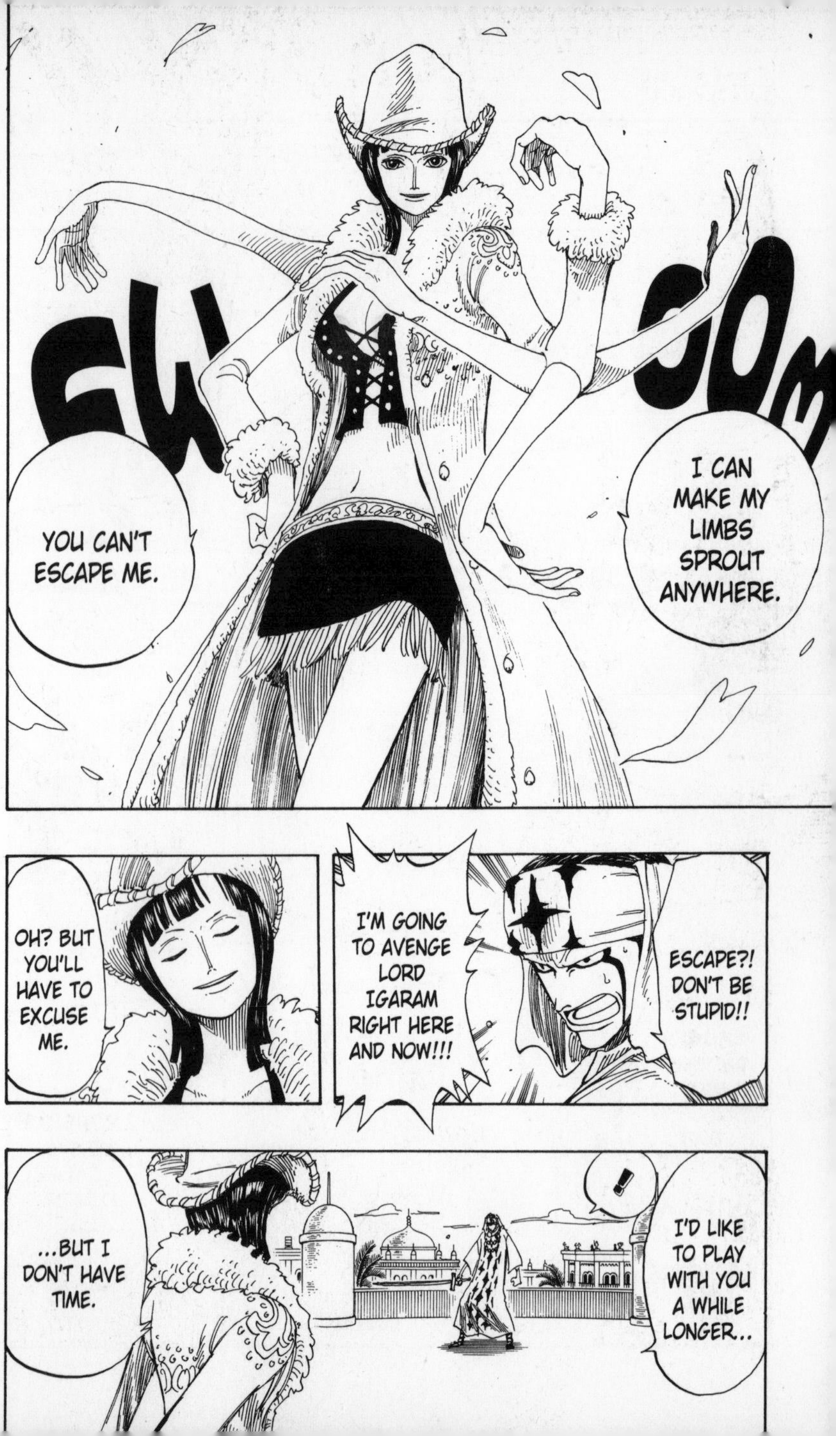
I CAN MAKE MY LIMBS SPROUT ANYWHERE.
YOU CAN'T ESCAPE ME.
ESCAPE?! DON'T BE STUPID!!
I'M GOING TO AVENGE LORD IGARAM RIGHT HERE AND NOW!!!
OH? BUT YOU'LL HAVE TO EXCUSE ME.
!
I'D LIKE TO PLAY WITH YOU A WHILE LONGER...
...BUT I DON'T HAVE TIME.

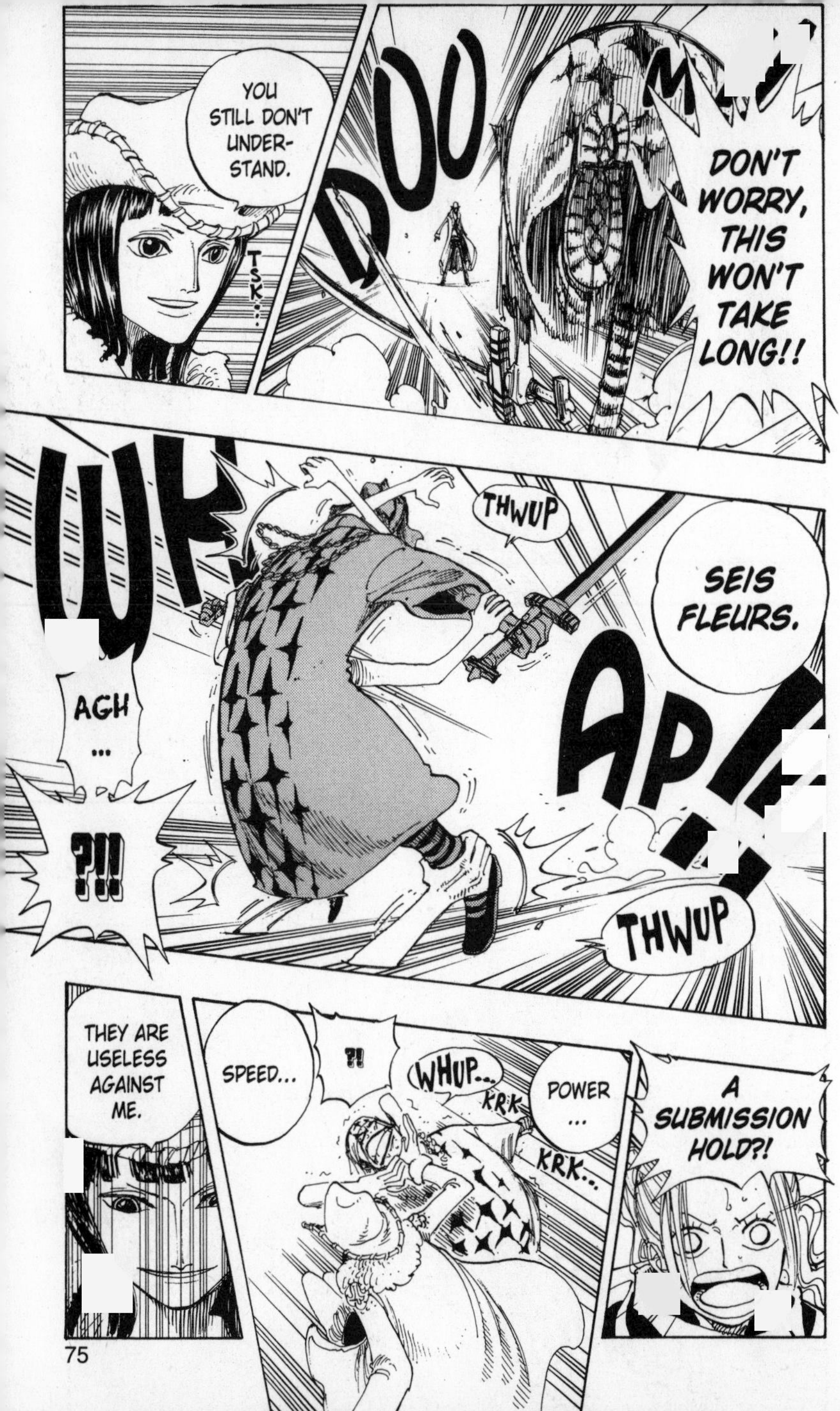
DOOM
DON'T WORRY, THIS WON'T TAKE LONG!!
YOU STILL DON'T UNDER-STAND.
TSK...
SEIS FLEURS.
THWUP
AP!!
THWUP
WH
AGH ...
?!!
A SUBMISSION HOLD?!
POWER ...
KRK...
KRK
WHUP...
?!
SPEED...
THEY ARE USELESS AGAINST ME.

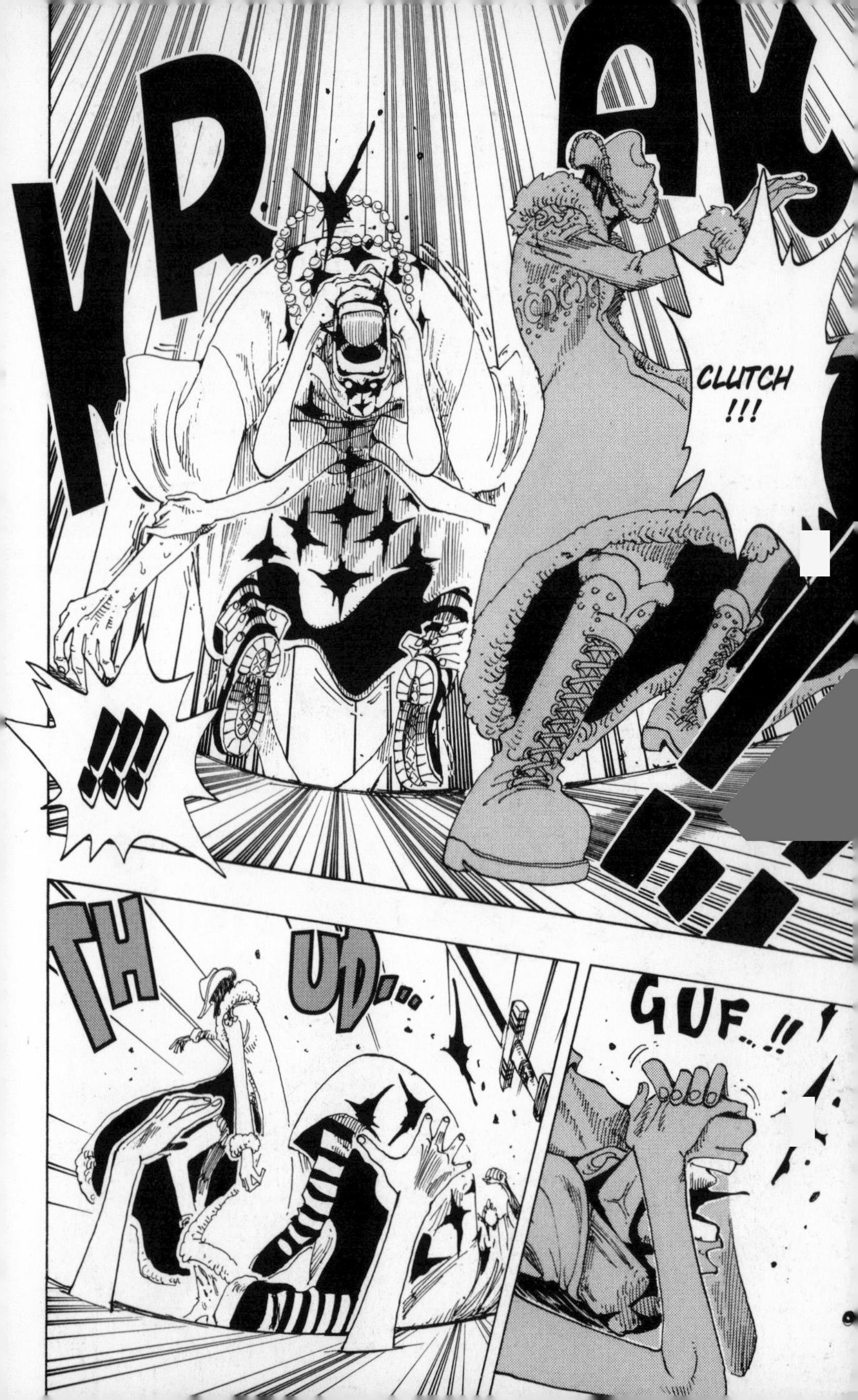
KRAK
CLUTCH !!!
!!!
GUF...!!
THUD...

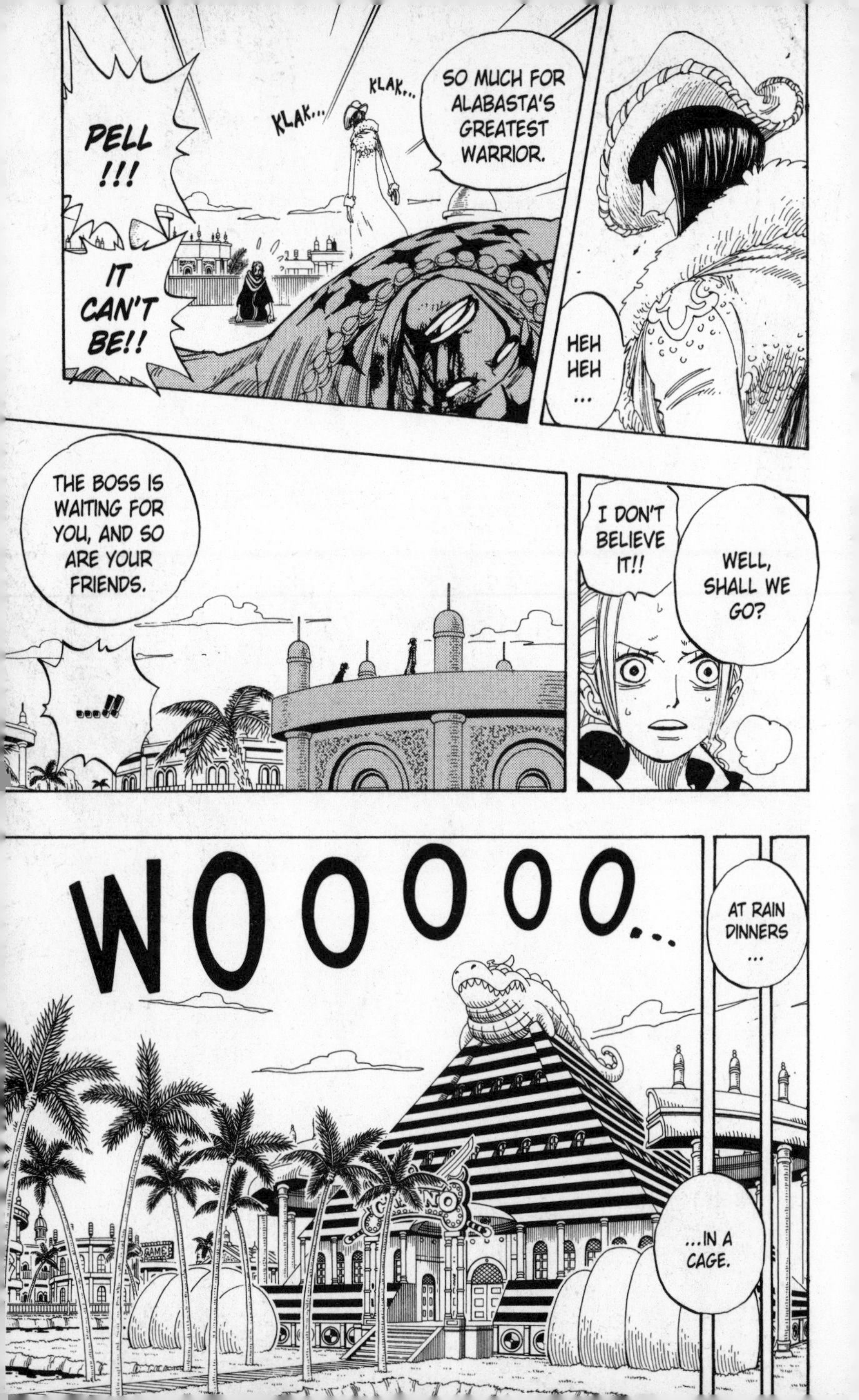
HEH HEH ...
SO MUCH FOR ALABASTA'S GREATEST WARRIOR.
KLAK...
KLAK...
PELL !!!
IT CAN'T BE!!
I DON'T BELIEVE IT!!
WELL, SHALL WE GO?
THE BOSS IS WAITING FOR YOU, AND SO ARE YOUR FRIENDS.
...!!
AT RAIN DINNERS ...
WOOOOO...
...IN A CAGE.
GAME

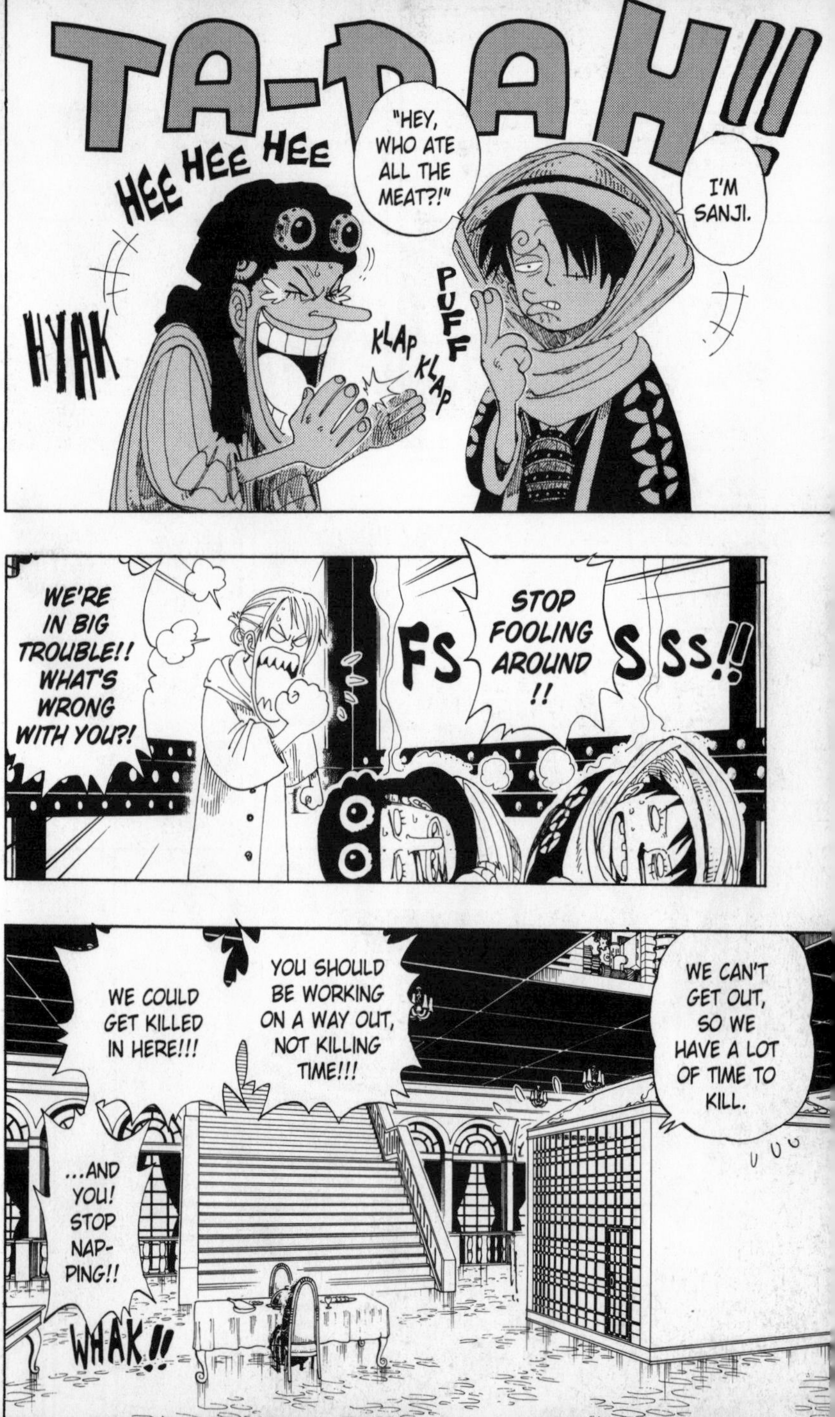
TA-DAH!!
I'M SANJI.
"HEY, WHO ATE ALL THE MEAT?!"
PUFF
KLAP KLAP
HEE HEE HEE
HYAK
FS SS!!
STOP FOOLING AROUND !!
WE'RE IN BIG TROUBLE!! WHAT'S WRONG WITH YOU?!
WE CAN'T GET OUT, SO WE HAVE A LOT OF TIME TO KILL.
YOU SHOULD BE WORKING ON A WAY OUT, NOT KILLING TIME!!!
WE COULD GET KILLED IN HERE!!!
...AND YOU! STOP NAP-PING!!
WHAK!!

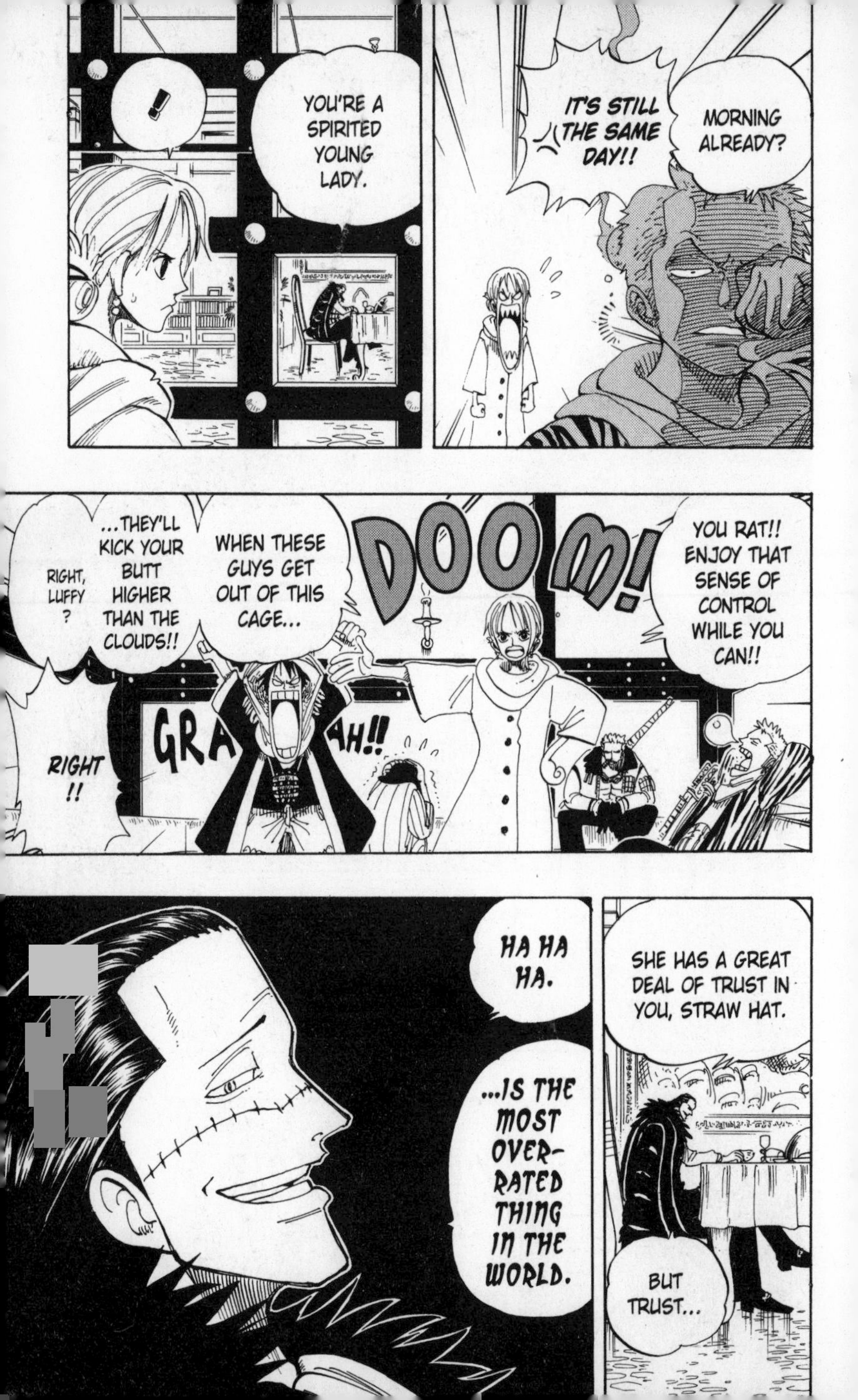
MORNING ALREADY?
IT'S STILL THE SAME DAY!!
YOU'RE A SPIRITED YOUNG LADY.
!
YOU RAT!! ENJOY THAT SENSE OF CONTROL WHILE YOU CAN!!
DOOM!
WHEN THESE GUYS GET OUT OF THIS CAGE...
...THEY'LL KICK YOUR BUTT HIGHER THAN THE CLOUDS!!
RIGHT, LUFFY?
GRA AH!!
RIGHT!!
SHE HAS A GREAT DEAL OF TRUST IN YOU, STRAW HAT.
BUT TRUST...
HA HA HA.
...IS THE MOST OVER-RATED THING IN THE WORLD.

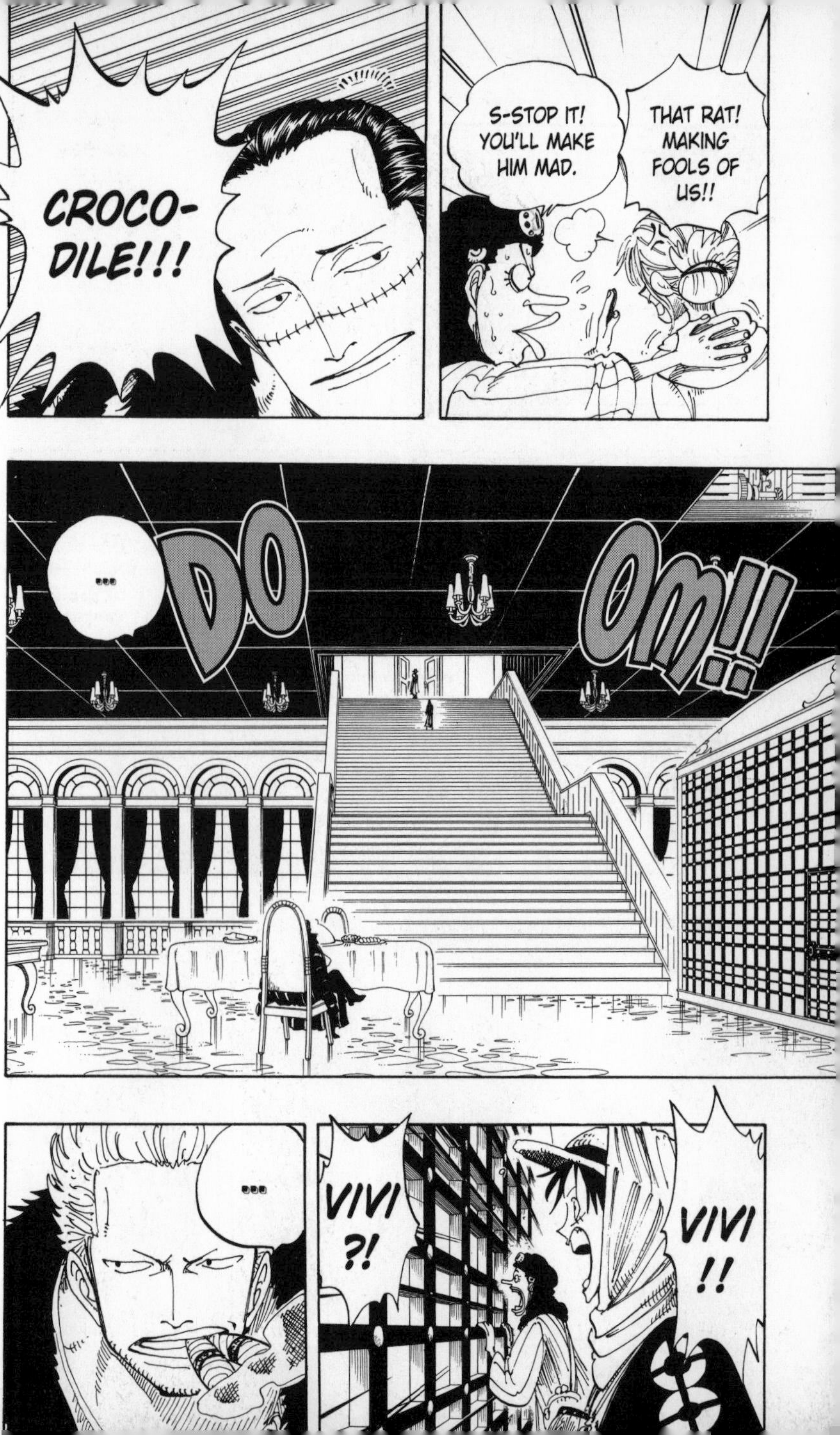
THAT RAT! MAKING FOOLS OF US!!
S-STOP IT! YOU'LL MAKE HIM MAD.
CROCO-DILE!!!
DO OM!!
...
VIVI !!
VIVI ?!
...

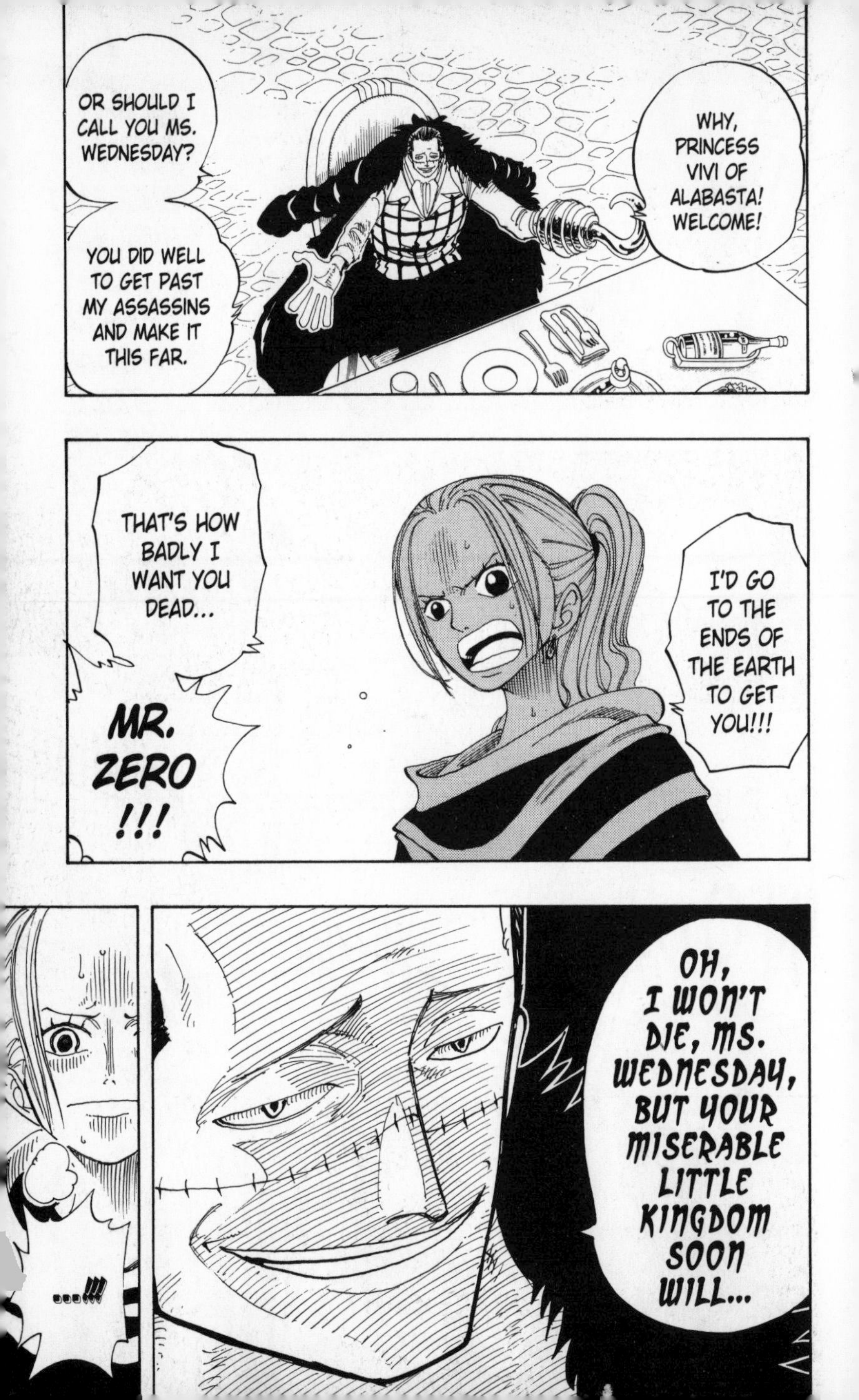
WHY, PRINCESS VIVI OF ALABASTA! WELCOME!
OR SHOULD I CALL YOU MS. WEDNESDAY?
YOU DID WELL TO GET PAST MY ASSASSINS AND MAKE IT THIS FAR.
I'D GO TO THE ENDS OF THE EARTH TO GET YOU!!!
THAT'S HOW BADLY I WANT YOU DEAD...
MR. ZERO!!!
OH, I WON'T DIE, MS. WEDNESDAY, BUT YOUR MISERABLE LITTLE KINGDOM SOON WILL...
...!!!

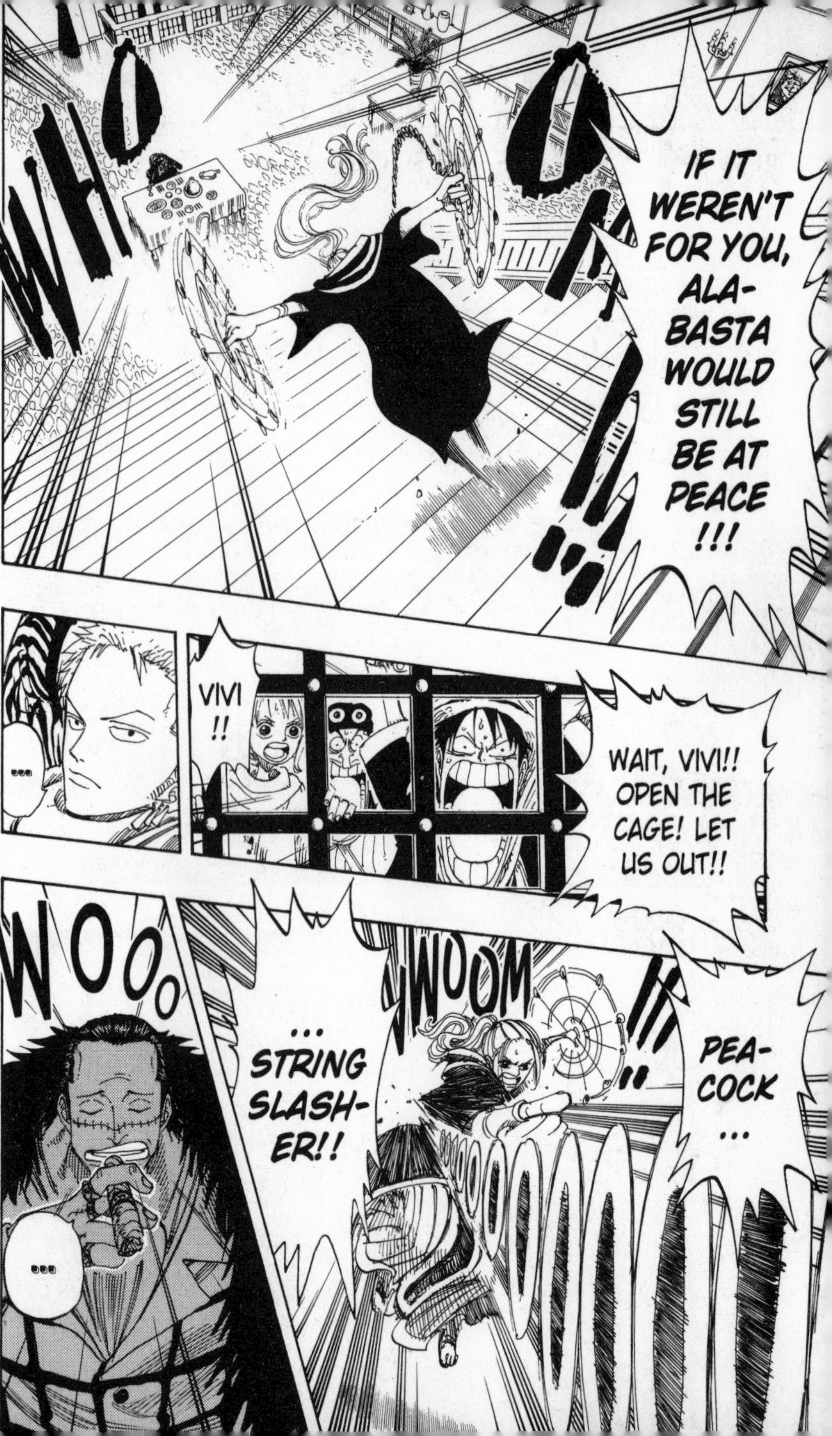
IF IT WEREN'T FOR YOU, ALA-BASTA WOULD STILL BE AT PEACE!!!
WAIT, VIVI!! OPEN THE CAGE! LET US OUT!!
VIVI !!
...
PEA-COCK ...
... STRING SLASH-ER!!
WOOM!!
WOOo
...

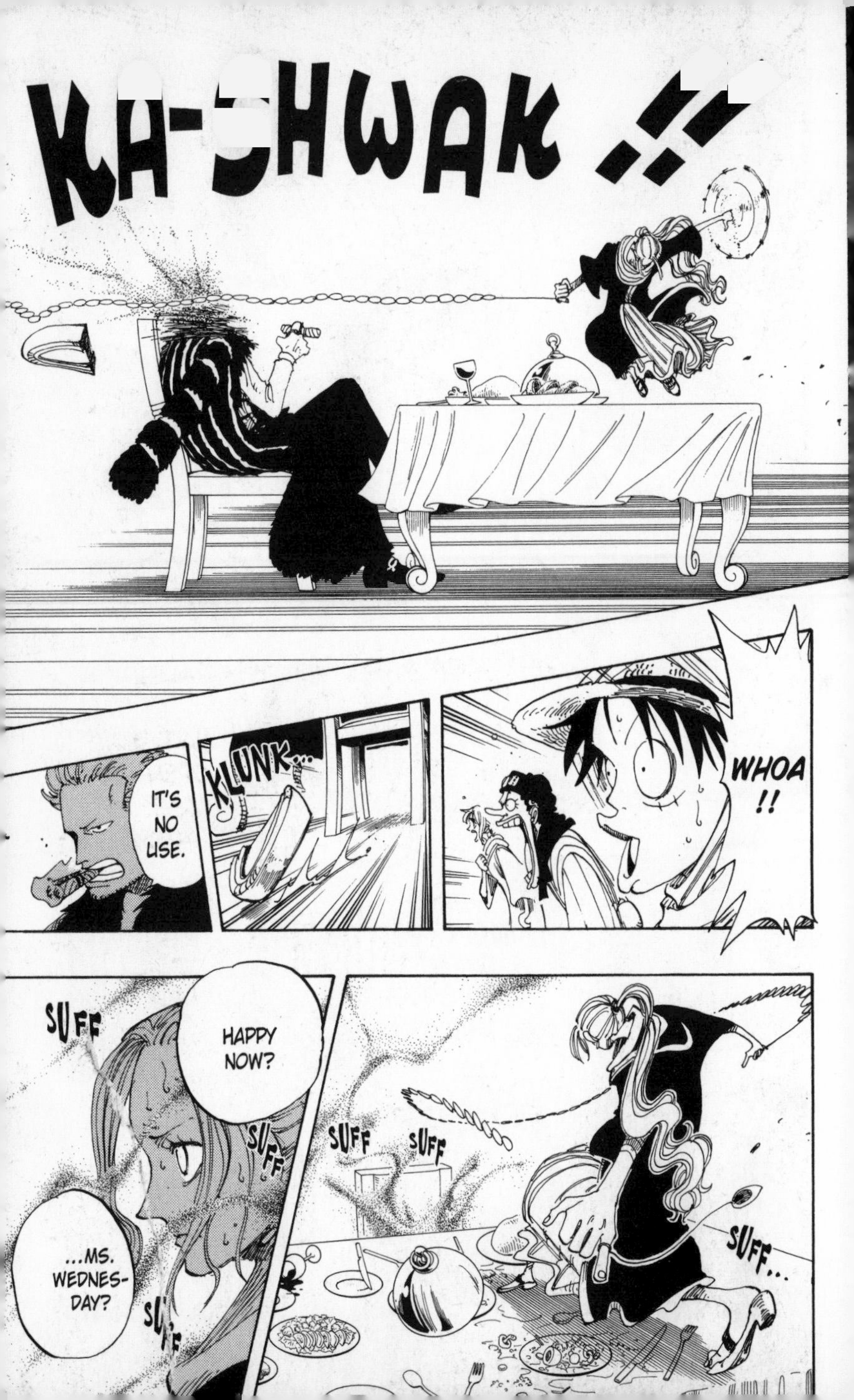
KA-SHWAK!!
WHOA!!
KLUNK...
IT'S NO USE.
SUFF
SUFF
SUFF...
SUFF
HAPPY NOW?
SUFF
...MS. WEDNES-DAY?
SUFF

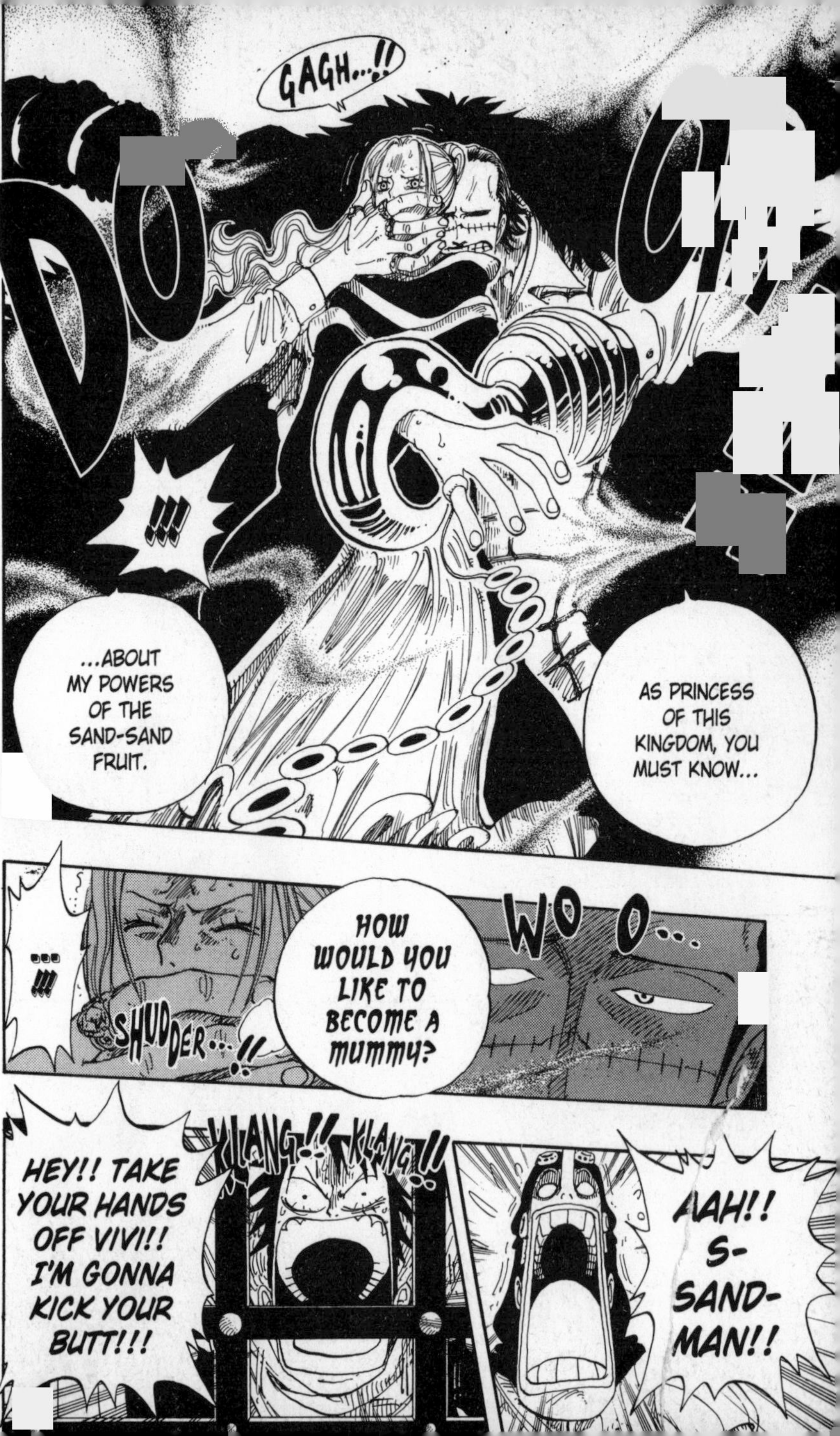
GAGH...!!
AS PRINCESS OF THIS KINGDOM, YOU MUST KNOW...
...ABOUT MY POWERS OF THE SAND-SAND FRUIT.
!!!
WOO...
HOW WOULD YOU LIKE TO BECOME A MUMMY?
SHUDDER...!!
...!!!
AAH!! S-SANDMAN!!
KLANG!! KLANG!!
HEY!! TAKE YOUR HANDS OFF VIVI!! I'M GONNA KICK YOUR BUTT!!!

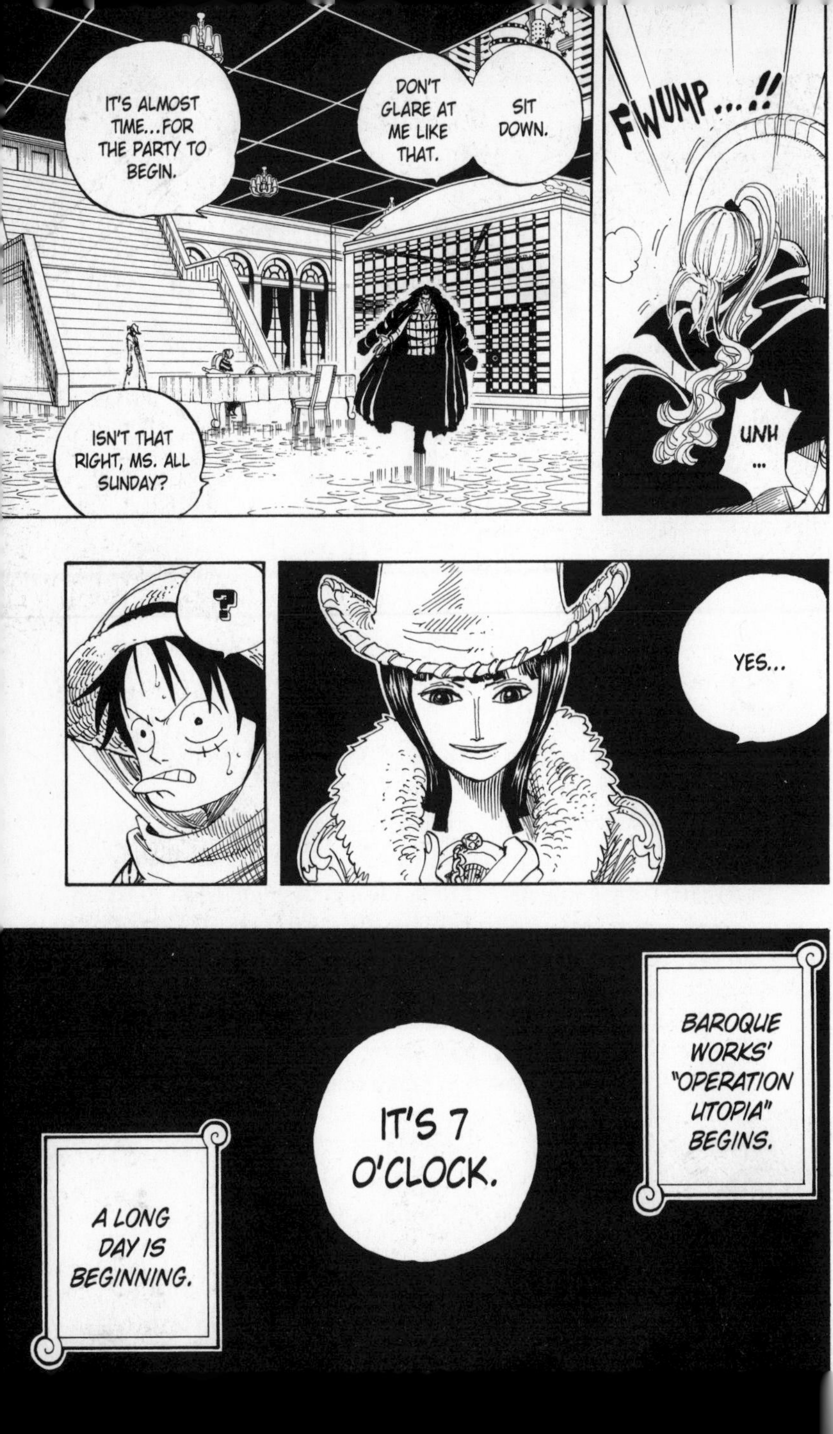
FWUMP...!!
UNH ...
SIT DOWN.
DON'T GLARE AT ME LIKE THAT.
IT'S ALMOST TIME...FOR THE PARTY TO BEGIN.
ISN'T THAT RIGHT, MS. ALL SUNDAY?
YES...
?
BAROQUE WORKS' "OPERATION UTOPIA" BEGINS.
IT'S 7 O'CLOCK.
A LONG DAY IS BEGINNING.

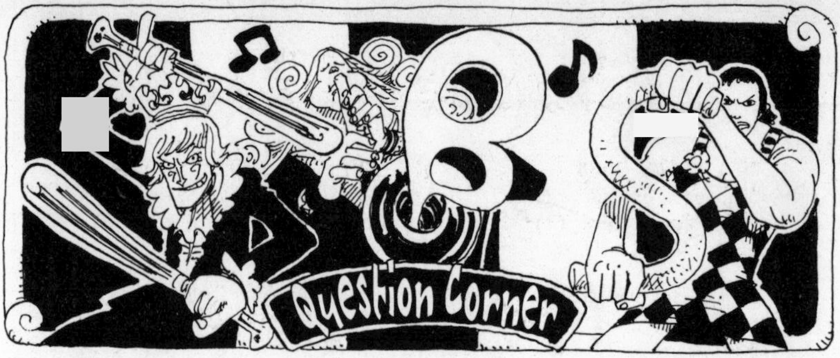
SBS
Question Corner

Q: Hey, Mr. Oda, does that mark that Ms. Golden Week drew on Luffy mean anything? Couldn't she just paint colors on him? Please tell me, 'kay?

--Lemon

A: Yes, that mark has a meaning.

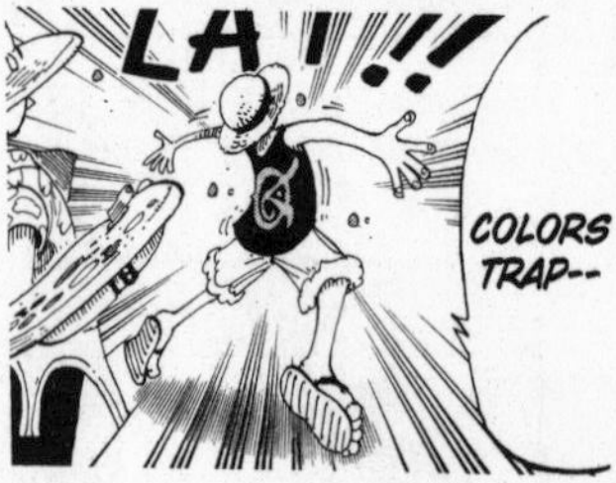
COLORS TRAP--

(That mark)

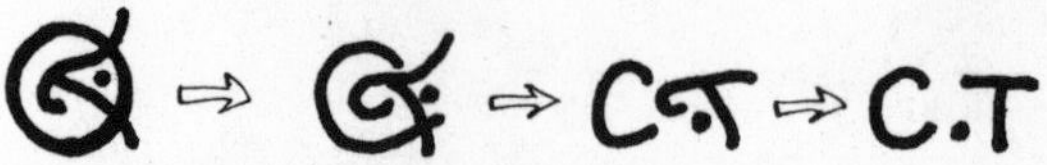
C.T
(Colors Trap)

Get it? Maybe you're thinking, "So what?" But it's better than nothing, right?

Q: Sensei, you went to college, correct? Also, were you in any manga or drawing clubs back in middle school or high school? I want to be a manga artist someday. (I'm in the eighth grade and I'm trying to figure out my future. Please tell me!)

A: I did go to college, but I dropped out after one year. I haven't had any formal art or manga training either. Actually, a lot of pro manga artists are like that. Since this is a serious question, I want to give you a serious answer. Regardless of the technical school you attend, I think the most dangerous thing you can do is to rely on other people.

Q: Hey, Oda!! Er, Sensei... Try this challenge!! Say "Roronoa" ten times!! Roronoa, Roronoa, Rororoa, Nononoa, Roronoa, Roroano... Okay, your turn!!

A: Sheesh-- You can't even do it yourself! Well, okay... Nonodo...chomp!! (I bit my tongue) Whaths nektht? (Covered with blood)

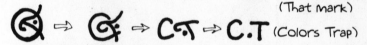

# Chapter 171:
# KOZA, LEADER OF THE REBELS

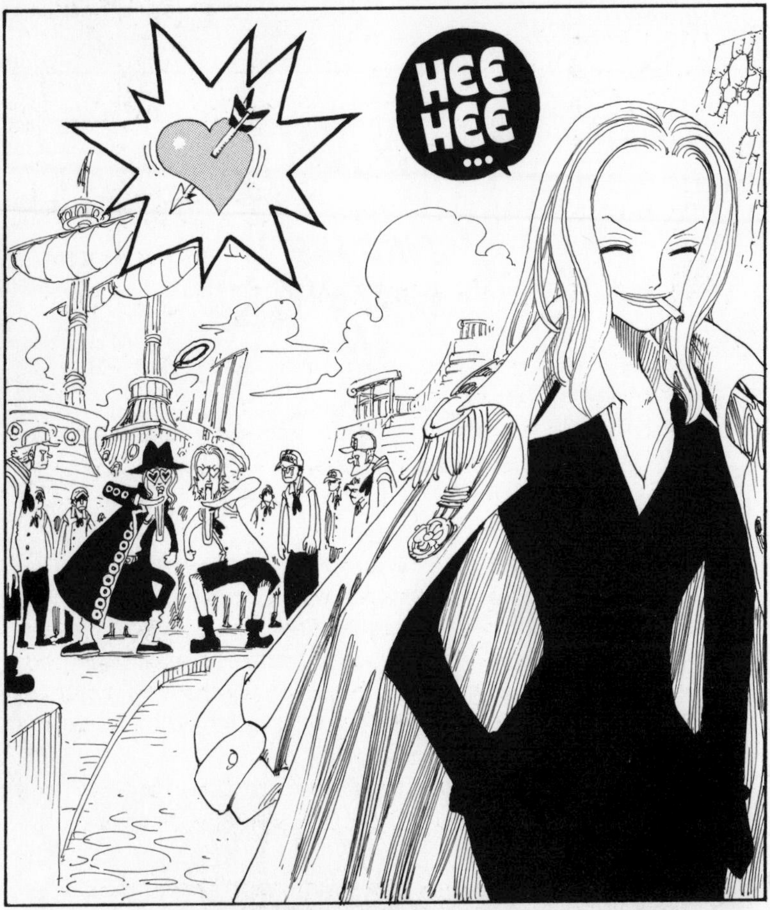
HEE HEE...

DJANGO'S DANCE PARADISE, VOL. 36:
"STOP!!! LOVE SHOCK♡ FEMALE OFFICER"

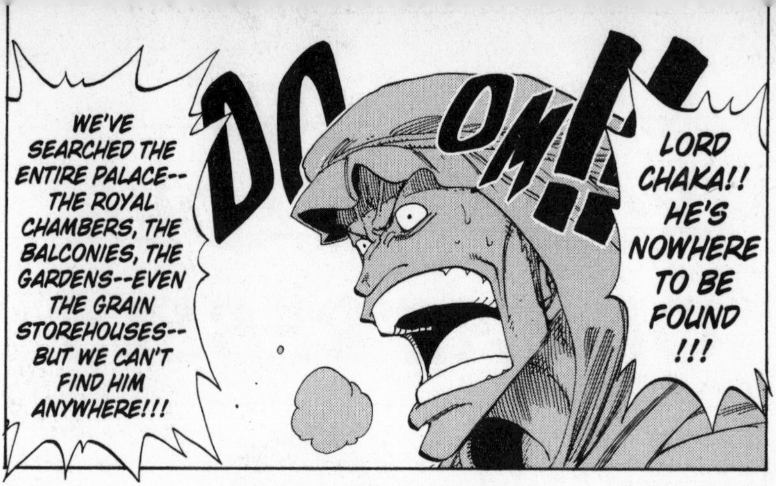
LORD CHAKA!! HE'S NOWHERE TO BE FOUND!!!
DOOM!!
WE'VE SEARCHED THE ENTIRE PALACE--THE ROYAL CHAMBERS, THE BALCONIES, THE GARDENS--EVEN THE GRAIN STOREHOUSES--BUT WE CAN'T FIND HIM ANYWHERE!!!

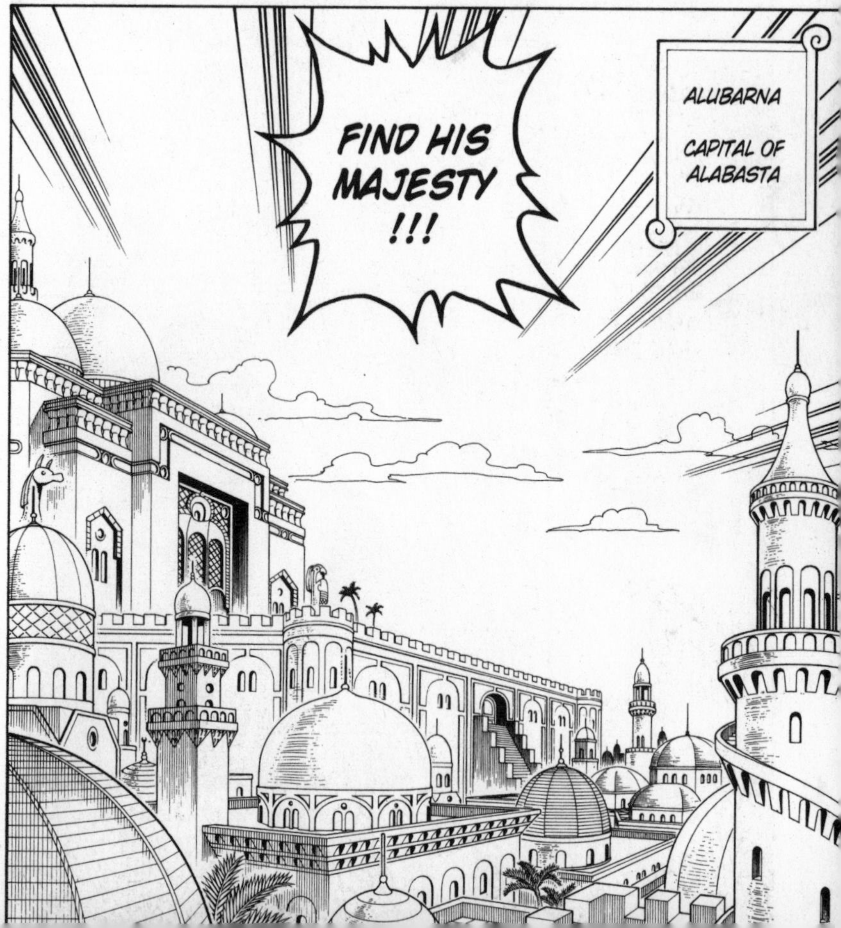
ALUBARNA
CAPITAL OF ALABASTA
FIND HIS MAJESTY!!!

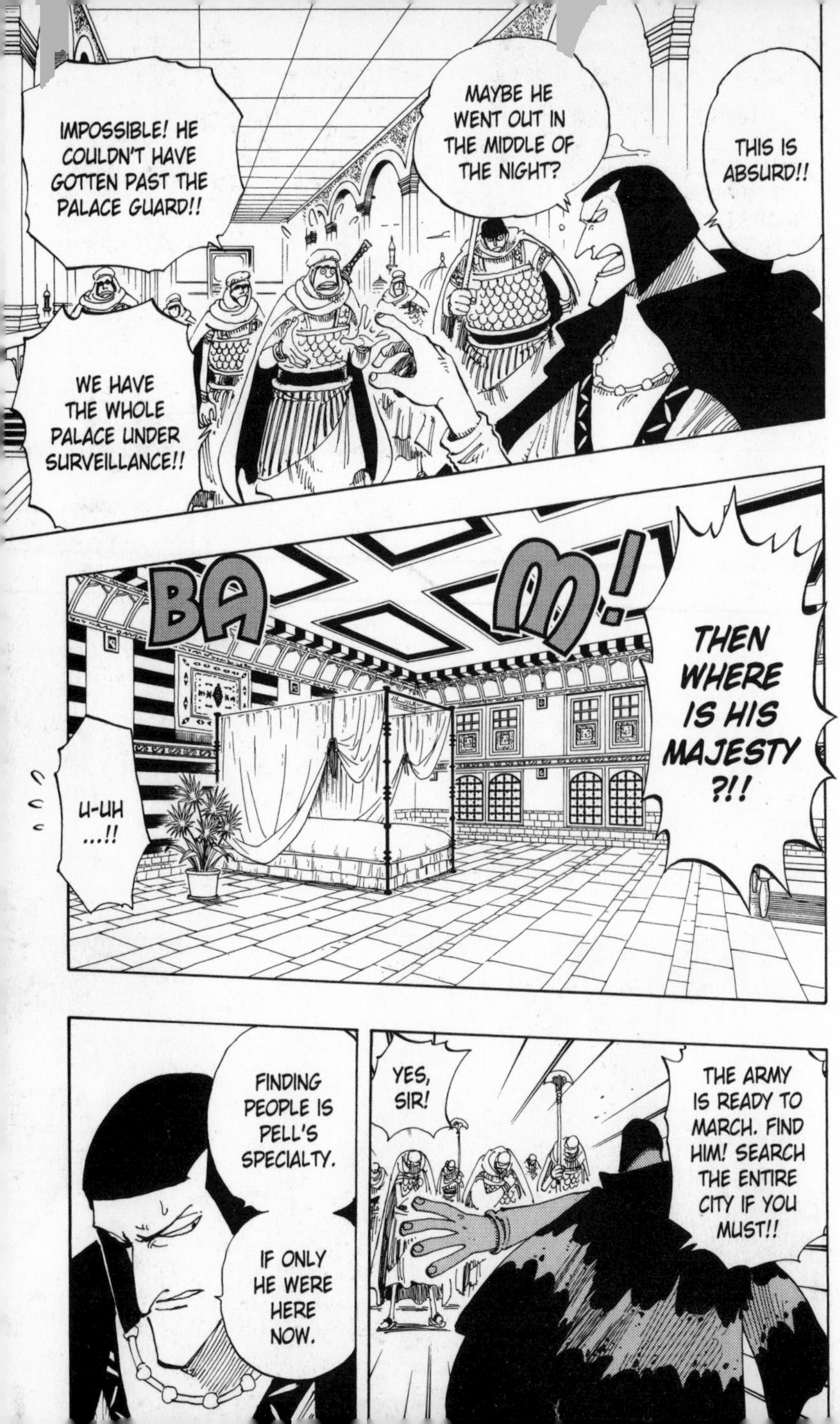
THIS IS ABSURD!!
MAYBE HE WENT OUT IN THE MIDDLE OF THE NIGHT?
IMPOSSIBLE! HE COULDN'T HAVE GOTTEN PAST THE PALACE GUARD!!
WE HAVE THE WHOLE PALACE UNDER SURVEILLANCE!!
BAM!
THEN WHERE IS HIS MAJESTY ?!!
U-UH ...!!
THE ARMY IS READY TO MARCH. FIND HIM! SEARCH THE ENTIRE CITY IF YOU MUST!!
YES, SIR!
FINDING PEOPLE IS PELL'S SPECIALTY.
IF ONLY HE WERE HERE NOW.

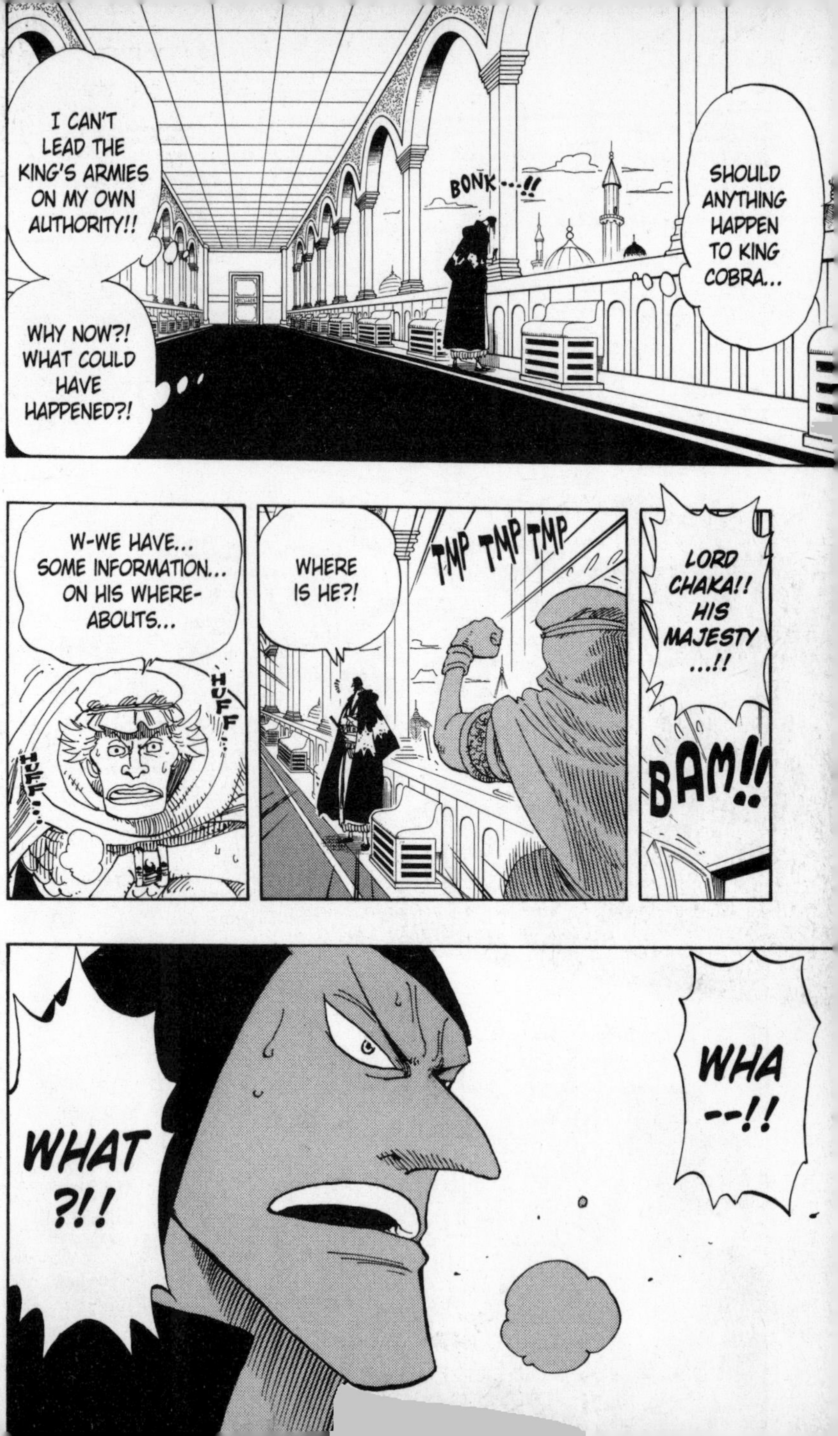
SHOULD ANYTHING HAPPEN TO KING COBRA...
BONK...!!
I CAN'T LEAD THE KING'S ARMIES ON MY OWN AUTHORITY!!
WHY NOW?! WHAT COULD HAVE HAPPENED?!
LORD CHAKA!! HIS MAJESTY ...!!
BAM!!
TMP TMP TMP
WHERE IS HE?!
W-WE HAVE... SOME INFORMATION... ON HIS WHERE-ABOUTS...
HUFF
HUFF
WHA--!!
WHAT ?!!

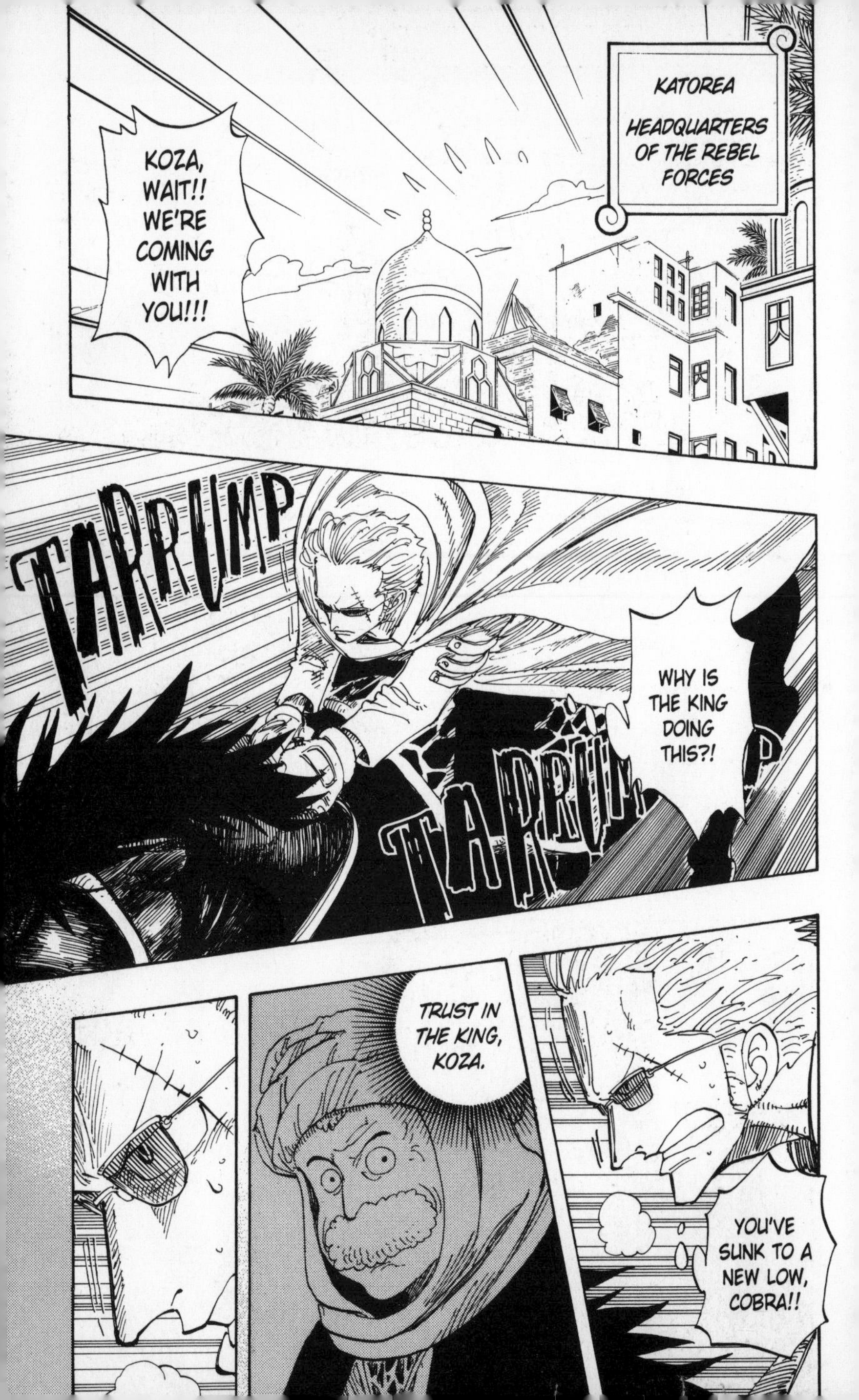
KATOREA
HEADQUARTERS OF THE REBEL FORCES
KOZA, WAIT!! WE'RE COMING WITH YOU!!!
TARRUMP
WHY IS THE KING DOING THIS?!
TARRUMP
YOU'VE SUNK TO A NEW LOW, COBRA!!
TRUST IN THE KING, KOZA.

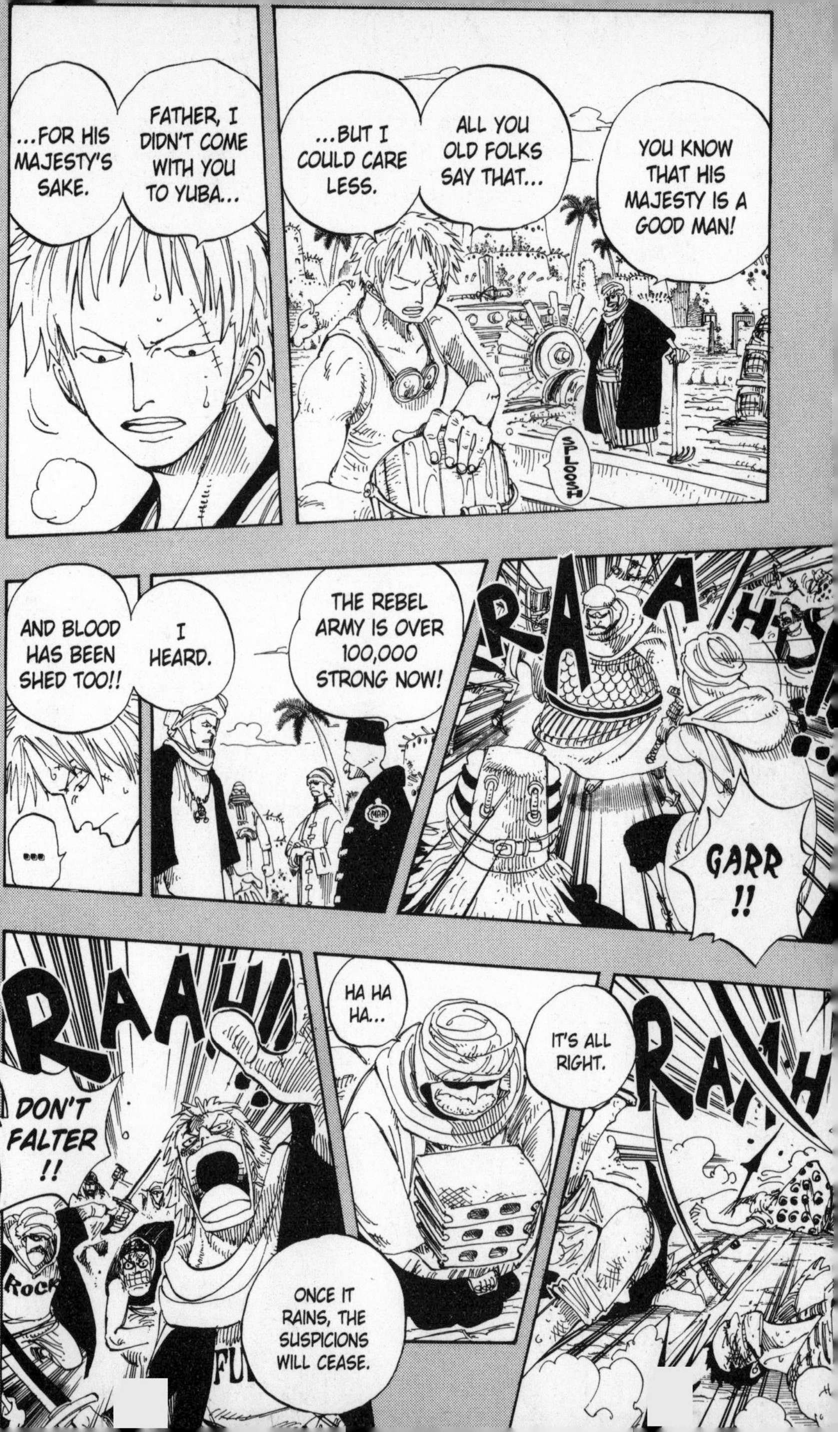
YOU KNOW THAT HIS MAJESTY IS A GOOD MAN!
ALL YOU OLD FOLKS SAY THAT...
...BUT I COULD CARE LESS.
SPLOOSH
FATHER, I DIDN'T COME WITH YOU TO YUBA...
...FOR HIS MAJESTY'S SAKE.
GARR !!
THE REBEL ARMY IS OVER 100,000 STRONG NOW!
I HEARD.
AND BLOOD HAS BEEN SHED TOO!!
...
IT'S ALL RIGHT.
HA HA HA...
ONCE IT RAINS, THE SUSPICIONS WILL CEASE.
DON'T FALTER !!

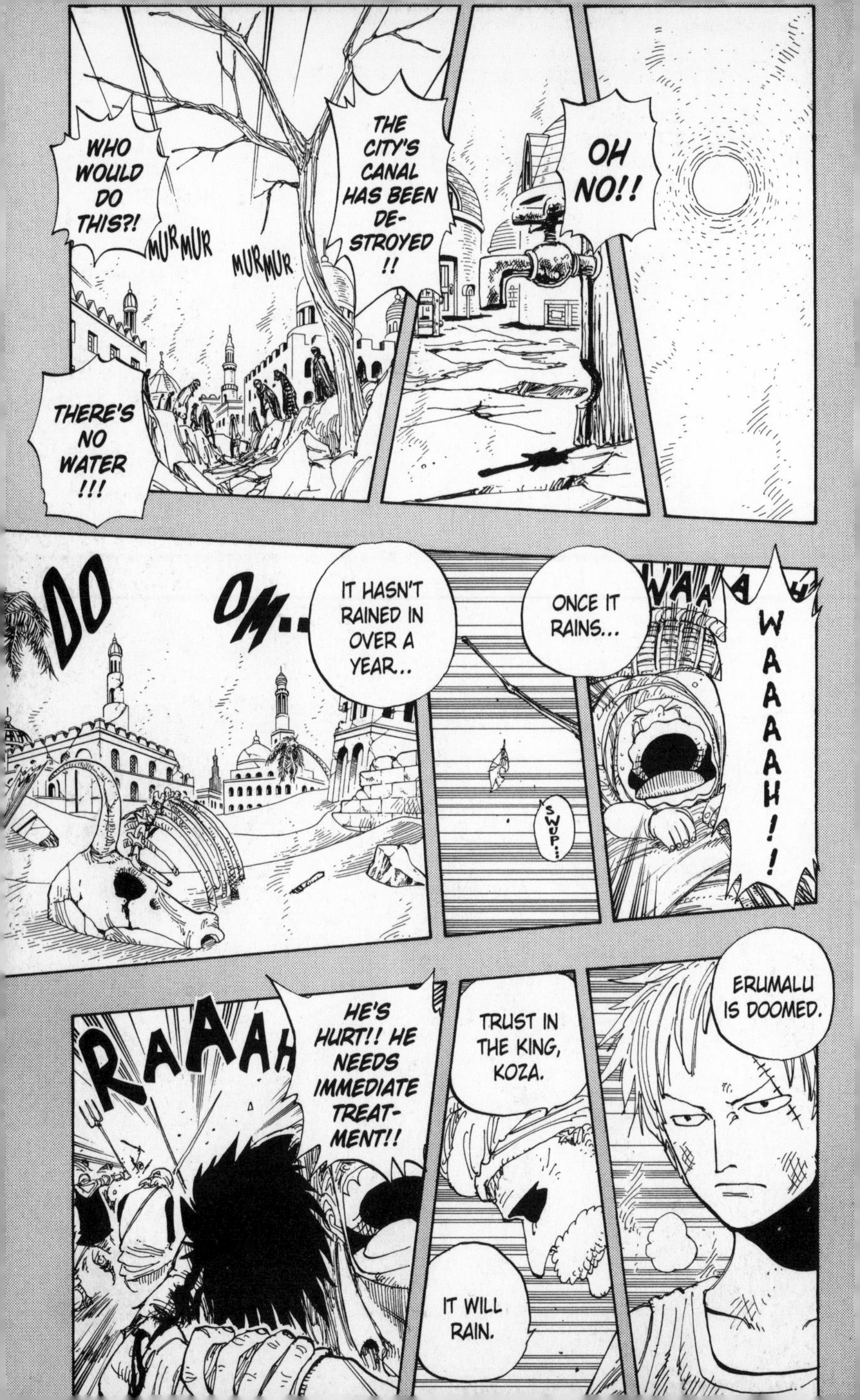
OH NO!!
THE CITY'S CANAL HAS BEEN DE-STROYED!!
WHO WOULD DO THIS?!
MUR MUR
MUR MUR
THERE'S NO WATER!!!
WAA A A H
WAAAAAH!!!
ONCE IT RAINS...
IT HASN'T RAINED IN OVER A YEAR...
SWUP...
DO OM...
ERUMALU IS DOOMED.
TRUST IN THE KING, KOZA.
IT WILL RAIN.
HE'S HURT!! HE NEEDS IMMEDIATE TREAT-MENT!!
RAAAAH

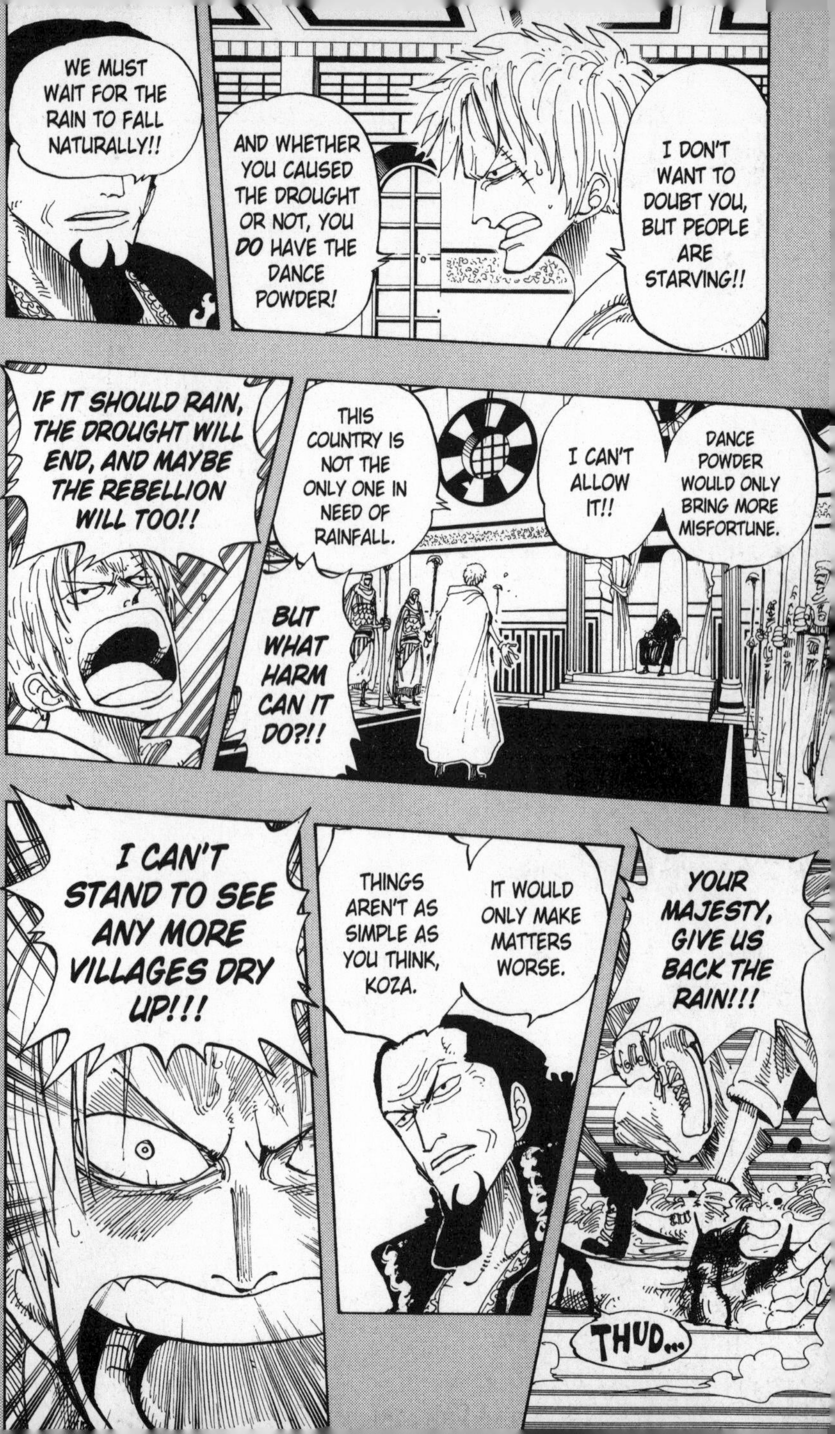
I DON'T WANT TO DOUBT YOU, BUT PEOPLE ARE STARVING!!
AND WHETHER YOU CAUSED THE DROUGHT OR NOT, YOU DO HAVE THE DANCE POWDER!
WE MUST WAIT FOR THE RAIN TO FALL NATURALLY!!
DANCE POWDER WOULD ONLY BRING MORE MISFORTUNE.
I CAN'T ALLOW IT!!
THIS COUNTRY IS NOT THE ONLY ONE IN NEED OF RAINFALL.
BUT WHAT HARM CAN IT DO?!!
IF IT SHOULD RAIN, THE DROUGHT WILL END, AND MAYBE THE REBELLION WILL TOO!!
YOUR MAJESTY, GIVE US BACK THE RAIN!!!
THUD...
IT WOULD ONLY MAKE MATTERS WORSE.
THINGS AREN'T AS SIMPLE AS YOU THINK, KOZA.
I CAN'T STAND TO SEE ANY MORE VILLAGES DRY UP!!!

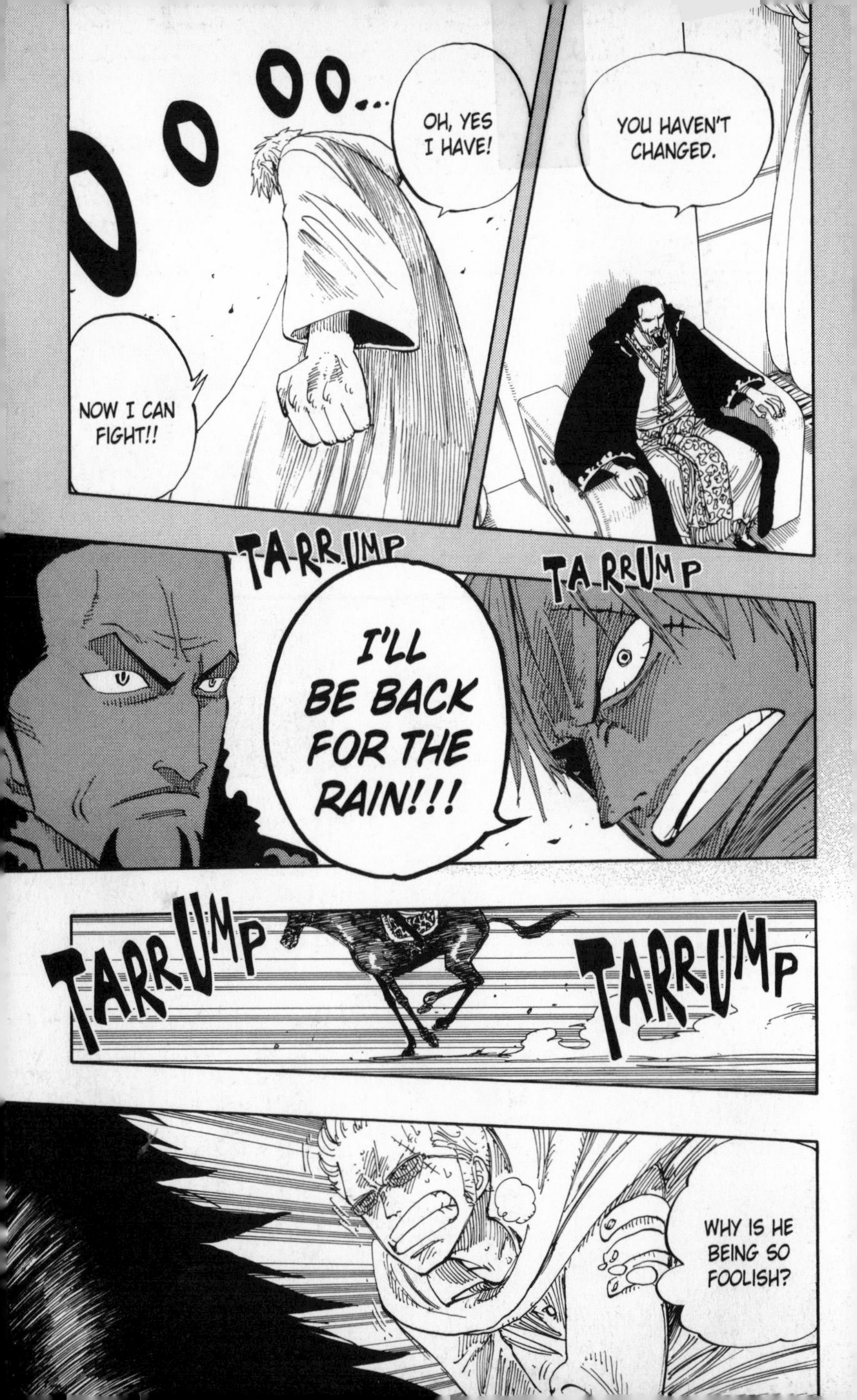
YOU HAVEN'T CHANGED.
OH, YES I HAVE!
OOOO...
NOW I CAN FIGHT!!
TARRUMP
TARRUMP
I'LL BE BACK FOR THE RAIN!!!
TARRUMP
TARRUMP
WHY IS HE BEING SO FOOLISH?

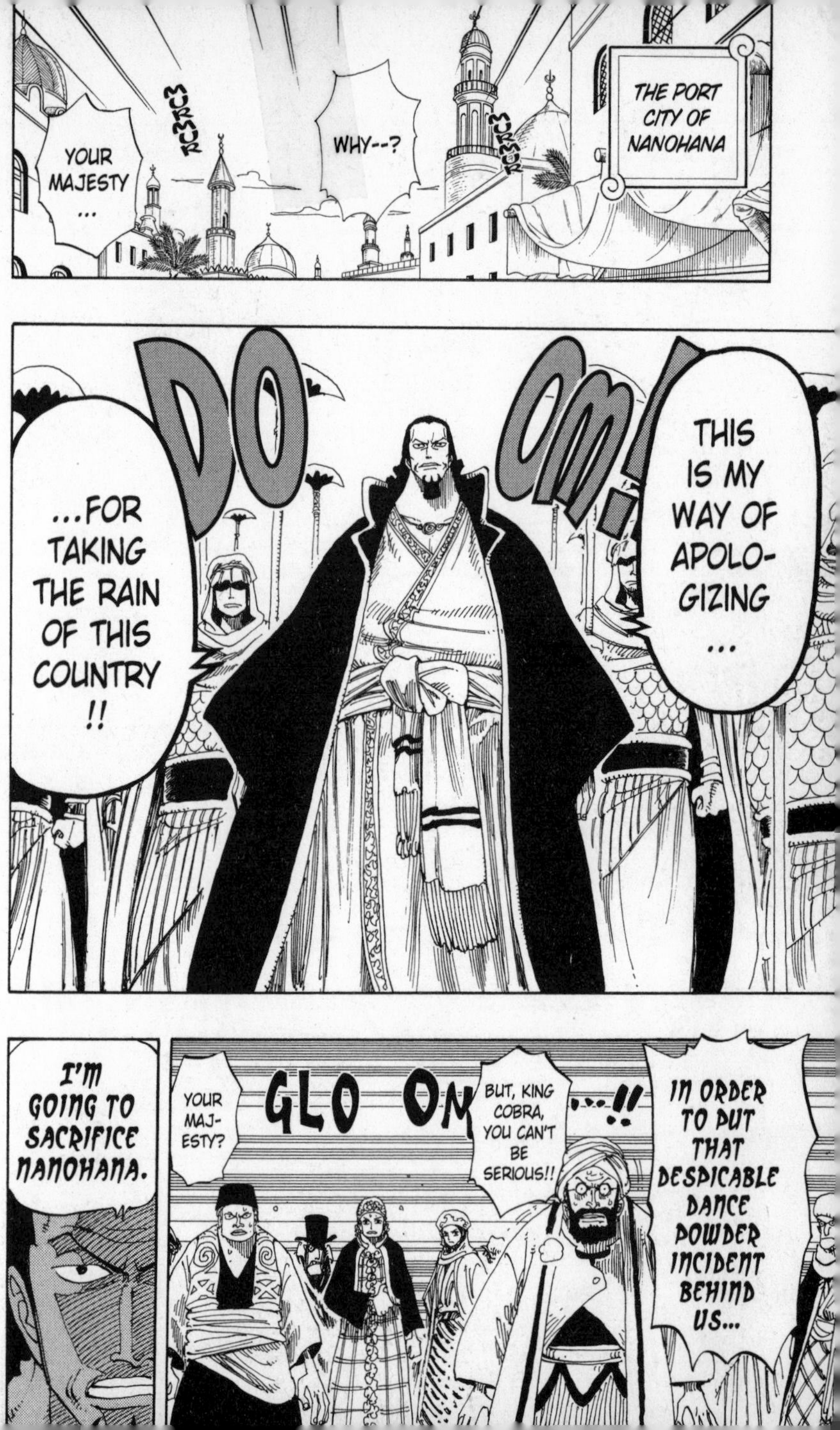
THE PORT CITY OF NANOHANA
MURMUR
WHY--?
MURMUR
YOUR MAJESTY ...
THIS IS MY WAY OF APOLOGIZING ...
DOOM!
...FOR TAKING THE RAIN OF THIS COUNTRY !!
IN ORDER TO PUT THAT DESPICABLE DANCE POWDER INCIDENT BEHIND US...
BUT, KING COBRA, YOU CAN'T BE SERIOUS!!
GLOOM...!!
YOUR MAJ-ESTY?
I'M GOING TO SACRIFICE NANOHANA.

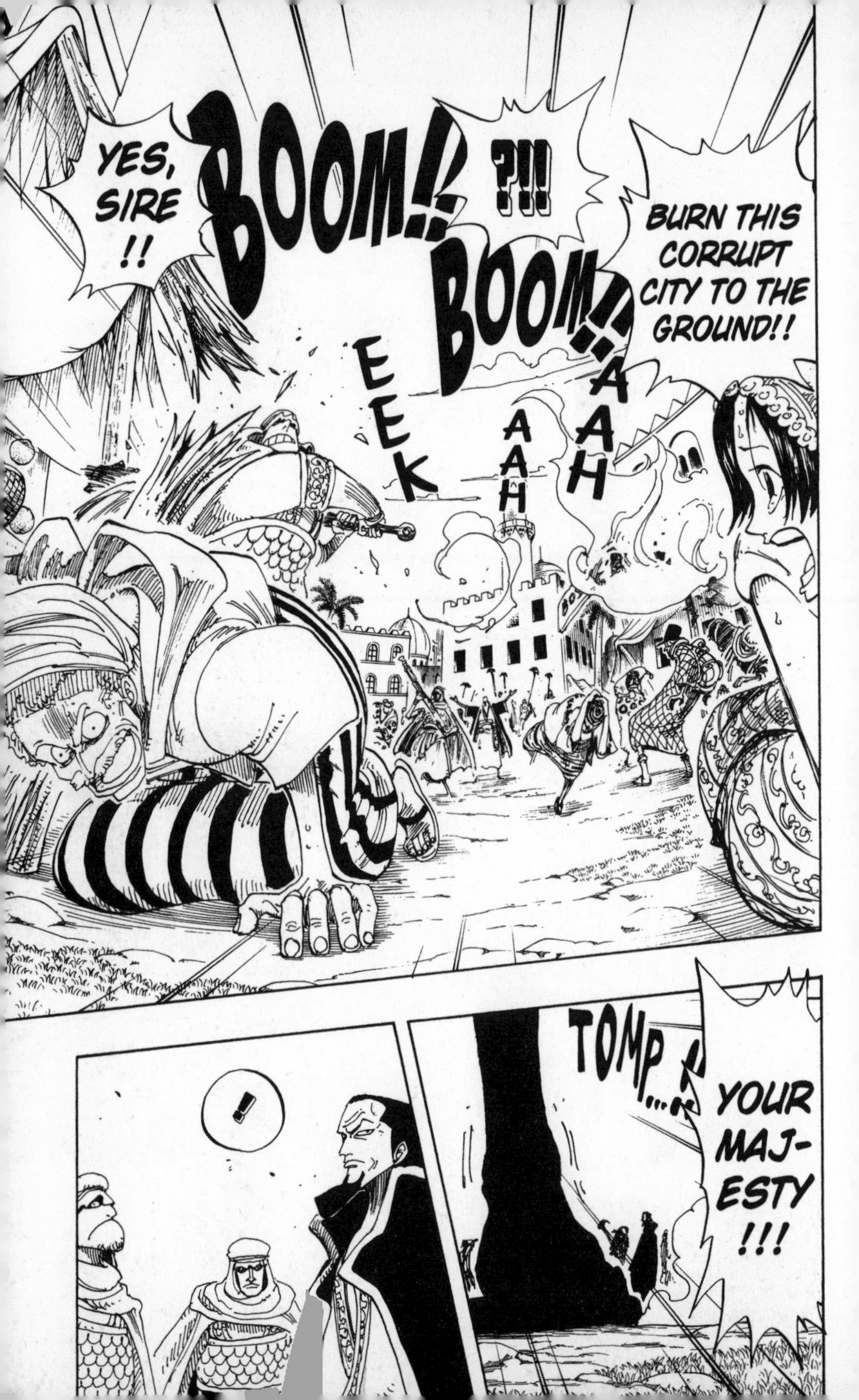
BURN THIS CORRUPT CITY TO THE GROUND!!
?!!
BOOM!!
BOOM!!
YES, SIRE !!
AAH
AAH
EEK
YOUR MAJ-ESTY !!!
TOMP...
!

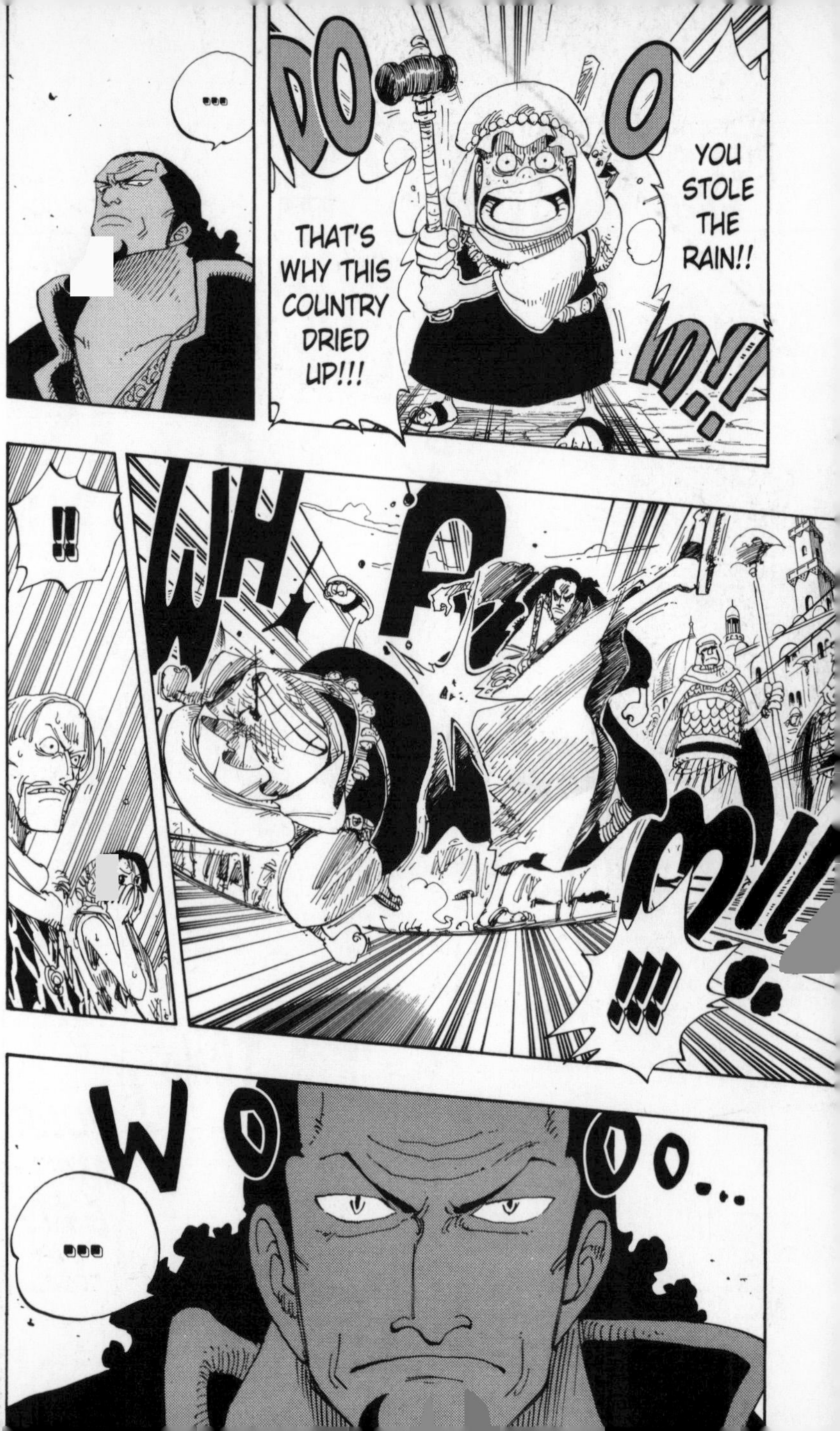
DOOOOM!!
YOU STOLE THE RAIN!!
THAT'S WHY THIS COUNTRY DRIED UP!!!
...
WHAM!!!
!!
WOOO...
...

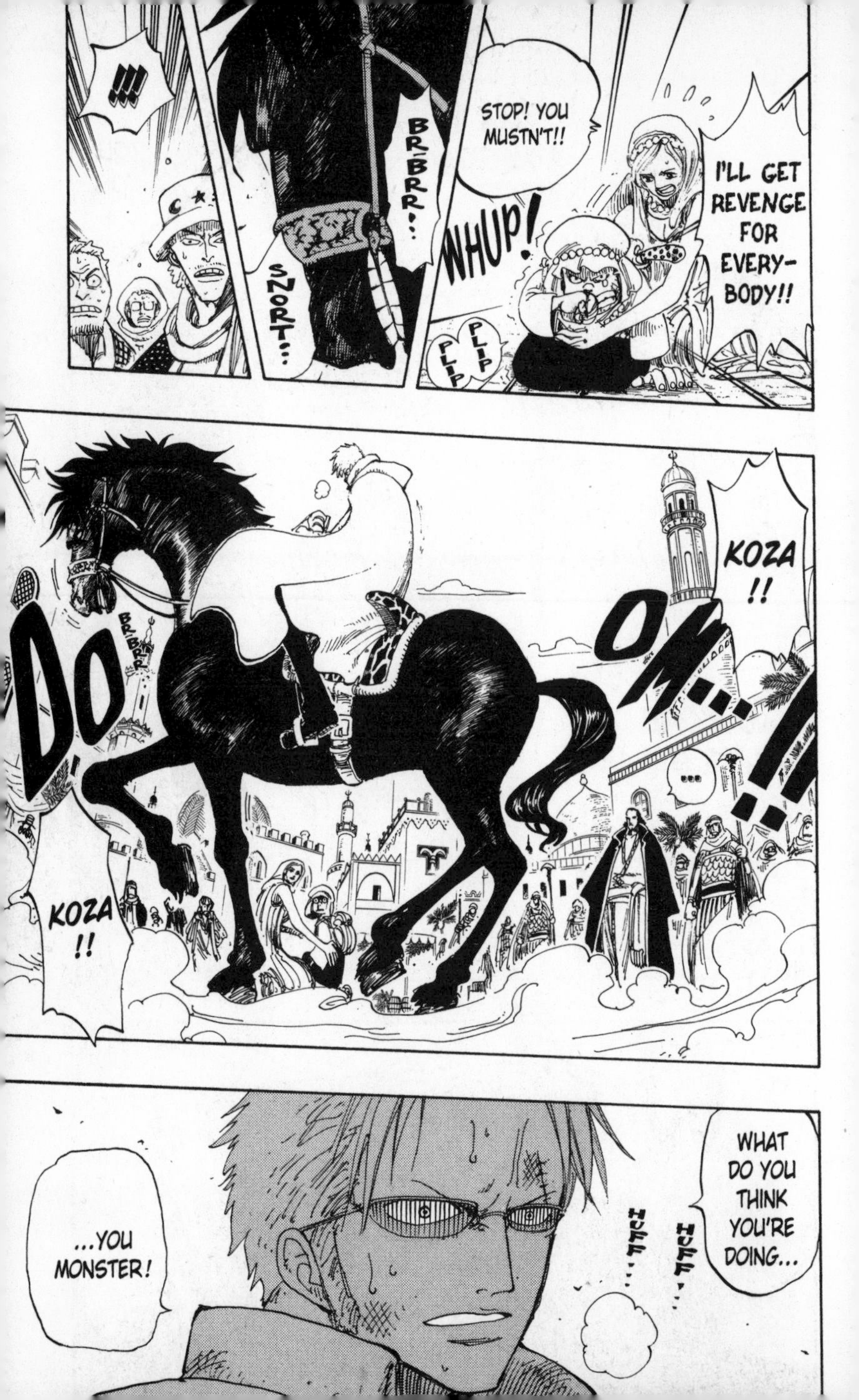
STOP! YOU MUSTN'T!!
I'LL GET REVENGE FOR EVERY-BODY!!
WHUP!
PLIP
PLIP
BR-BRR..
SNORT..
!!!
KOZA !!
...
DO
OM...!!
BR-BRR
KOZA !!
WHAT DO YOU THINK YOU'RE DOING...
HUFF..
HUFF..
...YOU MONSTER!

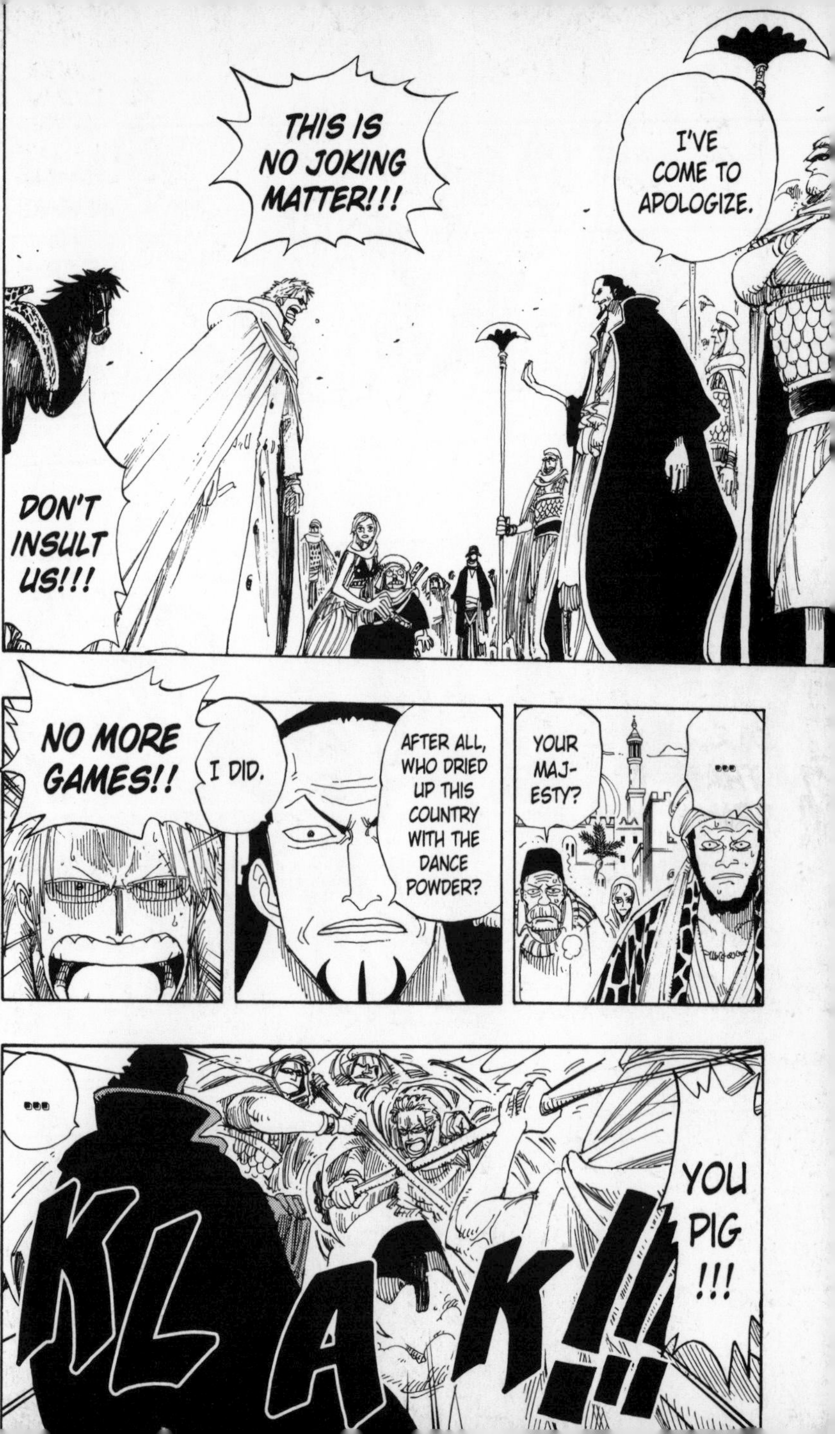
I'VE COME TO APOLOGIZE.
THIS IS NO JOKING MATTER!!!
DON'T INSULT US!!!
...
YOUR MAJESTY?
AFTER ALL, WHO DRIED UP THIS COUNTRY WITH THE DANCE POWDER?
I DID.
NO MORE GAMES!!
YOU PIG!!!
...
KLACK!!

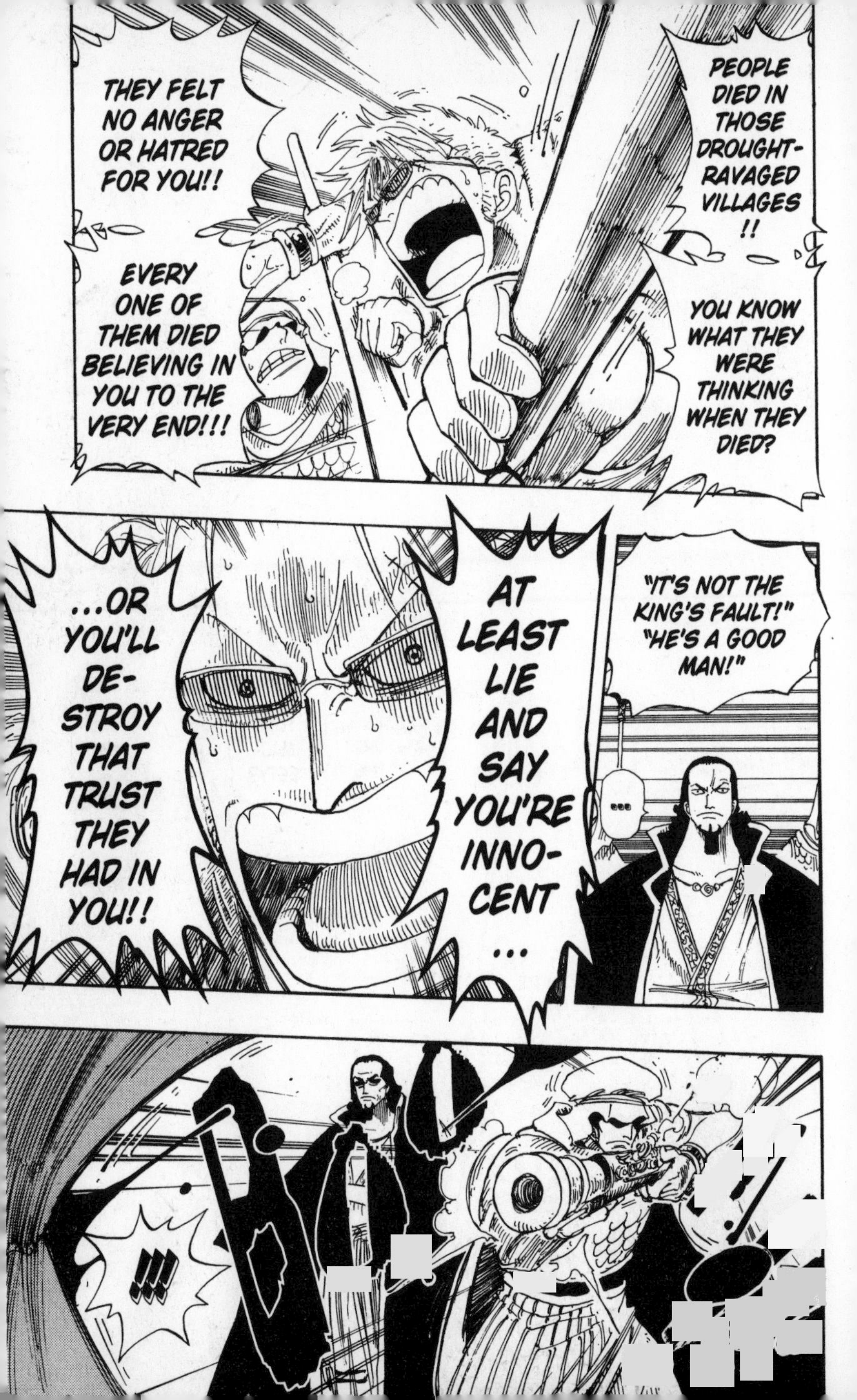
PEOPLE DIED IN THOSE DROUGHT-RAVAGED VILLAGES!!
YOU KNOW WHAT THEY WERE THINKING WHEN THEY DIED?
THEY FELT NO ANGER OR HATRED FOR YOU!!
EVERY ONE OF THEM DIED BELIEVING IN YOU TO THE VERY END!!!
"IT'S NOT THE KING'S FAULT!" "HE'S A GOOD MAN!"
...
AT LEAST LIE AND SAY YOU'RE INNOCENT...
...OR YOU'LL DE-STROY THAT TRUST THEY HAD IN YOU!!
!!!

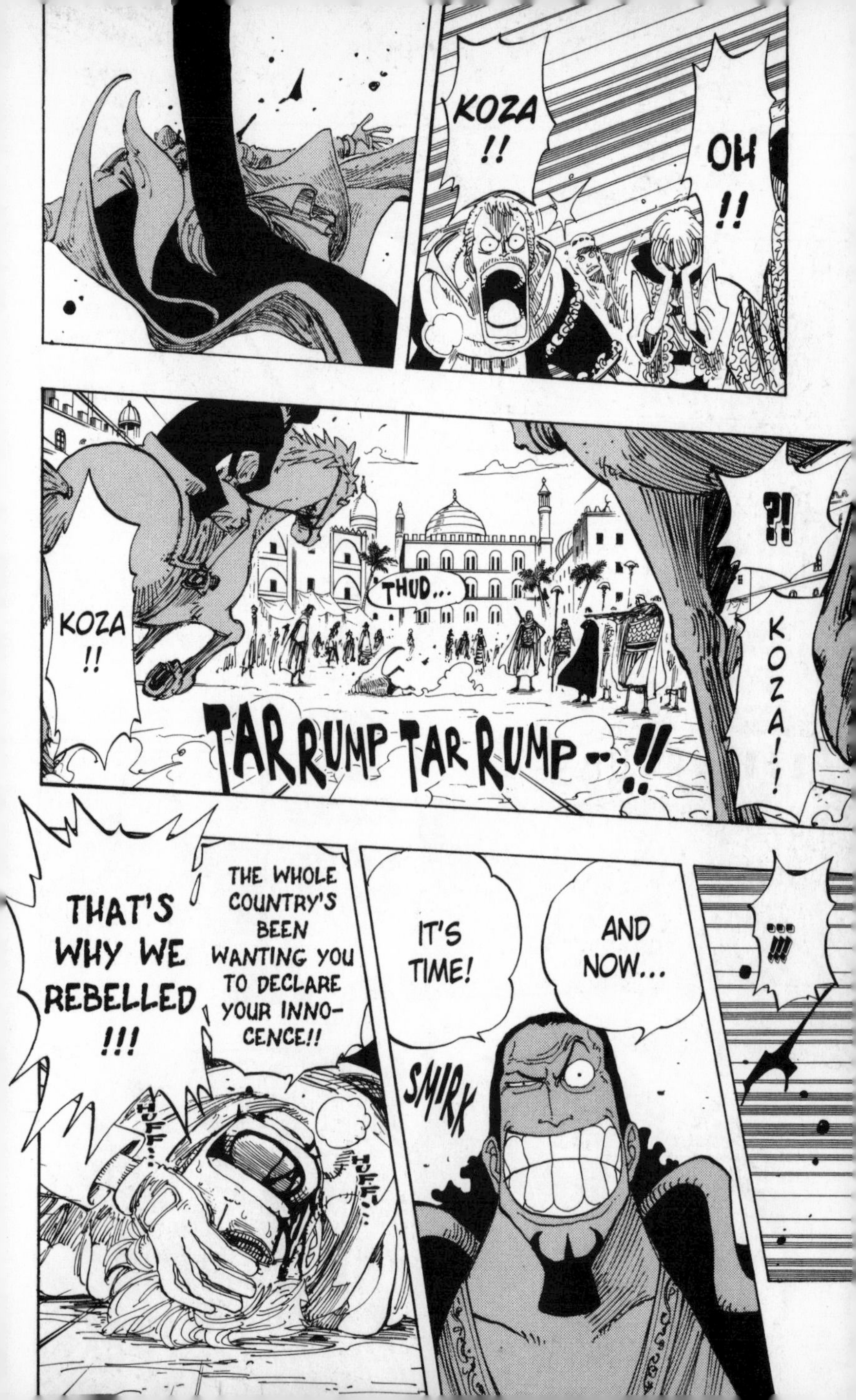
OH!!
KOZA!!
?!
KOZA!!
THUD...
TAR RUMP TAR RUMP--!!
KOZA!!
...!!!
AND NOW...
IT'S TIME!
SMIRK
THE WHOLE COUNTRY'S BEEN WANTING YOU TO DECLARE YOUR INNOCENCE!!
THAT'S WHY WE REBELLED!!!
HUFF...
HUFF...

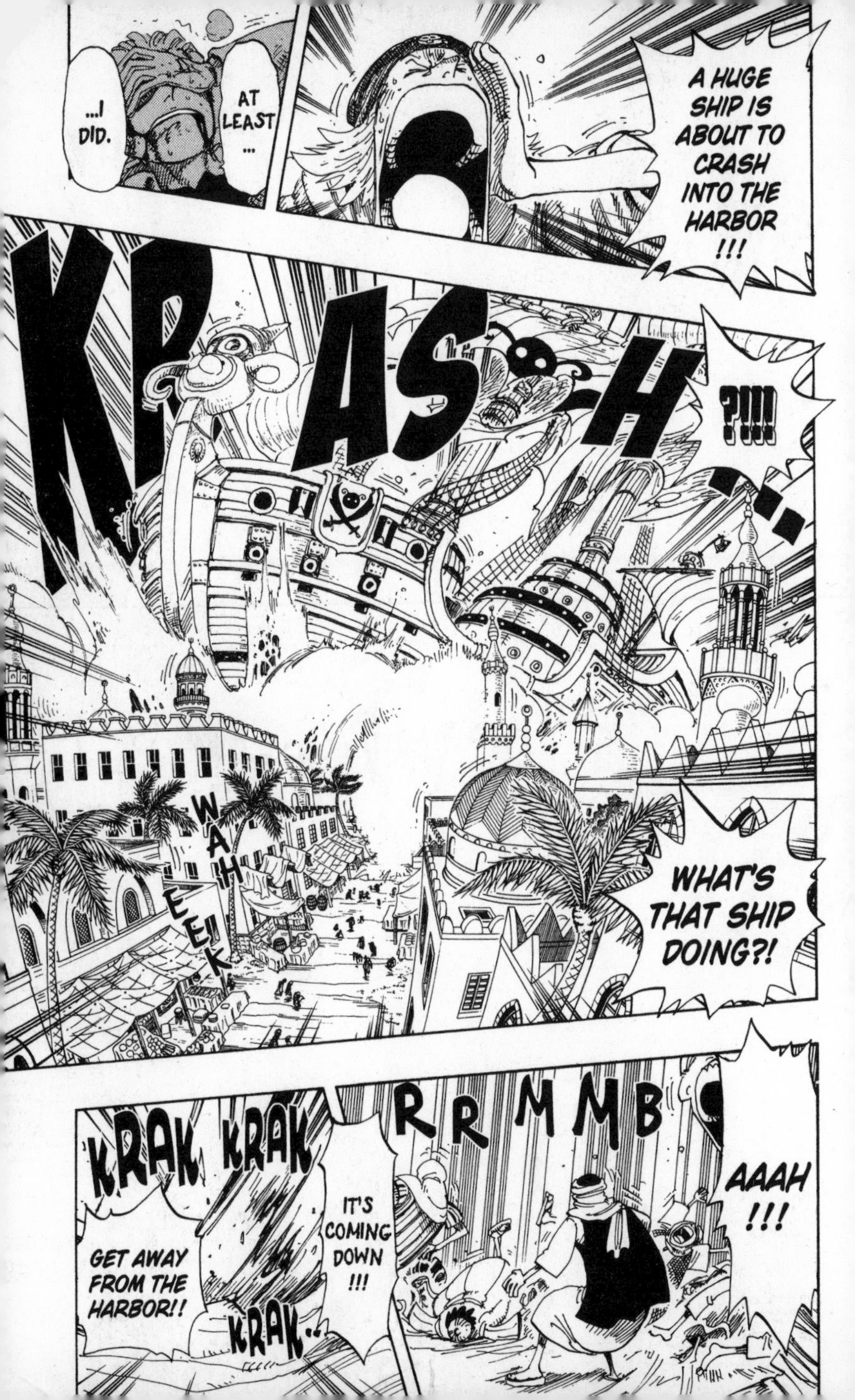
A HUGE SHIP IS ABOUT TO CRASH INTO THE HARBOR !!!
AT LEAST ...
...I DID.
KRASH
?!!!
...
WHAT'S THAT SHIP DOING?!
WAAH
EEEK
RRMMB
AAAH !!!
IT'S COMING DOWN !!!
KRAK KRAK
GET AWAY FROM THE HARBOR!!
KRAK..

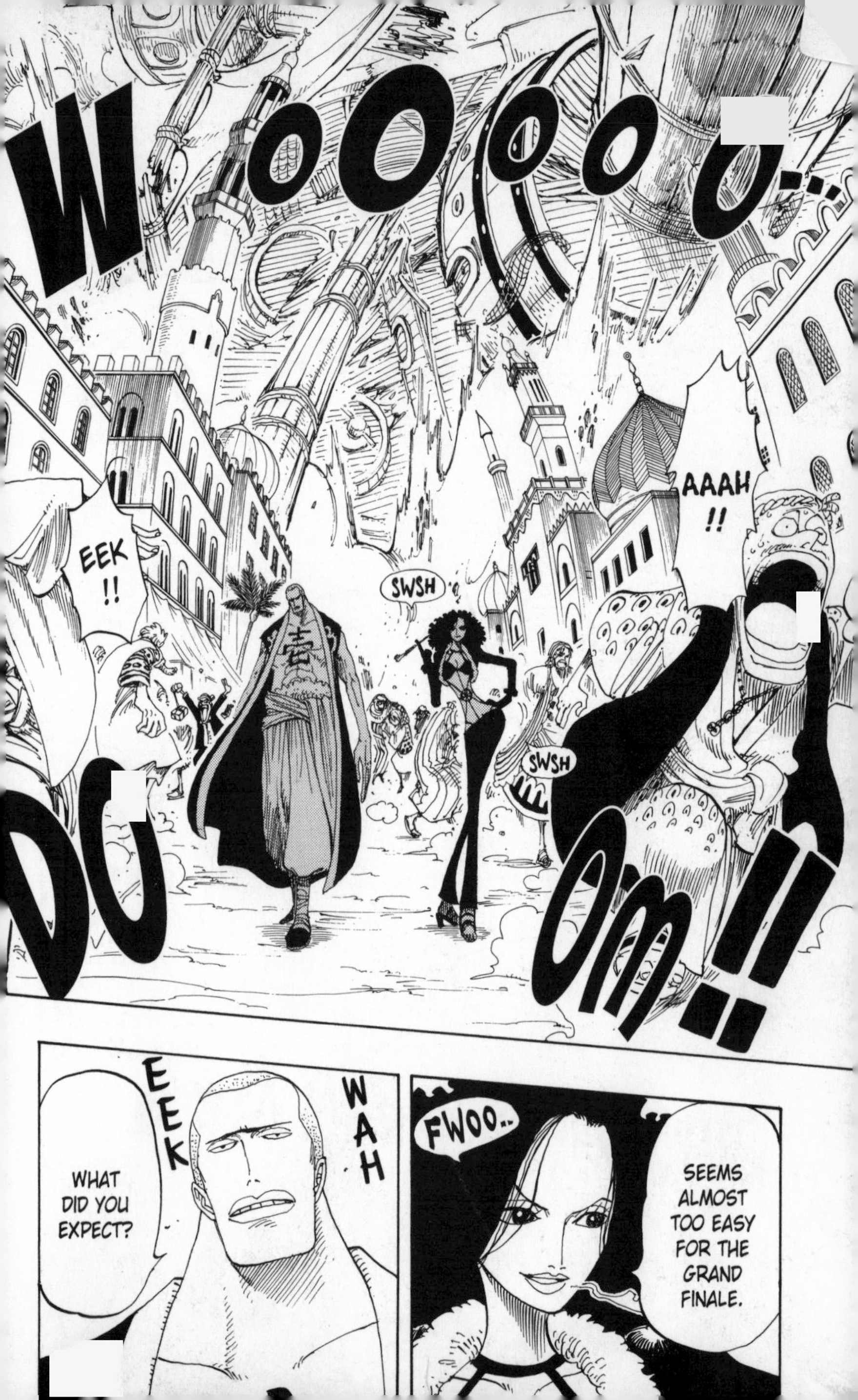
WOOOOOO...
AAAH!!
SWSH
EEK!!
SWSH
DOOM!!
FWOO..
SEEMS ALMOST TOO EASY FOR THE GRAND FINALE.
WAH
EEK
WHAT DID YOU EXPECT?

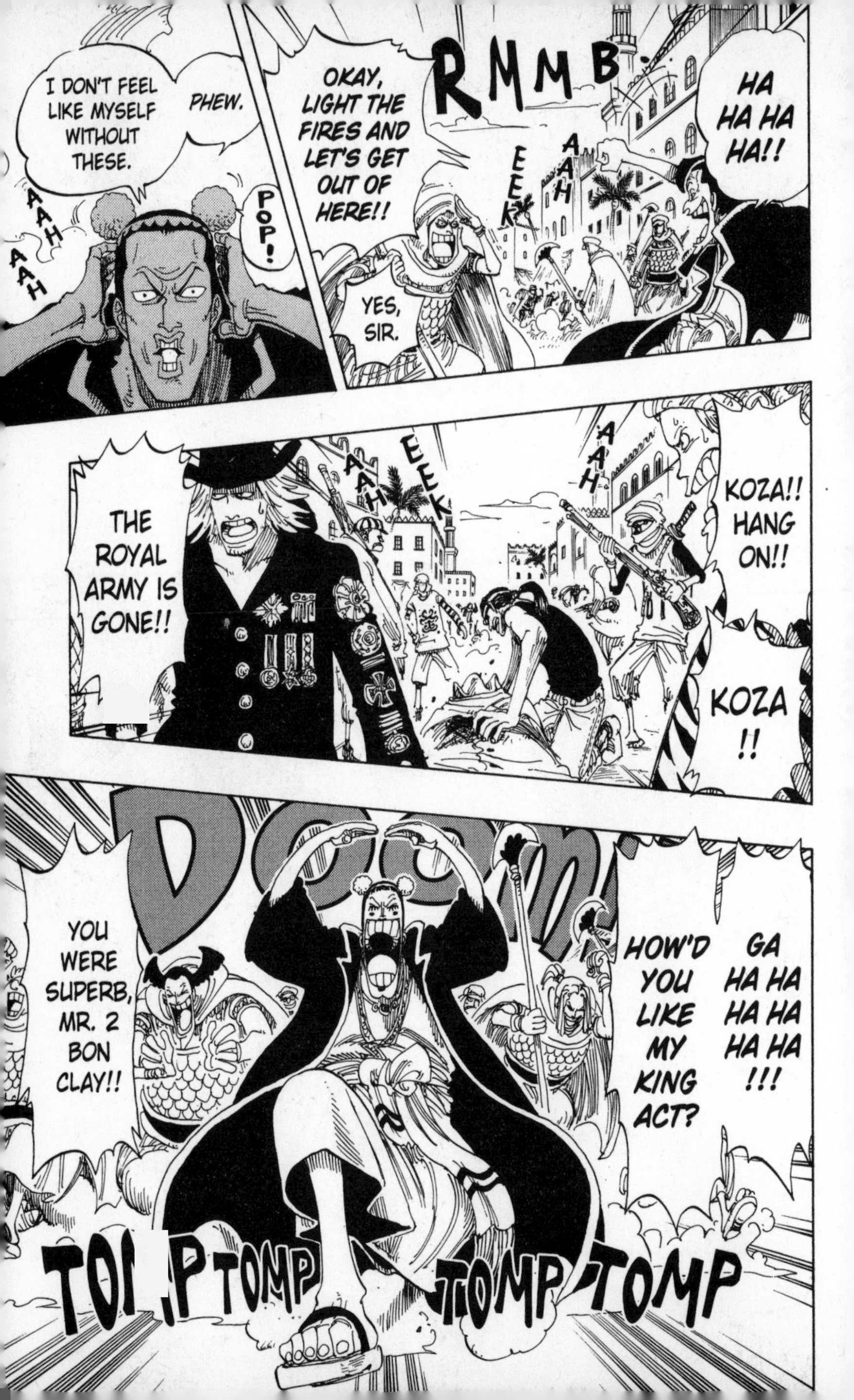
HA HA HA HA!!
RMMB
AAH
EEEK
OKAY, LIGHT THE FIRES AND LET'S GET OUT OF HERE!!
YES, SIR.
PHEW.
I DON'T FEEL LIKE MYSELF WITHOUT THESE.
POP!
AAH AAH
KOZA!! HANG ON!!
AAH
KOZA!!
EEEK
AAH
THE ROYAL ARMY IS GONE!!
GA HA HA HA HA HA HA!!!
HOW'D YOU LIKE MY KING ACT?
YOU WERE SUPERB, MR. 2 BON CLAY!!
TOMP TOMP
TOMP

# COLORING PAGE

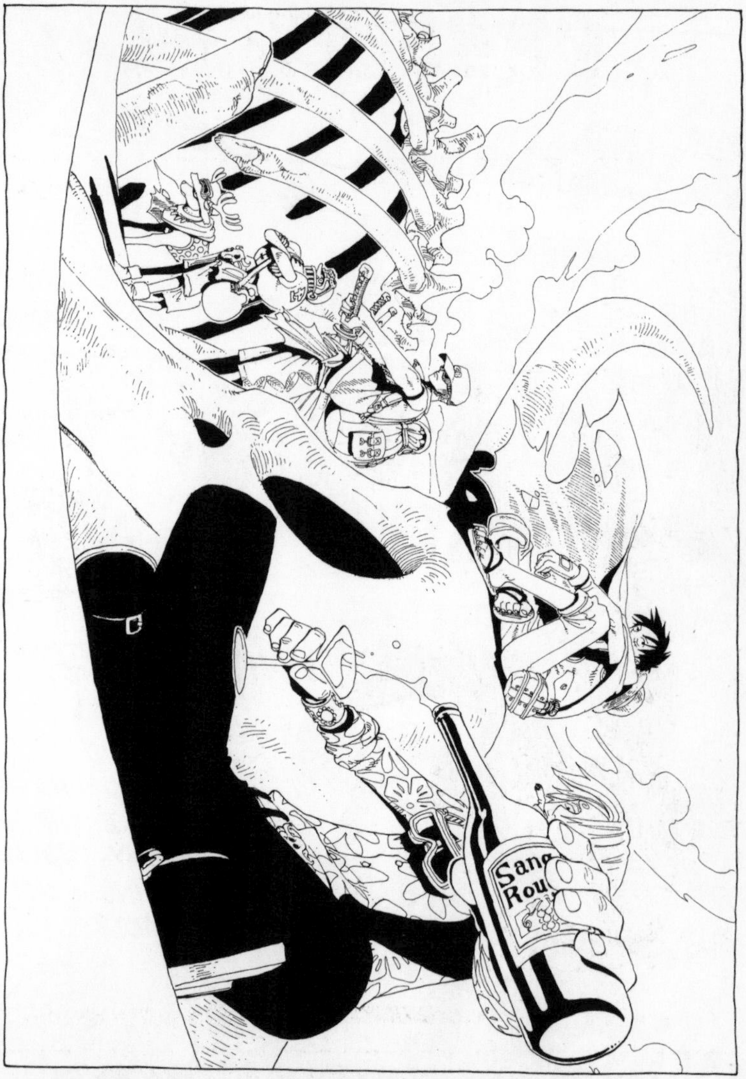

# Chapter 172:
# REBELLION

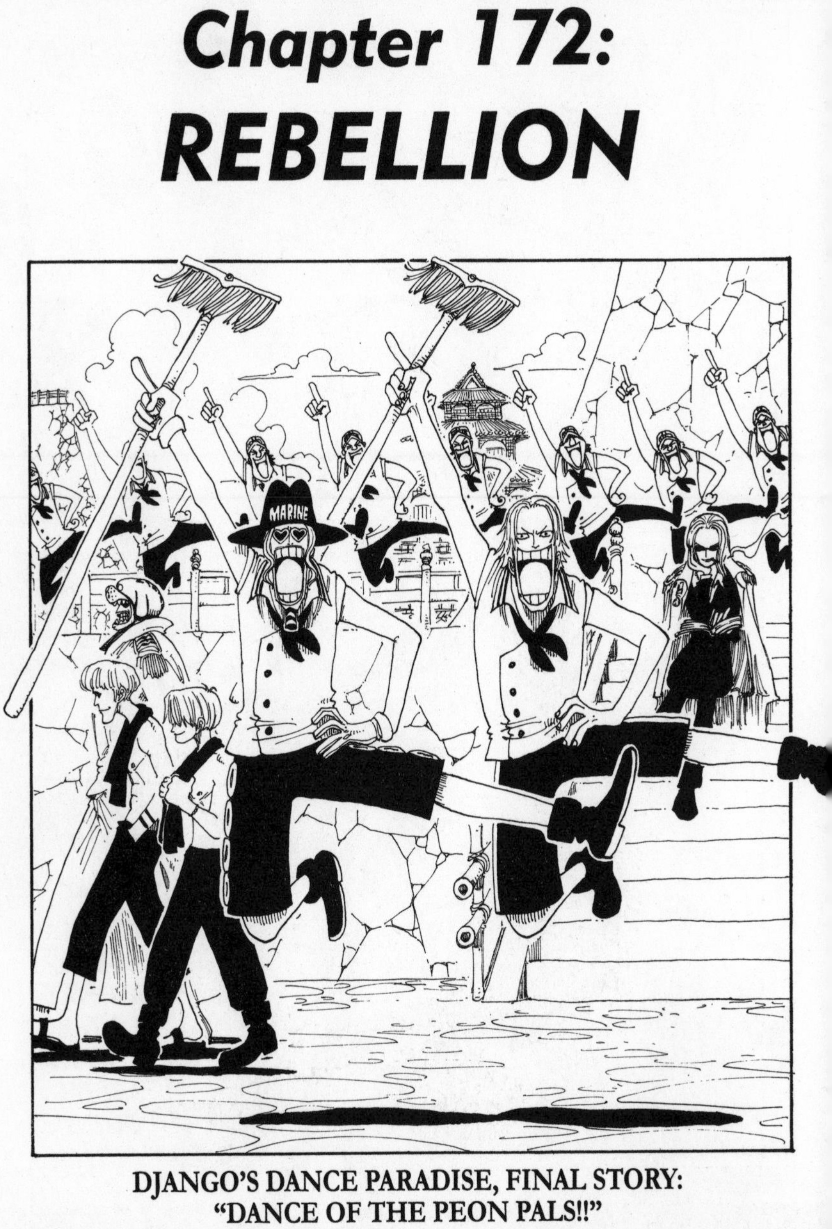
MARINE

DJANGO'S DANCE PARADISE, FINAL STORY:
"DANCE OF THE PEON PALS!!"

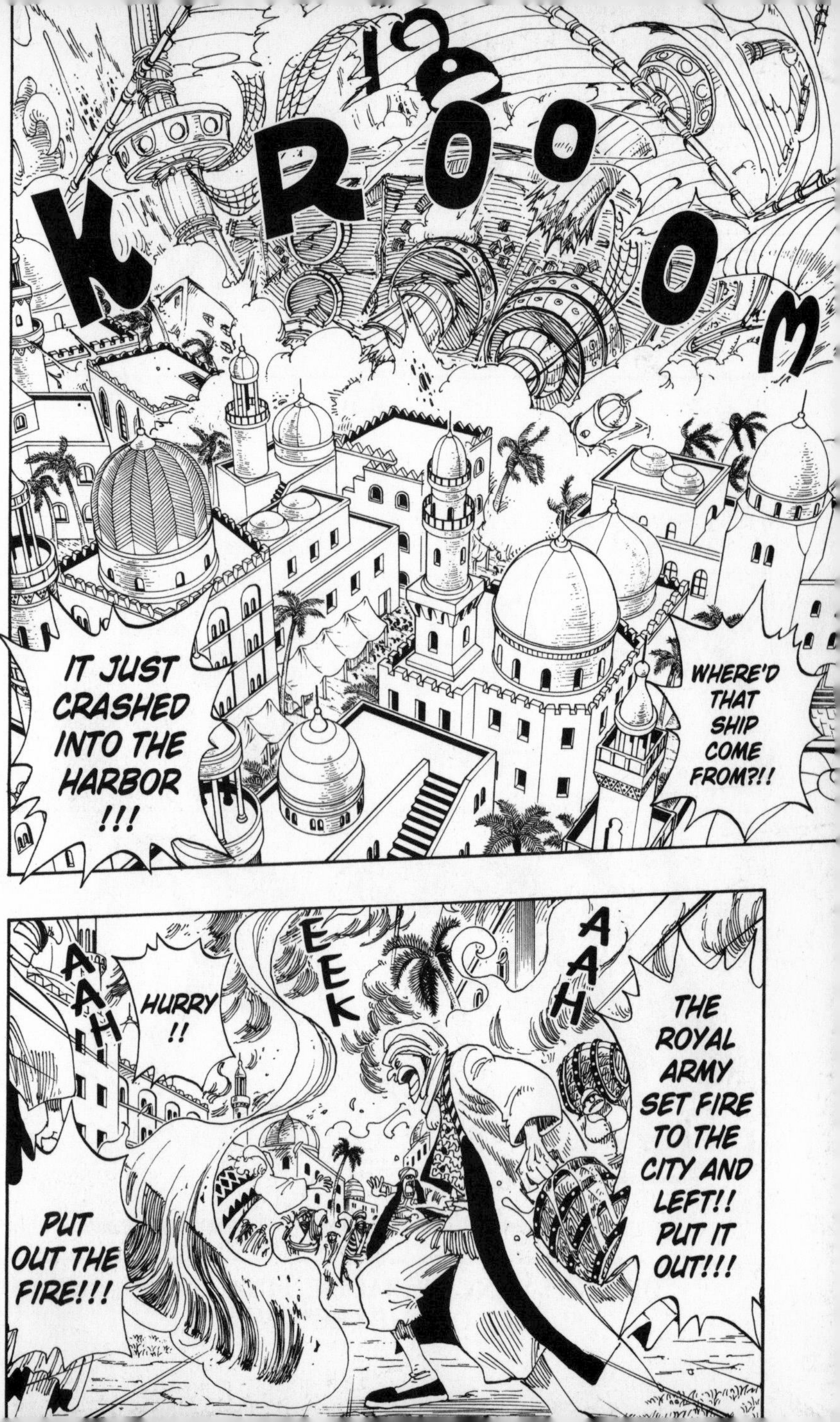
KROOOOM
WHERE'D THAT SHIP COME FROM?!!
IT JUST CRASHED INTO THE HARBOR !!!
THE ROYAL ARMY SET FIRE TO THE CITY AND LEFT!! PUT IT OUT!!!
AAH
EEK
HURRY !!
AAH
PUT OUT THE FIRE!!!

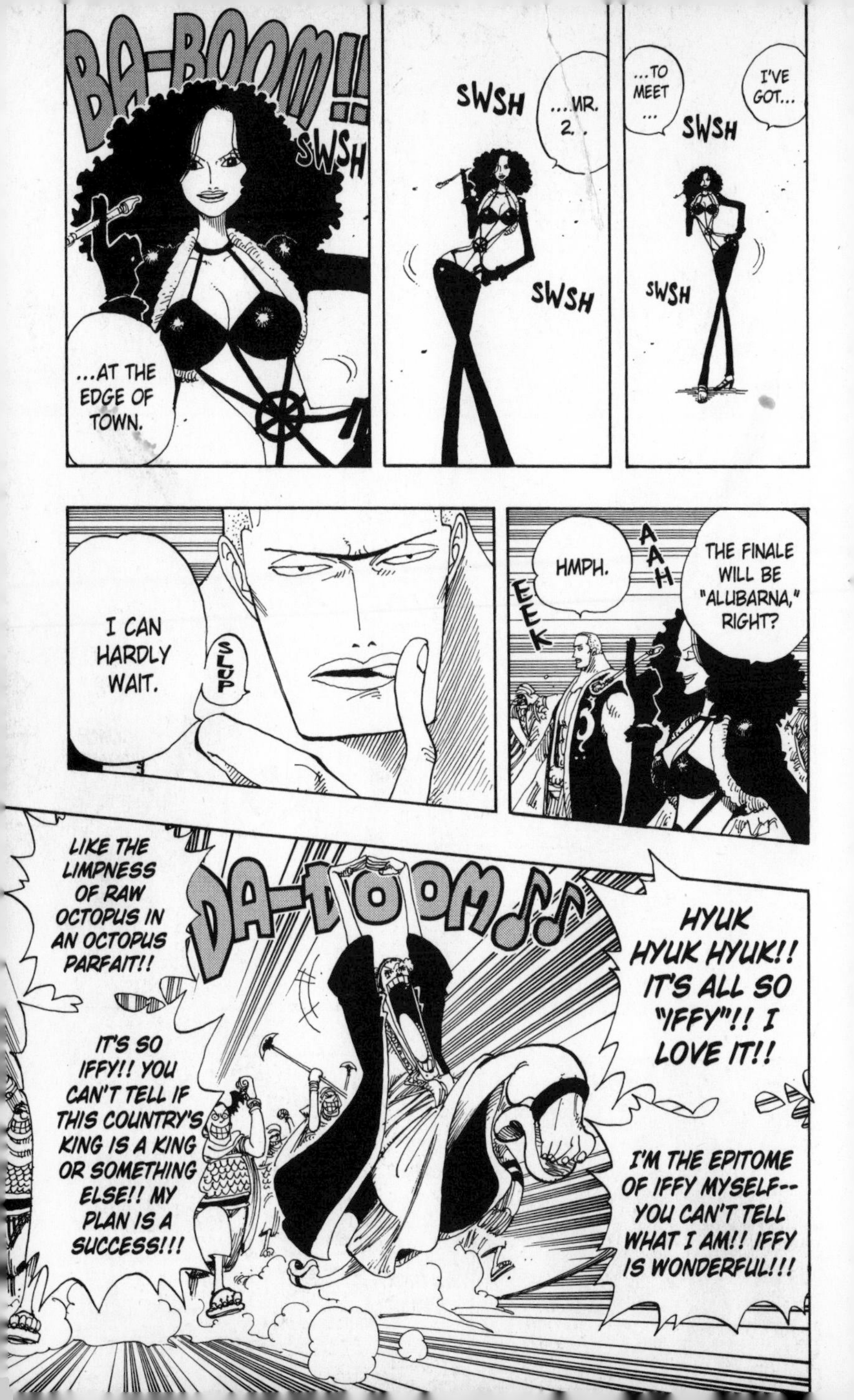

I'VE GOT...
...TO MEET...
SWSH
SWSH
....MR. 2..
SWSH
SWSH
BA-BOOM!!
SWSH
...AT THE EDGE OF TOWN.
THE FINALE WILL BE "ALUBARNA," RIGHT?
AAH
EEK
HMPH.
SLUP
I CAN HARDLY WAIT.
DA-DOOM
HYUK HYUK HYUK!! IT'S ALL SO "IFFY"!! I LOVE IT!!
LIKE THE LIMPNESS OF RAW OCTOPUS IN AN OCTOPUS PARFAIT!!
I'M THE EPITOME OF IFFY MYSELF-- YOU CAN'T TELL WHAT I AM!! IFFY IS WONDERFUL!!!
IT'S SO IFFY!! YOU CAN'T TELL IF THIS COUNTRY'S KING IS A KING OR SOMETHING ELSE!! MY PLAN IS A SUCCESS!!!

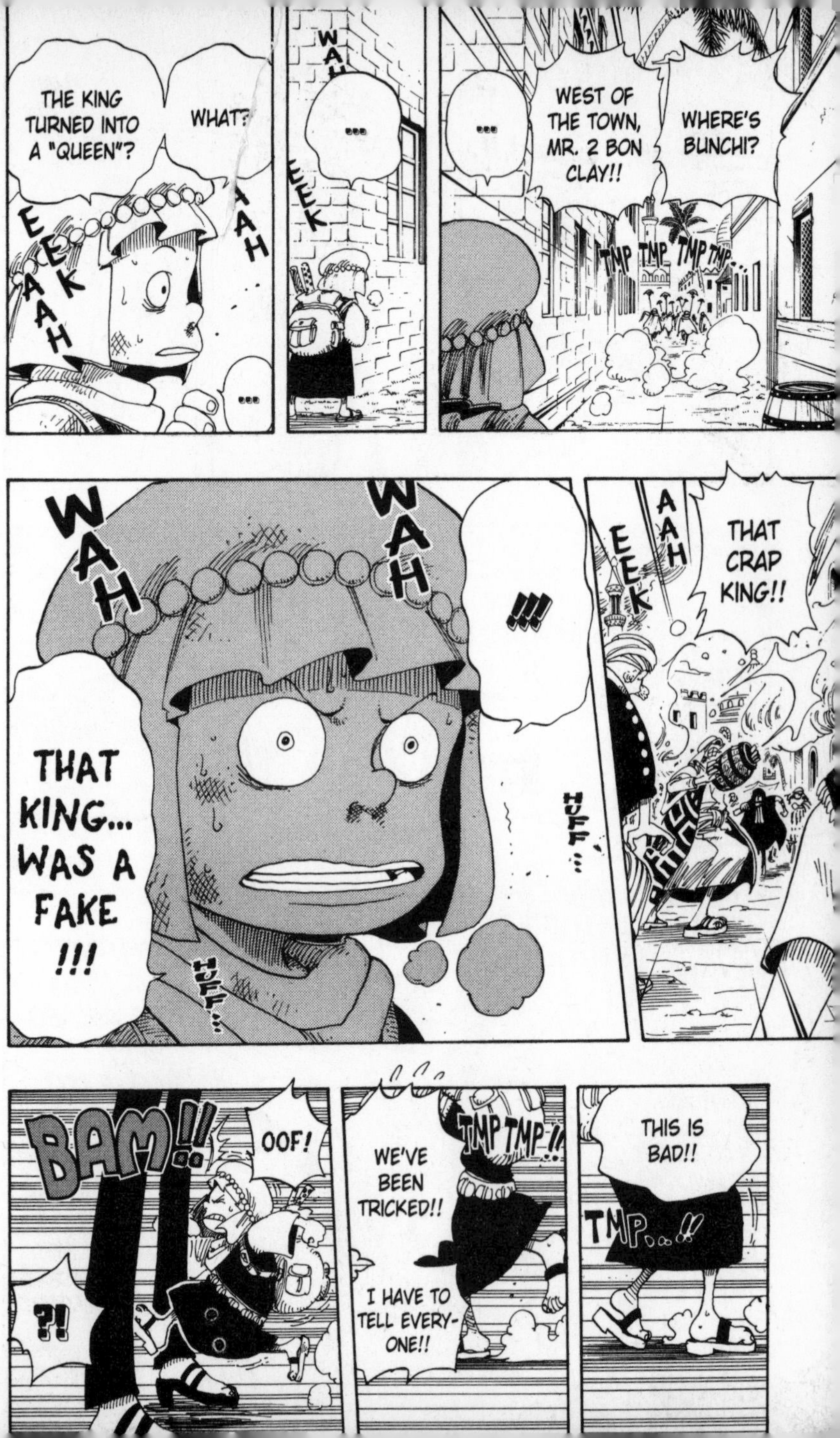
WHERE'S BUNCHI?
WEST OF THE TOWN, MR. 2 BON CLAY!!
...
TMP TMP TMP TMP...
WAH
...
EEK
WHAT?
THE KING TURNED INTO A "QUEEN"?
WAH
EEK
AAH
...
AAH
EEK
THAT CRAP KING!!
WAH
WAH
!!!
THAT KING... WAS A FAKE!!!
HUFF...
HUFF...
THIS IS BAD!!
TMP...!!
TMP TMP!!
WE'VE BEEN TRICKED!!
I HAVE TO TELL EVERY-ONE!!
BAM!!
OOF!
?!

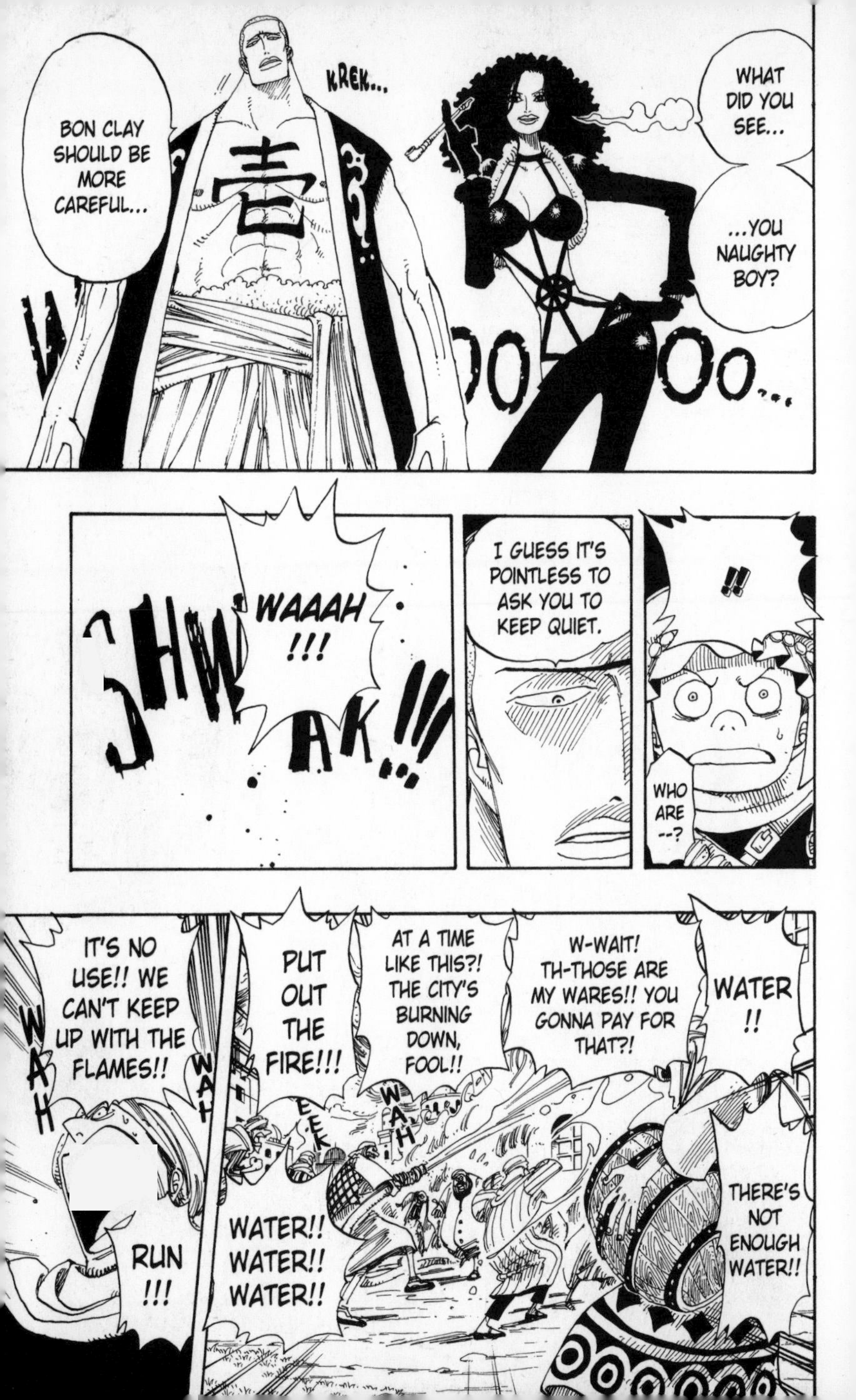
WHAT DID YOU SEE...
...YOU NAUGHTY BOY?
KREK...
BON CLAY SHOULD BE MORE CAREFUL...
!!
WHO ARE --?
I GUESS IT'S POINTLESS TO ASK YOU TO KEEP QUIET.
WAAAH !!!
SHW
AK!!!
WATER !!
THERE'S NOT ENOUGH WATER!!
W-WAIT! TH-THOSE ARE MY WARES!! YOU GONNA PAY FOR THAT?!
AT A TIME LIKE THIS?! THE CITY'S BURNING DOWN, FOOL!!
WAH
EEK
PUT OUT THE FIRE!!!
WATER!! WATER!! WATER!!
WAH
IT'S NO USE!! WE CAN'T KEEP UP WITH THE FLAMES!!
WAH
RUN !!!

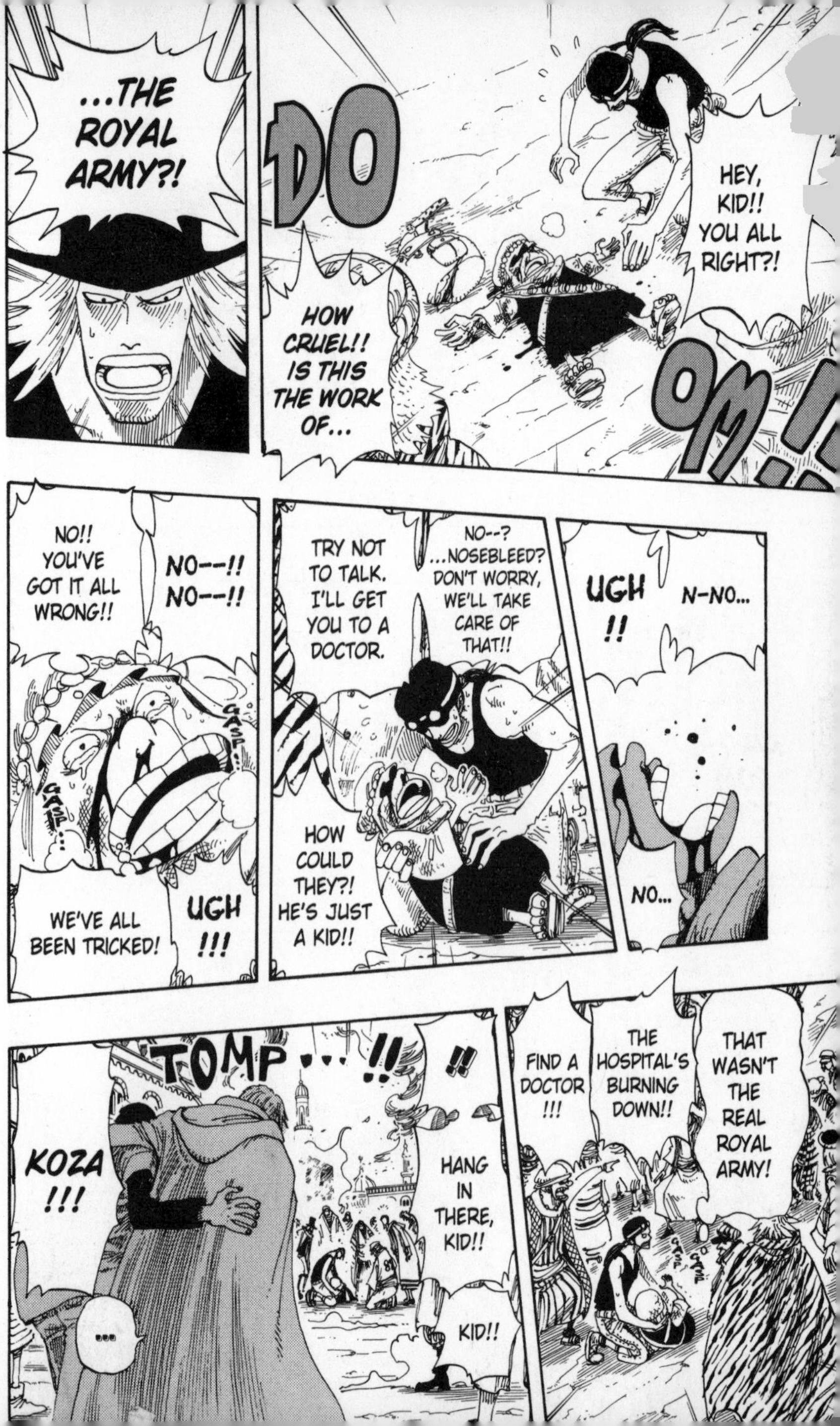
HEY, KID!! YOU ALL RIGHT?!
DO
OM!!
HOW CRUEL!! IS THIS THE WORK OF...
...THE ROYAL ARMY?!
N-NO...
UGH!!
NO...
NO--? ...NOSEBLEED? DON'T WORRY, WE'LL TAKE CARE OF THAT!!
TRY NOT TO TALK. I'LL GET YOU TO A DOCTOR.
HOW COULD THEY?! HE'S JUST A KID!!
NO--!! NO--!!
NO!! YOU'VE GOT IT ALL WRONG!!
GASP
GASP...
UGH!!!
WE'VE ALL BEEN TRICKED!
THAT WASN'T THE REAL ROYAL ARMY!
THE HOSPITAL'S BURNING DOWN!!
FIND A DOCTOR!!!
GASP
GASP
!!
HANG IN THERE, KID!!
KID!!
TOMP...!!
KOZA!!!
...

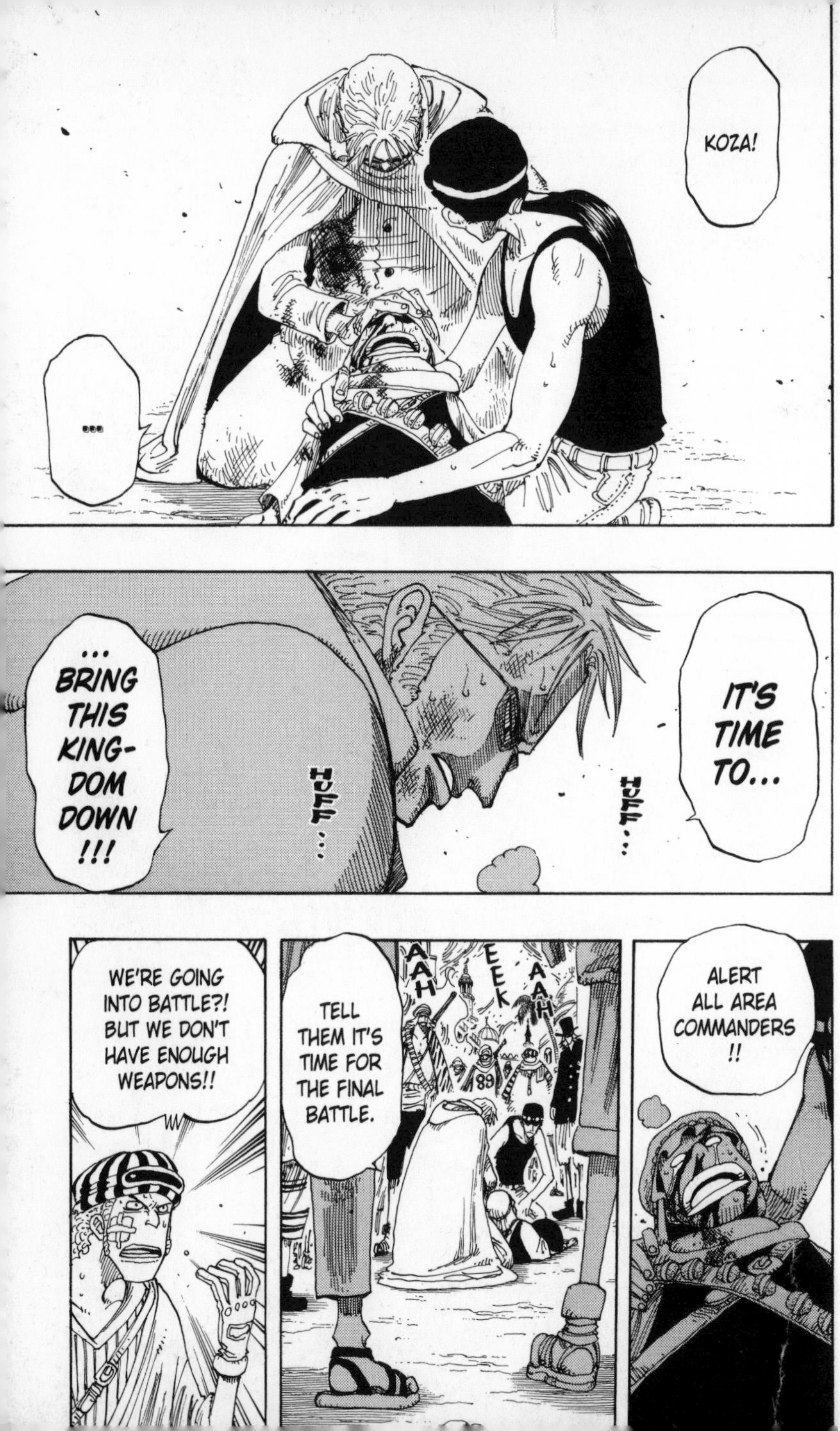
KOZA!
...
IT'S TIME TO...
HUFF...
HUFF...
...BRING THIS KING-DOM DOWN!!!
ALERT ALL AREA COMMANDERS !!
AAAH
EEK
AAH
TELL THEM IT'S TIME FOR THE FINAL BATTLE.
WE'RE GOING INTO BATTLE?! BUT WE DON'T HAVE ENOUGH WEAPONS!!

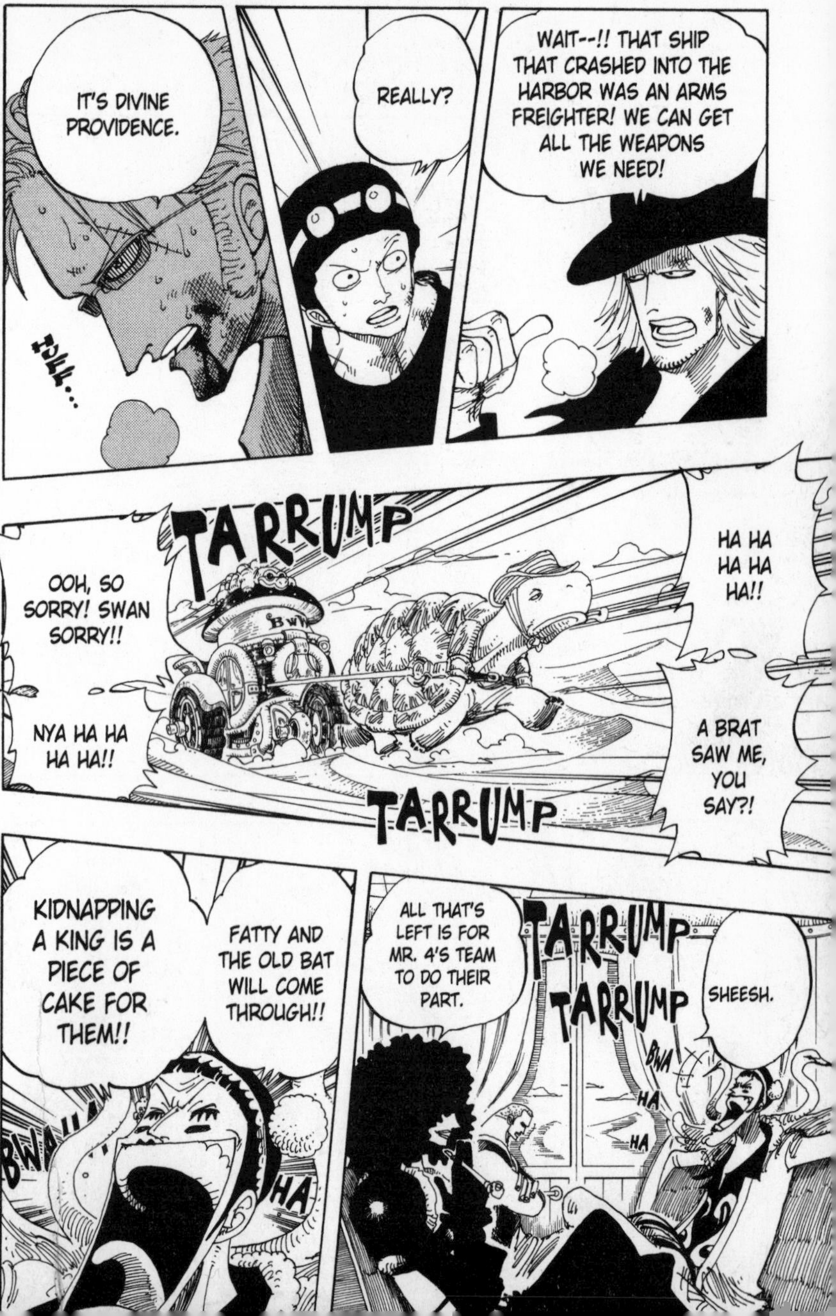
WAIT--!! THAT SHIP THAT CRASHED INTO THE HARBOR WAS AN ARMS FREIGHTER! WE CAN GET ALL THE WEAPONS WE NEED!
REALLY?
IT'S DIVINE PROVIDENCE.
HUFF...
HA HA HA HA HA!!
A BRAT SAW ME, YOU SAY?!
TARRUMP
OOH, SO SORRY! SWAN SORRY!!
NYA HA HA HA HA!!
TARRUMP
SHEESH.
TARRUMP
TARRUMP
BWA HA HA
ALL THAT'S LEFT IS FOR MR. 4'S TEAM TO DO THEIR PART.
FATTY AND THE OLD BAT WILL COME THROUGH!!
KIDNAPPING A KING IS A PIECE OF CAKE FOR THEM!!
BWA HA

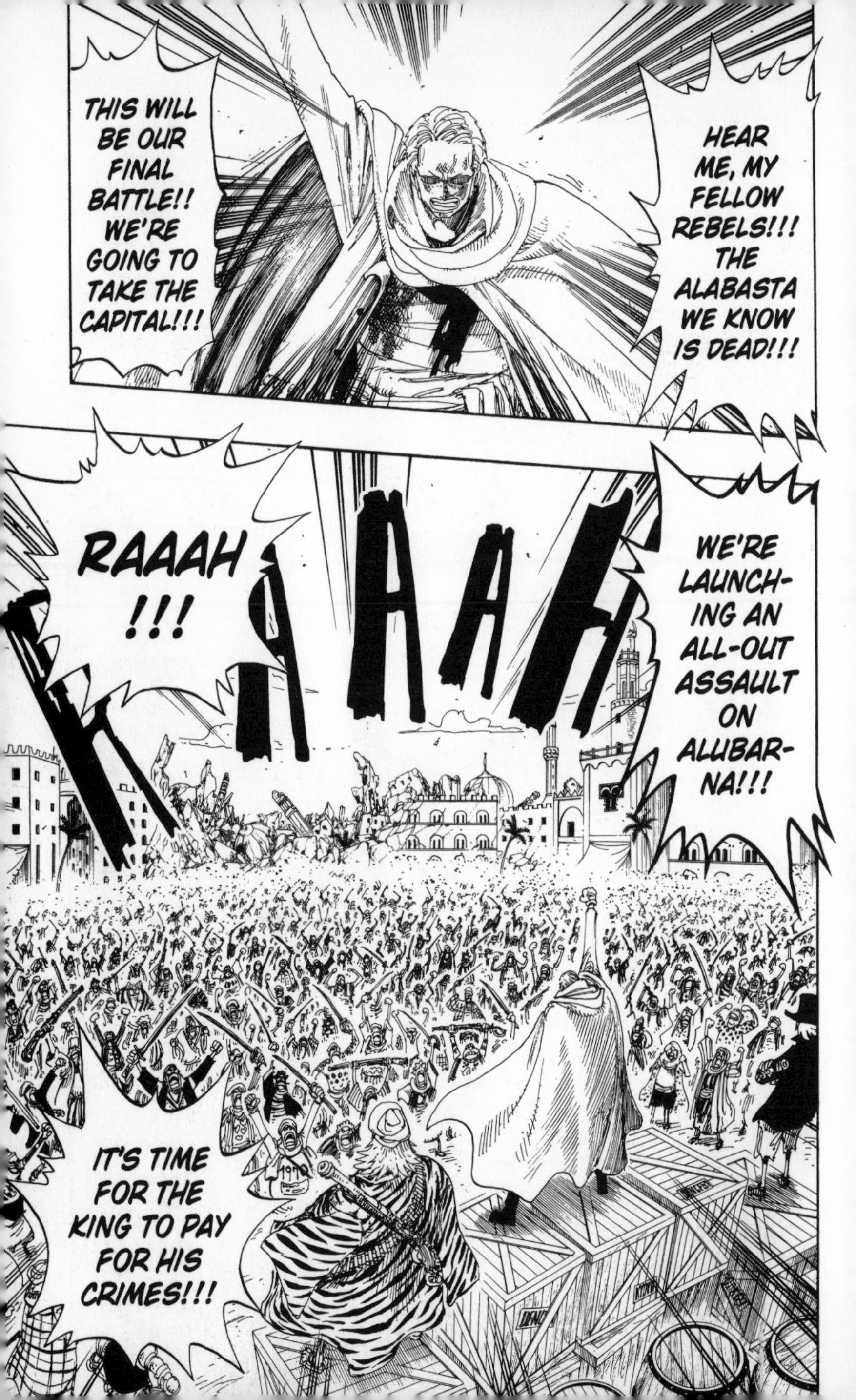
HEAR ME, MY FELLOW REBELS!!! THE ALABASTA WE KNOW IS DEAD!!!
THIS WILL BE OUR FINAL BATTLE!! WE'RE GOING TO TAKE THE CAPITAL!!!
WE'RE LAUNCH-ING AN ALL-OUT ASSAULT ON ALUBAR-NA!!!
RAAAH!!!
RAAAH
IT'S TIME FOR THE KING TO PAY FOR HIS CRIMES!!!

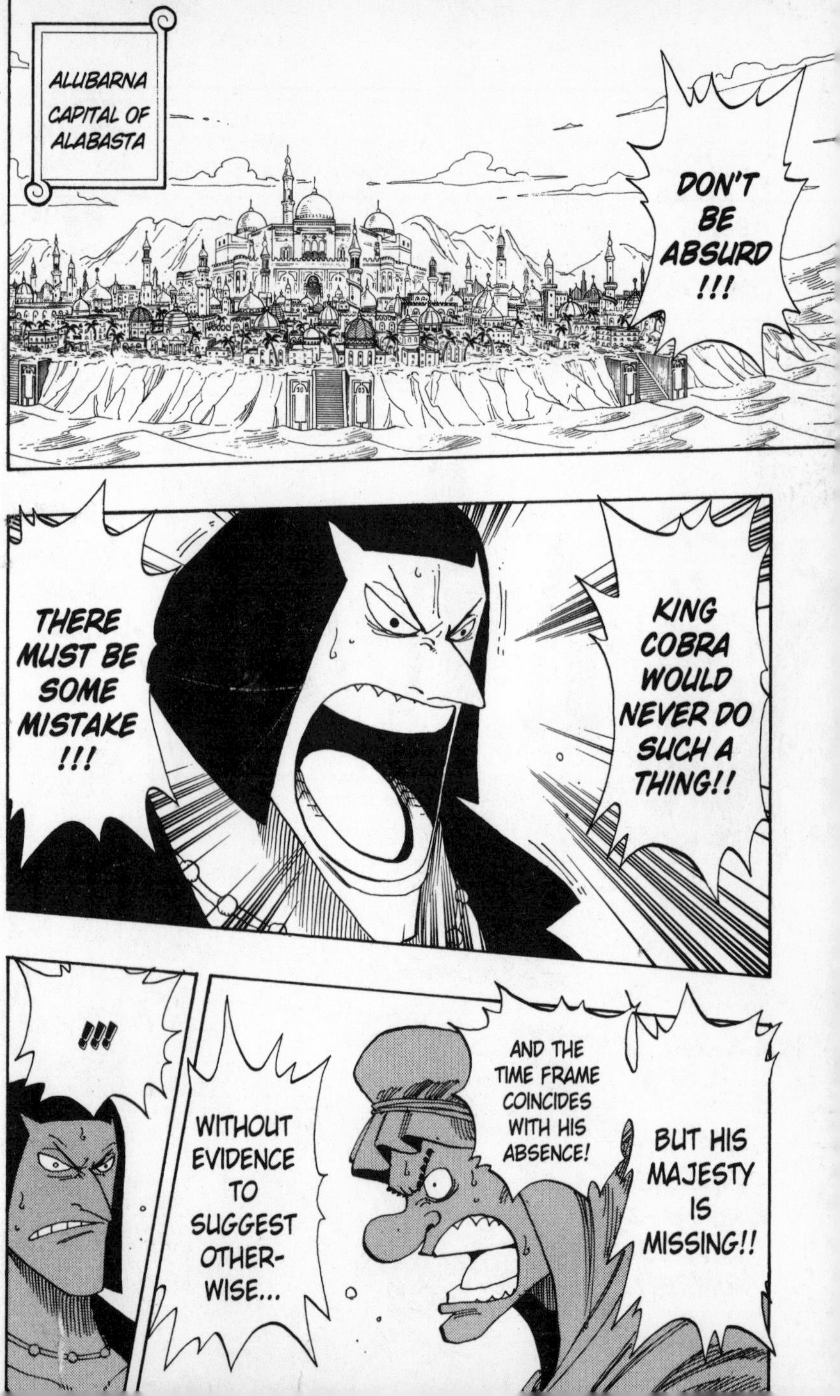
ALUBARNA CAPITAL OF ALABASTA
DON'T BE ABSURD!!!
KING COBRA WOULD NEVER DO SUCH A THING!!
THERE MUST BE SOME MISTAKE!!!
BUT HIS MAJESTY IS MISSING!!
AND THE TIME FRAME COINCIDES WITH HIS ABSENCE!
WITHOUT EVIDENCE TO SUGGEST OTHER-WISE...
!!!

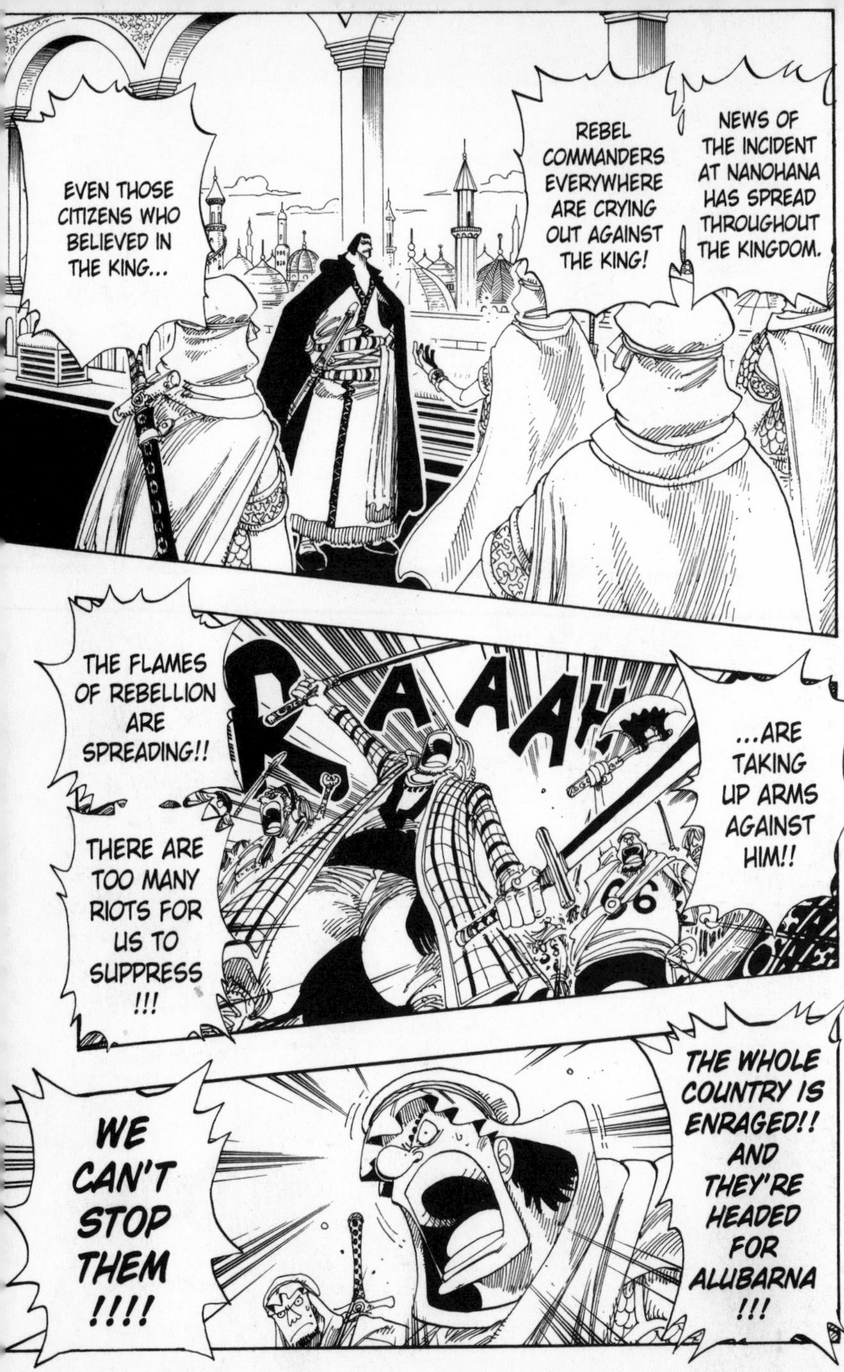
NEWS OF THE INCIDENT AT NANOHANA HAS SPREAD THROUGHOUT THE KINGDOM.
REBEL COMMANDERS EVERYWHERE ARE CRYING OUT AGAINST THE KING!
EVEN THOSE CITIZENS WHO BELIEVED IN THE KING...
...ARE TAKING UP ARMS AGAINST HIM!!
RAAAH
THE FLAMES OF REBELLION ARE SPREADING!!
THERE ARE TOO MANY RIOTS FOR US TO SUPPRESS!!!
THE WHOLE COUNTRY IS ENRAGED!! AND THEY'RE HEADED FOR ALUBARNA!!!
WE CAN'T STOP THEM!!!!

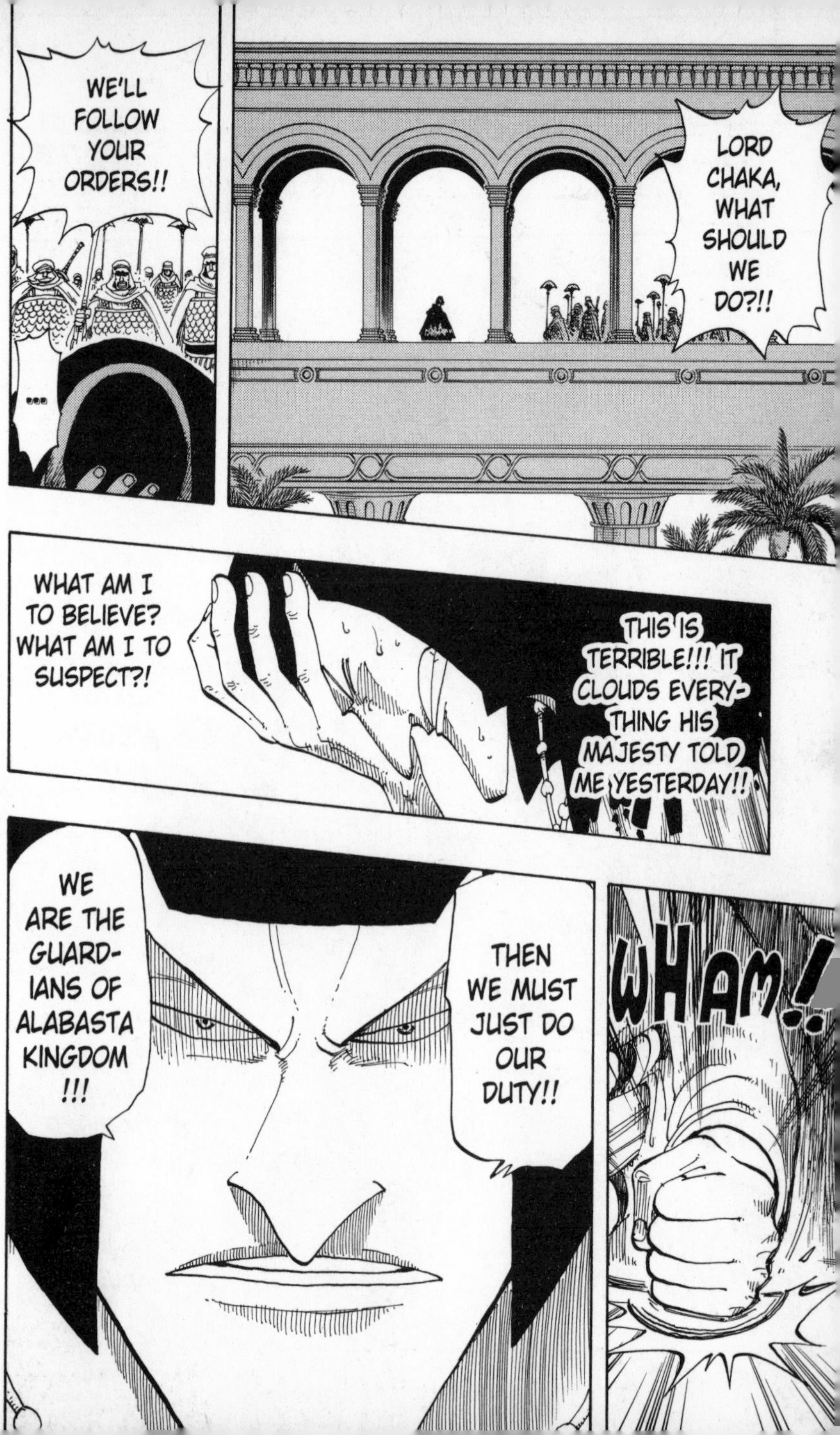
LORD CHAKA, WHAT SHOULD WE DO?!!
WE'LL FOLLOW YOUR ORDERS!!
...
THIS IS TERRIBLE!!! IT CLOUDS EVERY-THING HIS MAJESTY TOLD ME YESTERDAY!!
WHAT AM I TO BELIEVE? WHAT AM I TO SUSPECT?!
WHAM!!
THEN WE MUST JUST DO OUR DUTY!!
WE ARE THE GUARD-IANS OF ALABASTA KINGDOM!!!

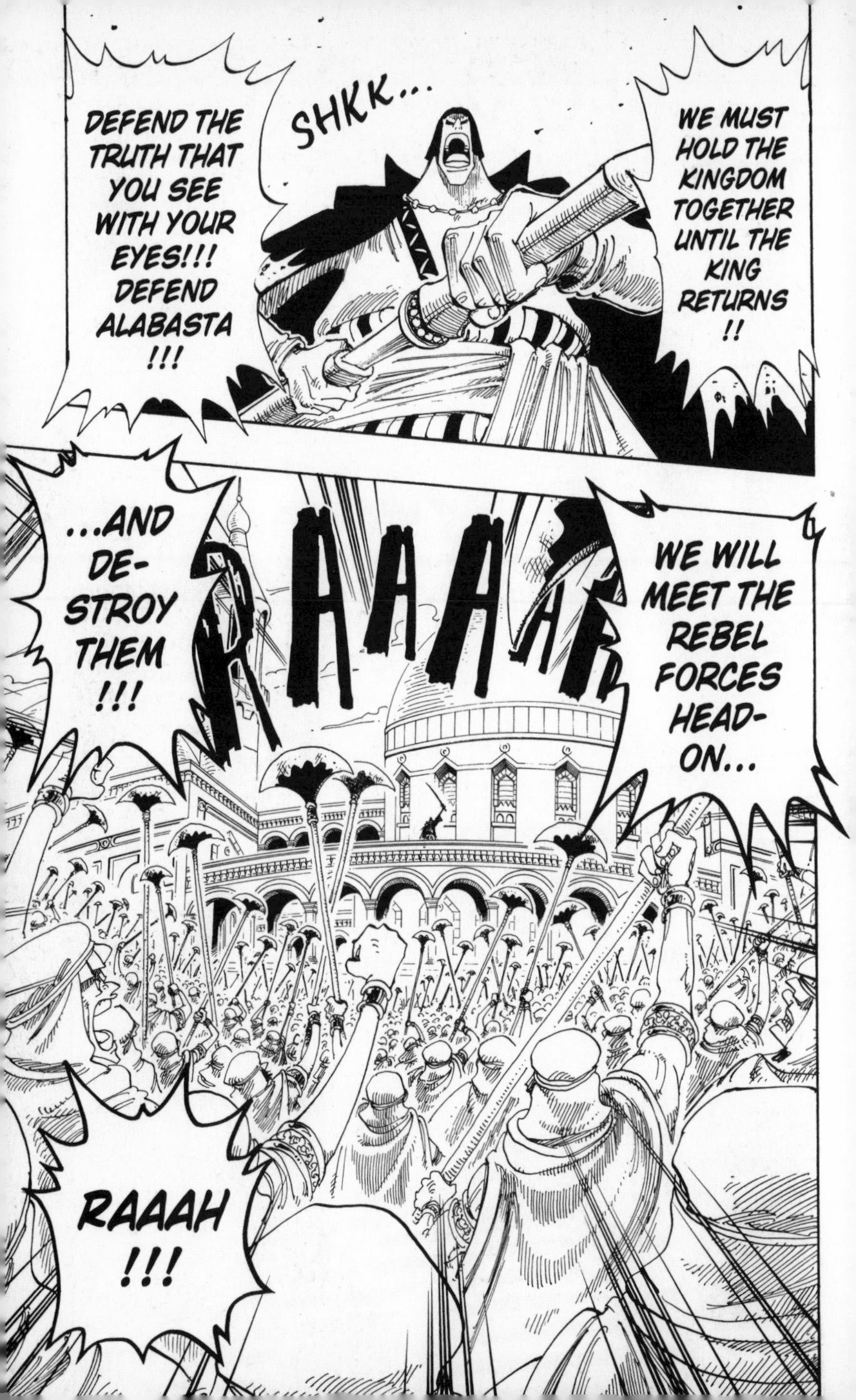
WE MUST HOLD THE KINGDOM TOGETHER UNTIL THE KING RETURNS!!
SHKK...
DEFEND THE TRUTH THAT YOU SEE WITH YOUR EYES!!! DEFEND ALABASTA!!!
WE WILL MEET THE REBEL FORCES HEAD-ON...
AAAA
...AND DE-STROY THEM!!!
RAAAH!!!

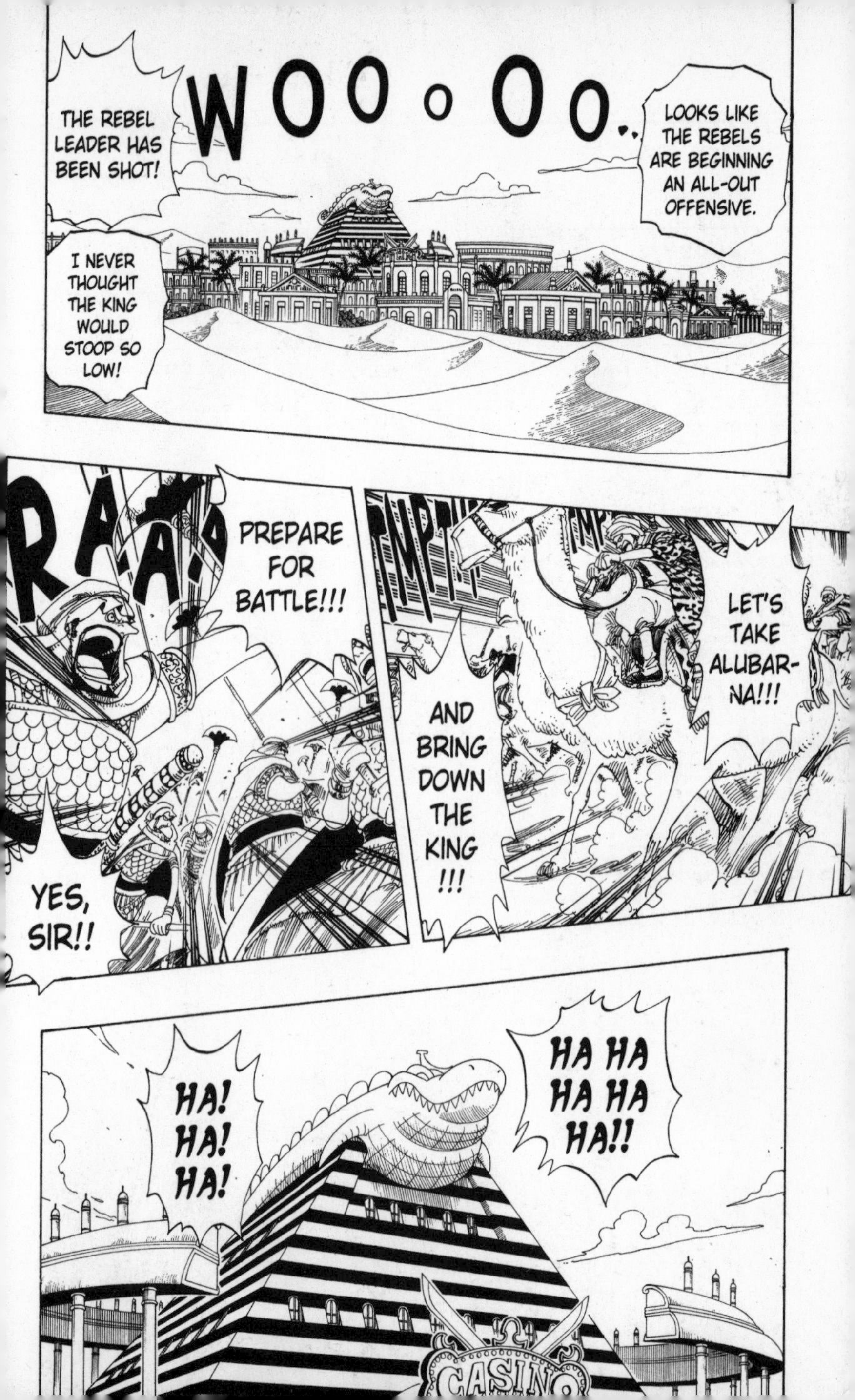
LOOKS LIKE THE REBELS ARE BEGINNING AN ALL-OUT OFFENSIVE.
WOOoOo..
THE REBEL LEADER HAS BEEN SHOT!
I NEVER THOUGHT THE KING WOULD STOOP SO LOW!
LET'S TAKE ALUBAR-NA!!!
AND BRING DOWN THE KING!!!
PREPARE FOR BATTLE!!!
YES, SIR!!
HA HA HA HA HA!!
HA! HA! HA!
CASINO

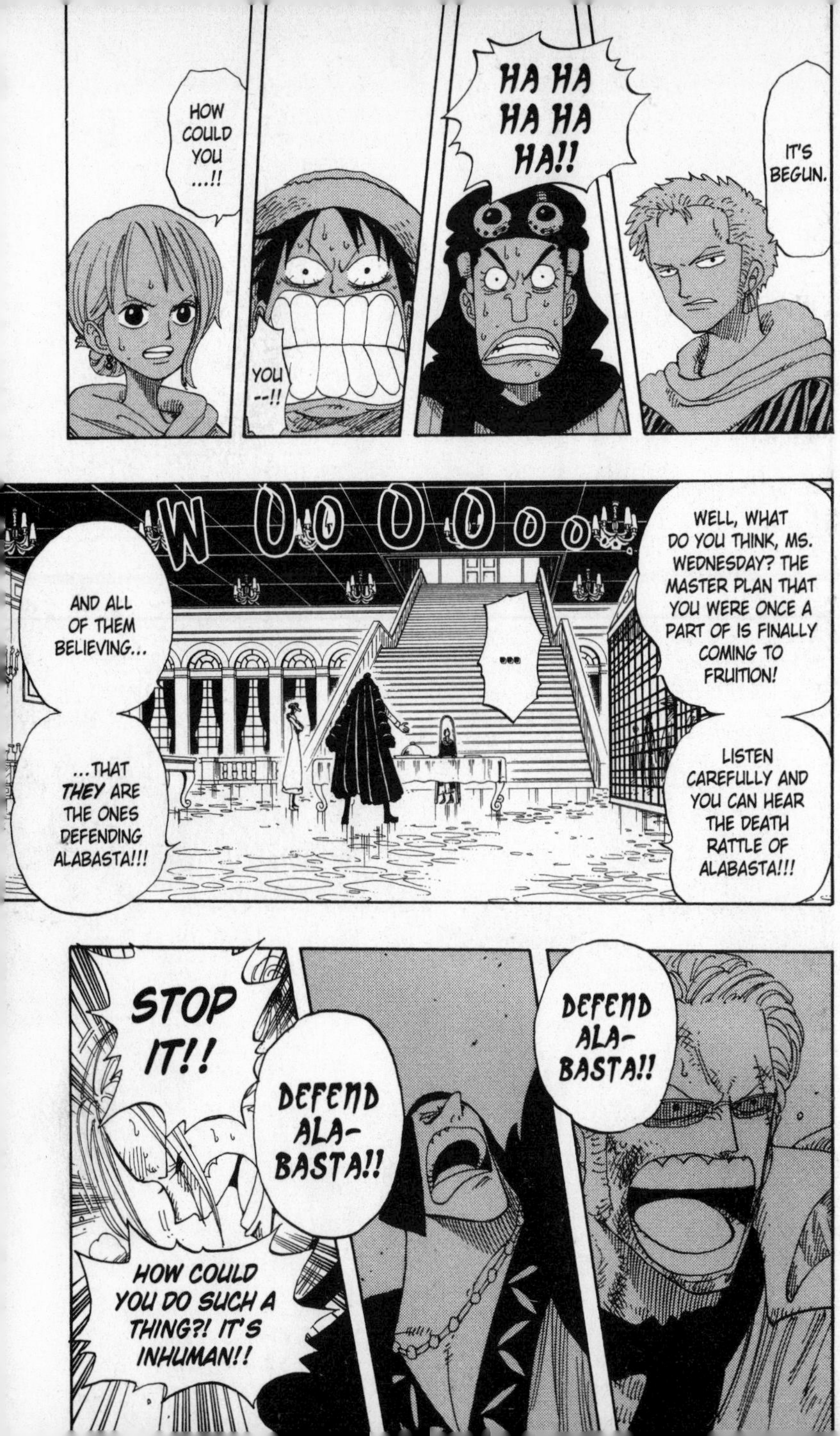
IT'S BEGUN.
HA HA HA HA HA!!
YOU --!!
HOW COULD YOU ...!!
WELL, WHAT DO YOU THINK, MS. WEDNESDAY? THE MASTER PLAN THAT YOU WERE ONCE A PART OF IS FINALLY COMING TO FRUITION!
LISTEN CAREFULLY AND YOU CAN HEAR THE DEATH RATTLE OF ALABASTA!!!
WOOOOOO
...
AND ALL OF THEM BELIEVING...
...THAT THEY ARE THE ONES DEFENDING ALABASTA!!!
DEFEND ALA-BASTA!!
DEFEND ALA-BASTA!!
STOP IT!!
HOW COULD YOU DO SUCH A THING?! IT'S INHUMAN!!

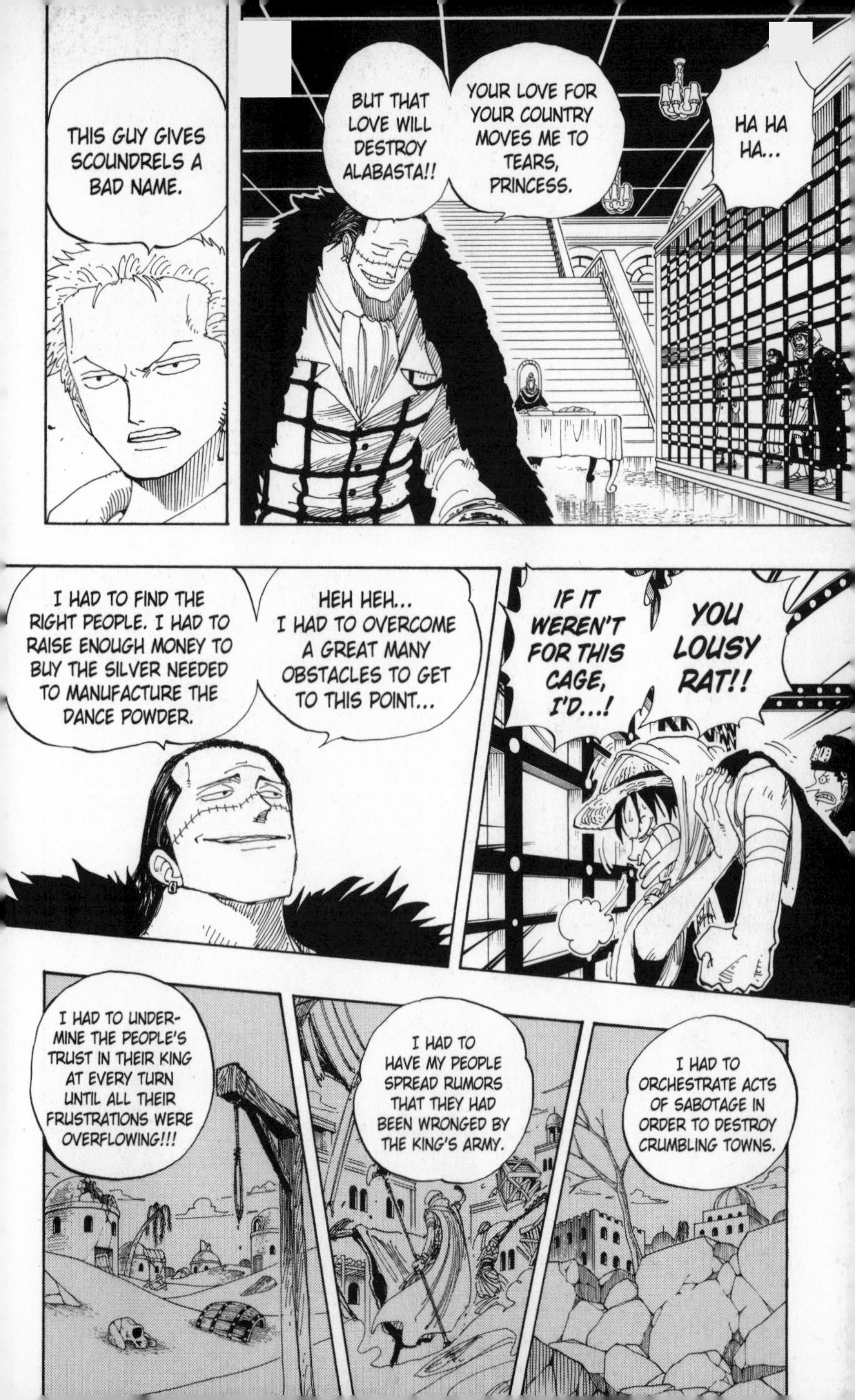
HA HA HA...
YOUR LOVE FOR YOUR COUNTRY MOVES ME TO TEARS, PRINCESS.
BUT THAT LOVE WILL DESTROY ALABASTA!!
THIS GUY GIVES SCOUNDRELS A BAD NAME.
YOU LOUSY RAT!!
IF IT WEREN'T FOR THIS CAGE, I'D...!
HEH HEH... I HAD TO OVERCOME A GREAT MANY OBSTACLES TO GET TO THIS POINT...
I HAD TO FIND THE RIGHT PEOPLE. I HAD TO RAISE ENOUGH MONEY TO BUY THE SILVER NEEDED TO MANUFACTURE THE DANCE POWDER.
I HAD TO ORCHESTRATE ACTS OF SABOTAGE IN ORDER TO DESTROY CRUMBLING TOWNS.
I HAD TO HAVE MY PEOPLE SPREAD RUMORS THAT THEY HAD BEEN WRONGED BY THE KING'S ARMY.
I HAD TO UNDER-MINE THE PEOPLE'S TRUST IN THEIR KING AT EVERY TURN UNTIL ALL THEIR FRUSTRATIONS WERE OVERFLOWING!!!

READ THIS WAY

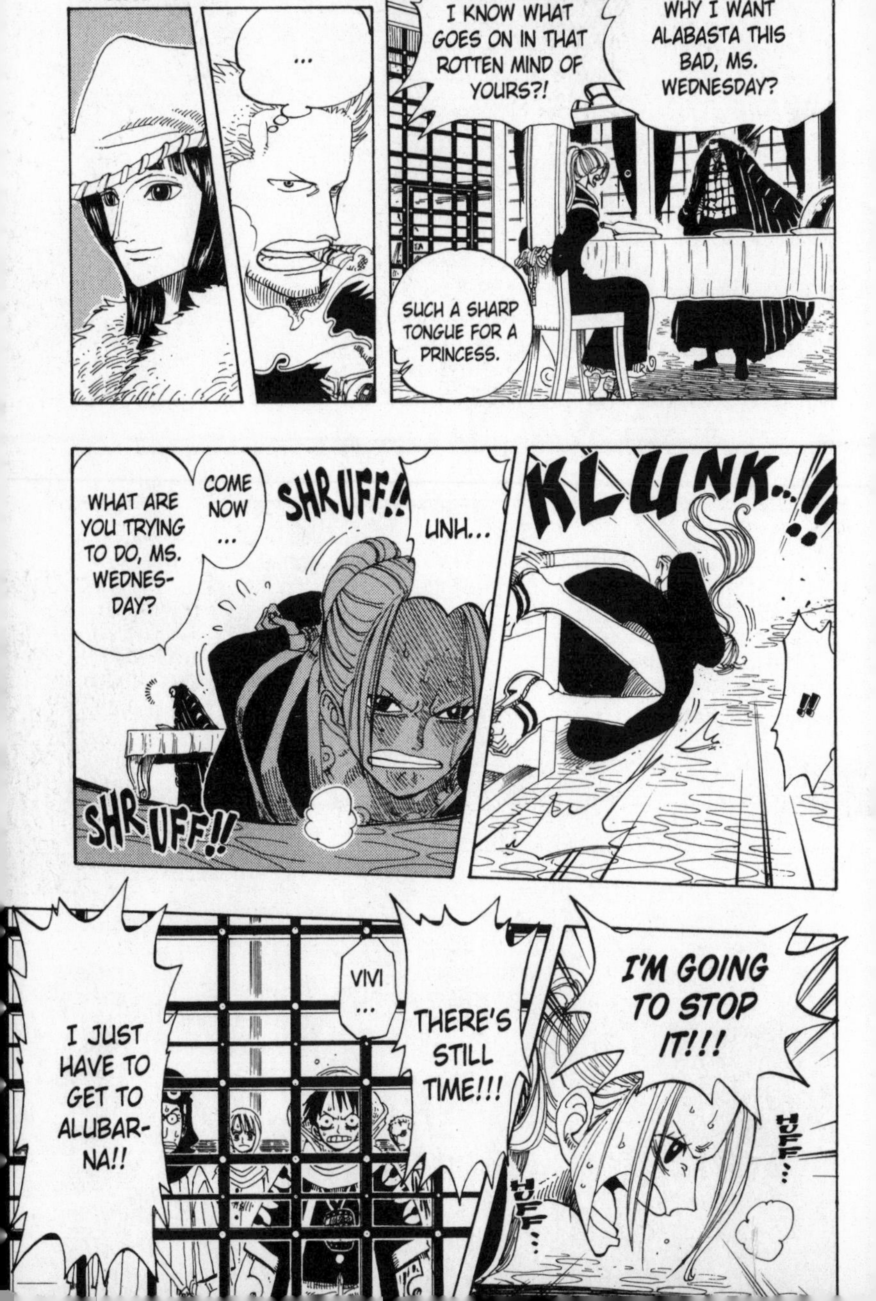

DO YOU KNOW WHY I WANT ALABASTA THIS BAD, MS. WEDNESDAY?
HOW SHOULD I KNOW WHAT GOES ON IN THAT ROTTEN MIND OF YOURS?!
SUCH A SHARP TONGUE FOR A PRINCESS.
...
KLUNK...!!
!!
UNH...
SHRUFF!!
COME NOW ...
WHAT ARE YOU TRYING TO DO, MS. WEDNES-DAY?
SHRUFF!!
I'M GOING TO STOP IT!!!
HUFF...
HUFF...
THERE'S STILL TIME!!!
VIVI ...
I JUST HAVE TO GET TO ALUBAR-NA!!

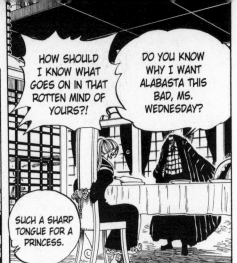

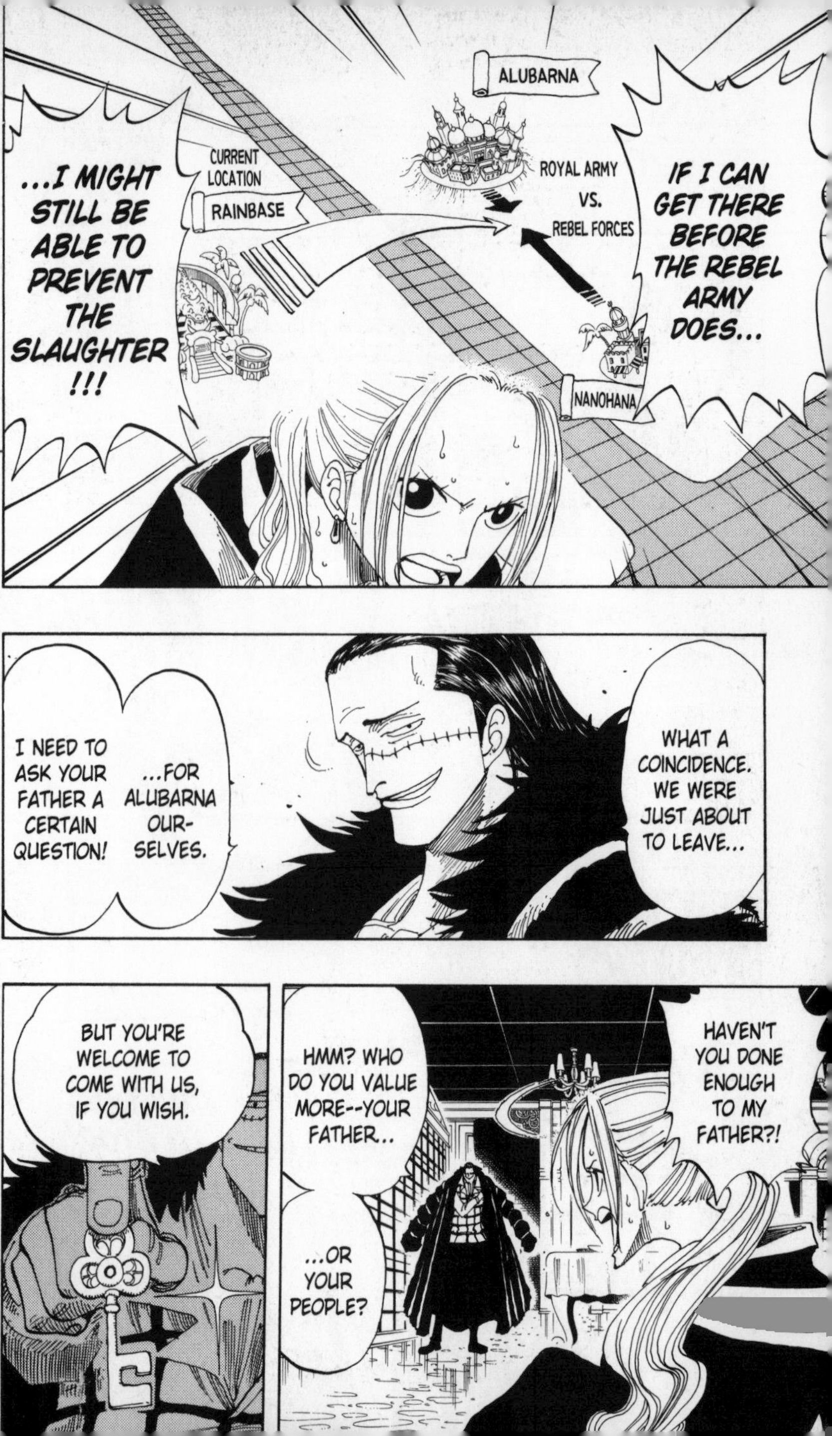
IF I CAN GET THERE BEFORE THE REBEL ARMY DOES...
ALUBARNA
ROYAL ARMY VS. REBEL FORCES
NANOHANA
CURRENT LOCATION
RAINBASE
...I MIGHT STILL BE ABLE TO PREVENT THE SLAUGHTER!!!
WHAT A COINCIDENCE. WE WERE JUST ABOUT TO LEAVE...
...FOR ALUBARNA OURSELVES.
I NEED TO ASK YOUR FATHER A CERTAIN QUESTION!
HAVEN'T YOU DONE ENOUGH TO MY FATHER?!
HMM? WHO DO YOU VALUE MORE--YOUR FATHER...
...OR YOUR PEOPLE?
BUT YOU'RE WELCOME TO COME WITH US, IF YOU WISH.

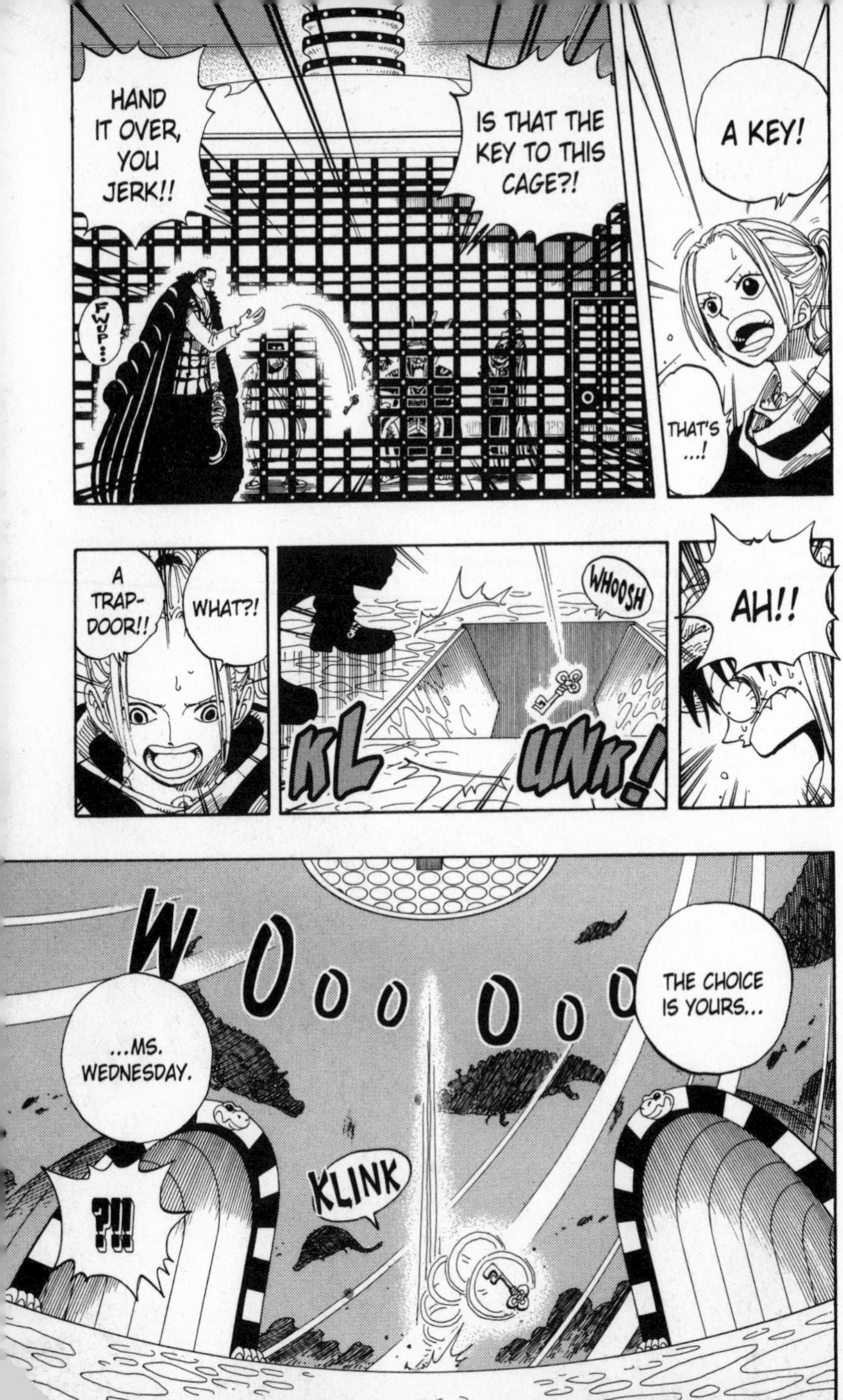
A KEY!
THAT'S ...!
IS THAT THE KEY TO THIS CAGE?!
HAND IT OVER, YOU JERK!!
FWUP...
AH!!
WHOOSH
KLUNK!
WHAT?!
A TRAP-DOOR!!
THE CHOICE IS YOURS...
WOOOOOOO
...MS. WEDNESDAY.
KLINK
?!!

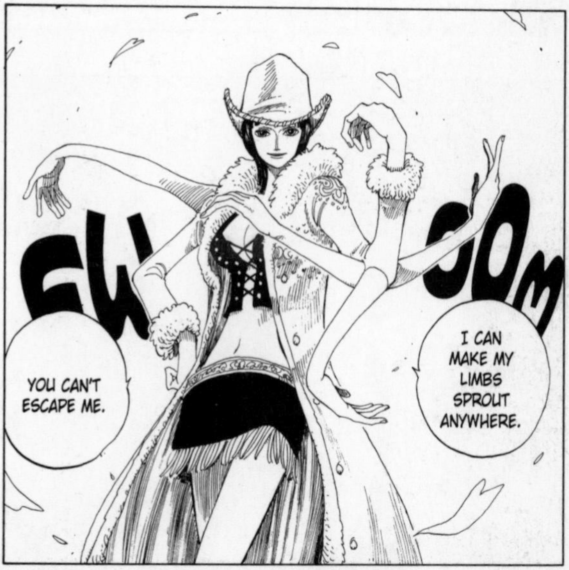
I CAN MAKE MY LIMBS SPROUT ANYWHERE.
YOU CAN'T ESCAPE ME.

# Chapter 173:
# BANANAGATOR

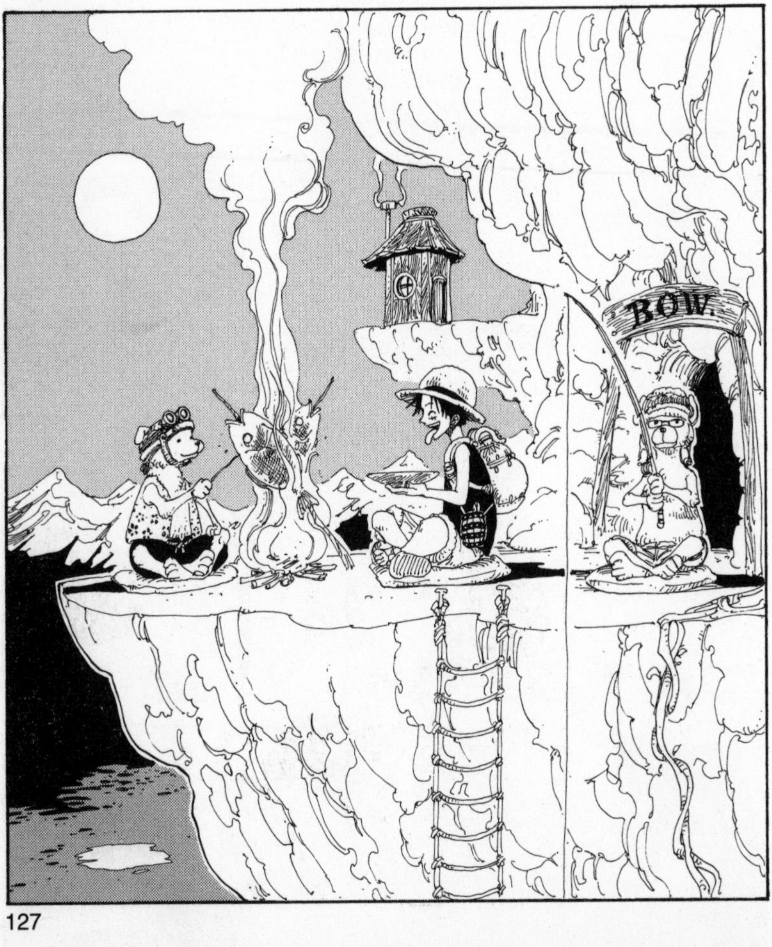
BOW.

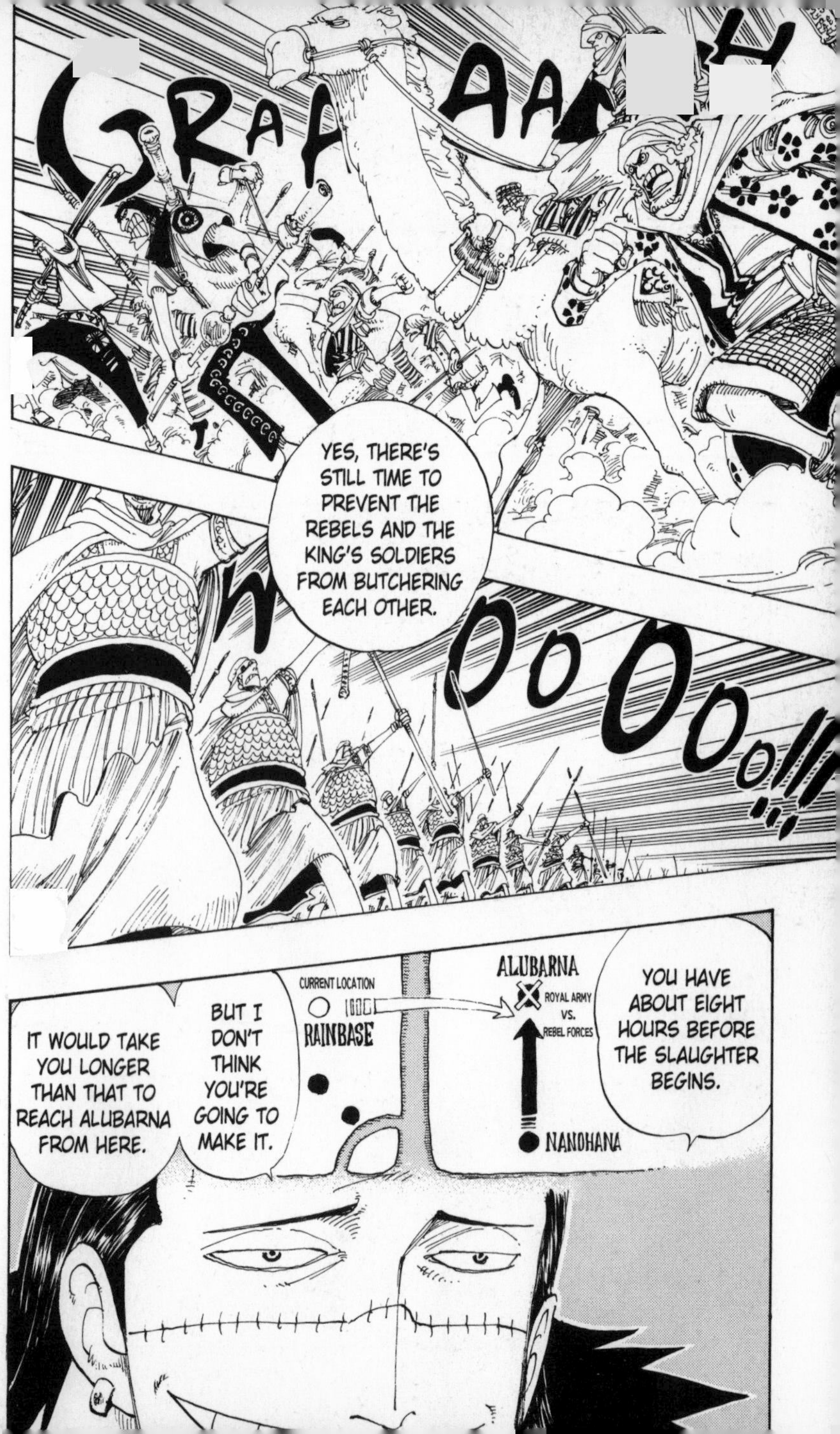
YES, THERE'S STILL TIME TO PREVENT THE REBELS AND THE KING'S SOLDIERS FROM BUTCHERING EACH OTHER.
YOU HAVE ABOUT EIGHT HOURS BEFORE THE SLAUGHTER BEGINS.
ALUBARNA
ROYAL ARMY VS. REBEL FORCES
NANOHANA
CURRENT LOCATION
RAINBASE
BUT I DON'T THINK YOU'RE GOING TO MAKE IT.
IT WOULD TAKE YOU LONGER THAN THAT TO REACH ALUBARNA FROM HERE.

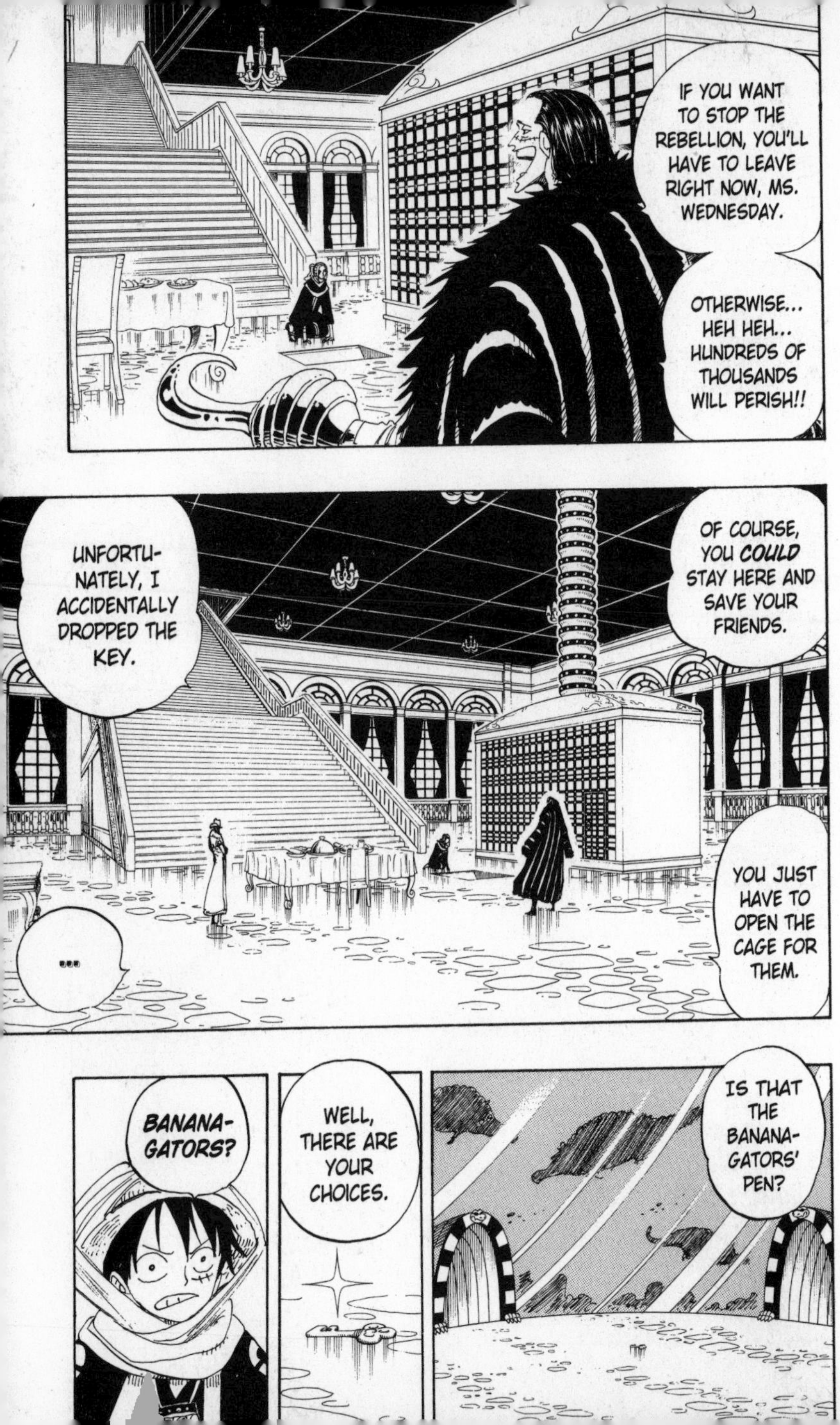
IF YOU WANT TO STOP THE REBELLION, YOU'LL HAVE TO LEAVE RIGHT NOW, MS. WEDNESDAY.
OTHERWISE... HEH HEH... HUNDREDS OF THOUSANDS WILL PERISH!!
OF COURSE, YOU *COULD* STAY HERE AND SAVE YOUR FRIENDS.
YOU JUST HAVE TO OPEN THE CAGE FOR THEM.
UNFORTUNATELY, I ACCIDENTALLY DROPPED THE KEY.
...
IS THAT THE BANANA-GATORS' PEN?
WELL, THERE ARE YOUR CHOICES.
*BANANA-GATORS?*

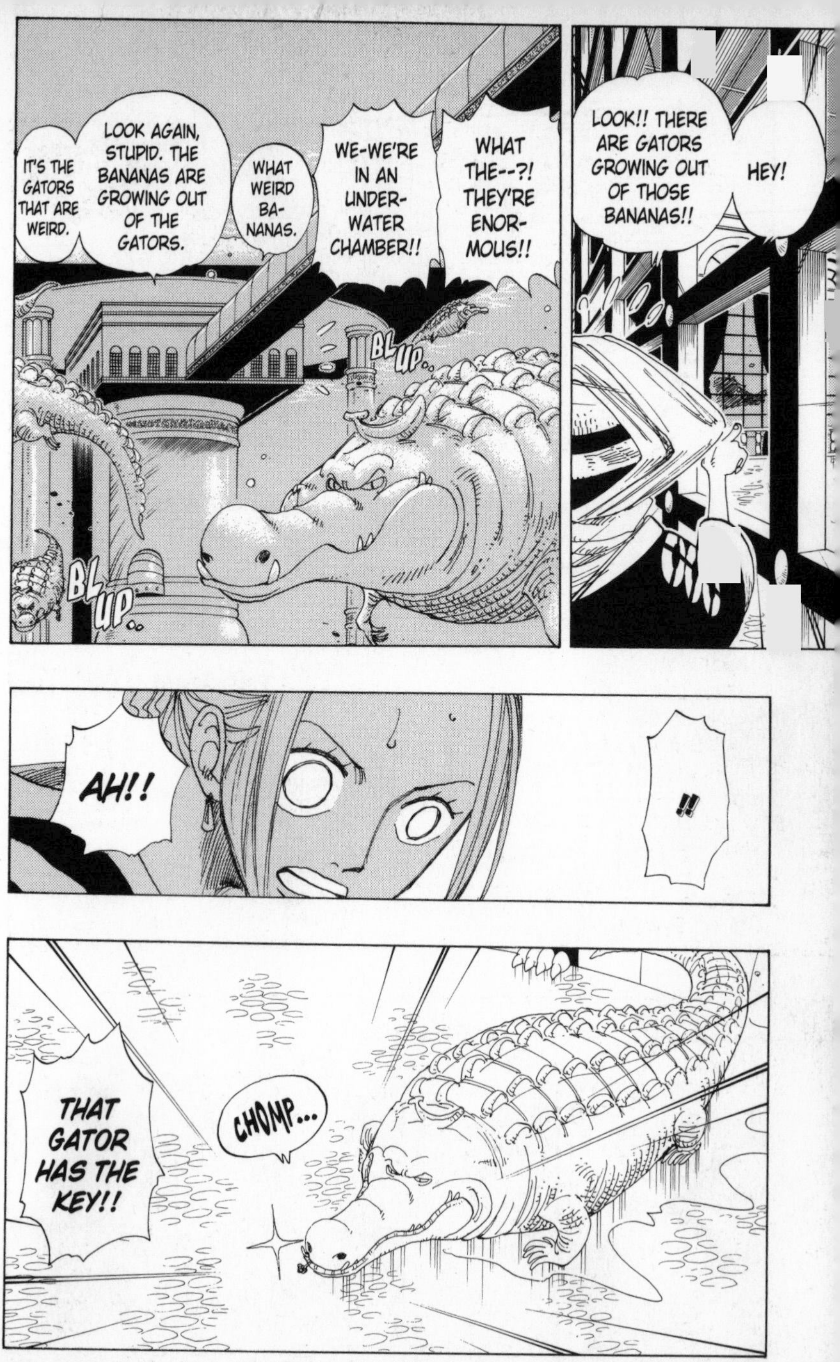
HEY!
LOOK!! THERE ARE GATORS GROWING OUT OF THOSE BANANAS!!
WHAT THE--?! THEY'RE ENORMOUS!!
WE-WE'RE IN AN UNDER-WATER CHAMBER!!
BLUP
WHAT WEIRD BA-NANAS.
LOOK AGAIN, STUPID. THE BANANAS ARE GROWING OUT OF THE GATORS.
IT'S THE GATORS THAT ARE WEIRD.
BLUP
!!
AH!!
CHOMP...
THAT GATOR HAS THE KEY!!

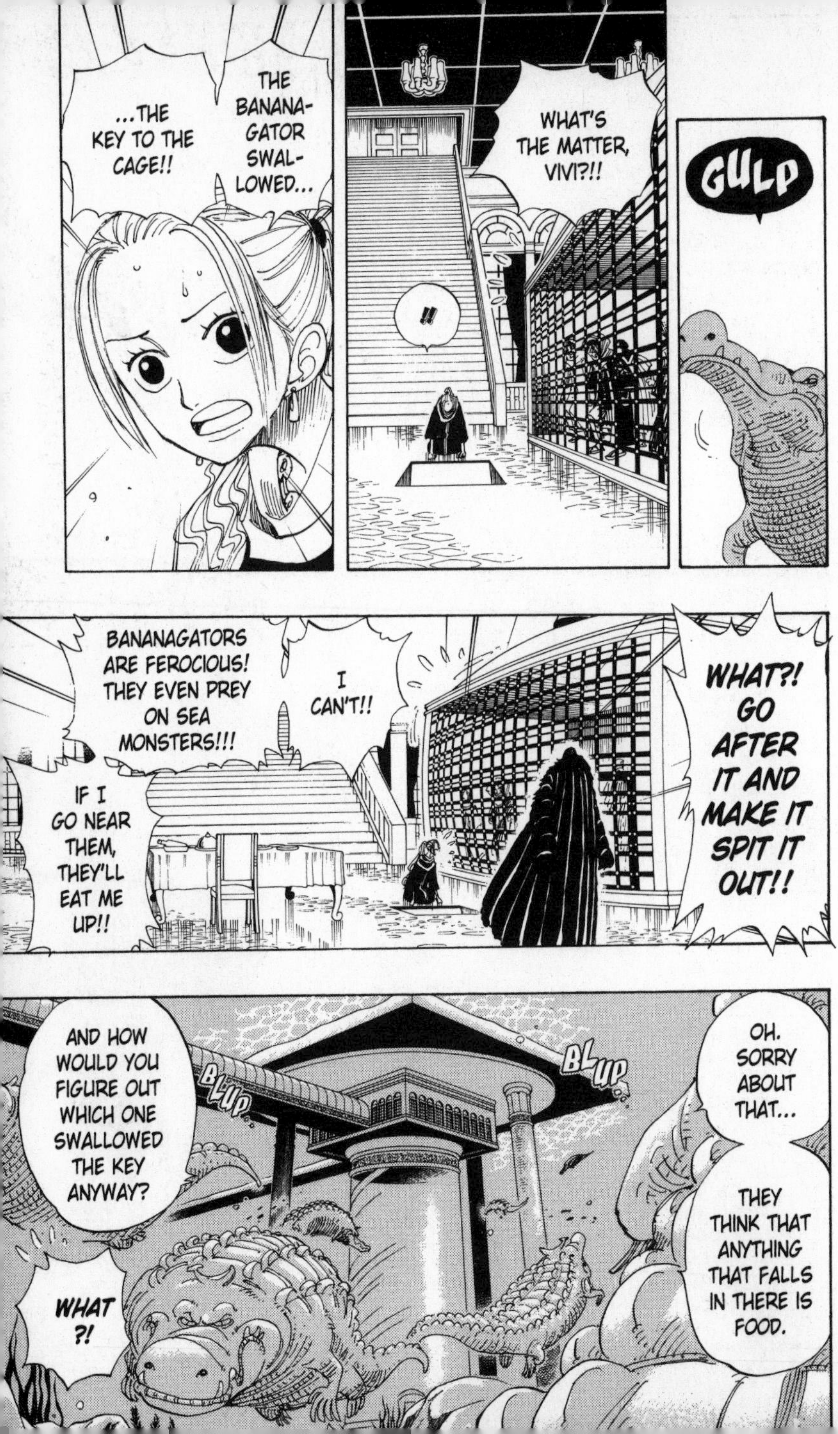
GULP
WHAT'S THE MATTER, VIVI?!!
!!
THE BANANA-GATOR SWAL-LOWED...
...THE KEY TO THE CAGE!!
WHAT?! GO AFTER IT AND MAKE IT SPIT IT OUT!!
I CAN'T!!
BANANAGATORS ARE FEROCIOUS! THEY EVEN PREY ON SEA MONSTERS!!!
IF I GO NEAR THEM, THEY'LL EAT ME UP!!
OH. SORRY ABOUT THAT...
THEY THINK THAT ANYTHING THAT FALLS IN THERE IS FOOD.
BLUP
BLUP
AND HOW WOULD YOU FIGURE OUT WHICH ONE SWALLOWED THE KEY ANYWAY?
WHAT?!

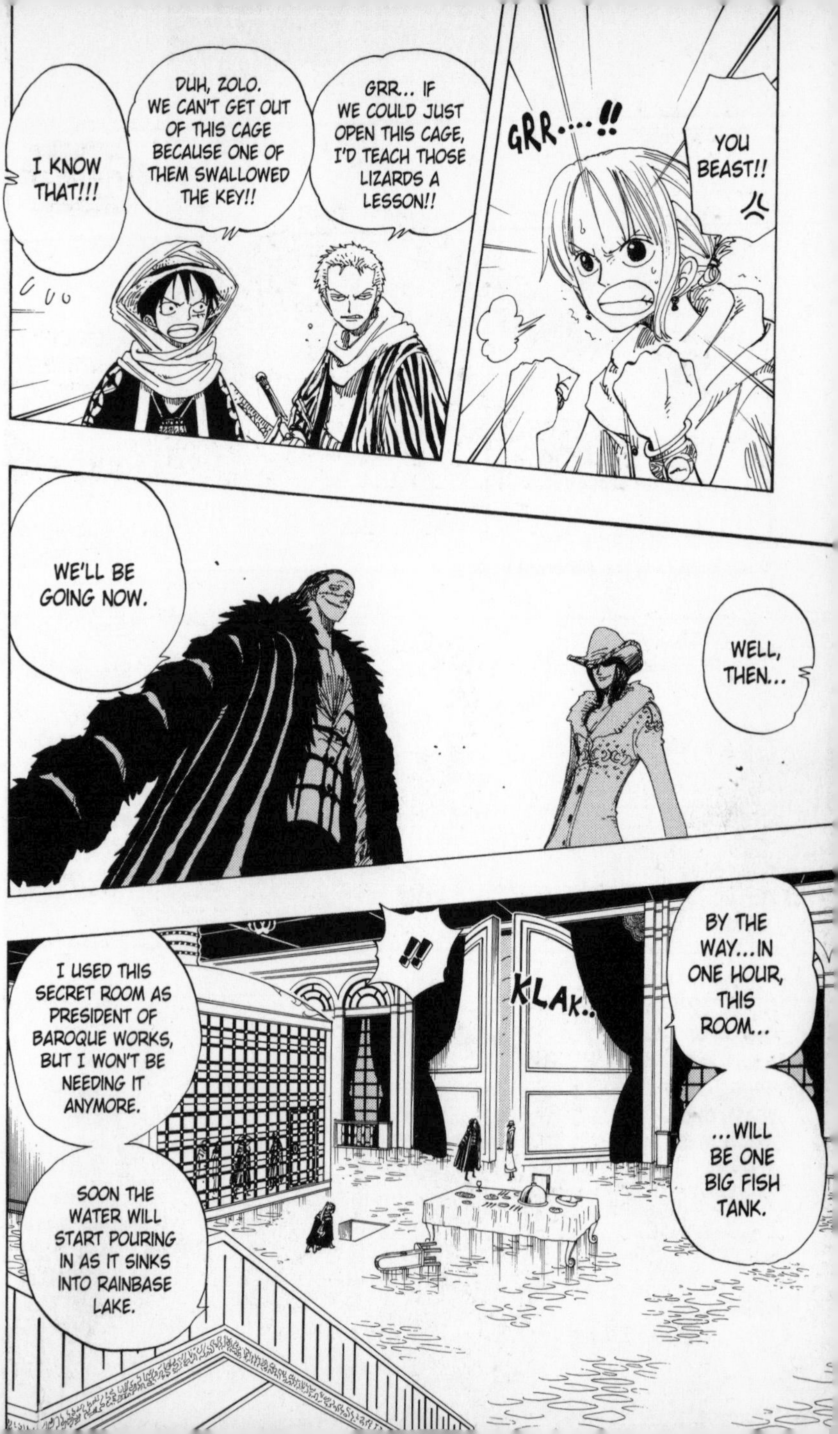
YOU BEAST!!
GRR....!!
GRR... IF WE COULD JUST OPEN THIS CAGE, I'D TEACH THOSE LIZARDS A LESSON!!
DUH, ZOLO. WE CAN'T GET OUT OF THIS CAGE BECAUSE ONE OF THEM SWALLOWED THE KEY!!
I KNOW THAT!!!
WELL, THEN...
WE'LL BE GOING NOW.
BY THE WAY...IN ONE HOUR, THIS ROOM...
...WILL BE ONE BIG FISH TANK.
!!
KLAK..
I USED THIS SECRET ROOM AS PRESIDENT OF BAROQUE WORKS, BUT I WON'T BE NEEDING IT ANYMORE.
SOON THE WATER WILL START POURING IN AS IT SINKS INTO RAINBASE LAKE.

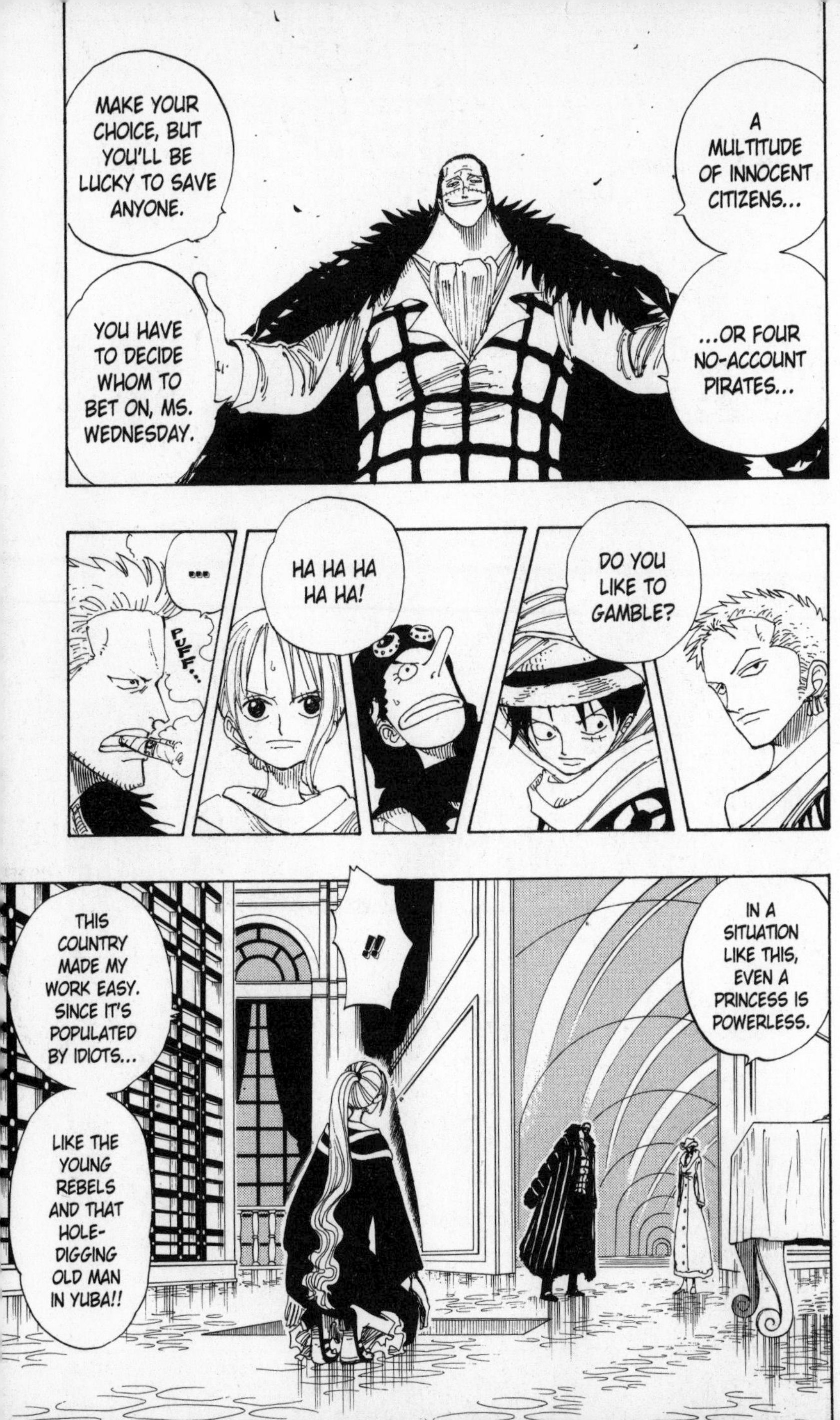
A MULTITUDE OF INNOCENT CITIZENS...
...OR FOUR NO-ACCOUNT PIRATES...
YOU HAVE TO DECIDE WHOM TO BET ON, MS. WEDNESDAY.
MAKE YOUR CHOICE, BUT YOU'LL BE LUCKY TO SAVE ANYONE.
DO YOU LIKE TO GAMBLE?
HA HA HA HA HA!
...
PUFF...
IN A SITUATION LIKE THIS, EVEN A PRINCESS IS POWERLESS.
!!
THIS COUNTRY MADE MY WORK EASY. SINCE IT'S POPULATED BY IDIOTS...
LIKE THE YOUNG REBELS AND THAT HOLE-DIGGING OLD MAN IN YUBA!!

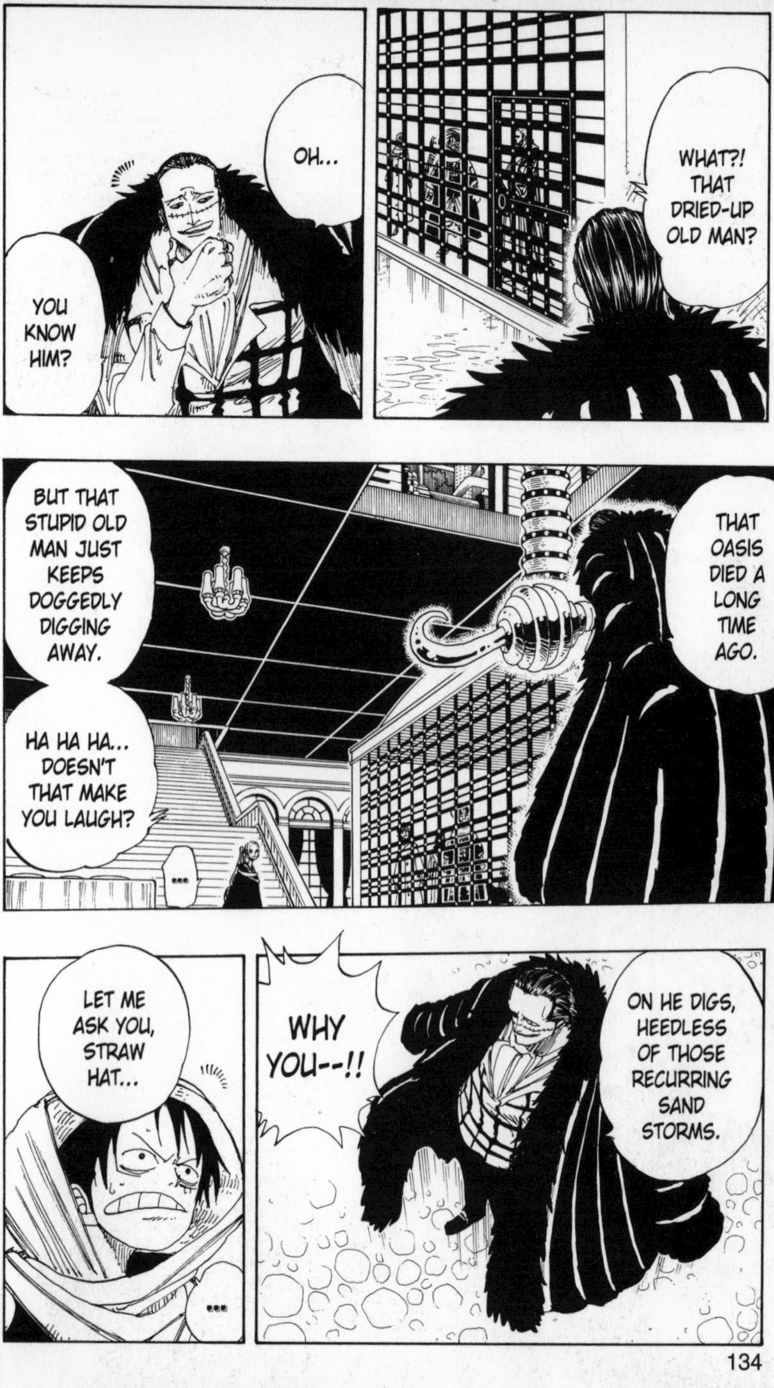
WHAT?! THAT DRIED-UP OLD MAN?
OH...
YOU KNOW HIM?
THAT OASIS DIED A LONG TIME AGO.
BUT THAT STUPID OLD MAN JUST KEEPS DOGGEDLY DIGGING AWAY.
HA HA HA... DOESN'T THAT MAKE YOU LAUGH?
...
ON HE DIGS, HEEDLESS OF THOSE RECURRING SAND STORMS.
WHY YOU--!!
LET ME ASK YOU, STRAW HAT...
...

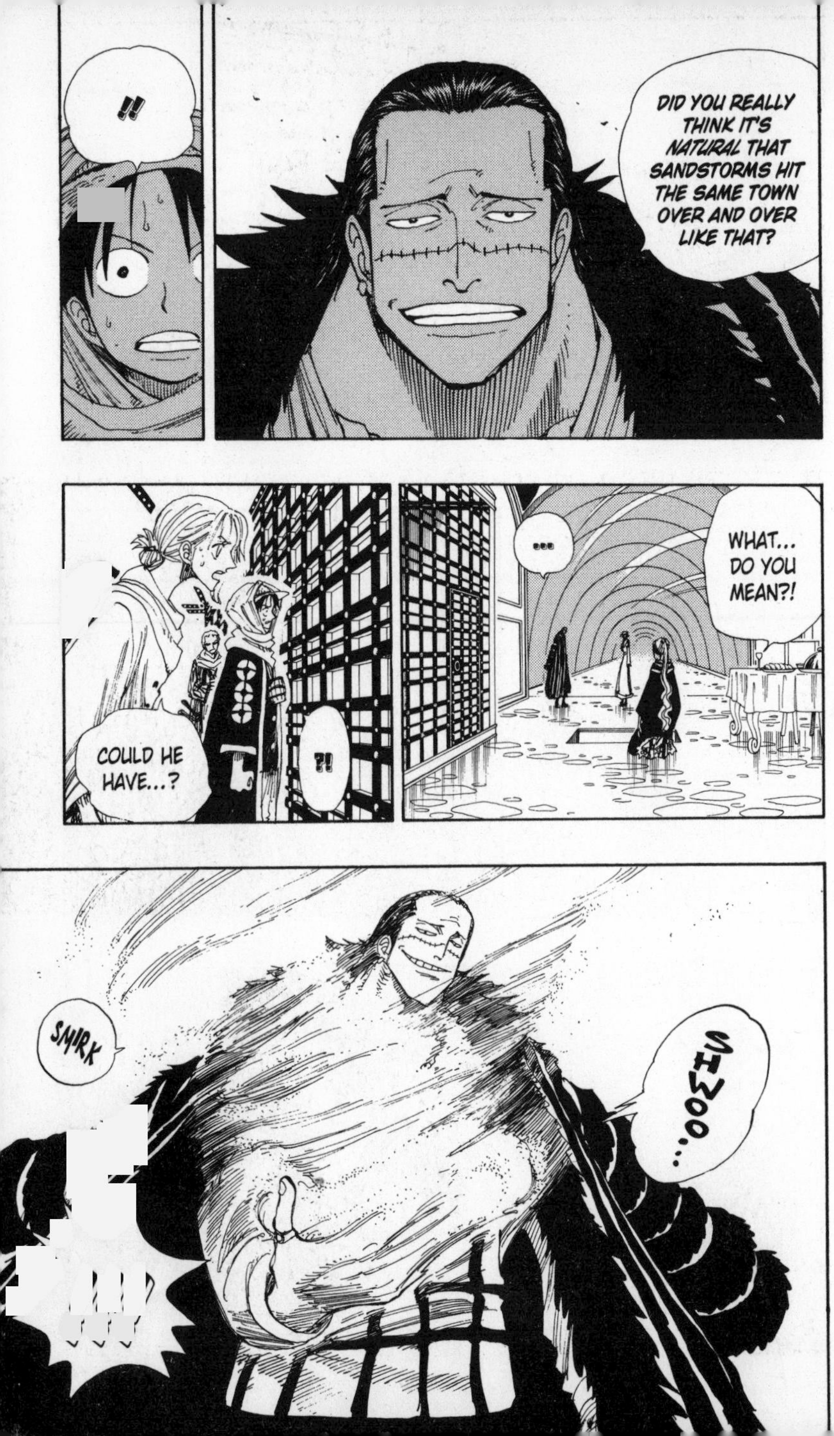
DID YOU REALLY THINK IT'S NATURAL THAT SANDSTORMS HIT THE SAME TOWN OVER AND OVER LIKE THAT?
!!
WHAT... DO YOU MEAN?!
...
?!
COULD HE HAVE...?
SHWOO...
SMIRK

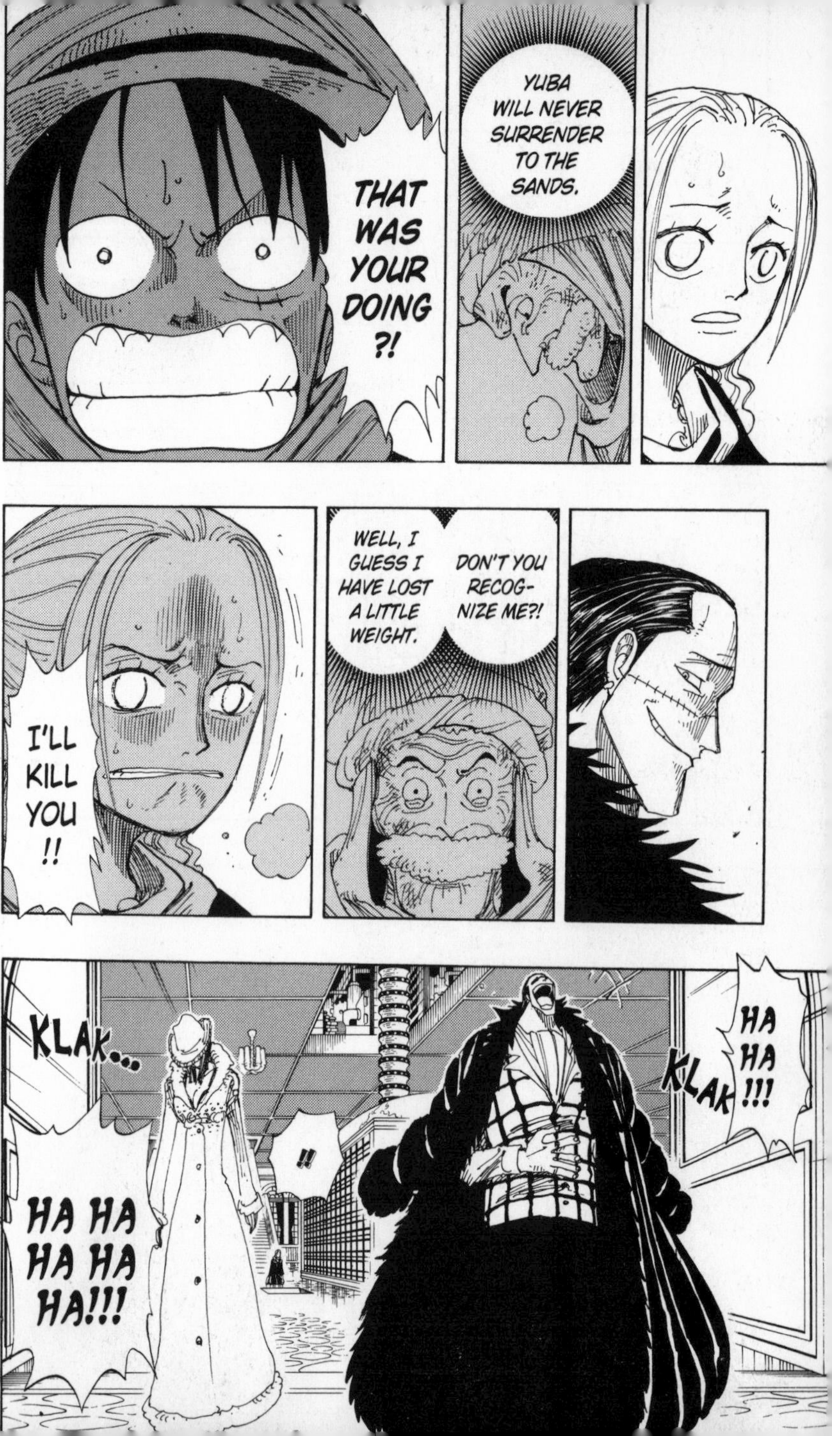
YUBA WILL NEVER SURRENDER TO THE SANDS.
THAT WAS YOUR DOING ?!
DON'T YOU RECOGNIZE ME?!
WELL, I GUESS I HAVE LOST A LITTLE WEIGHT.
I'LL KILL YOU !!
HA HA !!!
KLAK
!!
KLAK...
HA HA HA HA HA!!!

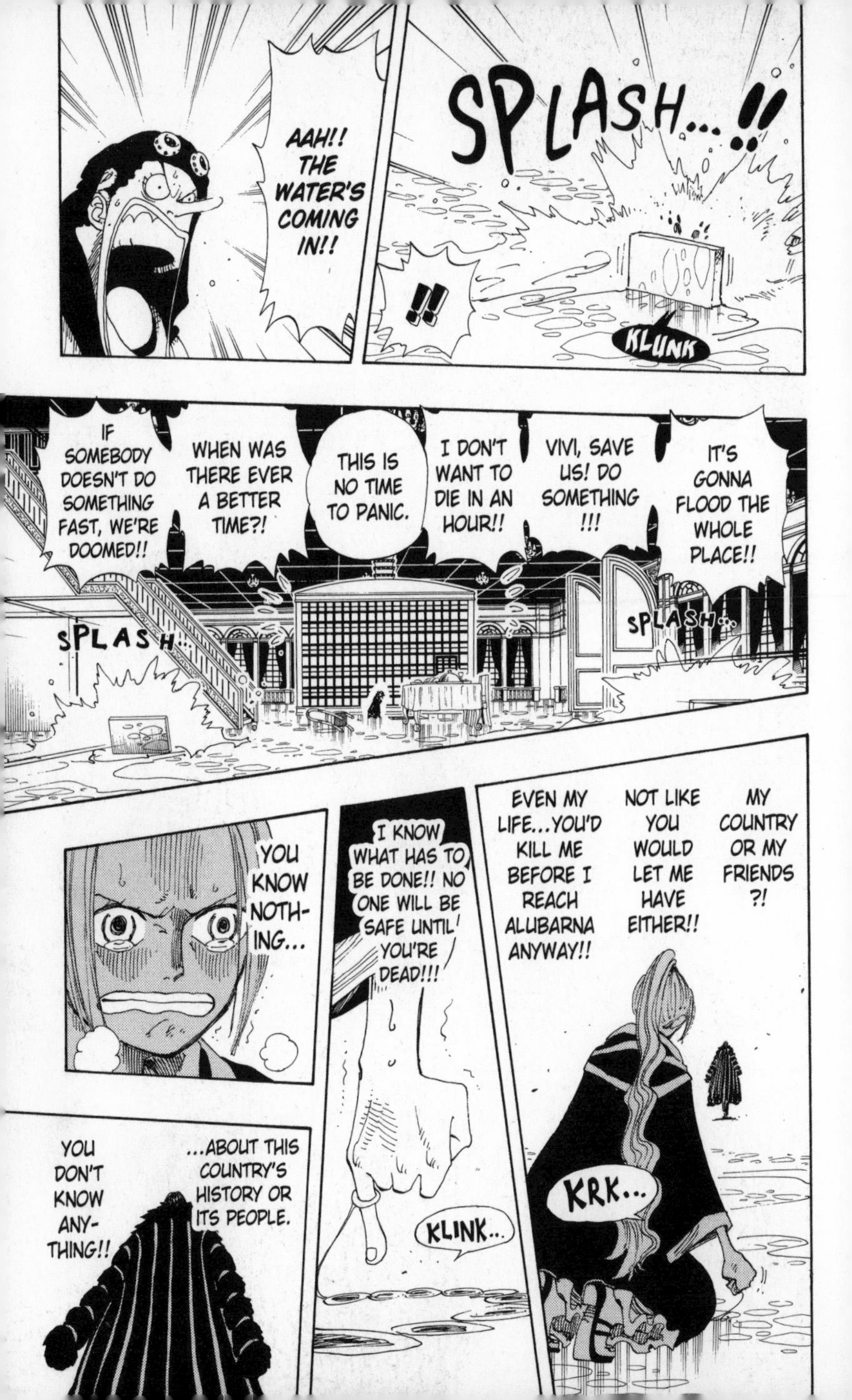
SPLASH...!!
!!
KLUNK
AAH!! THE WATER'S COMING IN!!
IT'S GONNA FLOOD THE WHOLE PLACE!!
VIVI, SAVE US! DO SOMETHING!!!
I DON'T WANT TO DIE IN AN HOUR!!
THIS IS NO TIME TO PANIC.
WHEN WAS THERE EVER A BETTER TIME?!
IF SOMEBODY DOESN'T DO SOMETHING FAST, WE'RE DOOMED!!
SPLASH...
SPLASH...
MY COUNTRY OR MY FRIENDS?!
NOT LIKE YOU WOULD LET ME HAVE EITHER!!
EVEN MY LIFE...YOU'D KILL ME BEFORE I REACH ALUBARNA ANYWAY!!
KRK...
I KNOW WHAT HAS TO BE DONE!! NO ONE WILL BE SAFE UNTIL YOU'RE DEAD!!!
KLINK...
YOU KNOW NOTHING...
...ABOUT THIS COUNTRY'S HISTORY OR ITS PEOPLE.
YOU DON'T KNOW ANYTHING!!

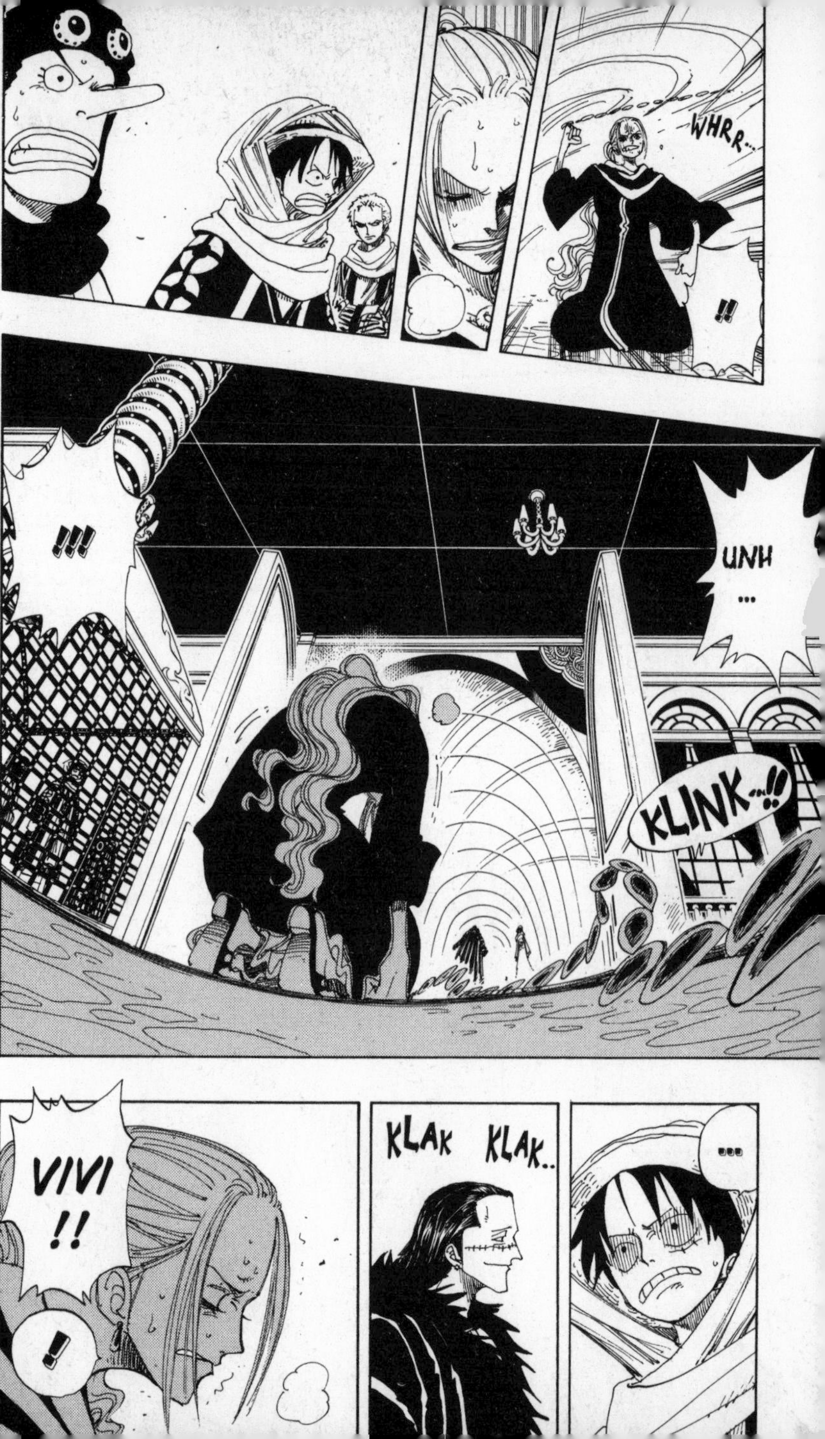
WHRR...
!!
UNH ...
KLINK...!!
!!!
...
KLAK KLAK..
VIVI !!
!

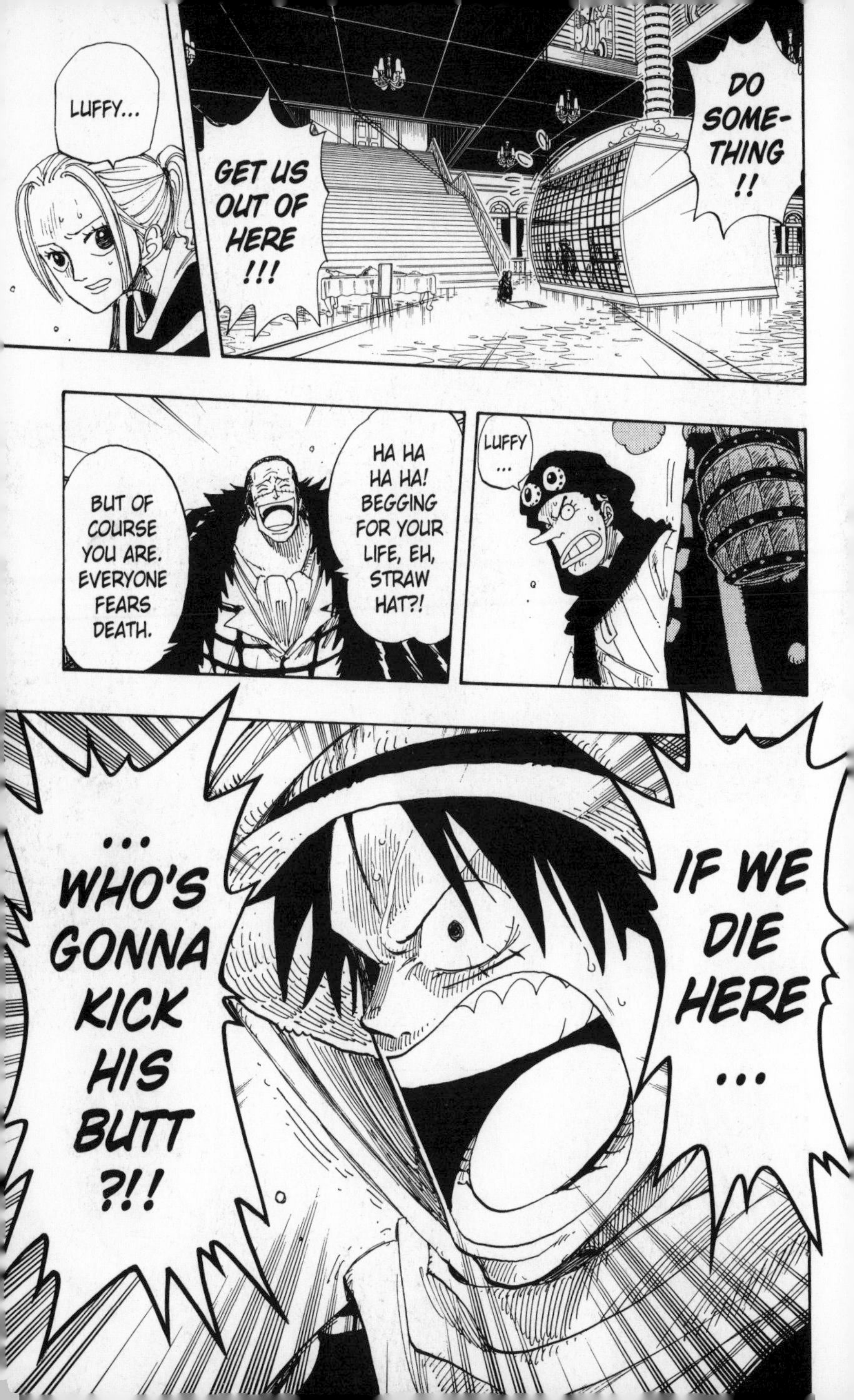
DO SOMETHING!!
GET US OUT OF HERE!!!
LUFFY...
LUFFY ...
HA HA HA HA! BEGGING FOR YOUR LIFE, EH, STRAW HAT?!
BUT OF COURSE YOU ARE. EVERYONE FEARS DEATH.
IF WE DIE HERE ...
... WHO'S GONNA KICK HIS BUTT ?!!

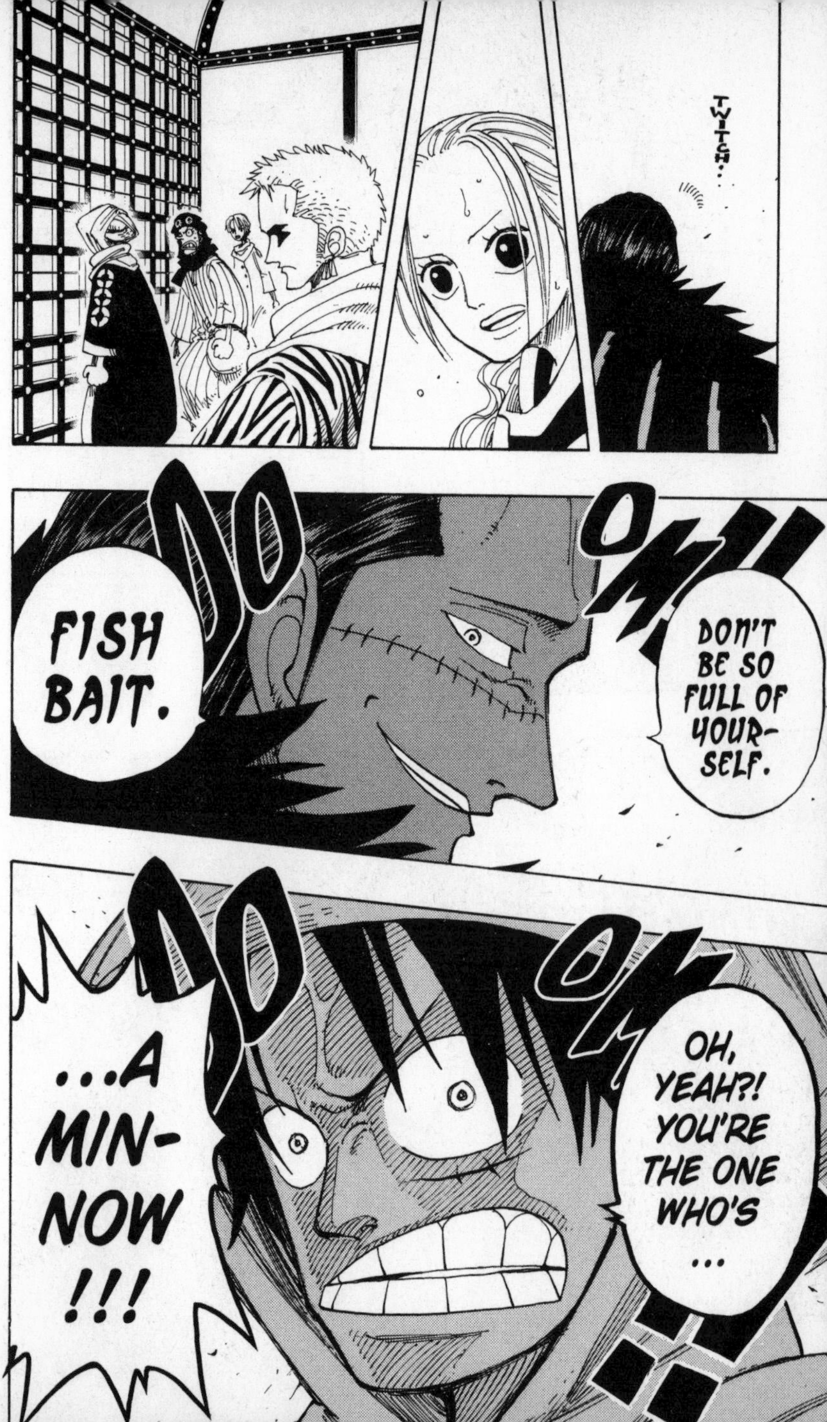
TWITCH...
DON'T BE SO FULL OF YOUR-SELF.
FISH BAIT.
OH, YEAH?! YOU'RE THE ONE WHO'S ...
...A MIN-NOW!!!

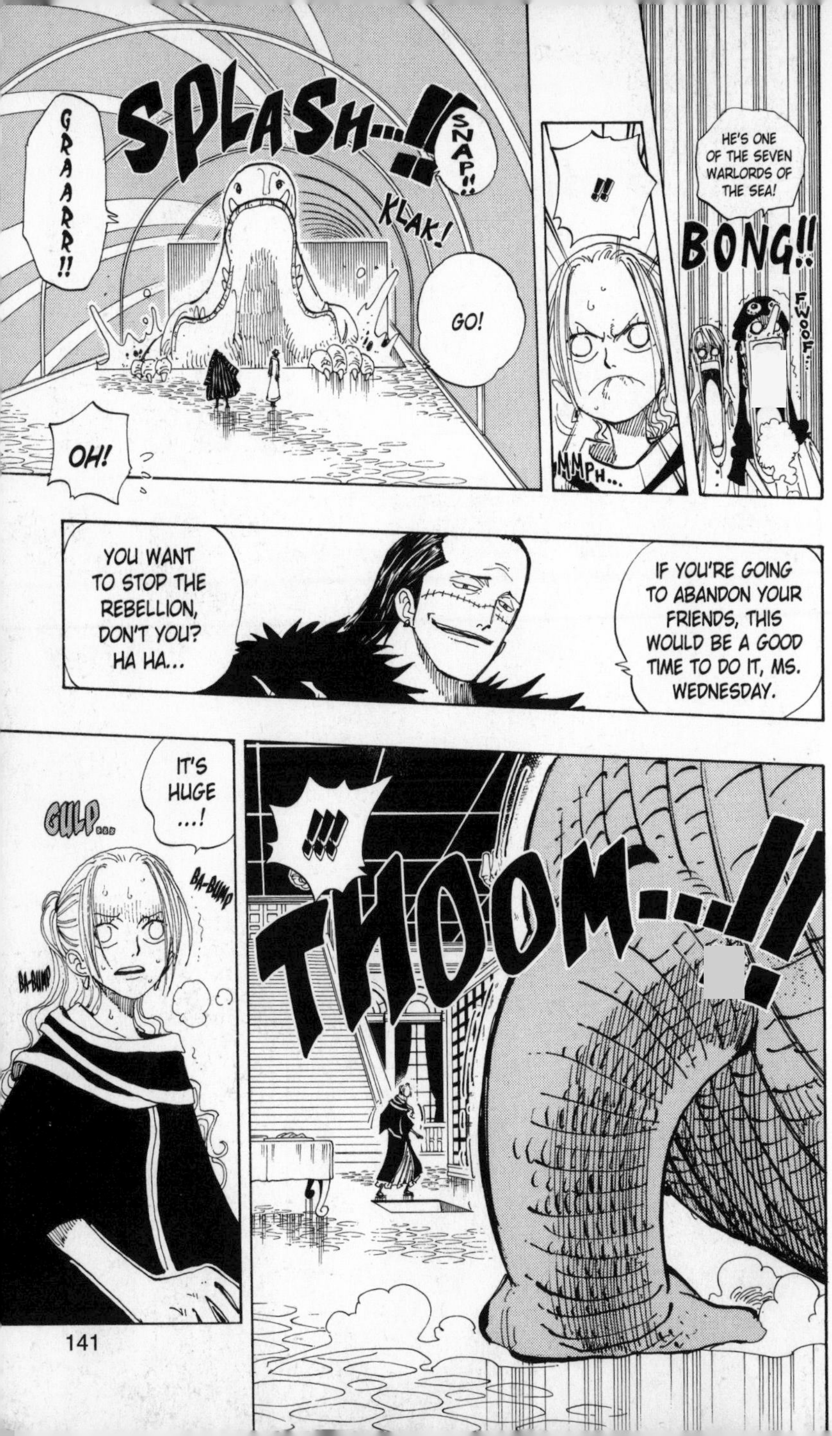

HE'S ONE OF THE SEVEN WARLORDS OF THE SEA!
BONG!!
FWOOF...
!!
MMPH...
SNAP!!
SPLASH...!!
GRAAARR!!
KLAK!
GO!
OH!
IF YOU'RE GOING TO ABANDON YOUR FRIENDS, THIS WOULD BE A GOOD TIME TO DO IT, MS. WEDNESDAY.
YOU WANT TO STOP THE REBELLION, DON'T YOU? HA HA...
!!!
THOOM...!!
IT'S HUGE ...!
GULP...
BA-BUMP
BA-BUMP

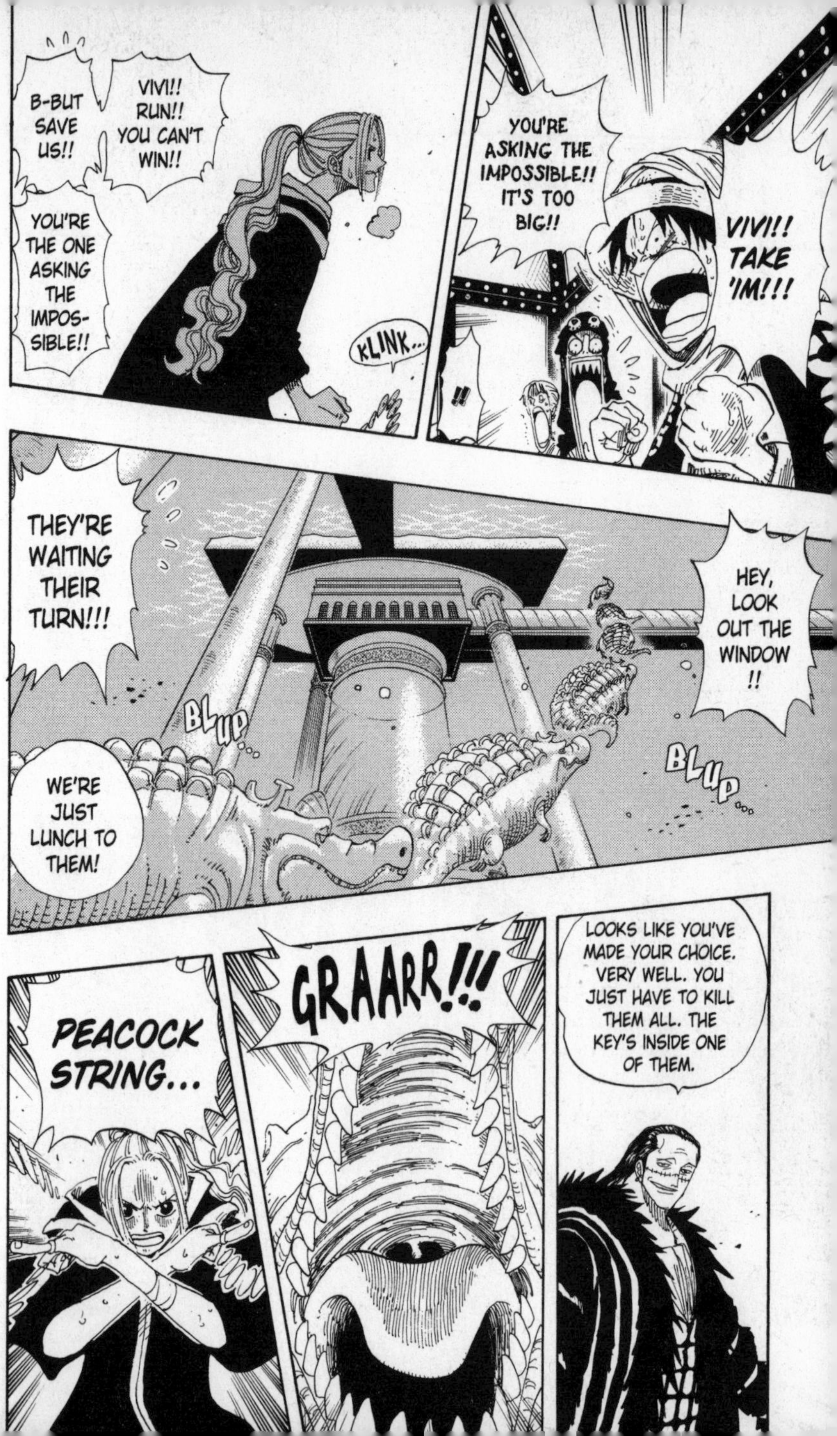
VIVI!! TAKE 'IM!!!
YOU'RE ASKING THE IMPOSSIBLE!! IT'S TOO BIG!!
VIVI!! RUN!! YOU CAN'T WIN!!
B-BUT SAVE US!!
YOU'RE THE ONE ASKING THE IMPOS-SIBLE!!
KLINK...
HEY, LOOK OUT THE WINDOW!!
BLUP...
THEY'RE WAITING THEIR TURN!!!
BLUP...
WE'RE JUST LUNCH TO THEM!
LOOKS LIKE YOU'VE MADE YOUR CHOICE. VERY WELL. YOU JUST HAVE TO KILL THEM ALL. THE KEY'S INSIDE ONE OF THEM.
GRAARR!!!
PEACOCK STRING...

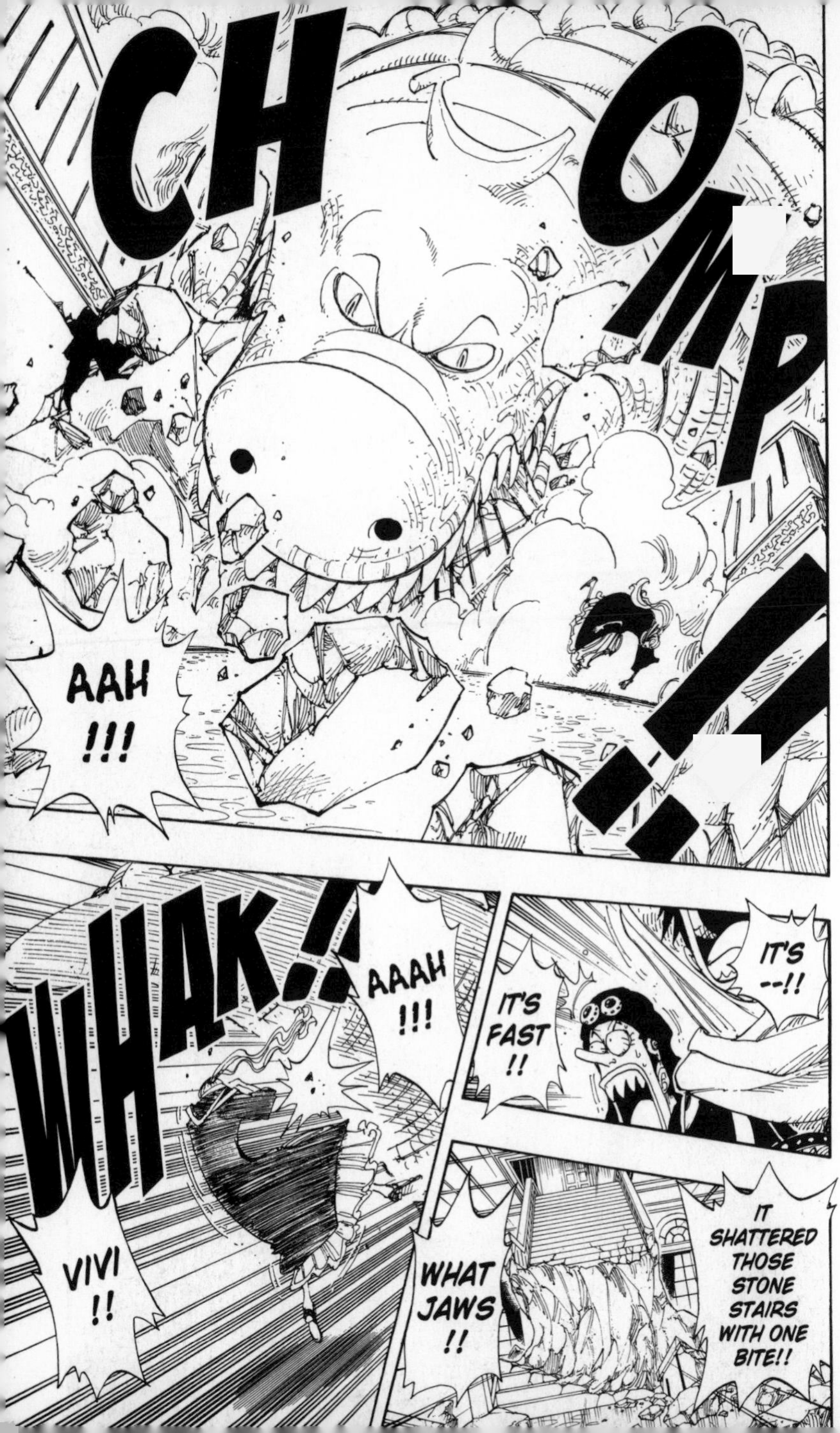
CHOMP!!
AAH!!!
IT'S--!!
IT'S FAST!!
IT SHATTERED THOSE STONE STAIRS WITH ONE BITE!!
WHAT JAWS!!
WHAK!!
AAAH!!!
VIVI!!

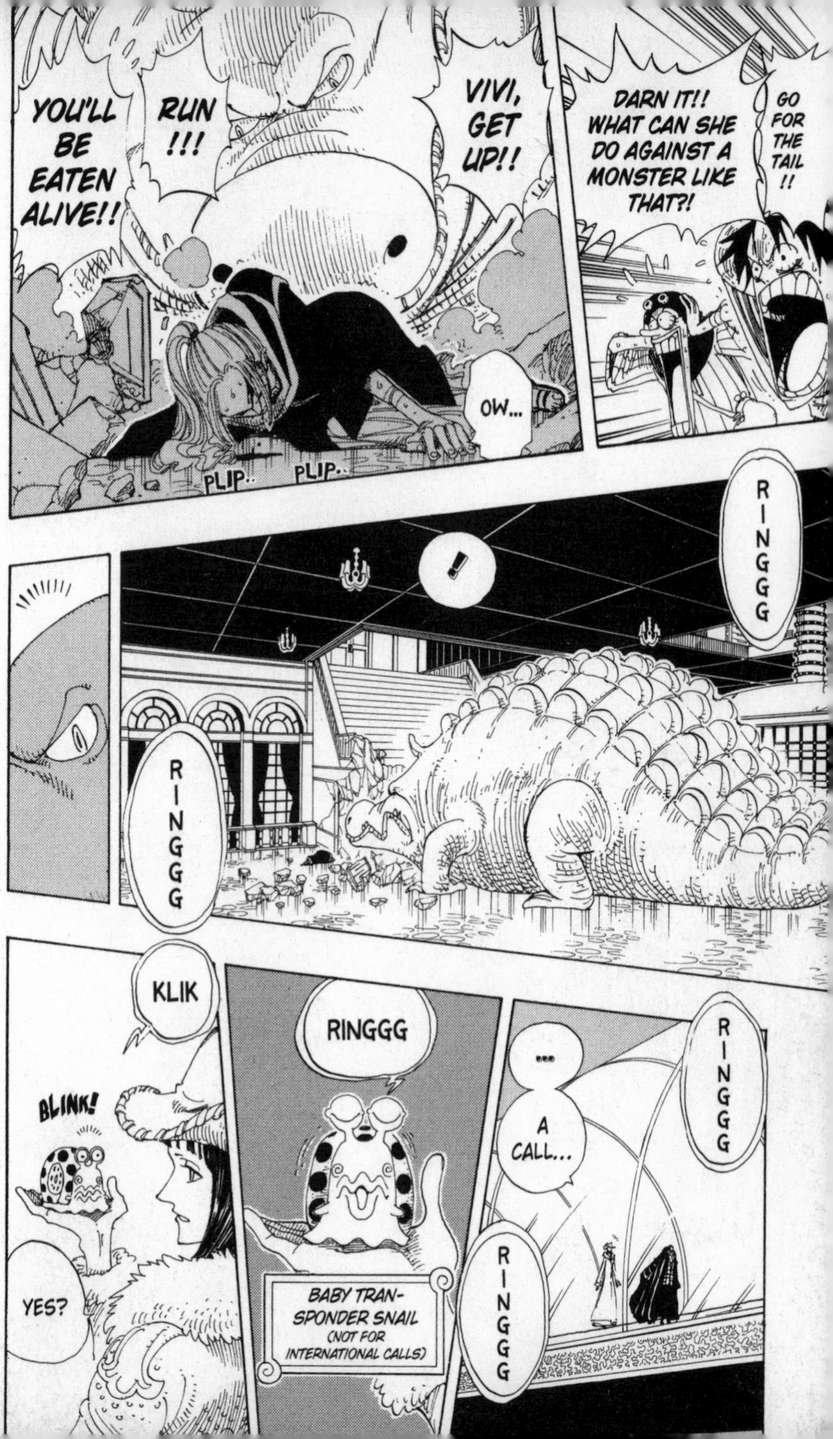
GO FOR THE TAIL!!
DARN IT!! WHAT CAN SHE DO AGAINST A MONSTER LIKE THAT?!
VIVI, GET UP!!
RUN!!!
YOU'LL BE EATEN ALIVE!!
OW...
PLIP.. PLIP..
RINGGG
!
RINGGG
RINGGG
...
A CALL...
RINGGG
RINGGG
BABY TRAN-SPONDER SNAIL (NOT FOR INTERNATIONAL CALLS)
KLIK
BLINK!
YES?

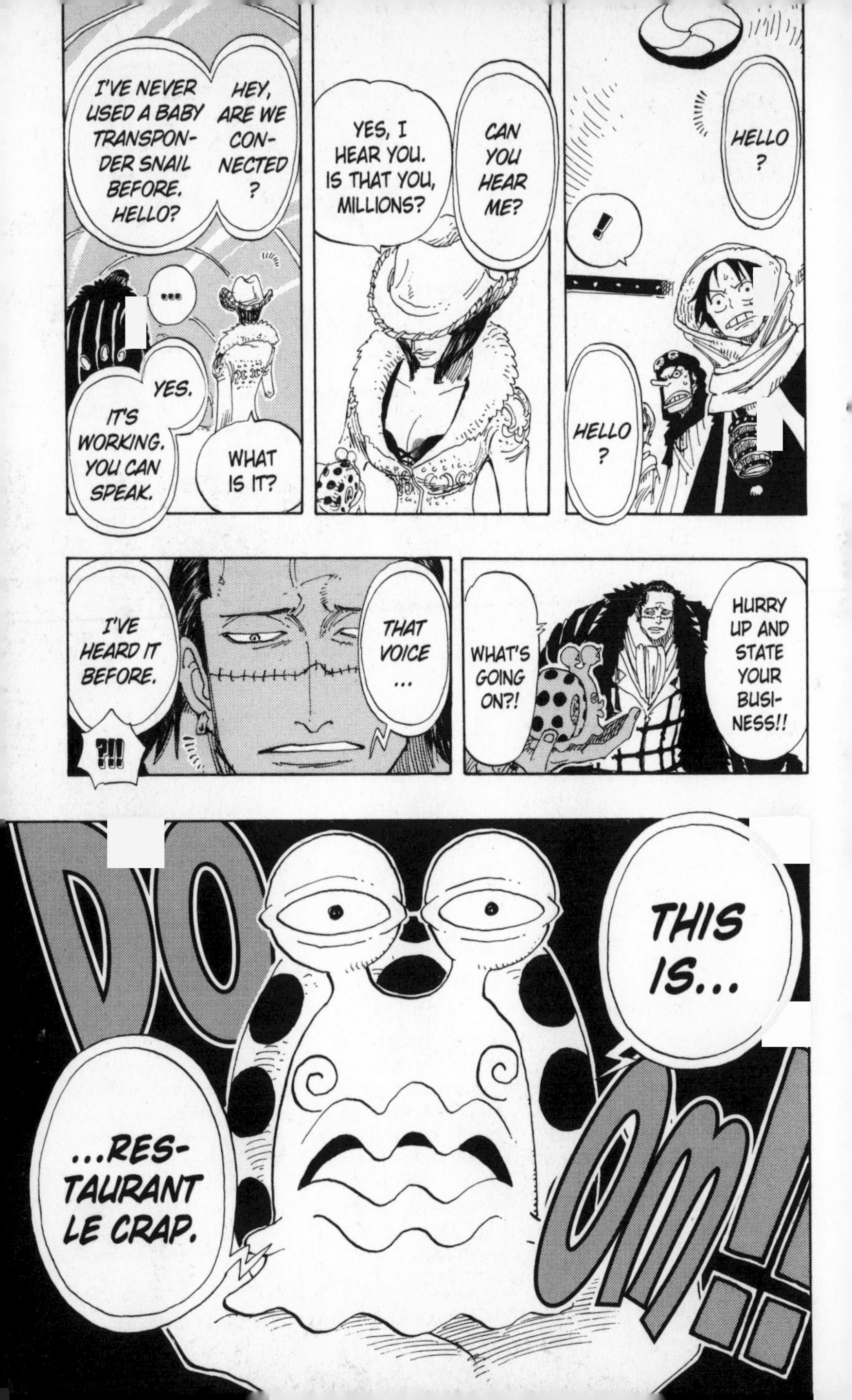
HELLO ?
!
HELLO ?
CAN YOU HEAR ME?
YES, I HEAR YOU. IS THAT YOU, MILLIONS?
HEY, ARE WE CONNECTED ?
I'VE NEVER USED A BABY TRANSPONDER SNAIL BEFORE. HELLO?
...
YES. IT'S WORKING. YOU CAN SPEAK.
WHAT IS IT?
HURRY UP AND STATE YOUR BUSINESS!!
WHAT'S GOING ON?!
THAT VOICE ...
I'VE HEARD IT BEFORE.
?!!
THIS IS...
...RESTAURANT LE CRAP.
DOOM!!

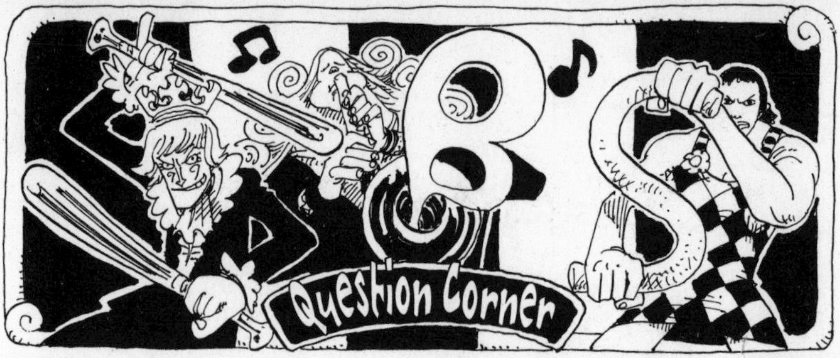
Question Corner

Reader: Oda Sensei!! I found something rather surprising!! It's about the courier who appears on pages 117-118 of volume 18. His T-shirt says "half-fledged" there, but it says "full-fledged" on page 69!! What's going on with him? Please tell me!!

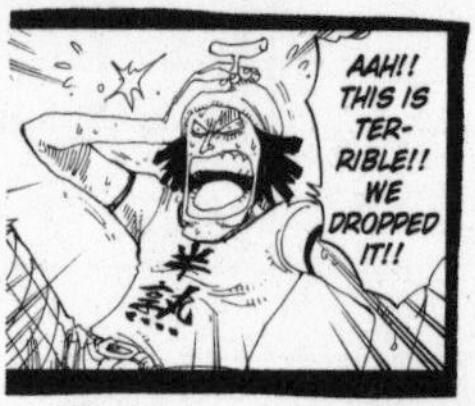
AAH!! THIS IS TERRIBLE!! WE DROPPED IT!!
(Flashback scene of the courier)

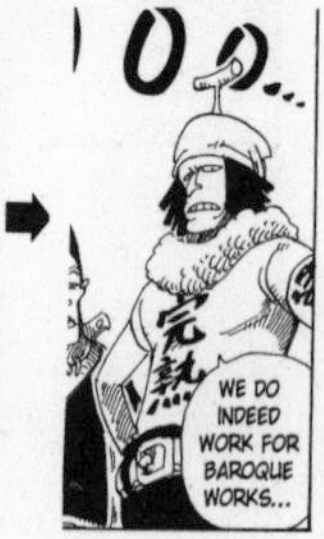
OD...
WE DO INDEED WORK FOR BAROQUE WORKS...
(The courier now)

Oda: He matured.

Reader: Are Transponder Snails animals or machines?

Oda: They're living things, like bugs.

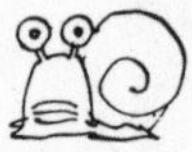

Baby Transponder Snail

They are small and easy to carry. However, they have a weak signal and cannot be used to communicate between islands.

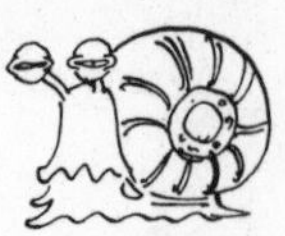

Transponder Snail

These are big and inconvenient to carry around, but they have a strong signal so they can communicate with distant islands. They can also be used to send faxes by connecting an attachment.

Different species

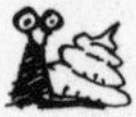

Black Transponder Snail

These remain small even when mature. They like to eavesdrop and do not like to communicate with their fellow Snails. They are used as listening devices.

The important thing is that Transponder Snails do not mind captivity by humans because they get fed.

# Chapter 174:
# MR. PRINCE

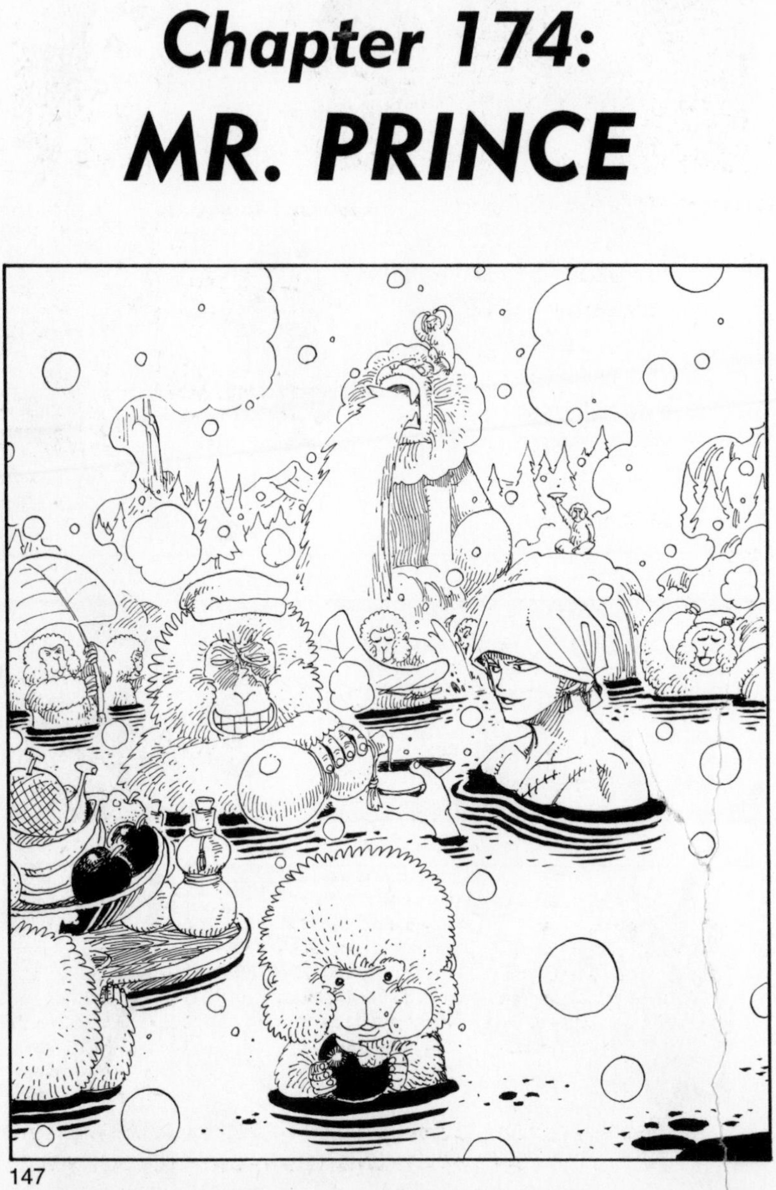

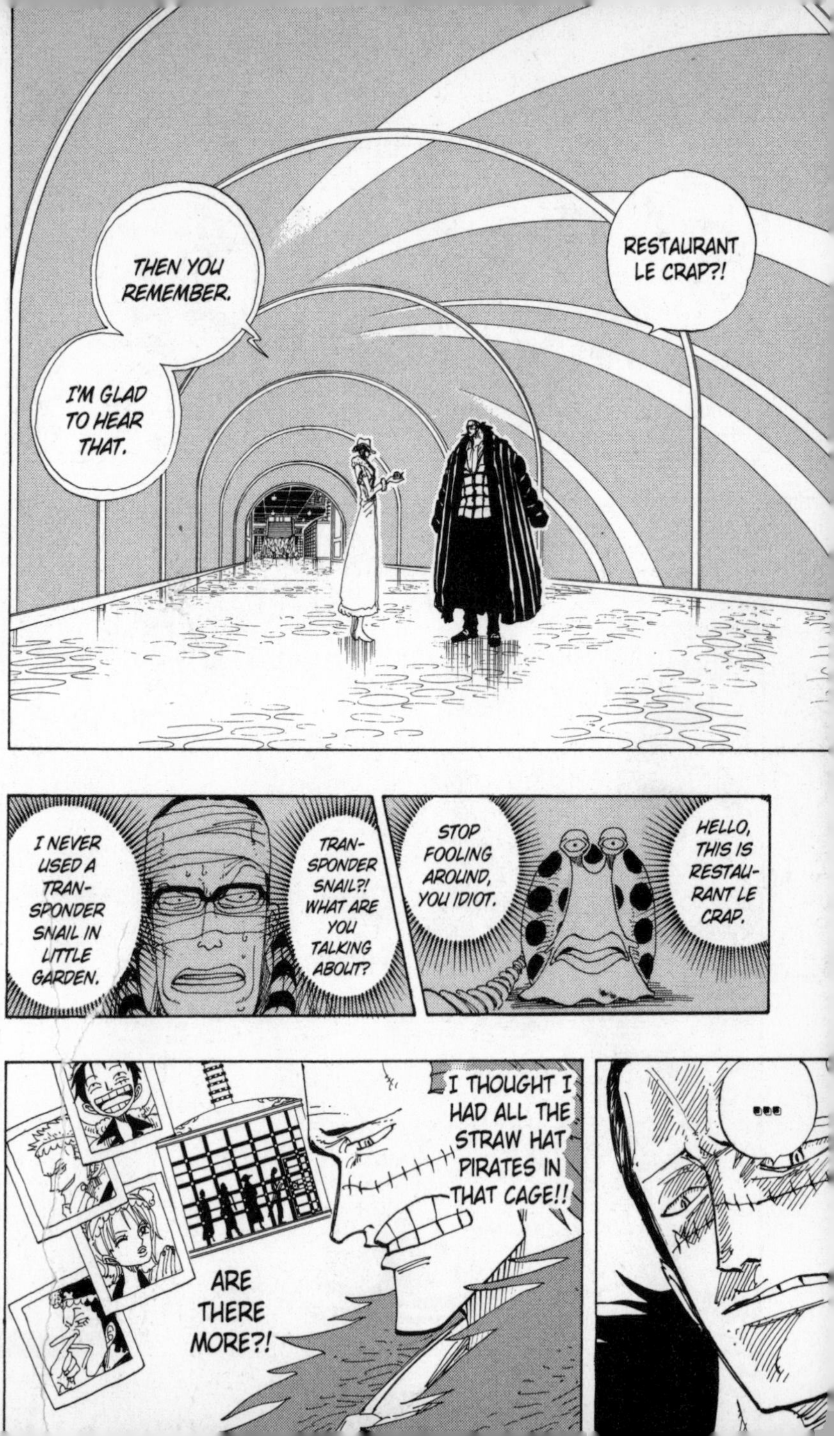
RESTAURANT LE CRAP?!
THEN YOU REMEMBER.
I'M GLAD TO HEAR THAT.
HELLO, THIS IS RESTAU-RANT LE CRAP.
STOP FOOLING AROUND, YOU IDIOT.
TRAN-SPONDER SNAIL?! WHAT ARE YOU TALKING ABOUT?
I NEVER USED A TRAN-SPONDER SNAIL IN LITTLE GARDEN.
...
I THOUGHT I HAD ALL THE STRAW HAT PIRATES IN THAT CAGE!!
ARE THERE MORE?!

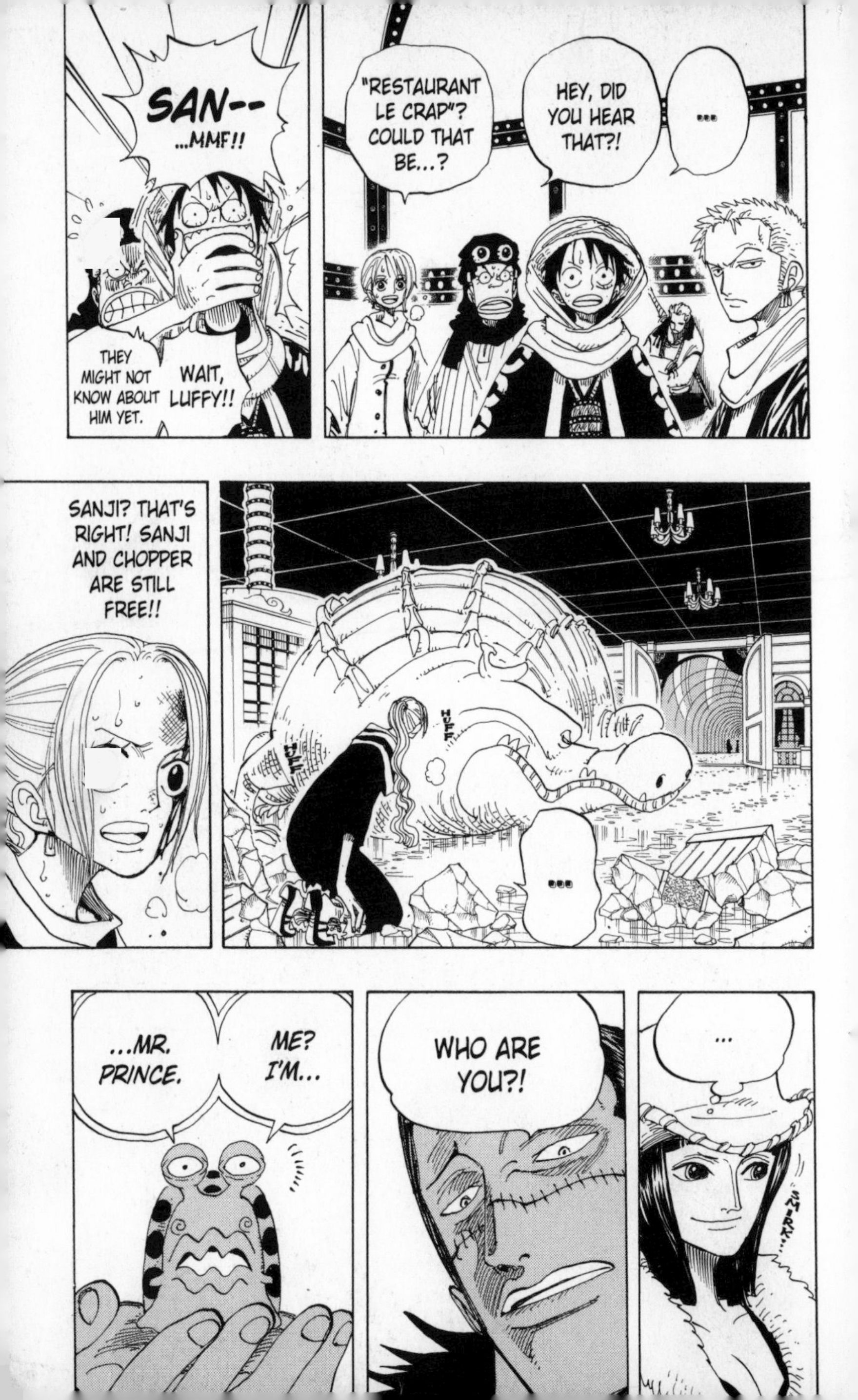
...
HEY, DID YOU HEAR THAT?!
"RESTAURANT LE CRAP"? COULD THAT BE...?
SAN-- ...MMF!!
WAIT, LUFFY!!
THEY MIGHT NOT KNOW ABOUT HIM YET.
HUFF
HUFF
...
SANJI? THAT'S RIGHT! SANJI AND CHOPPER ARE STILL FREE!!
...
SMIRK...
WHO ARE YOU?!
ME? I'M...
...MR. PRINCE.

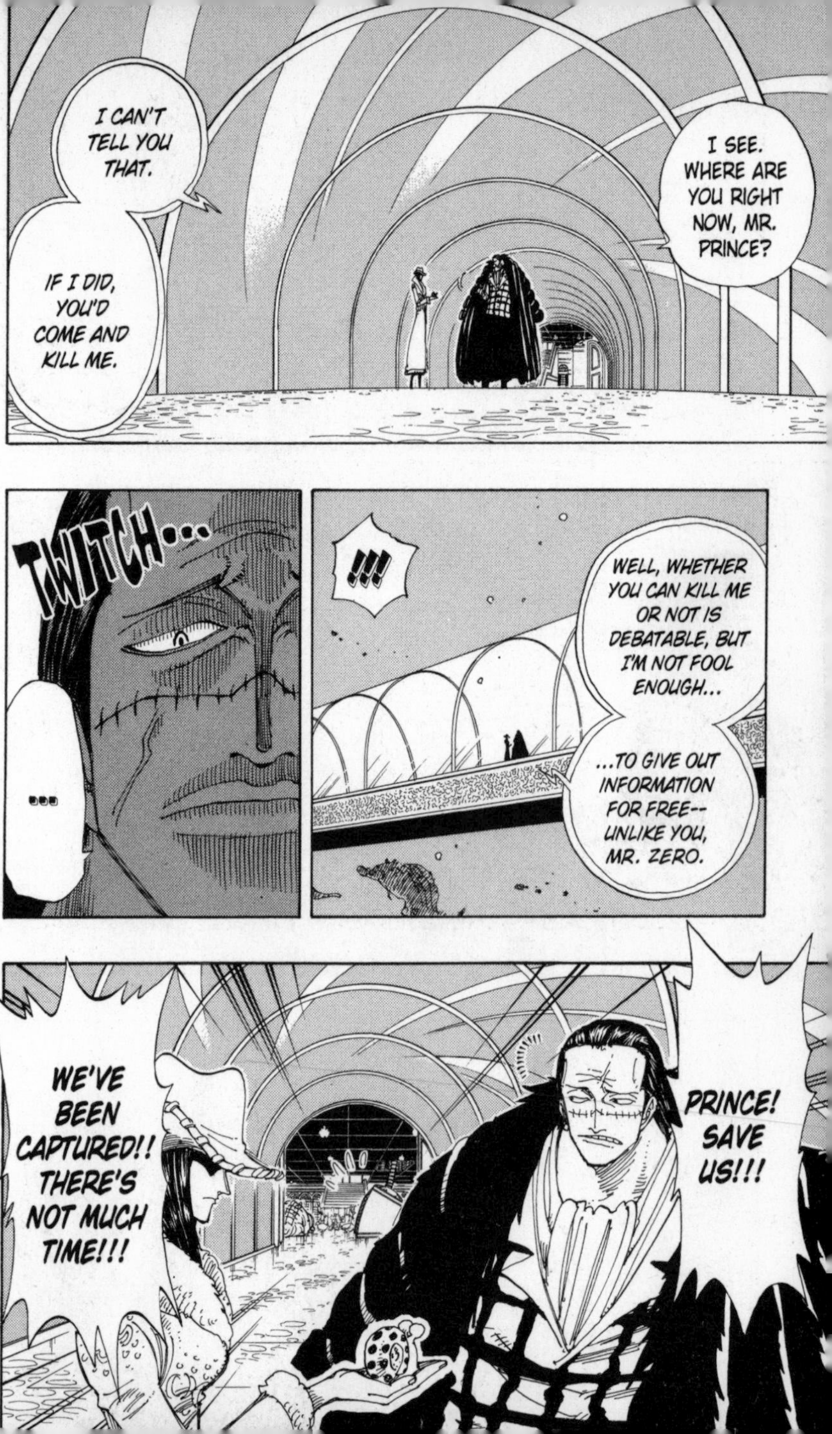
I SEE. WHERE ARE YOU RIGHT NOW, MR. PRINCE?
I CAN'T TELL YOU THAT.
IF I DID, YOU'D COME AND KILL ME.
WELL, WHETHER YOU CAN KILL ME OR NOT IS DEBATABLE, BUT I'M NOT FOOL ENOUGH...
...TO GIVE OUT INFORMATION FOR FREE-- UNLIKE YOU, MR. ZERO.
!!!
TWITCH...
...
PRINCE! SAVE US!!!
WE'VE BEEN CAPTURED!! THERE'S NOT MUCH TIME!!!

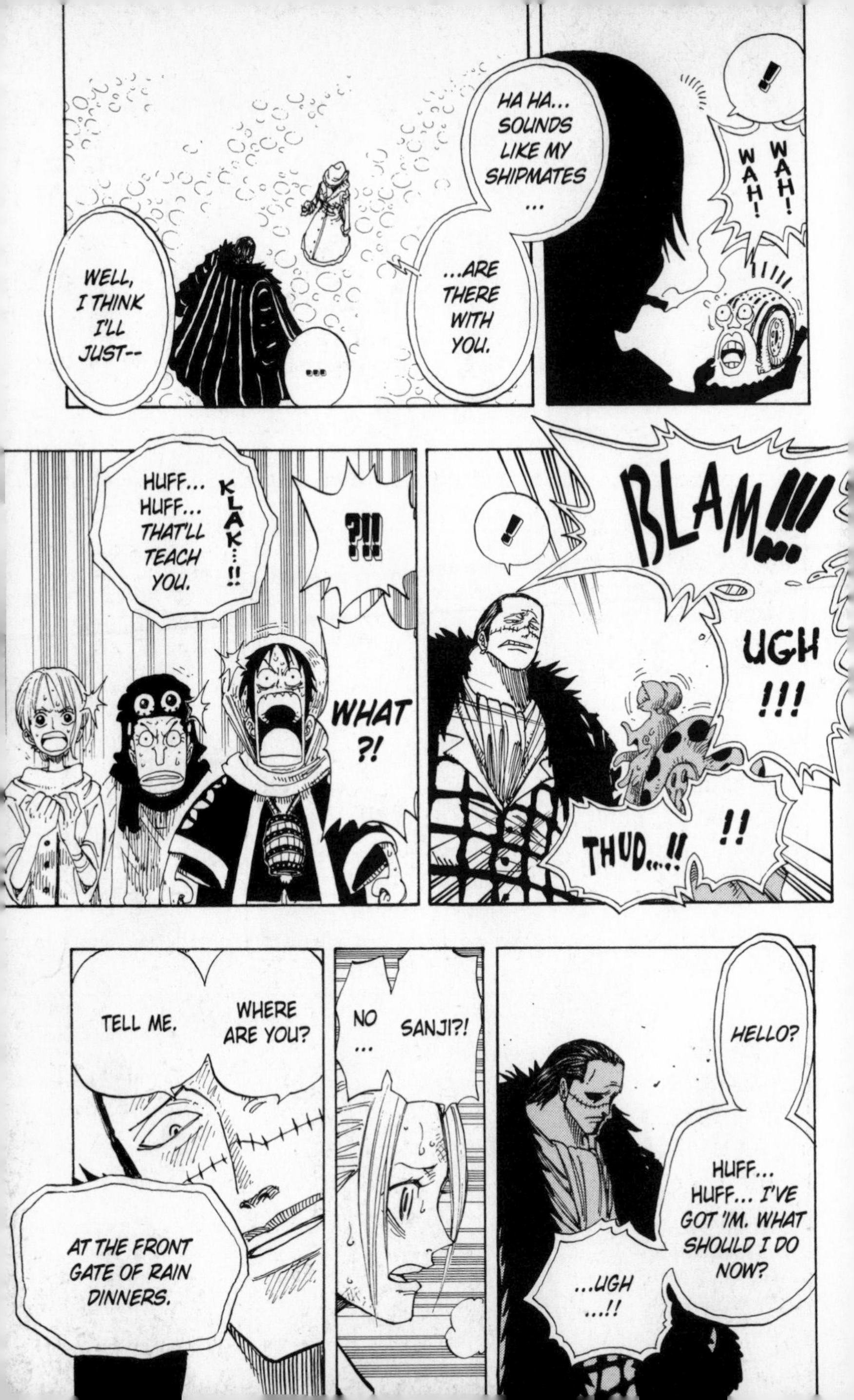
!
WAH! WAH!
HA HA... SOUNDS LIKE MY SHIPMATES ...
...ARE THERE WITH YOU.
...
WELL, I THINK I'LL JUST--
BLAM!!!...
!
UGH !!!
!!
THUD...!!
?!!
WHAT ?!
HUFF... HUFF... THAT'LL TEACH YOU.
KLAK...!!
HELLO?
HUFF... HUFF... I'VE GOT 'IM. WHAT SHOULD I DO NOW?
...UGH ...!!
SANJI?!
NO ...
WHERE ARE YOU?
TELL ME.
AT THE FRONT GATE OF RAIN DINNERS.

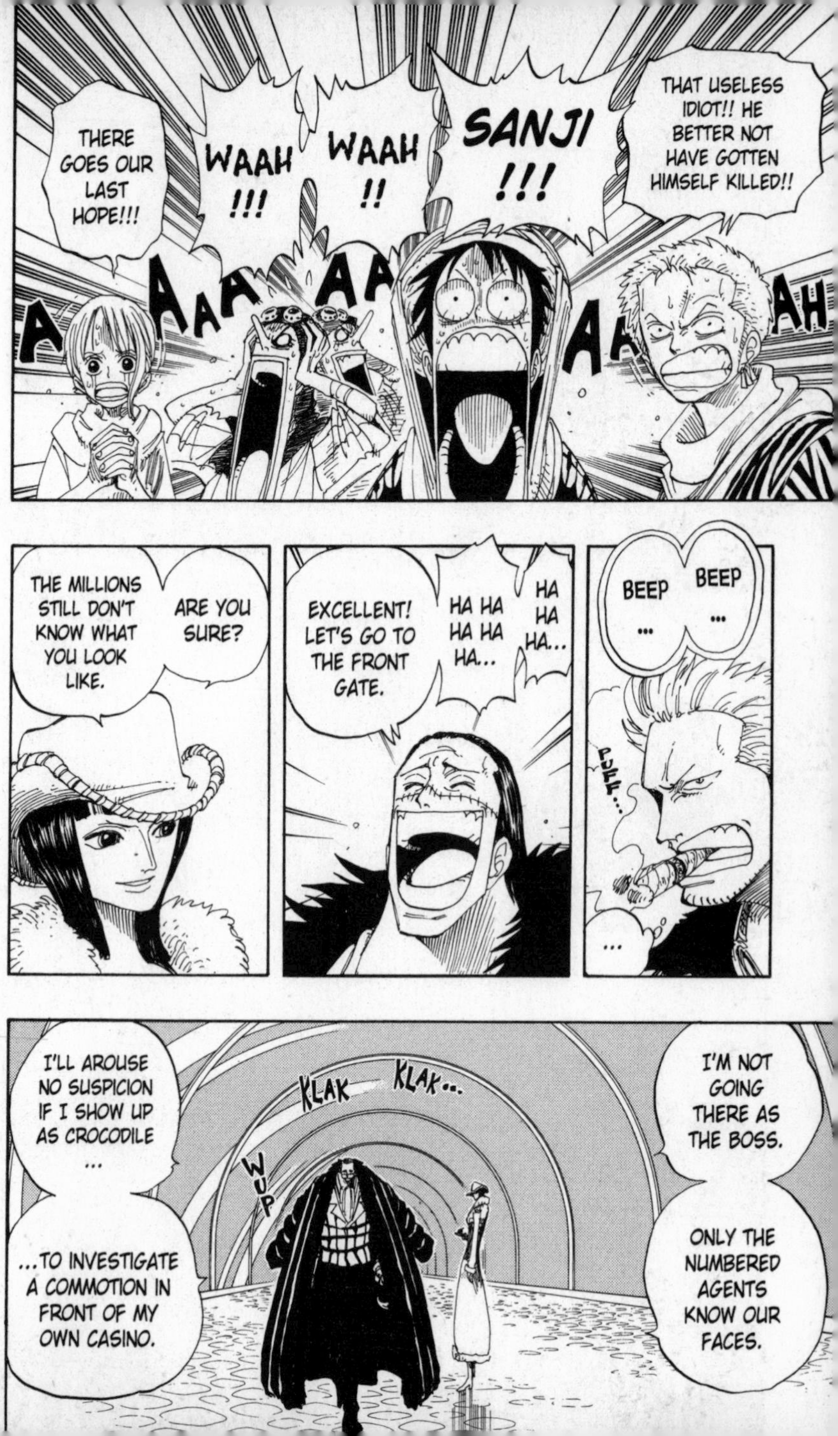
THAT USELESS IDIOT!! HE BETTER NOT HAVE GOTTEN HIMSELF KILLED!!
AH
SANJI !!!
WAAH !!
WAAH !!!
THERE GOES OUR LAST HOPE!!!
A AAA AA AA
BEEP ...
BEEP ...
PUFF...
...
HA HA HA...
HA HA HA HA HA...
EXCELLENT! LET'S GO TO THE FRONT GATE.
ARE YOU SURE?
THE MILLIONS STILL DON'T KNOW WHAT YOU LOOK LIKE.
I'M NOT GOING THERE AS THE BOSS.
ONLY THE NUMBERED AGENTS KNOW OUR FACES.
KLAK KLAK...
WUP
I'LL AROUSE NO SUSPICION IF I SHOW UP AS CROCODILE ...
...TO INVESTIGATE A COMMOTION IN FRONT OF MY OWN CASINO.

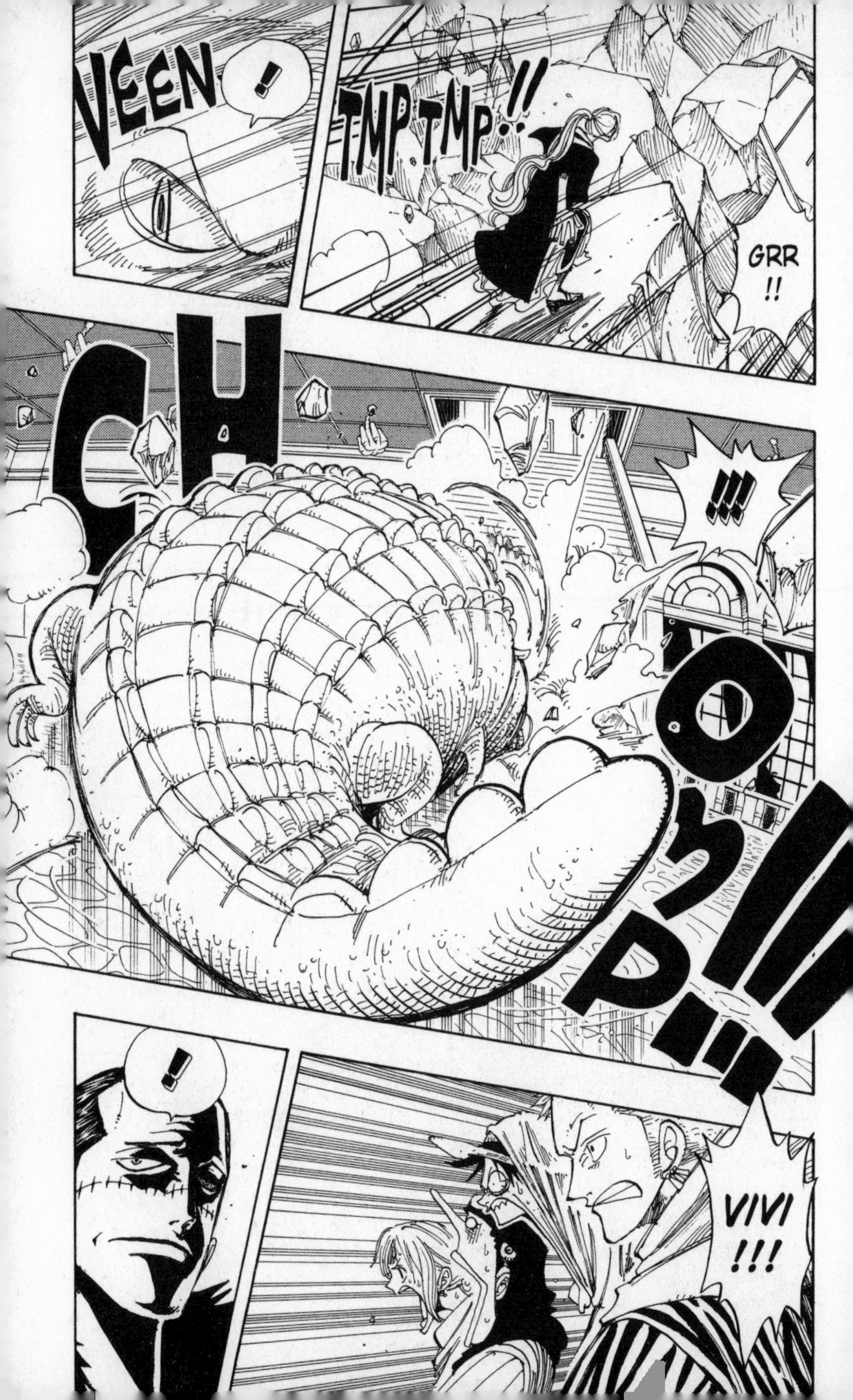
TMP TMP!!
GRR !!
!
VEEN
!!!
CH
VIVI !!!
!

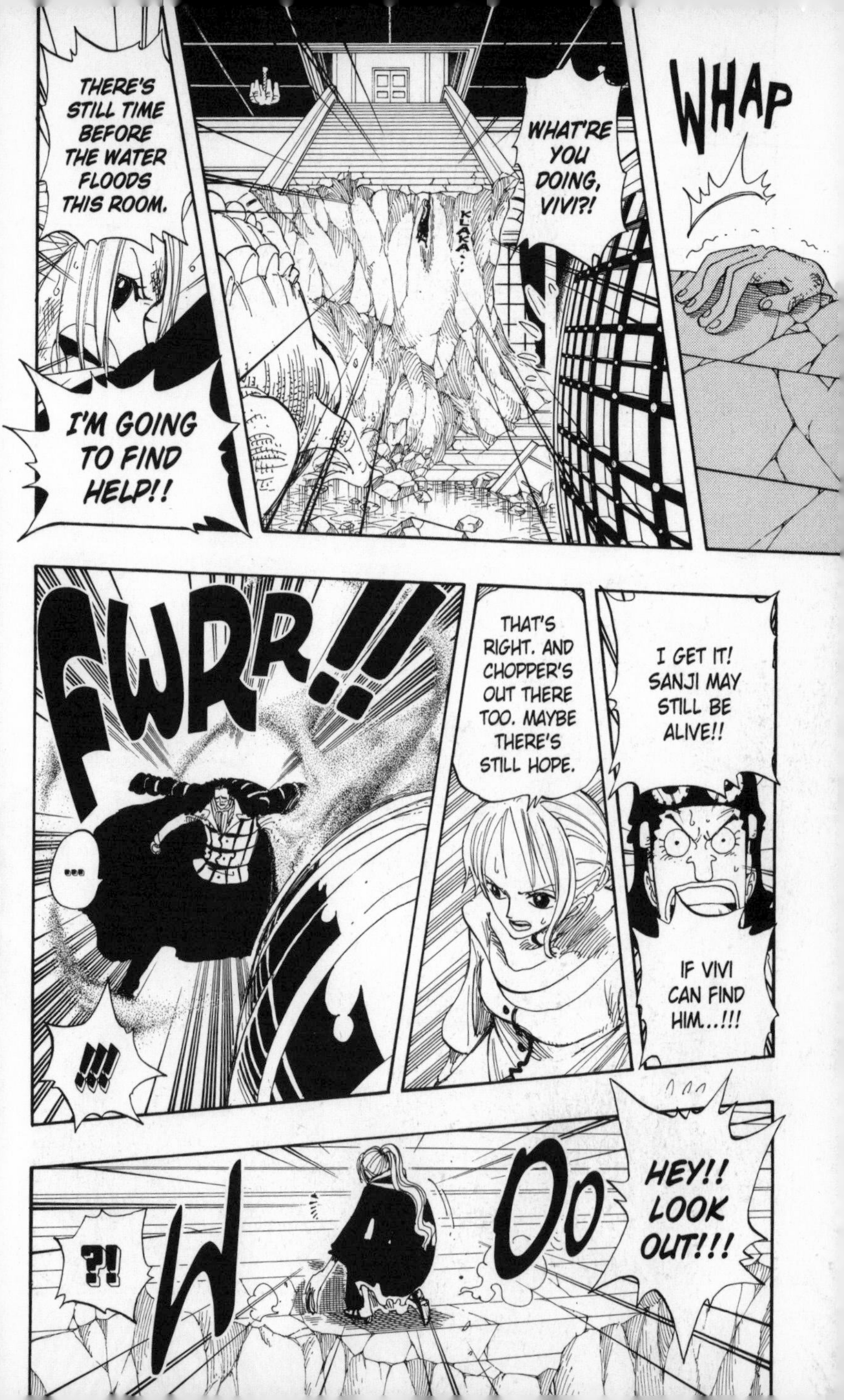
WHAP
WHAT'RE YOU DOING, VIVI?!
KLAKA...
THERE'S STILL TIME BEFORE THE WATER FLOODS THIS ROOM.
I'M GOING TO FIND HELP!!
I GET IT! SANJI MAY STILL BE ALIVE!!
IF VIVI CAN FIND HIM...!!!
THAT'S RIGHT. AND CHOPPER'S OUT THERE TOO. MAYBE THERE'S STILL HOPE.
FWRR!!
...
!!!
HEY!! LOOK OUT!!!
?!

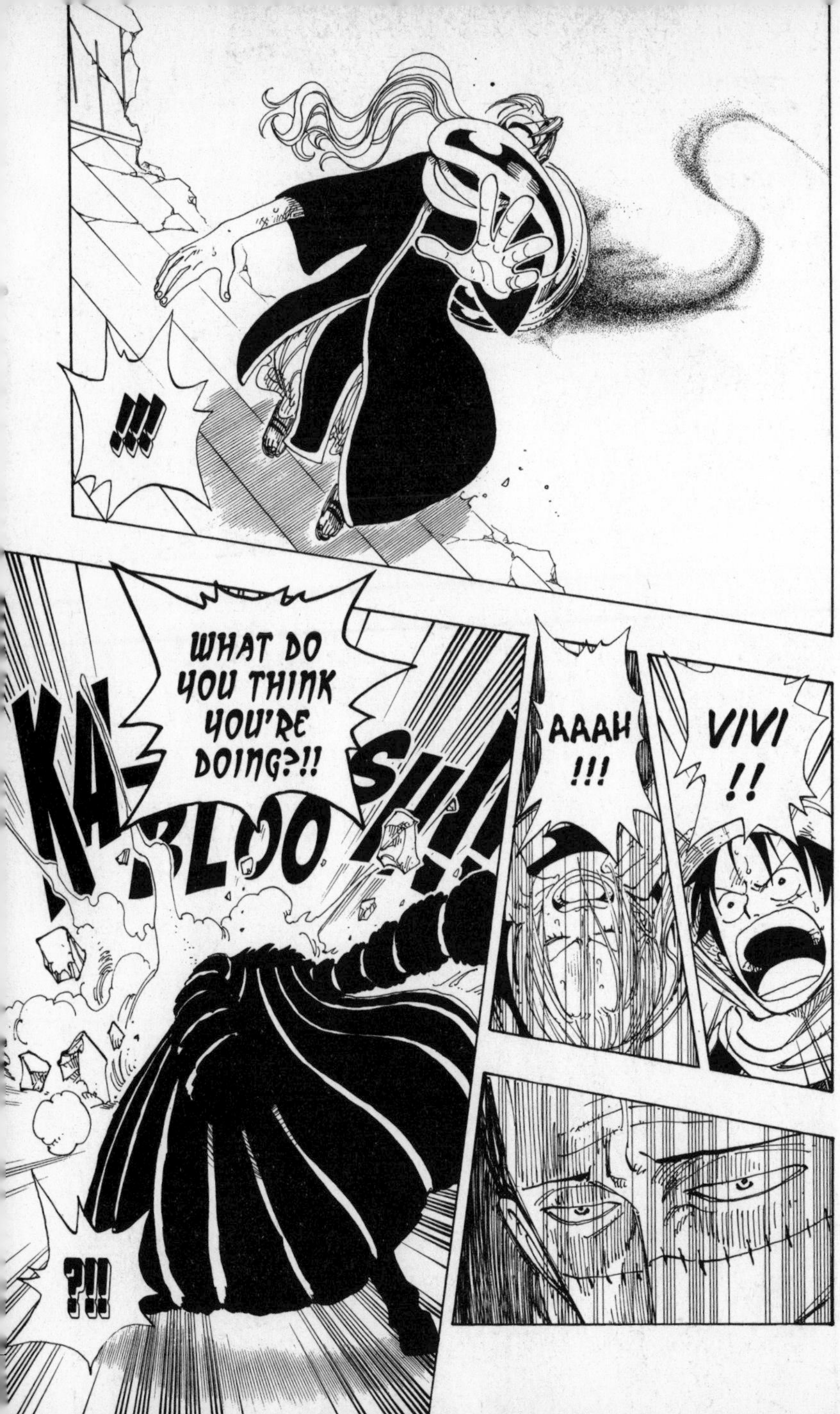
!!!
VIVI !!
AAAH !!!
WHAT DO YOU THINK YOU'RE DOING?!!
KA-BLOOSH!!
?!!

CHING!!!

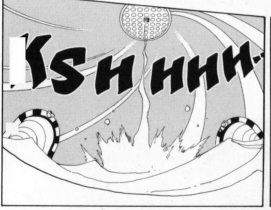

KSHHHH...

SPLOOSH...

...MMOO...

KLANG-KLANG!!!

VIVI, WAKE UP!!!

THE GATOR'S COMING!!

VEEN

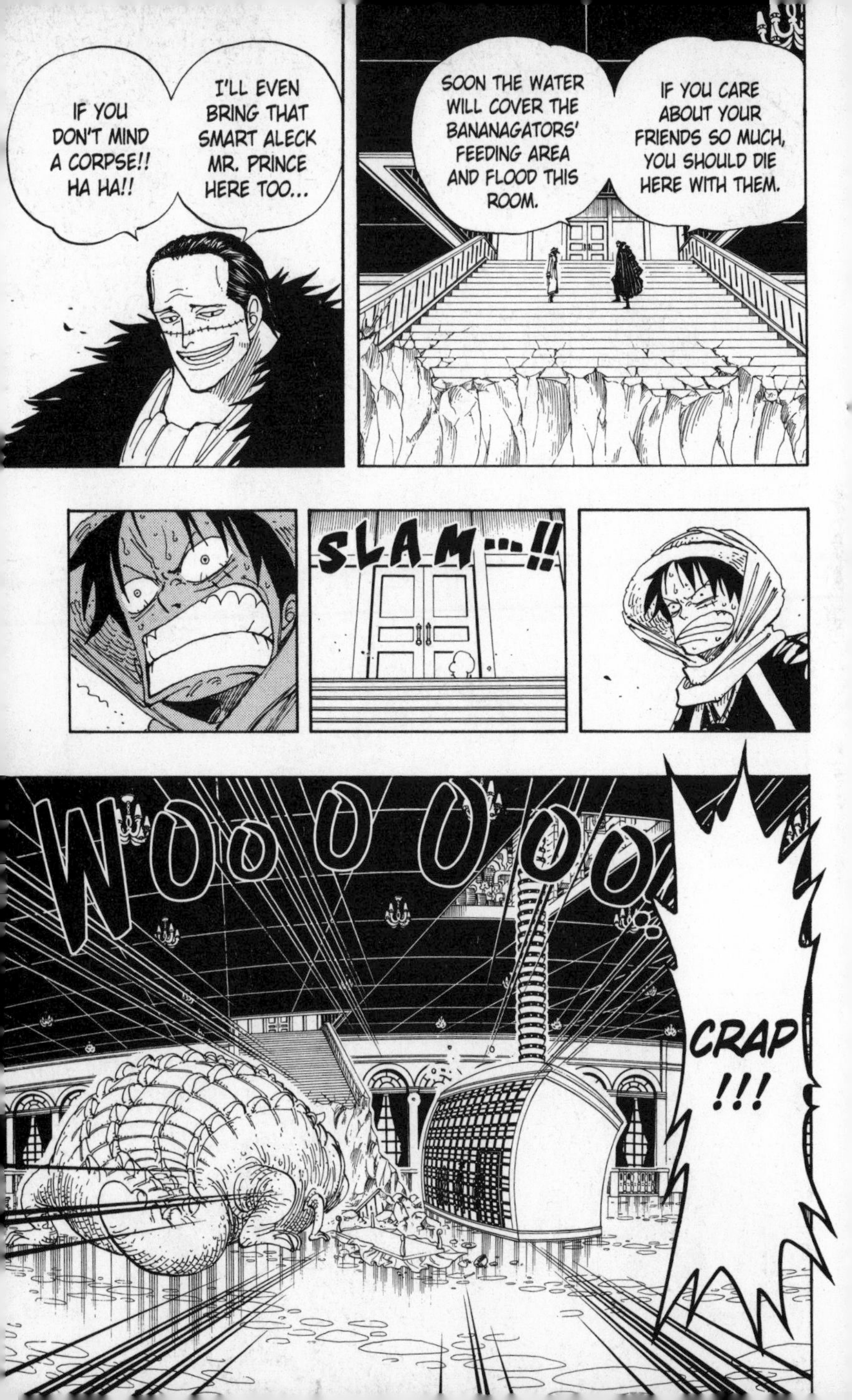
IF YOU CARE ABOUT YOUR FRIENDS SO MUCH, YOU SHOULD DIE HERE WITH THEM.
SOON THE WATER WILL COVER THE BANANAGATORS' FEEDING AREA AND FLOOD THIS ROOM.
I'LL EVEN BRING THAT SMART ALECK MR. PRINCE HERE TOO...
IF YOU DON'T MIND A CORPSE!! HA HA!!
SLAM...!!
CRAP!!!
WOOOOOOO

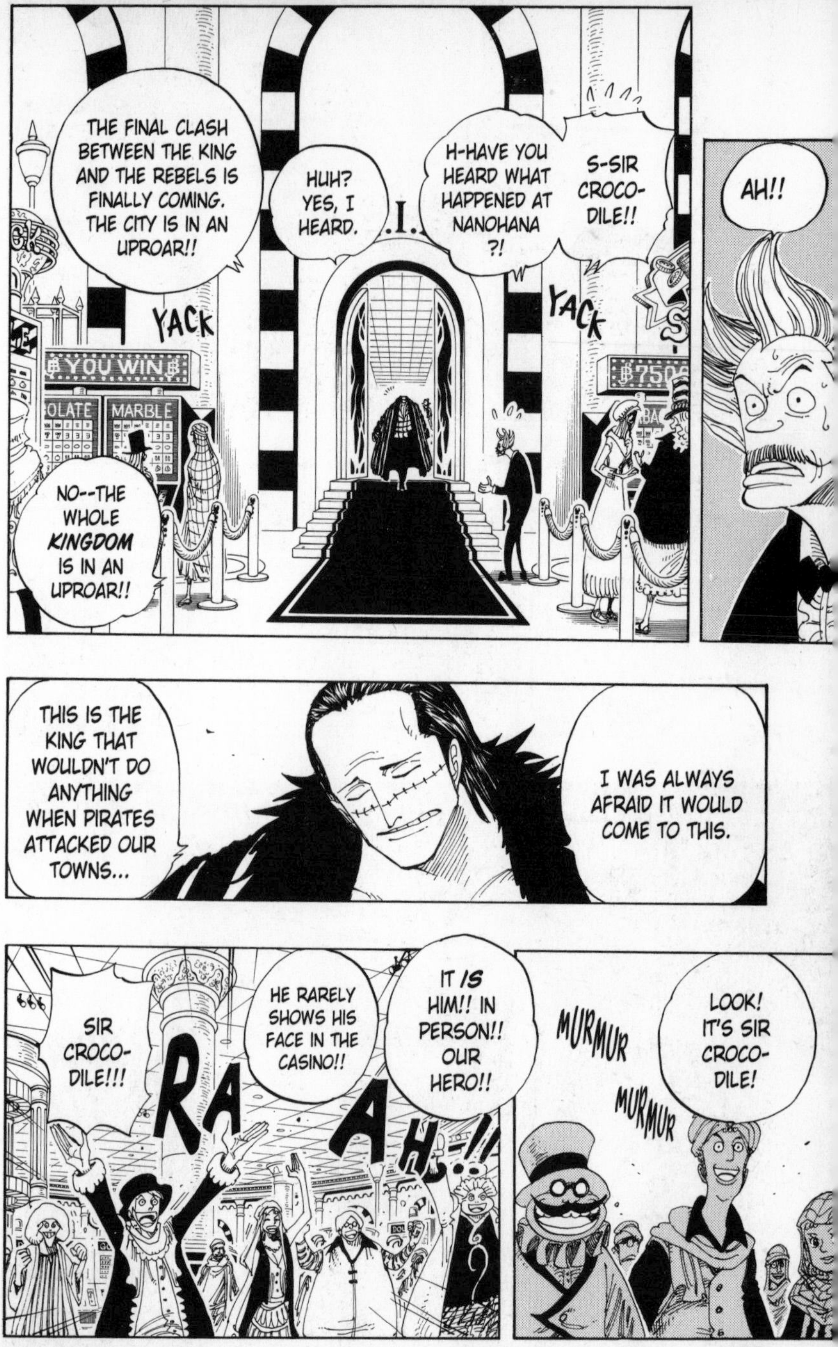
AH!!
S-SIR CROCODILE!!
H-HAVE YOU HEARD WHAT HAPPENED AT NANOHANA?!
YACK
HUH? YES, I HEARD.
THE FINAL CLASH BETWEEN THE KING AND THE REBELS IS FINALLY COMING. THE CITY IS IN AN UPROAR!!
YACK
YOU WIN
MARBLE
NO--THE WHOLE *KINGDOM* IS IN AN UPROAR!!
I WAS ALWAYS AFRAID IT WOULD COME TO THIS.
THIS IS THE KING THAT WOULDN'T DO ANYTHING WHEN PIRATES ATTACKED OUR TOWNS...
LOOK! IT'S SIR CROCODILE!
MURMUR
MURMUR
IT *IS* HIM!! IN PERSON!! OUR HERO!!
HE RARELY SHOWS HIS FACE IN THE CASINO!!
SIR CROCODILE!!!
RAAH!!

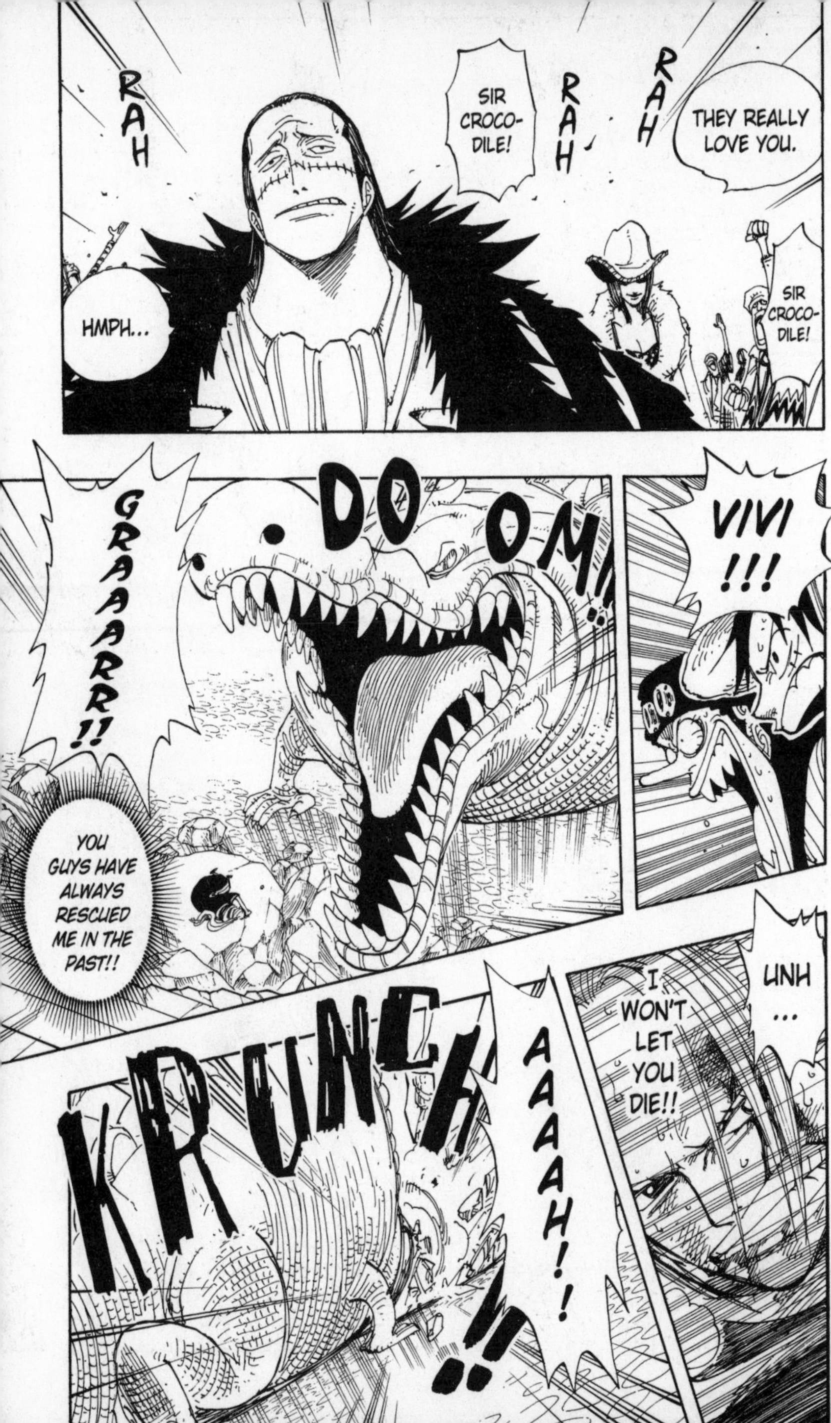
RAH
THEY REALLY LOVE YOU.
RAH
SIR CROCODILE!
RAH
SIR CROCODILE!
HMPH...
VIVI!!!
DOOM!!
GRAAAARRR!!
YOU GUYS HAVE ALWAYS RESCUED ME IN THE PAST!!
UNH...
I WON'T LET YOU DIE!!
AAAAAH!!
KRUNCH!!

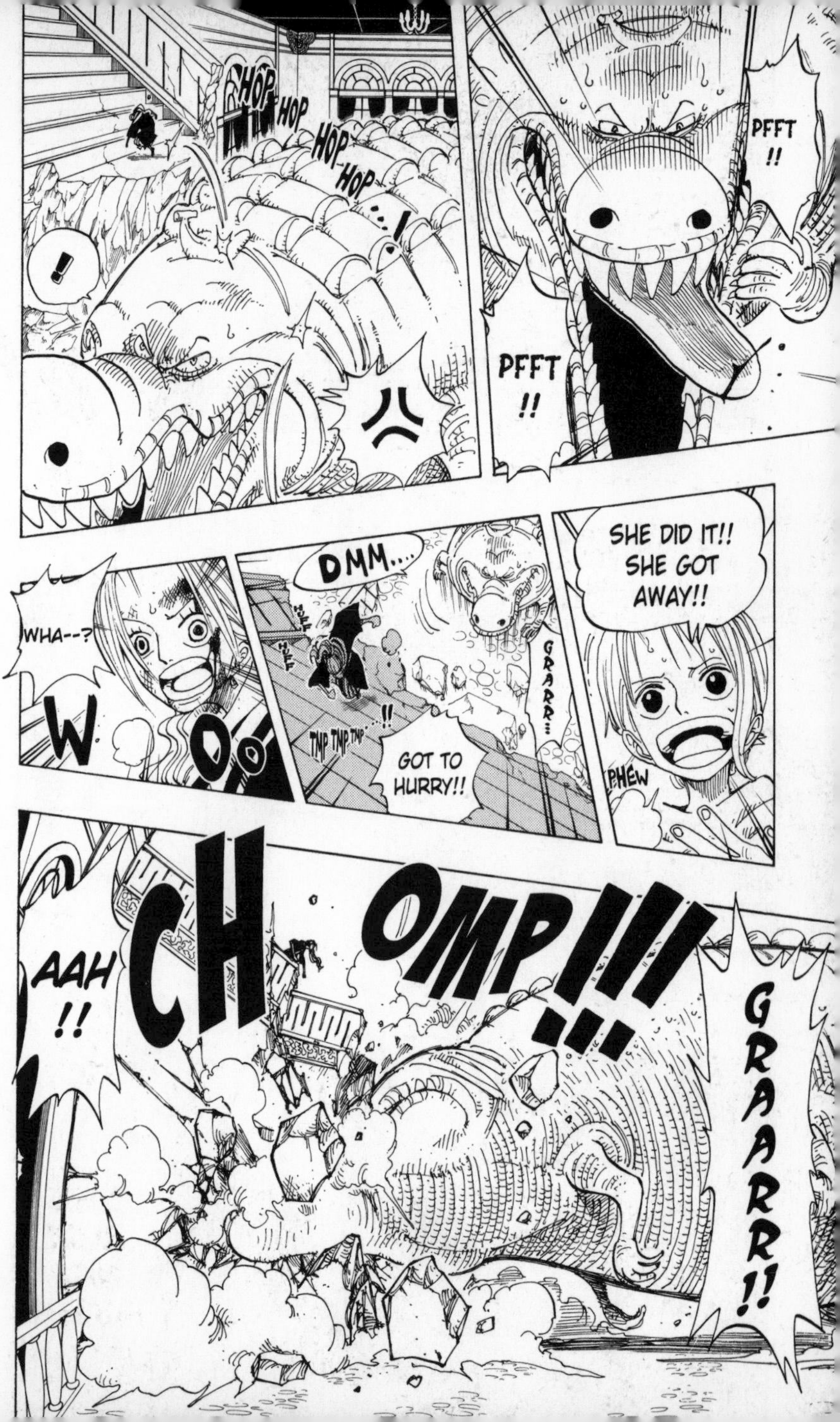
PFFT!!
PFFT!!
HOP HOP HOP HOP
...!
!
SHE DID IT!! SHE GOT AWAY!!
PHEW
DMM....
GRARR...
HUFF
TMP TMP TMP
...!!
GOT TO HURRY!!
WHA--?
WOO
GRAARR!!
CHOMP!!!
AAH!!

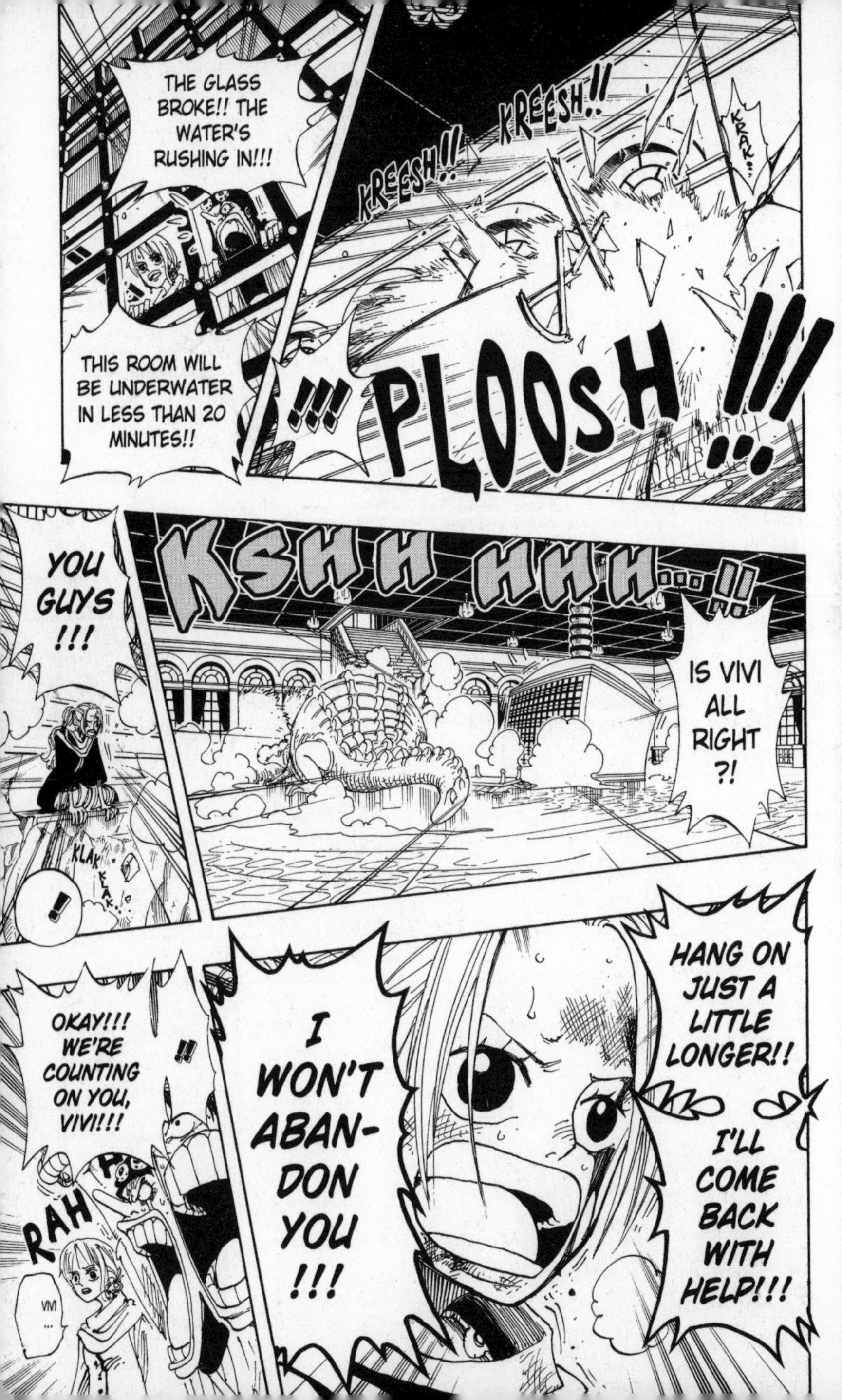
KRAK
KREESH!!
KREESH!!
PLOOSH!!!...
!!!
THE GLASS BROKE!! THE WATER'S RUSHING IN!!!
THIS ROOM WILL BE UNDERWATER IN LESS THAN 20 MINUTES!!
KSHHH HHH...!!
IS VIVI ALL RIGHT?!
YOU GUYS!!!
KLAK KLAK
!
HANG ON JUST A LITTLE LONGER!!
I'LL COME BACK WITH HELP!!!
I WON'T ABAN-DON YOU!!!
OKAY!!! WE'RE COUNTING ON YOU, VIVI!!!
!!
RAH
VIVI...

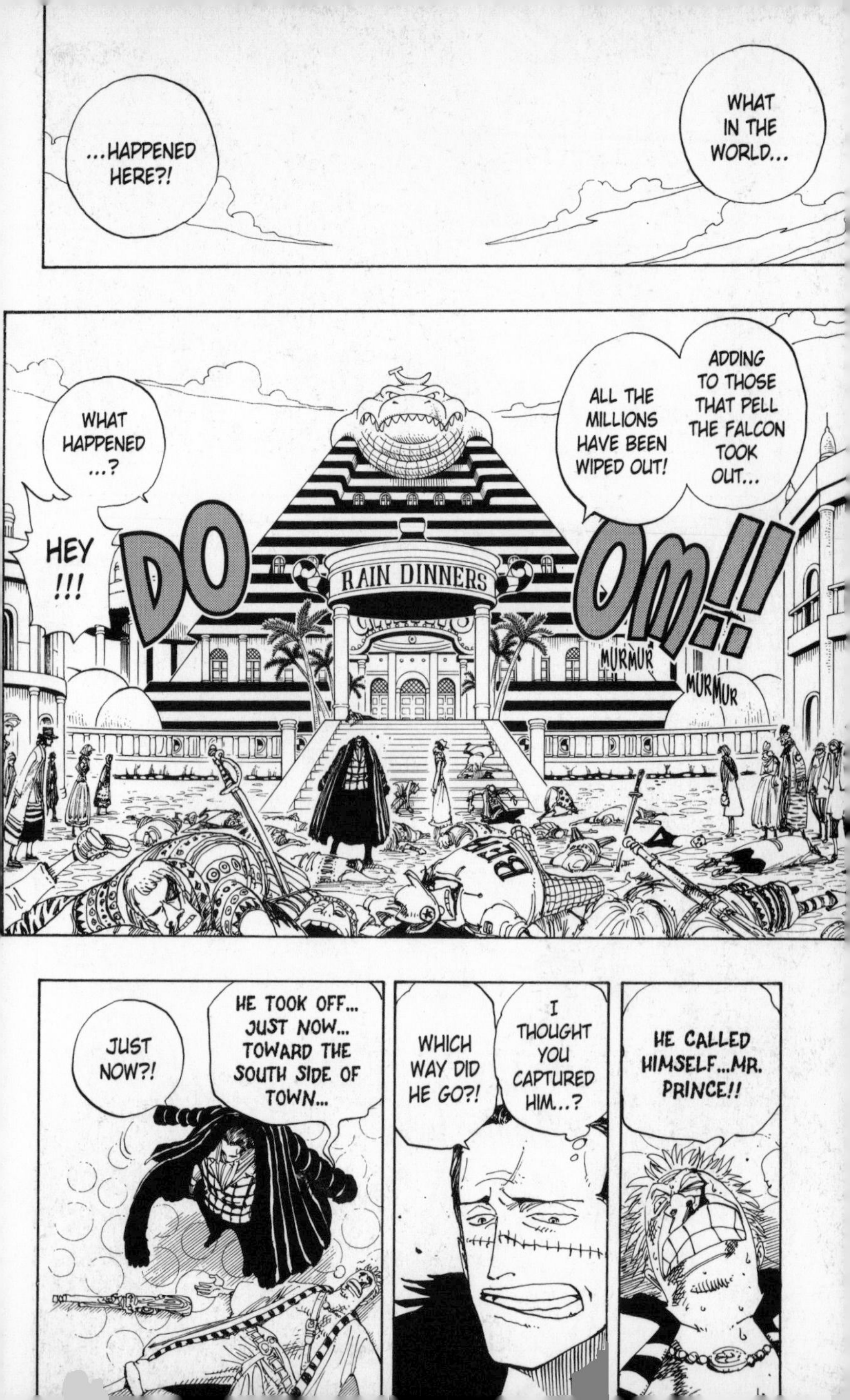
WHAT IN THE WORLD...
...HAPPENED HERE?!
ADDING TO THOSE THAT PELL THE FALCON TOOK OUT...
ALL THE MILLIONS HAVE BEEN WIPED OUT!
RAIN DINNERS
DOOM!!
MURMUR
MURMUR
HEY !!!
WHAT HAPPENED ...?
HE CALLED HIMSELF...MR. PRINCE!!
I THOUGHT YOU CAPTURED HIM...?
WHICH WAY DID HE GO?!
HE TOOK OFF... JUST NOW... TOWARD THE SOUTH SIDE OF TOWN...
JUST NOW?!

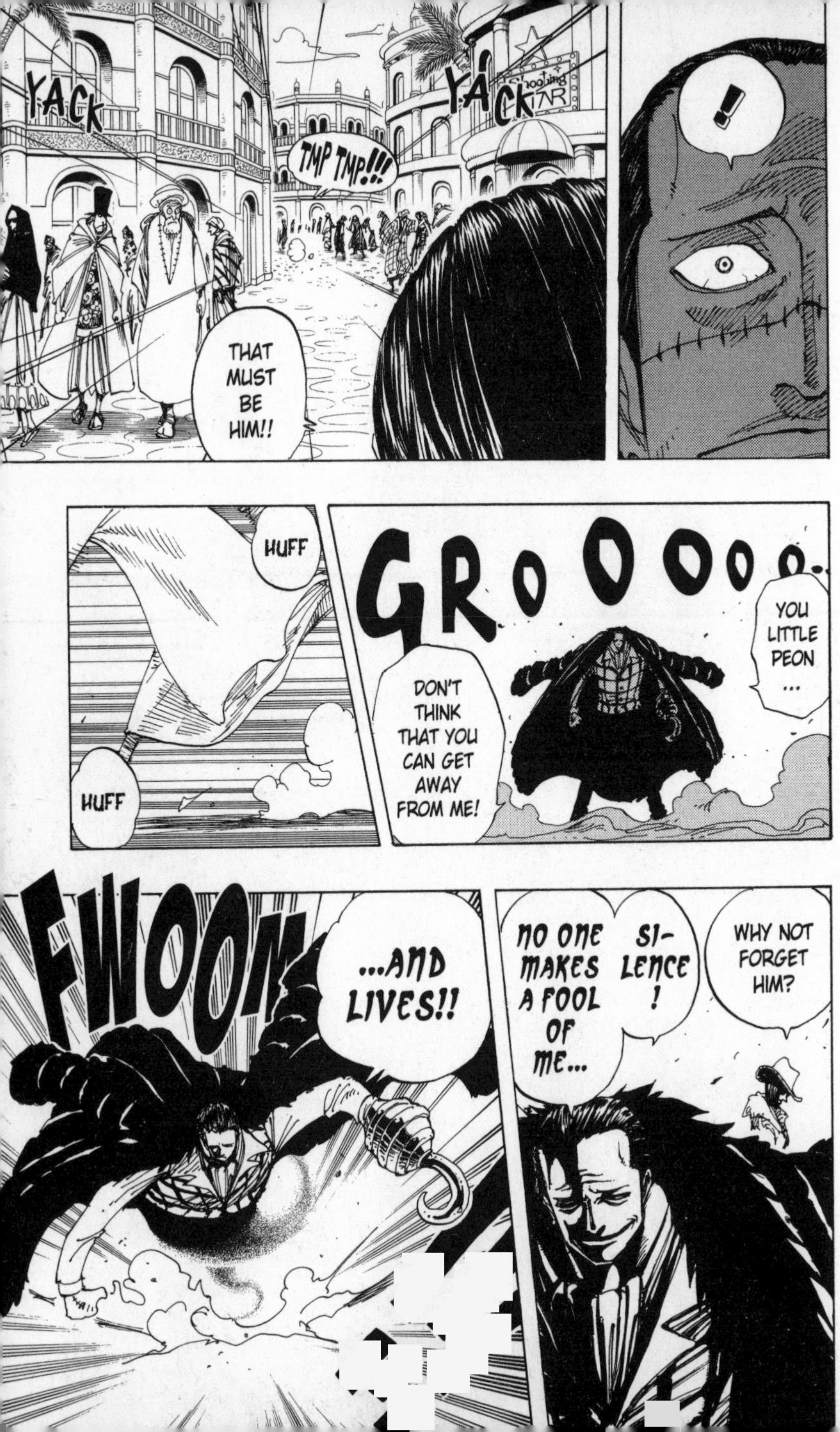
!
YACK
Shooting STAR
TMP TMP!!!
YACK
THAT MUST BE HIM!!
GROOOOO
YOU LITTLE PEON ...
DON'T THINK THAT YOU CAN GET AWAY FROM ME!
HUFF
HUFF
WHY NOT FORGET HIM?
SI-LENCE!
NO ONE MAKES A FOOL OF ME...
FWOOM
...AND LIVES!!

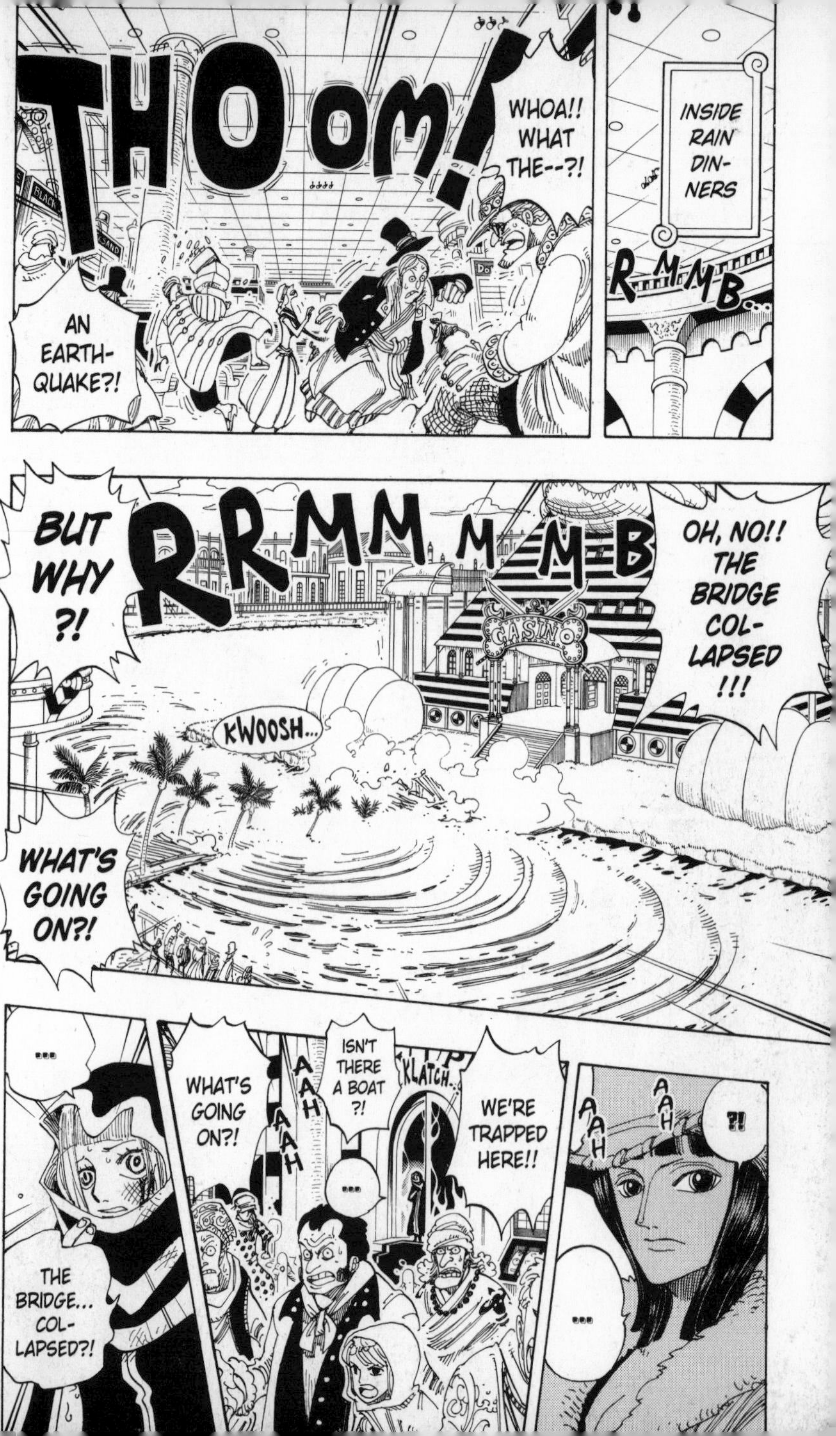
INSIDE RAIN DINNERS
RMMB...
THOOM!
WHOA!! WHAT THE--?!
AN EARTHQUAKE?!
OH, NO!! THE BRIDGE COLLAPSED!!!
RRMMMMB
KWOOSH...
BUT WHY?!
WHAT'S GOING ON?!
?!
AAH
...
WE'RE TRAPPED HERE!!
KLATCH...
ISN'T THERE A BOAT?!
AAH
AAH
...
WHAT'S GOING ON?!
...
THE BRIDGE... COLLAPSED?!

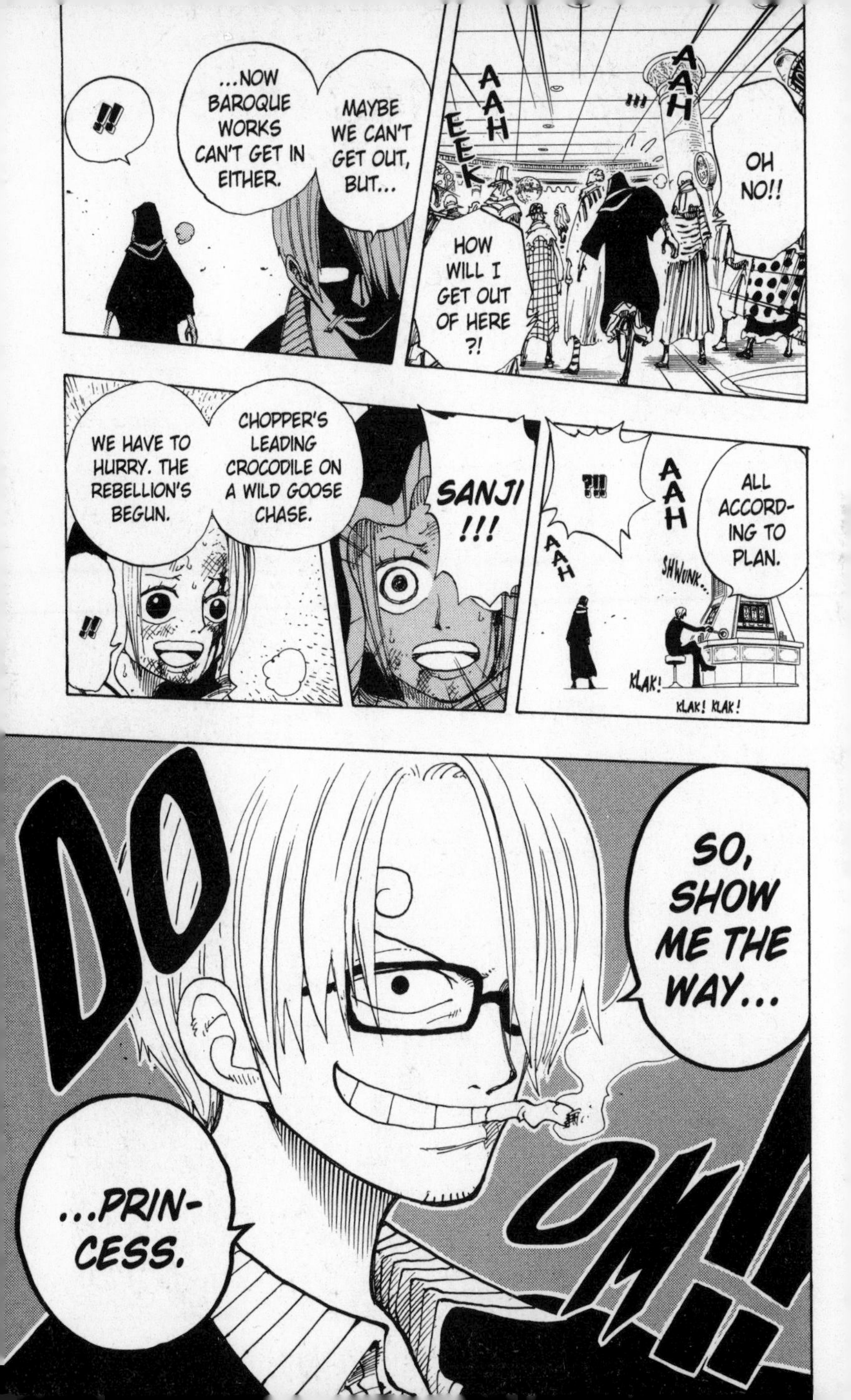
OH NO!!
AAH
!!!
AAH
EEEK
HOW WILL I GET OUT OF HERE ?!
MAYBE WE CAN'T GET OUT, BUT...
...NOW BAROQUE WORKS CAN'T GET IN EITHER.
!!
ALL ACCORD-ING TO PLAN.
AAH
?!!
AAH
SHWUNK...
KLAK!
KLAK! KLAK!
SANJI !!!
CHOPPER'S LEADING CROCODILE ON A WILD GOOSE CHASE.
WE HAVE TO HURRY. THE REBELLION'S BEGUN.
!!
SO, SHOW ME THE WAY...
...PRIN-CESS.
DOOM!!

# Chapter 175: RELEASE

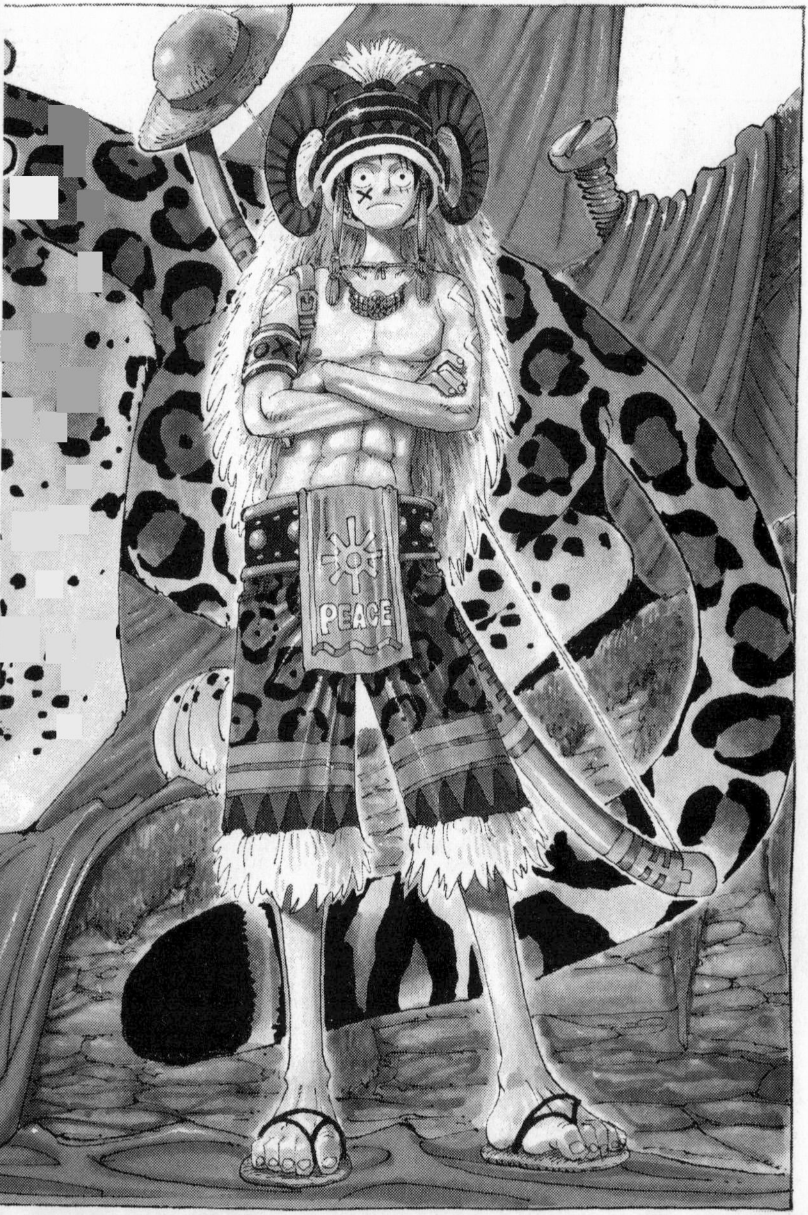
PEACE

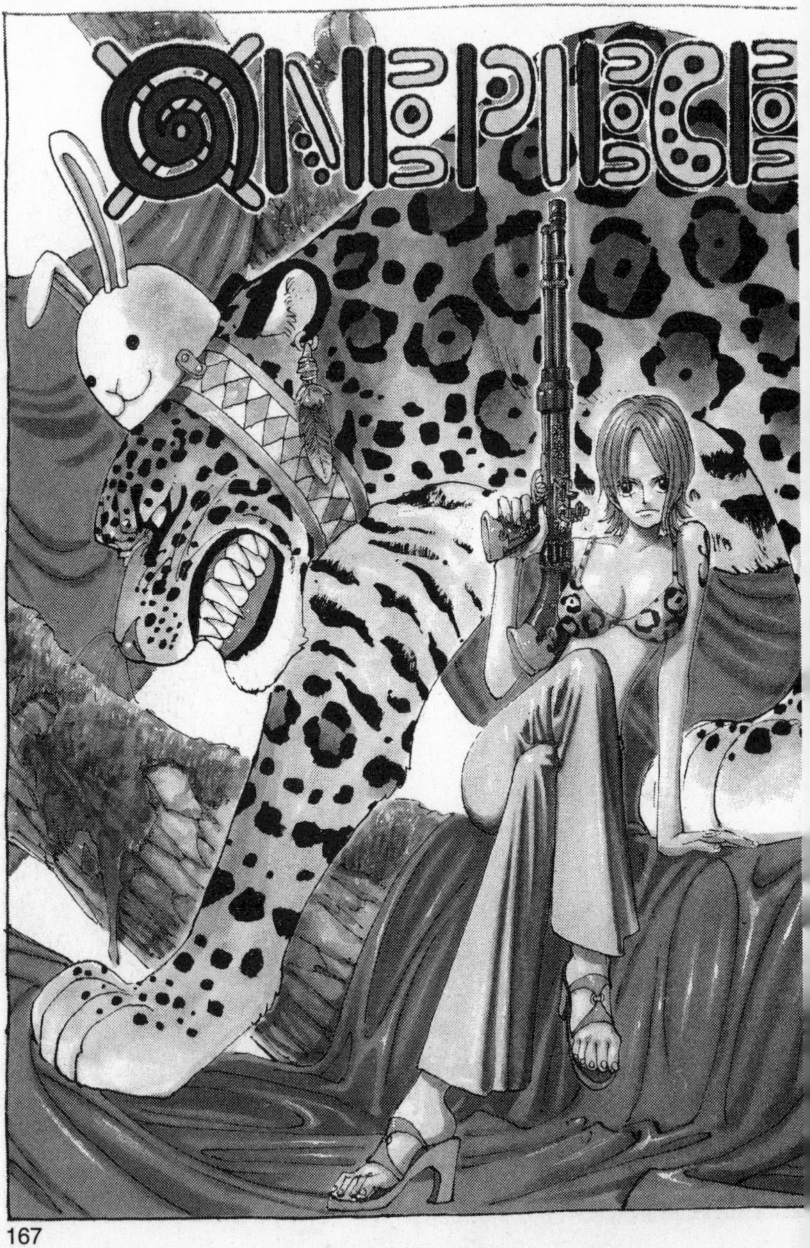
ONE PIECE

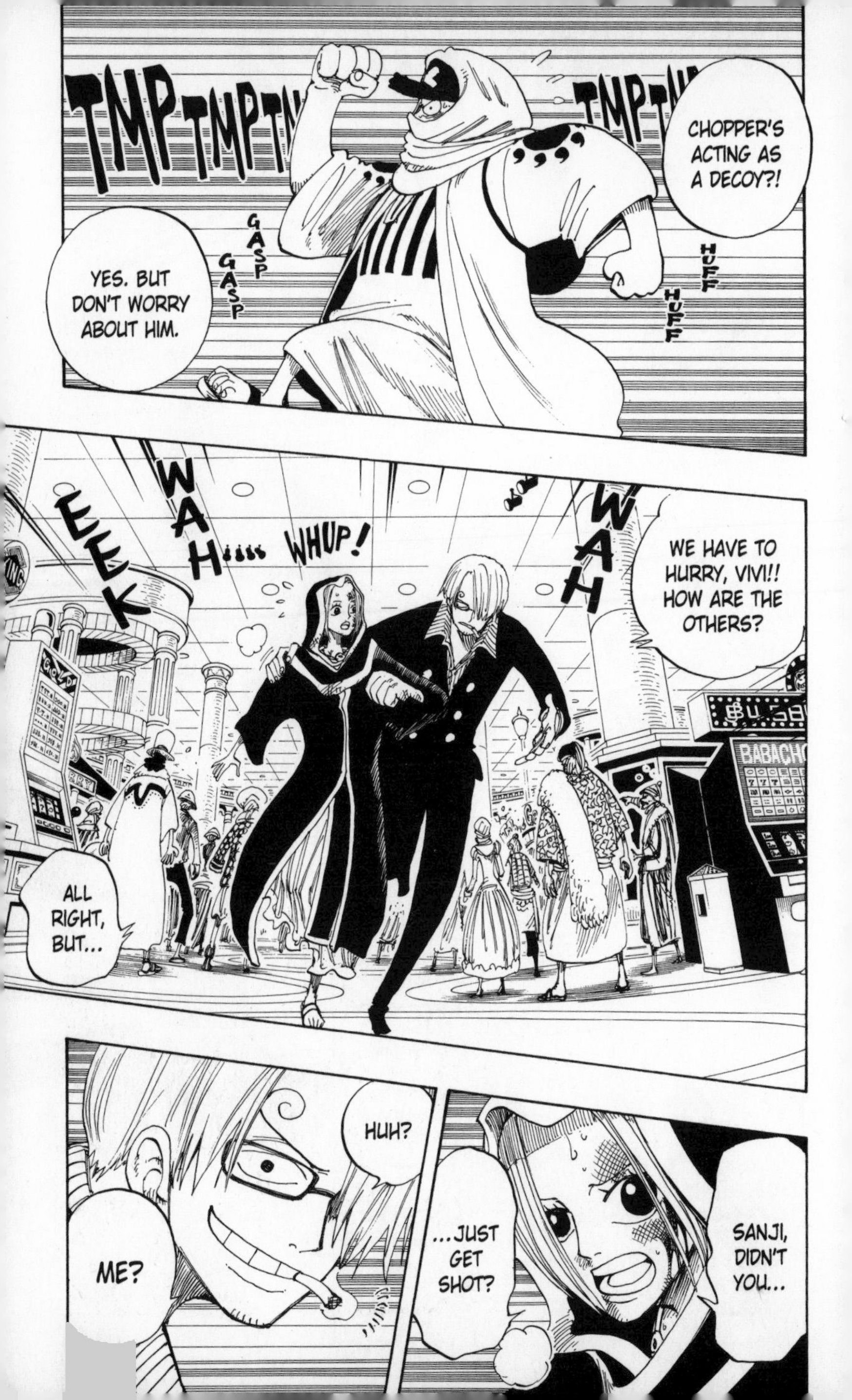

TMPTM
CHOPPER'S ACTING AS A DECOY?!
TMP TMPTM
HUFF HUFF
GASP GASP
YES. BUT DON'T WORRY ABOUT HIM.
WAH WAH
WE HAVE TO HURRY, VIVI!! HOW ARE THE OTHERS?
WHUP!
WAH...
EEK
BABACHO
GOLD
ALL RIGHT, BUT...
SANJI, DIDN'T YOU...
...JUST GET SHOT?
HUH?
ME?

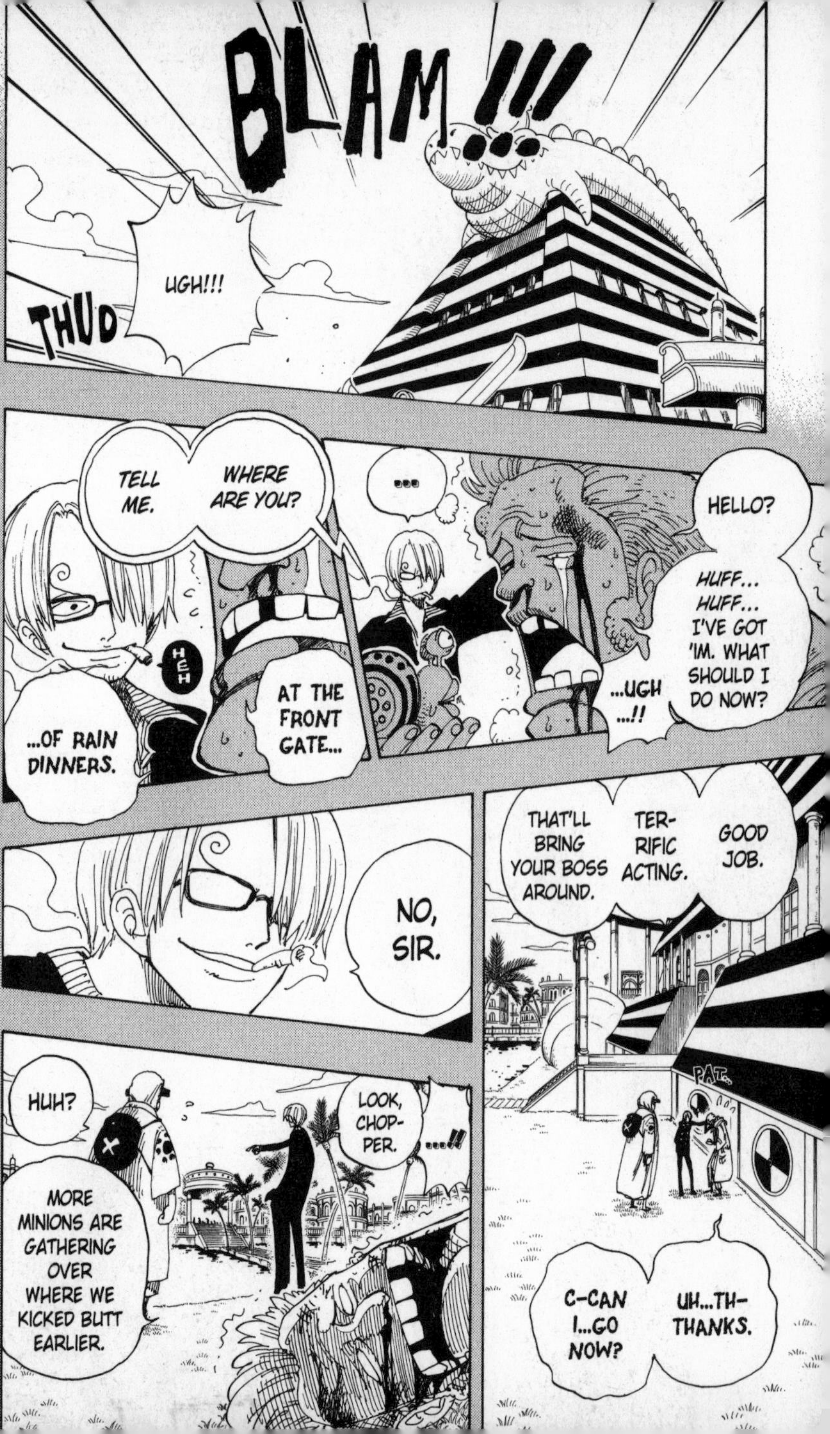
BLAM!!!
UGH!!!
THUD
HELLO?
HUFF... HUFF... I'VE GOT 'IM. WHAT SHOULD I DO NOW?
...UGH ...!!
...
WHERE ARE YOU?
TELL ME.
AT THE FRONT GATE...
HEH
...OF RAIN DINNERS.
GOOD JOB.
TER-RIFIC ACTING.
THAT'LL BRING YOUR BOSS AROUND.
PAT...
UH...TH-THANKS.
C-CAN I...GO NOW?
NO, SIR.
LOOK, CHOP-PER.
...!!
HUH?
MORE MINIONS ARE GATHERING OVER WHERE WE KICKED BUTT EARLIER.

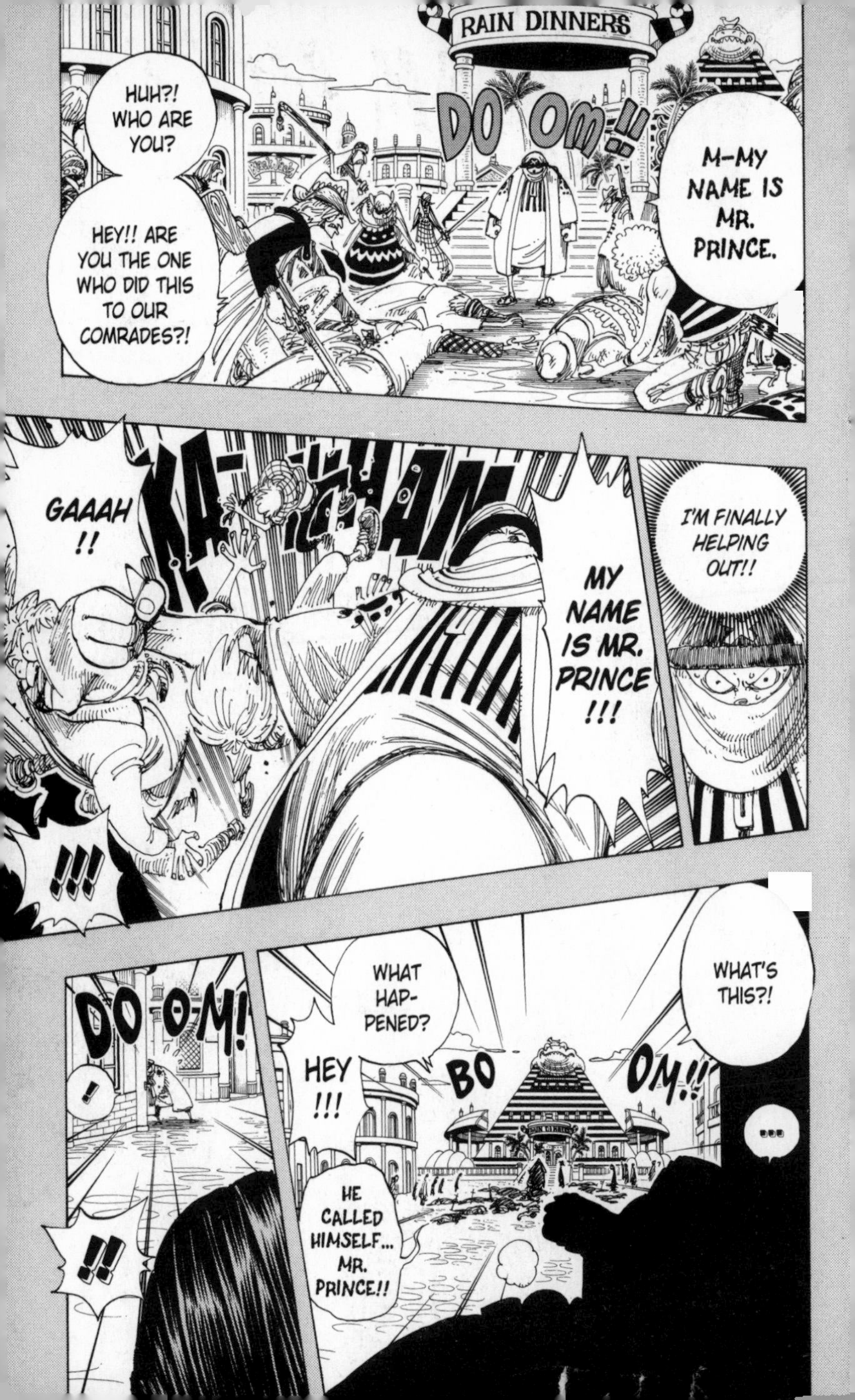
RAIN DINNERS
DOOM!!
M-MY NAME IS MR. PRINCE.
HUH?! WHO ARE YOU?
HEY!! ARE YOU THE ONE WHO DID THIS TO OUR COMRADES?!
I'M FINALLY HELPING OUT!!
MY NAME IS MR. PRINCE!!!
GAAAH!!
!!!
WHAT'S THIS?!
...
BOOM!!
WHAT HAPPENED?
HEY!!!
HE CALLED HIMSELF... MR. PRINCE!!
DOOM!
!
!!

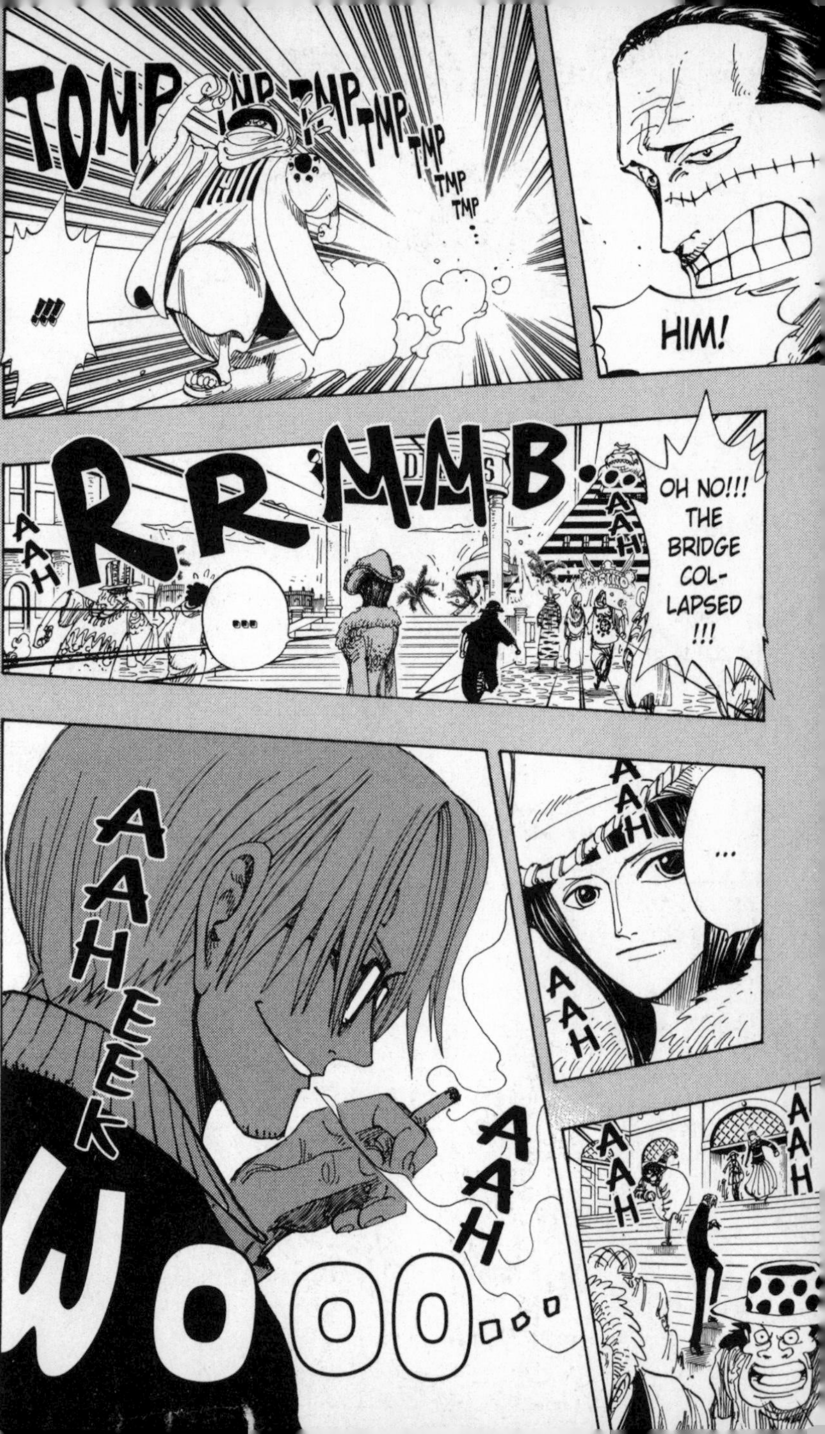
HIM!
TOMP
TMP TMP TMP TMP TMP TMP
!!!
OH NO!!! THE BRIDGE COL-LAPSED!!!
AAH
AAH
RRMMB
...
AAH
...
AAH
AAH
AAH
AAH
AAHEEEK
WOOOO...

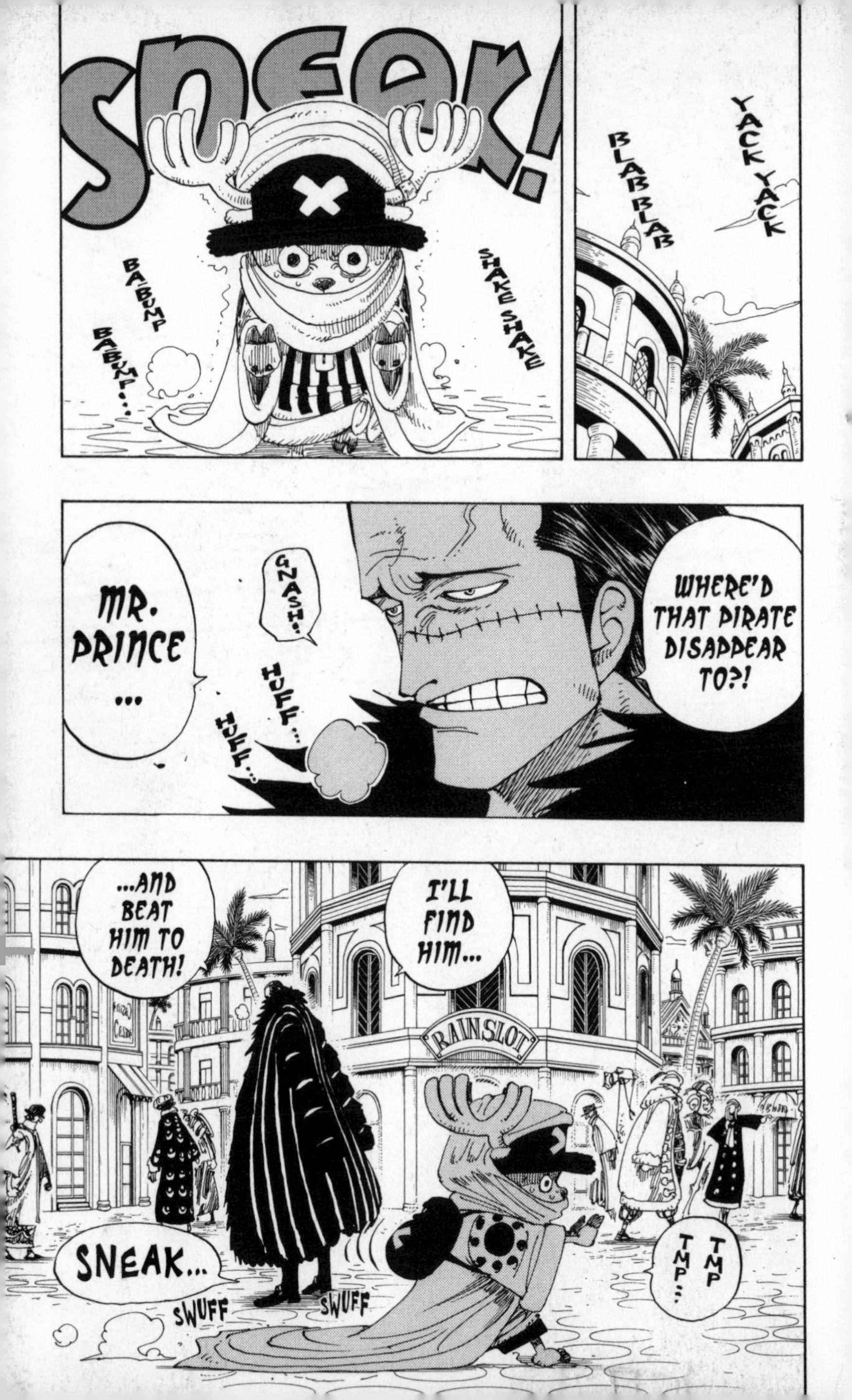
YACK YACK
BLAB BLAB
SNEAK!
SHAKE SHAKE
BA-BUMP
BA-BUMP...
WHERE'D THAT PIRATE DISAPPEAR TO?!
GNASH...
HUFF...
HUFF...
MR. PRINCE ...
I'LL FIND HIM...
...AND BEAT HIM TO DEATH!
RAINSLOT
TMP TMP...
SWUFF
SWUFF
SNEAK...

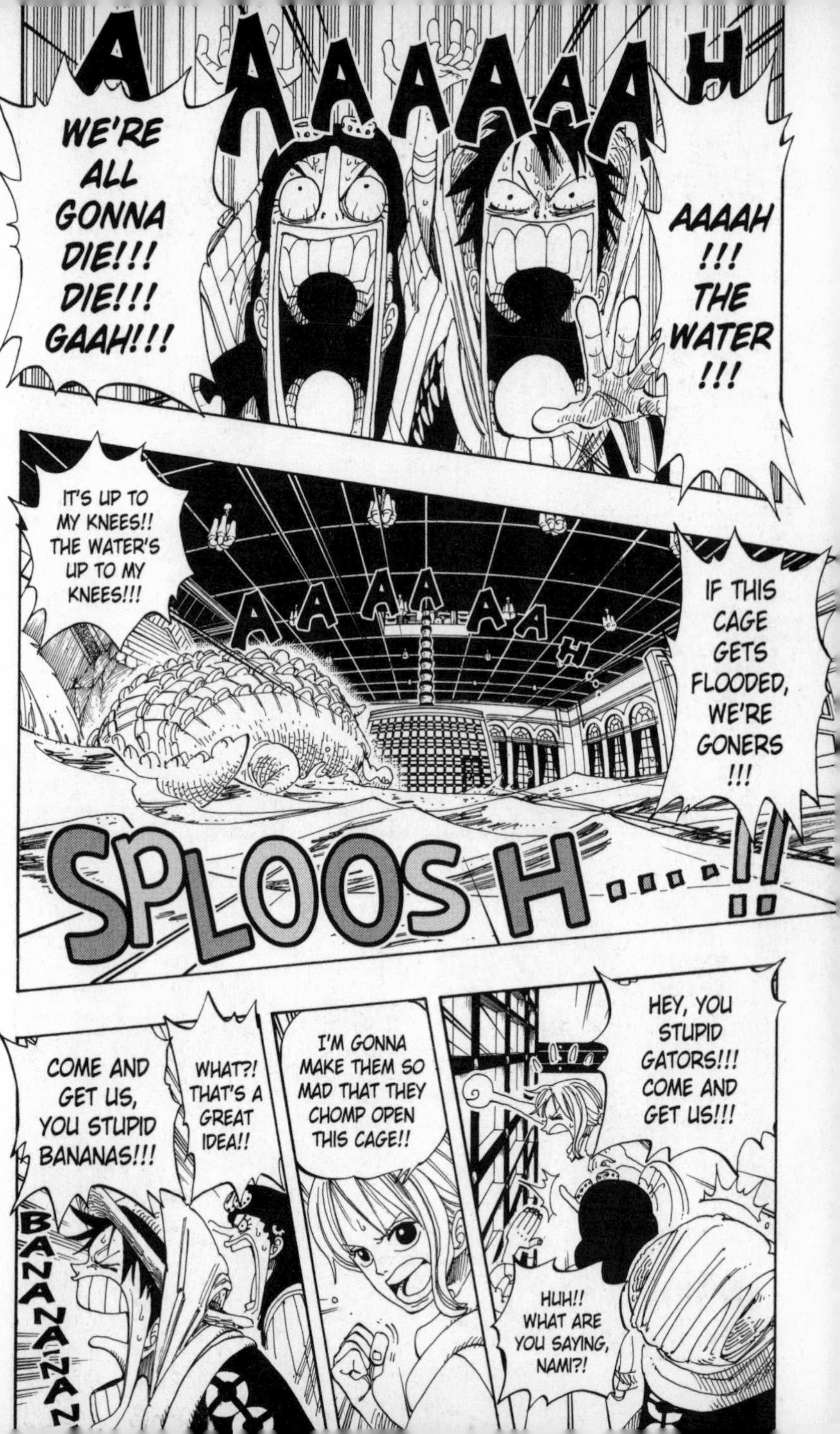
AAAAAAAH
AAAAH!!! THE WATER!!!
WE'RE ALL GONNA DIE!!! DIE!!! GAAH!!!
IF THIS CAGE GETS FLOODED, WE'RE GONERS!!!
AAAAAAH
IT'S UP TO MY KNEES!! THE WATER'S UP TO MY KNEES!!!
SPLOOSH....!!
HEY, YOU STUPID GATORS!!! COME AND GET US!!!
HUH!! WHAT ARE YOU SAYING, NAMI?!
I'M GONNA MAKE THEM SO MAD THAT THEY CHOMP OPEN THIS CAGE!!
WHAT?! THAT'S A GREAT IDEA!!
COME AND GET US, YOU STUPID BANANAS!!!
BANANANANAN

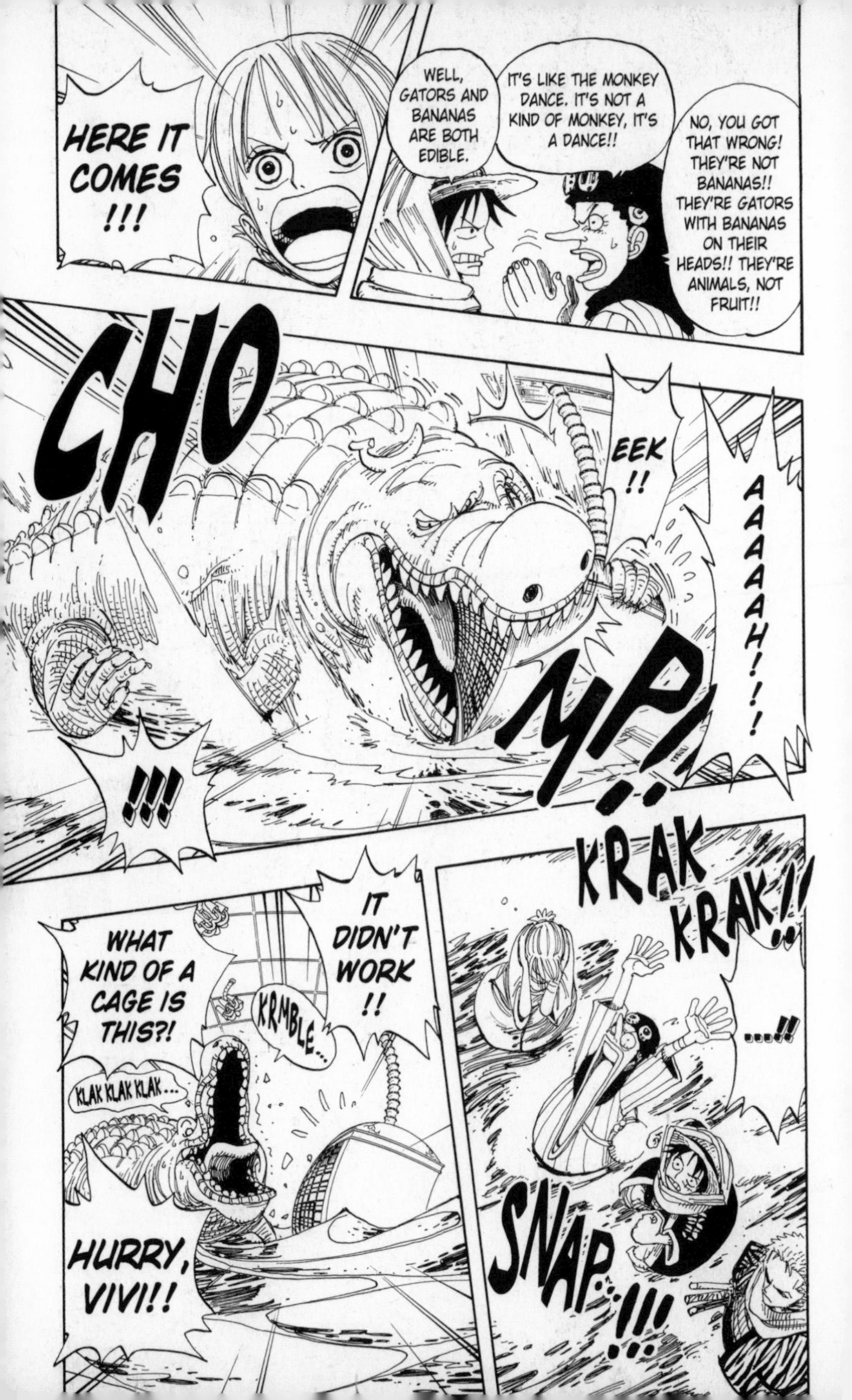
NO, YOU GOT THAT WRONG! THEY'RE NOT BANANAS!! THEY'RE GATORS WITH BANANAS ON THEIR HEADS!! THEY'RE ANIMALS, NOT FRUIT!!
IT'S LIKE THE MONKEY DANCE. IT'S NOT A KIND OF MONKEY, IT'S A DANCE!!
WELL, GATORS AND BANANAS ARE BOTH EDIBLE.
HERE IT COMES!!!
AAAAAAH!!!
EEK!!
CHO
MP!!
!!!
KRAK KRAK!!
...!!
SNAP!!!
IT DIDN'T WORK!!
KRMBLE...
WHAT KIND OF A CAGE IS THIS?!
KLAK KLAK KLAK...
HURRY, VIVI!!

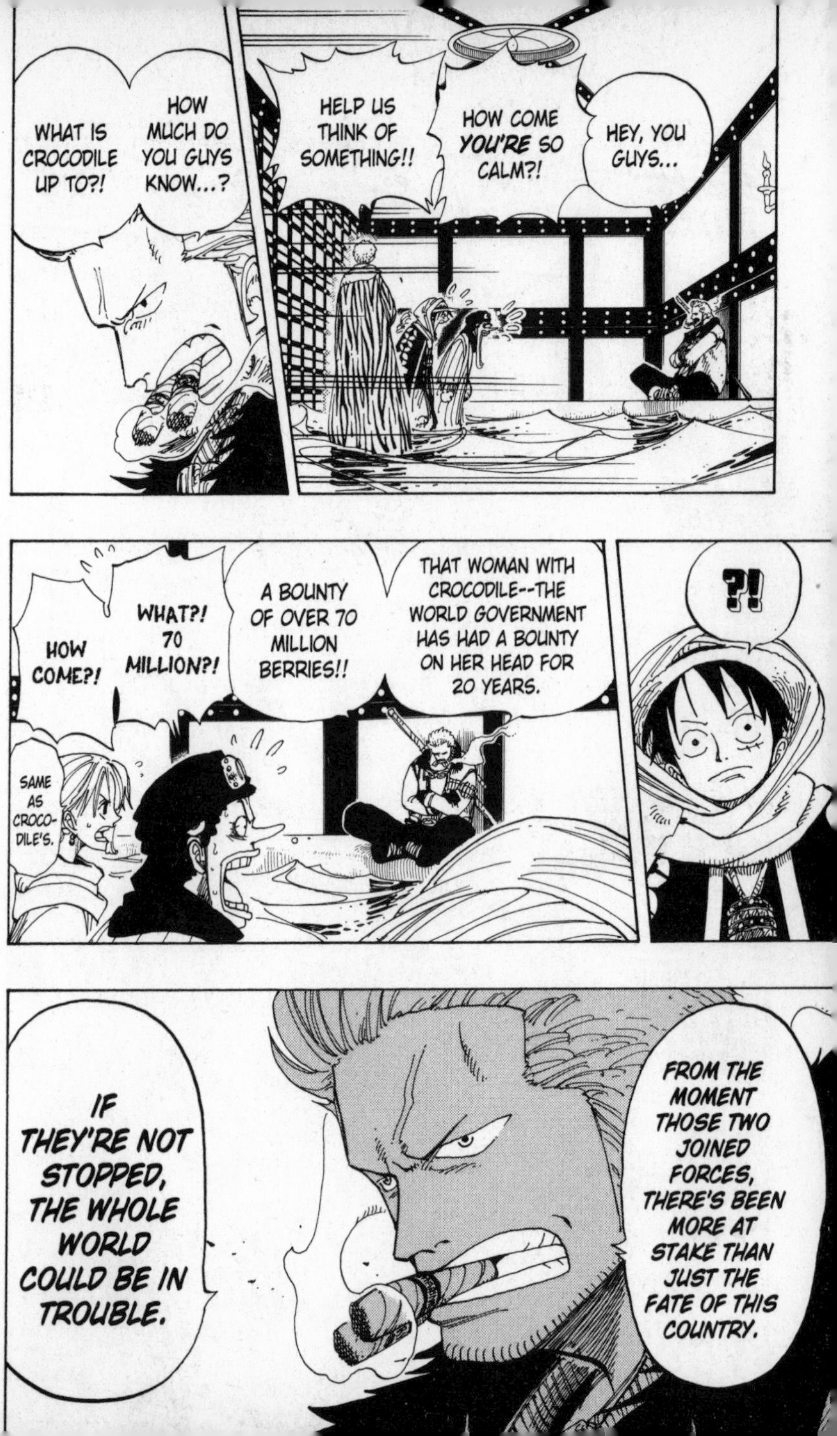
HEY, YOU GUYS...
HOW COME YOU'RE SO CALM?!
HELP US THINK OF SOMETHING!!
HOW MUCH DO YOU GUYS KNOW...?
WHAT IS CROCODILE UP TO?!
?!
THAT WOMAN WITH CROCODILE--THE WORLD GOVERNMENT HAS HAD A BOUNTY ON HER HEAD FOR 20 YEARS.
A BOUNTY OF OVER 70 MILLION BERRIES!!
WHAT?! 70 MILLION?!
HOW COME?!
SAME AS CROCO-DILE'S.
FROM THE MOMENT THOSE TWO JOINED FORCES, THERE'S BEEN MORE AT STAKE THAN JUST THE FATE OF THIS COUNTRY.
IF THEY'RE NOT STOPPED, THE WHOLE WORLD COULD BE IN TROUBLE.

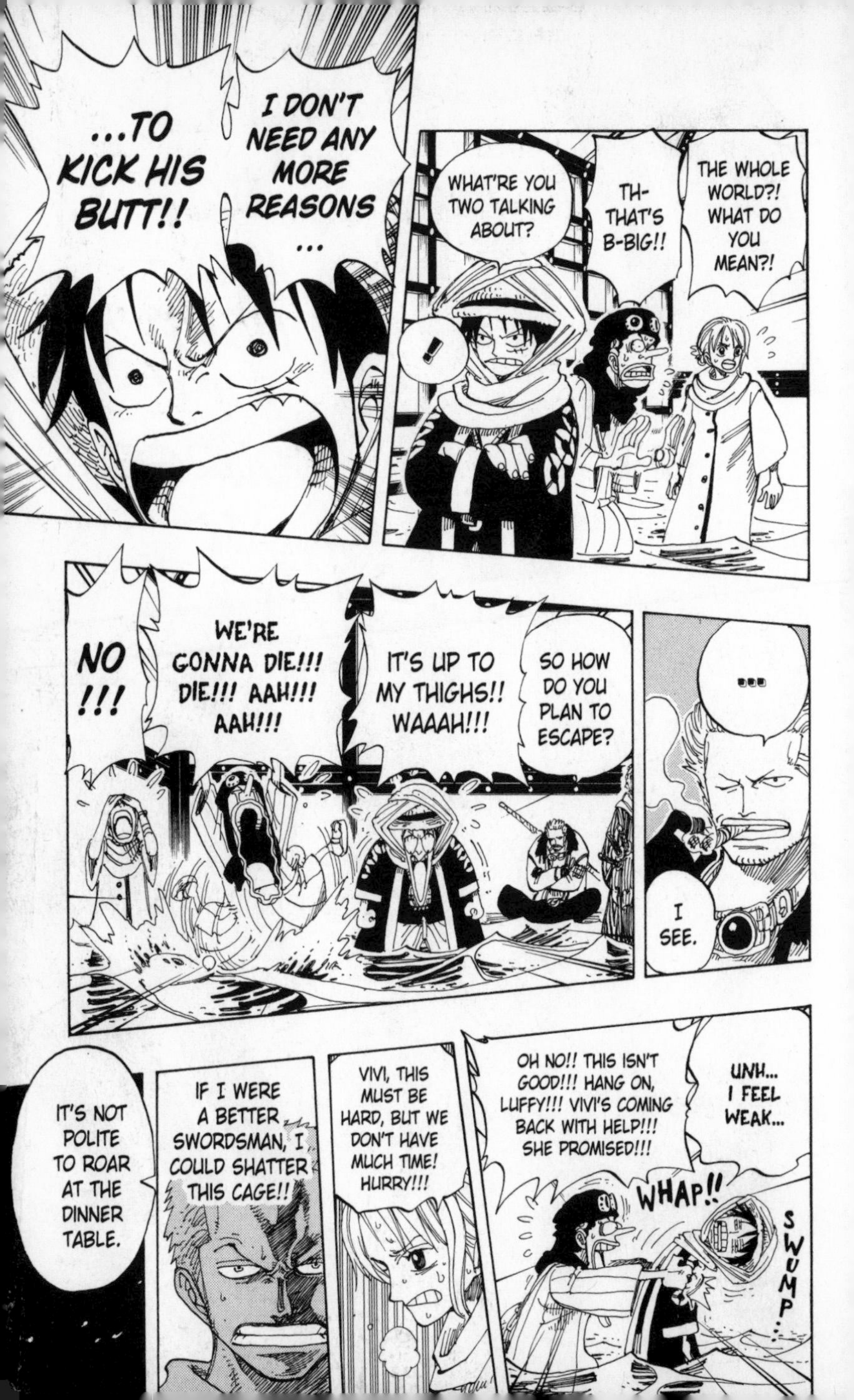
I DON'T NEED ANY MORE REASONS ...
...TO KICK HIS BUTT!!
THE WHOLE WORLD?! WHAT DO YOU MEAN?!
TH- THAT'S B-BIG!!
WHAT'RE YOU TWO TALKING ABOUT?
!
...
I SEE.
SO HOW DO YOU PLAN TO ESCAPE?
IT'S UP TO MY THIGHS!! WAAAH!!!
WE'RE GONNA DIE!!! DIE!!! AAH!!! AAH!!!
NO !!!
UNH... I FEEL WEAK...
OH NO!! THIS ISN'T GOOD!!! HANG ON, LUFFY!!! VIVI'S COMING BACK WITH HELP!!! SHE PROMISED!!!
SWUMP..!
WHAP!!
VIVI, THIS MUST BE HARD, BUT WE DON'T HAVE MUCH TIME! HURRY!!!
IF I WERE A BETTER SWORDSMAN, I COULD SHATTER THIS CAGE!!
IT'S NOT POLITE TO ROAR AT THE DINNER TABLE.

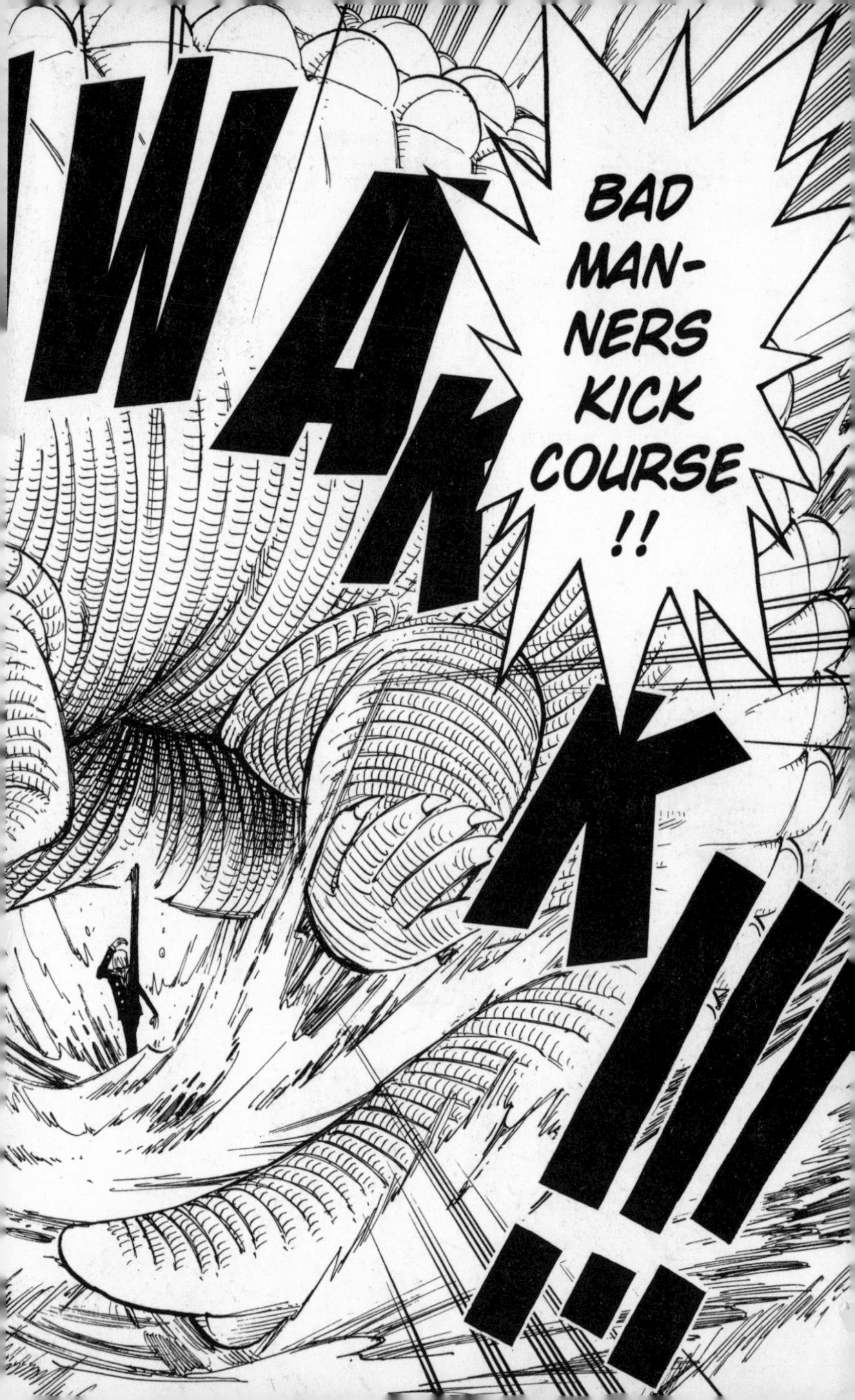
WHAK!!
BAD MAN-NERS KICK COURSE!!

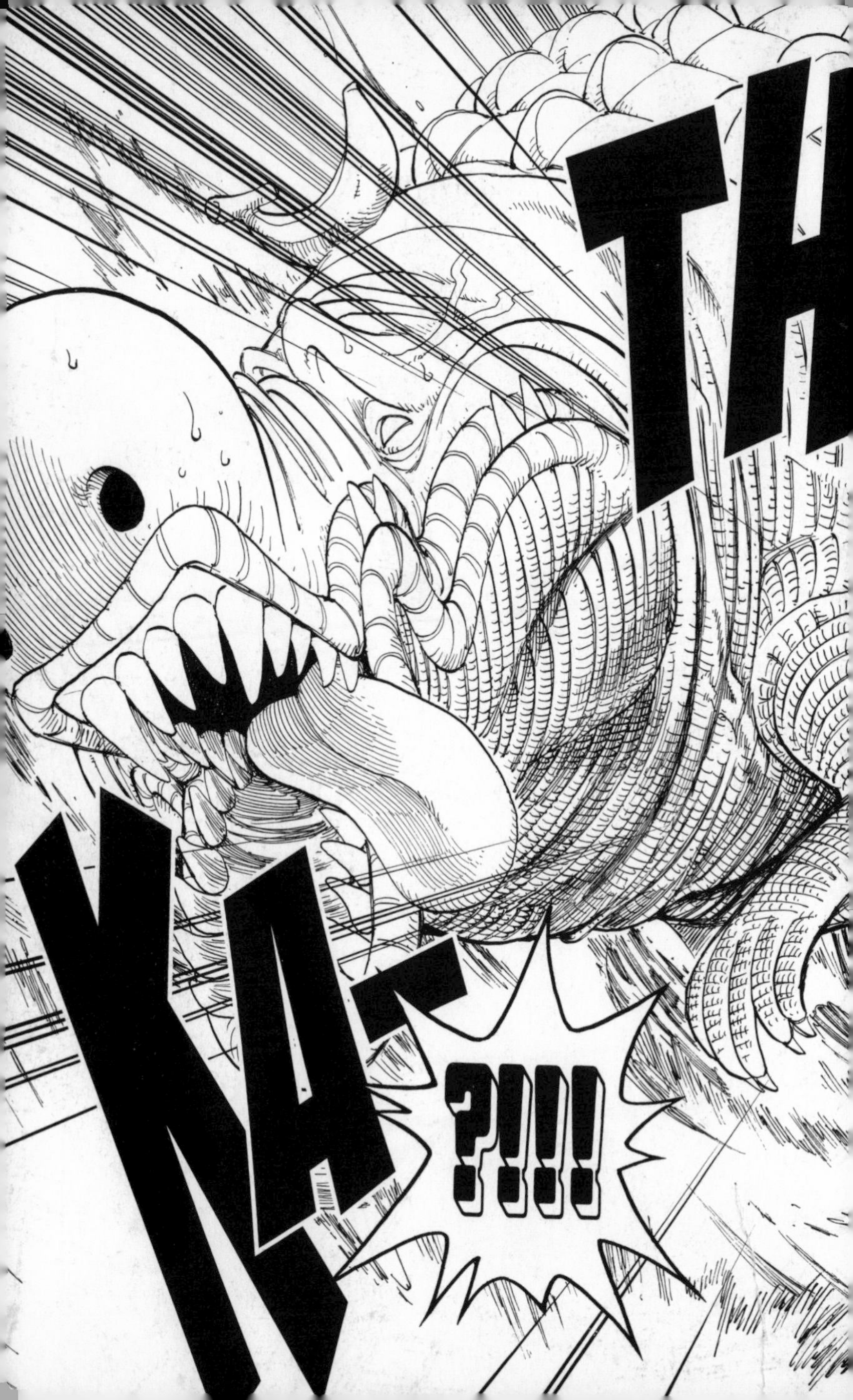
TH
KA-
?!!!

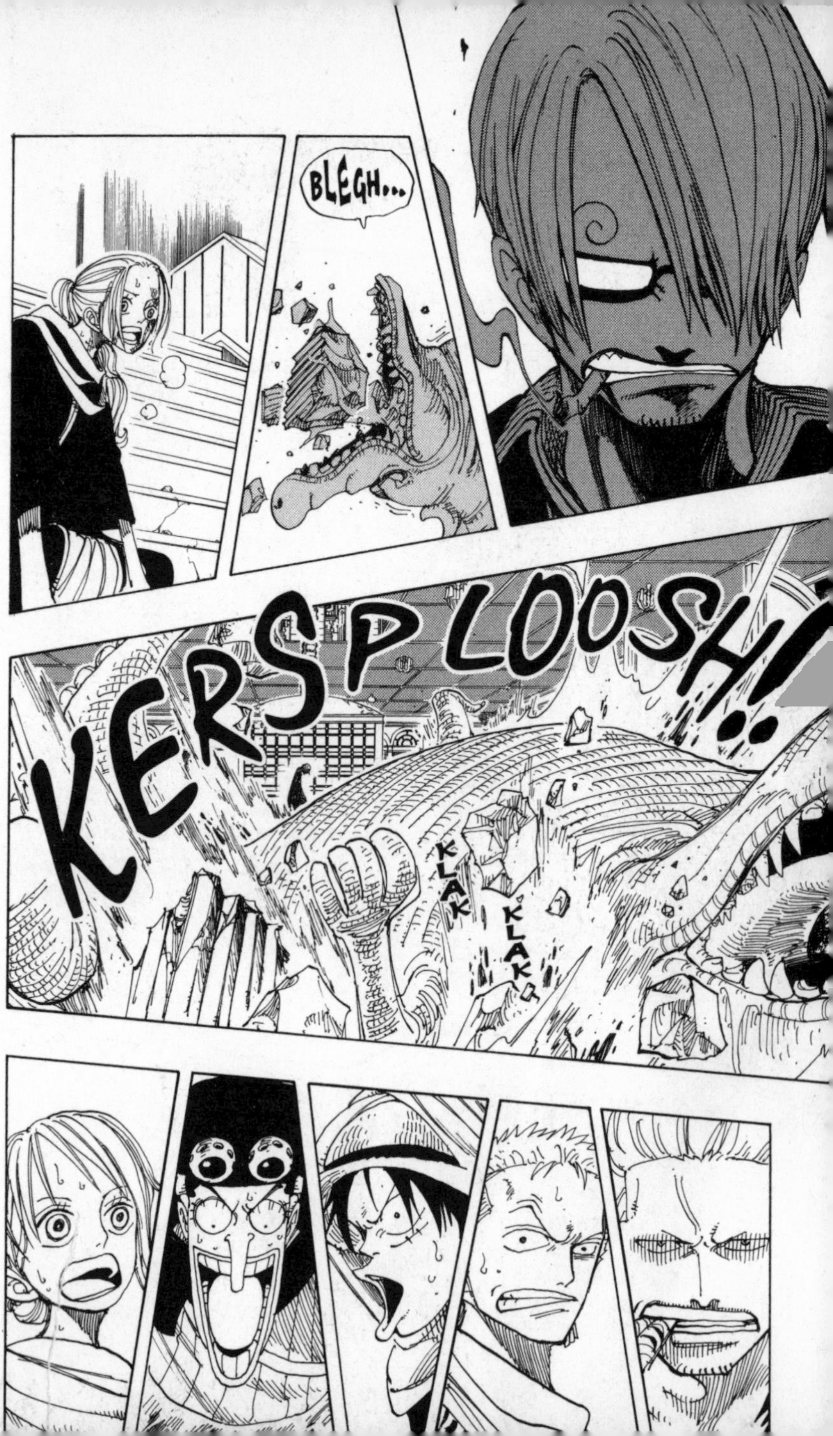
BLEGH...
KERSPLOOSH!!
KLAK
KLAK

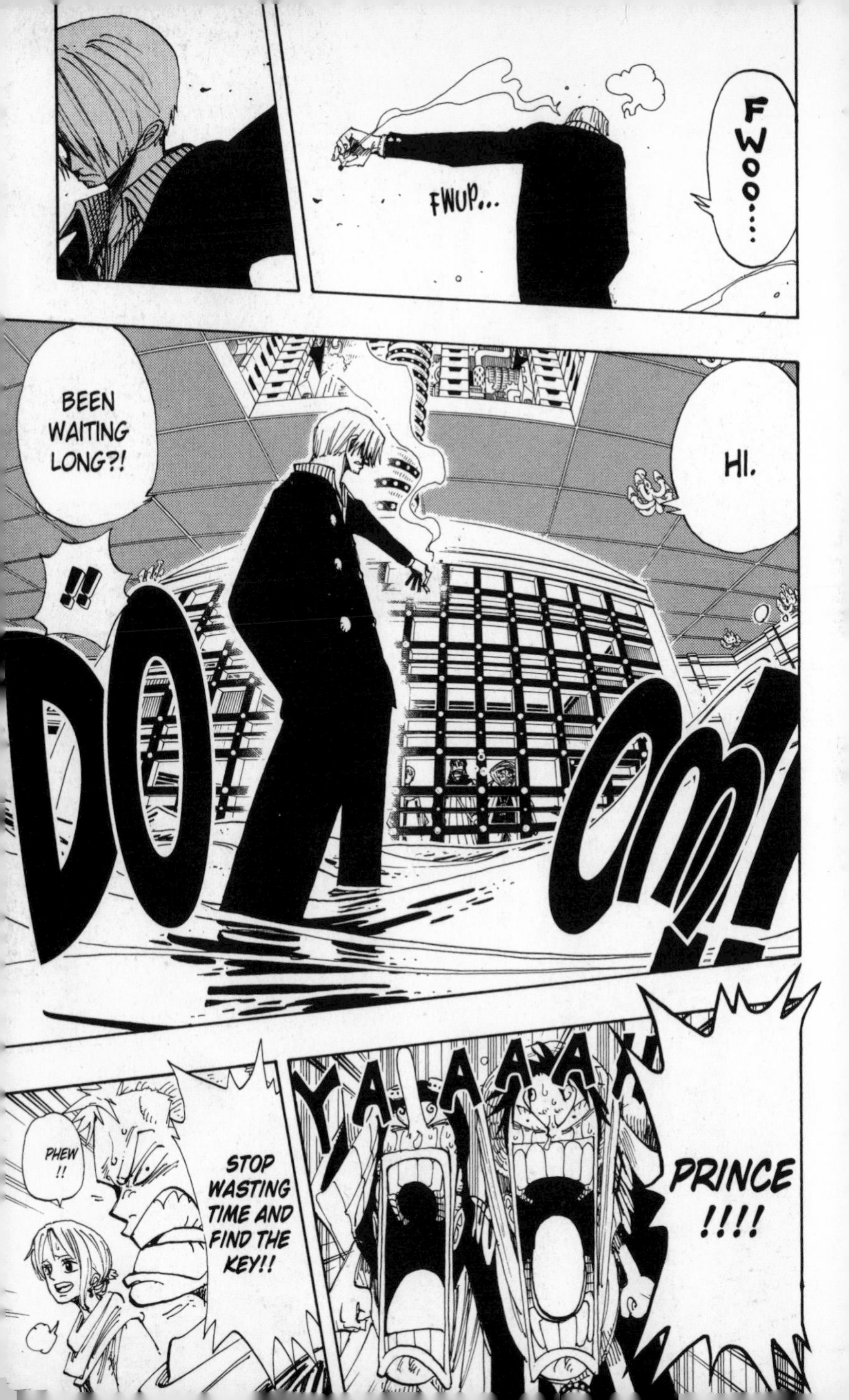
FWOO....
FWUP...
HI.
BEEN WAITING LONG?!
!!
DOOM!
YAAAAH
PRINCE !!!!
STOP WASTING TIME AND FIND THE KEY!!
PHEW !!

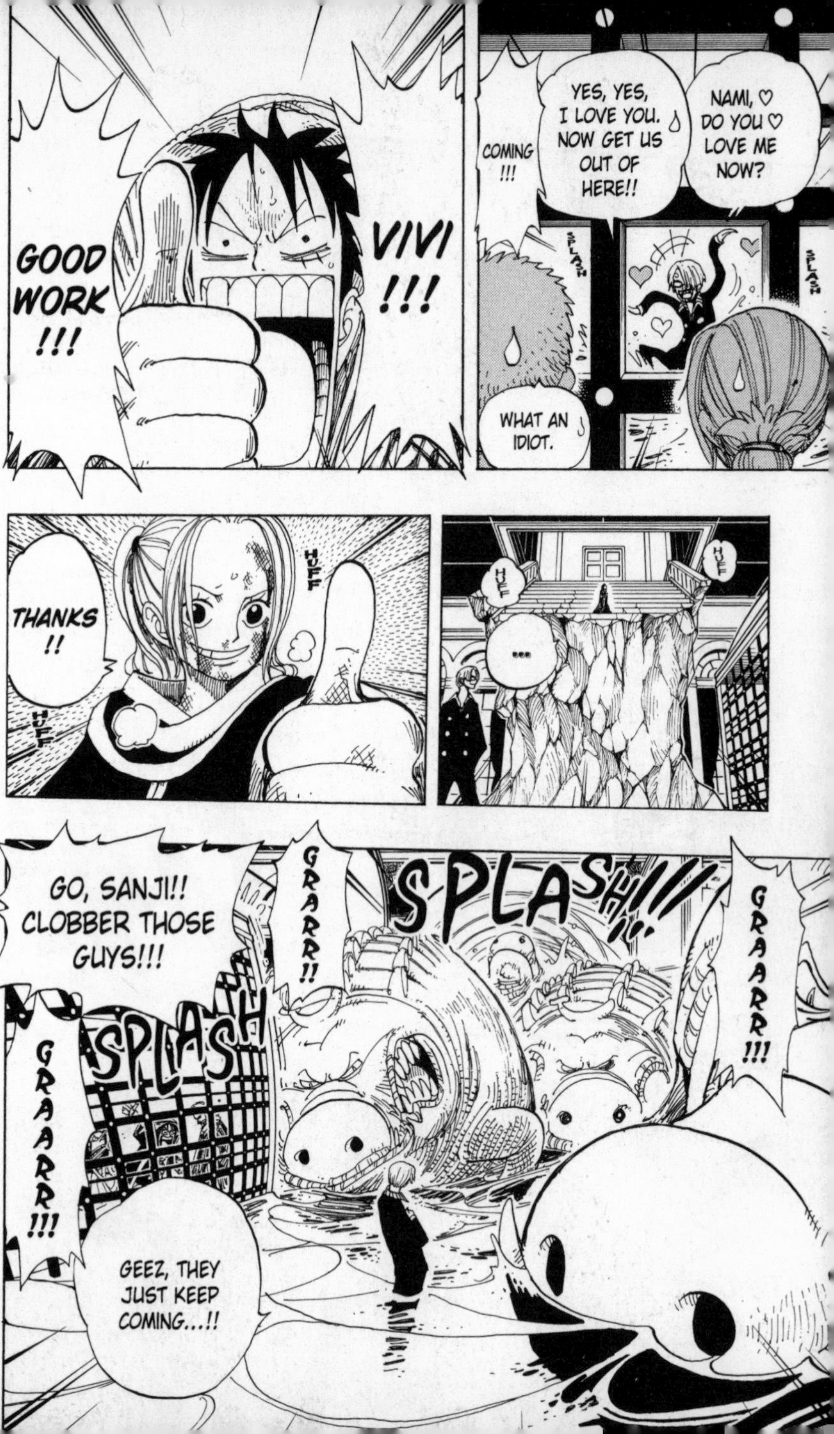
NAMI, ♡ DO YOU ♡ LOVE ME NOW?
YES, YES, I LOVE YOU. NOW GET US OUT OF HERE!!
COMING !!!
SPLASH
SPLASH
WHAT AN IDIOT.
VIVI !!!
GOOD WORK !!!
HUFF
HUFF
...
HUFF
THANKS !!
HUFF
GRAAARR !!!
SPLASH!!!
GRAARR !!
GO, SANJI!! CLOBBER THOSE GUYS!!!
SPLASH
GRAAARR !!!
GEEZ, THEY JUST KEEP COMING...!!

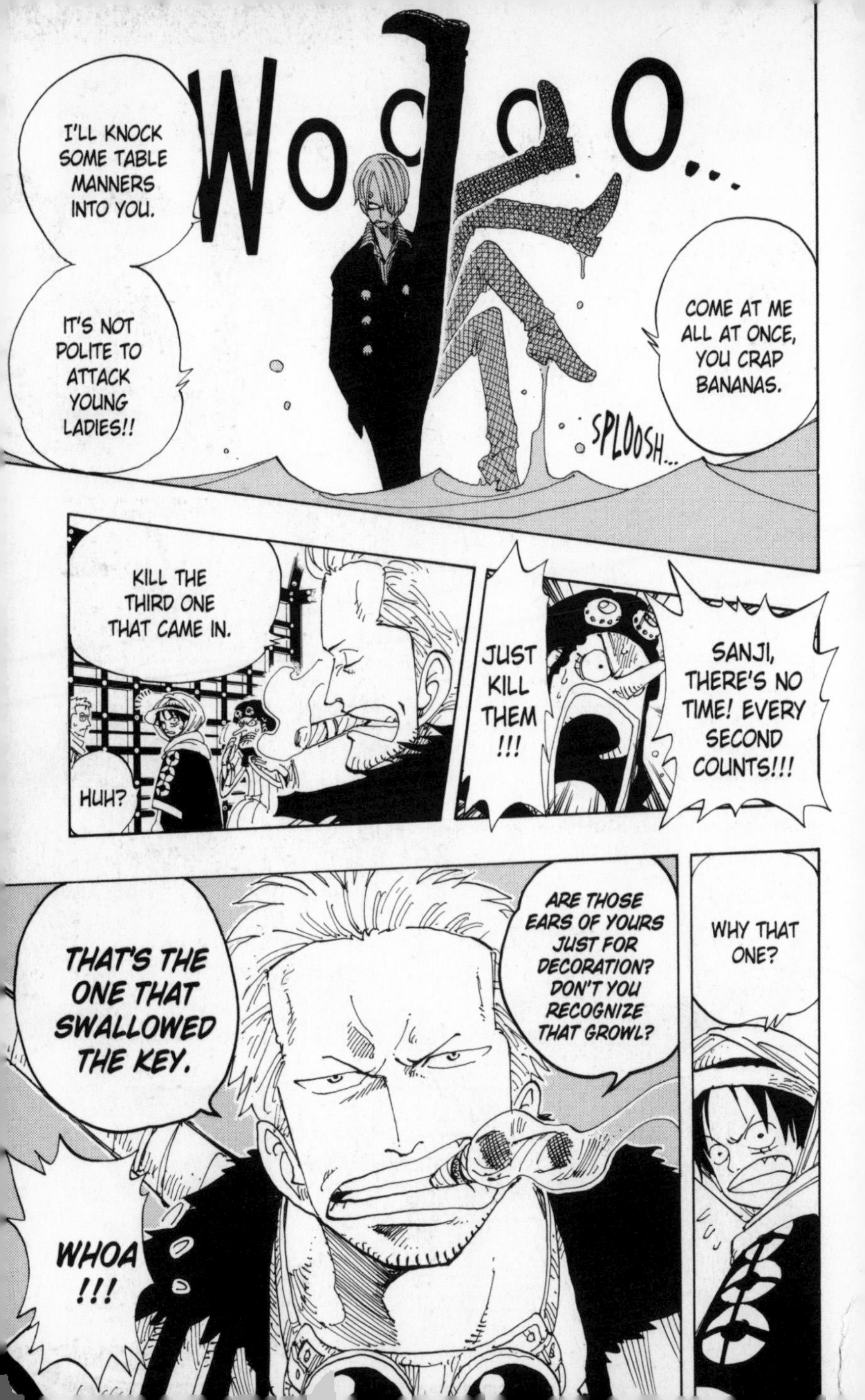
Wodooo...
I'LL KNOCK SOME TABLE MANNERS INTO YOU.
IT'S NOT POLITE TO ATTACK YOUNG LADIES!!
COME AT ME ALL AT ONCE, YOU CRAP BANANAS.
SPLOOSH...
SANJI, THERE'S NO TIME! EVERY SECOND COUNTS!!!
JUST KILL THEM!!!
KILL THE THIRD ONE THAT CAME IN.
HUH?
WHY THAT ONE?
ARE THOSE EARS OF YOURS JUST FOR DECORATION? DON'T YOU RECOGNIZE THAT GROWL?
THAT'S THE ONE THAT SWALLOWED THE KEY.
WHOA!!!

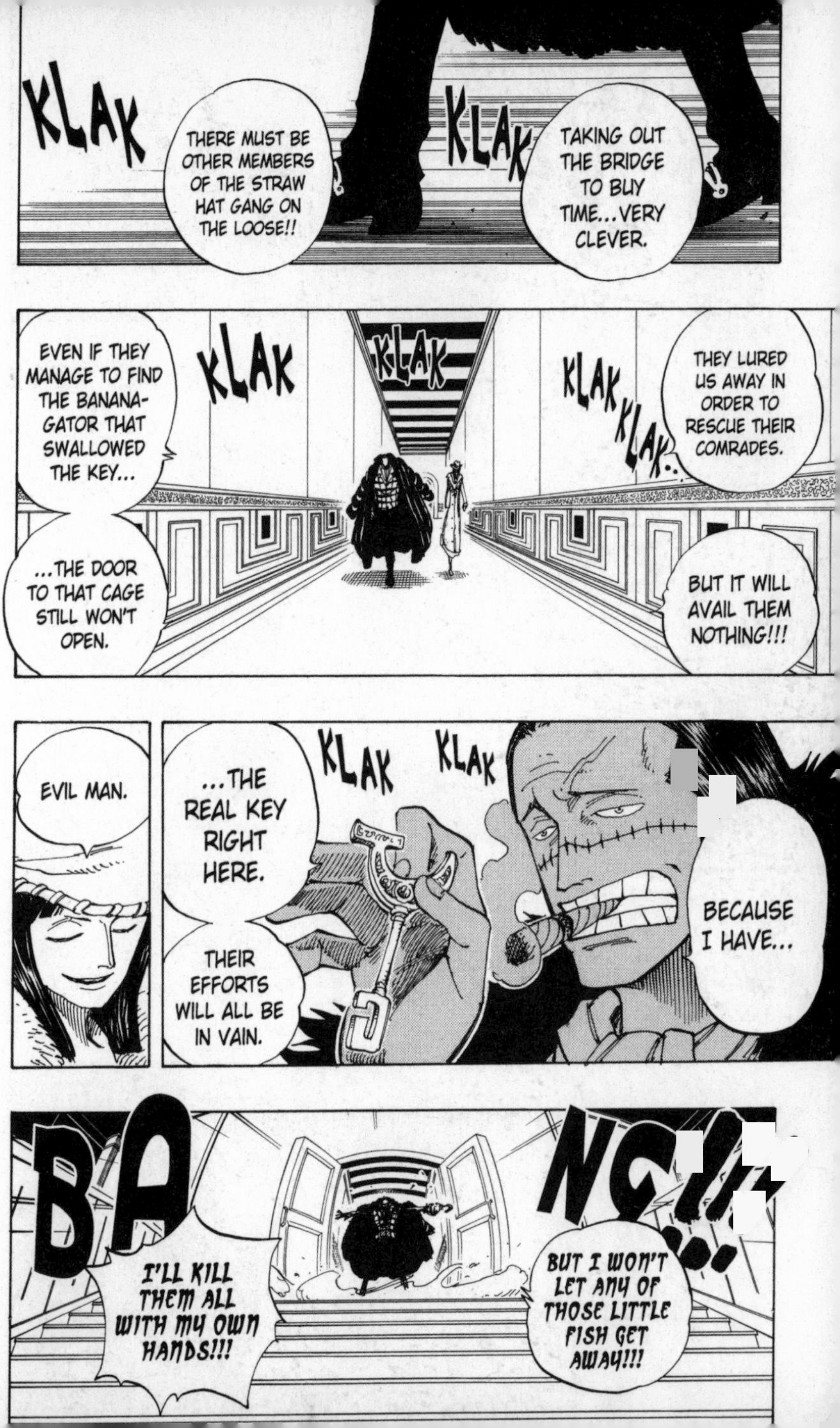
TAKING OUT THE BRIDGE TO BUY TIME...VERY CLEVER.
KLAK
THERE MUST BE OTHER MEMBERS OF THE STRAW HAT GANG ON THE LOOSE!!
KLAK
THEY LURED US AWAY IN ORDER TO RESCUE THEIR COMRADES.
KLAK KLAK..
BUT IT WILL AVAIL THEM NOTHING!!!
KLAK
KLAK
EVEN IF THEY MANAGE TO FIND THE BANANA-GATOR THAT SWALLOWED THE KEY...
...THE DOOR TO THAT CAGE STILL WON'T OPEN.
BECAUSE I HAVE...
KLAK
KLAK
...THE REAL KEY RIGHT HERE.
THEIR EFFORTS WILL ALL BE IN VAIN.
EVIL MAN.
BANG!!...
BUT I WON'T LET ANY OF THOSE LITTLE FISH GET AWAY!!!
I'LL KILL THEM ALL WITH MY OWN HANDS!!!

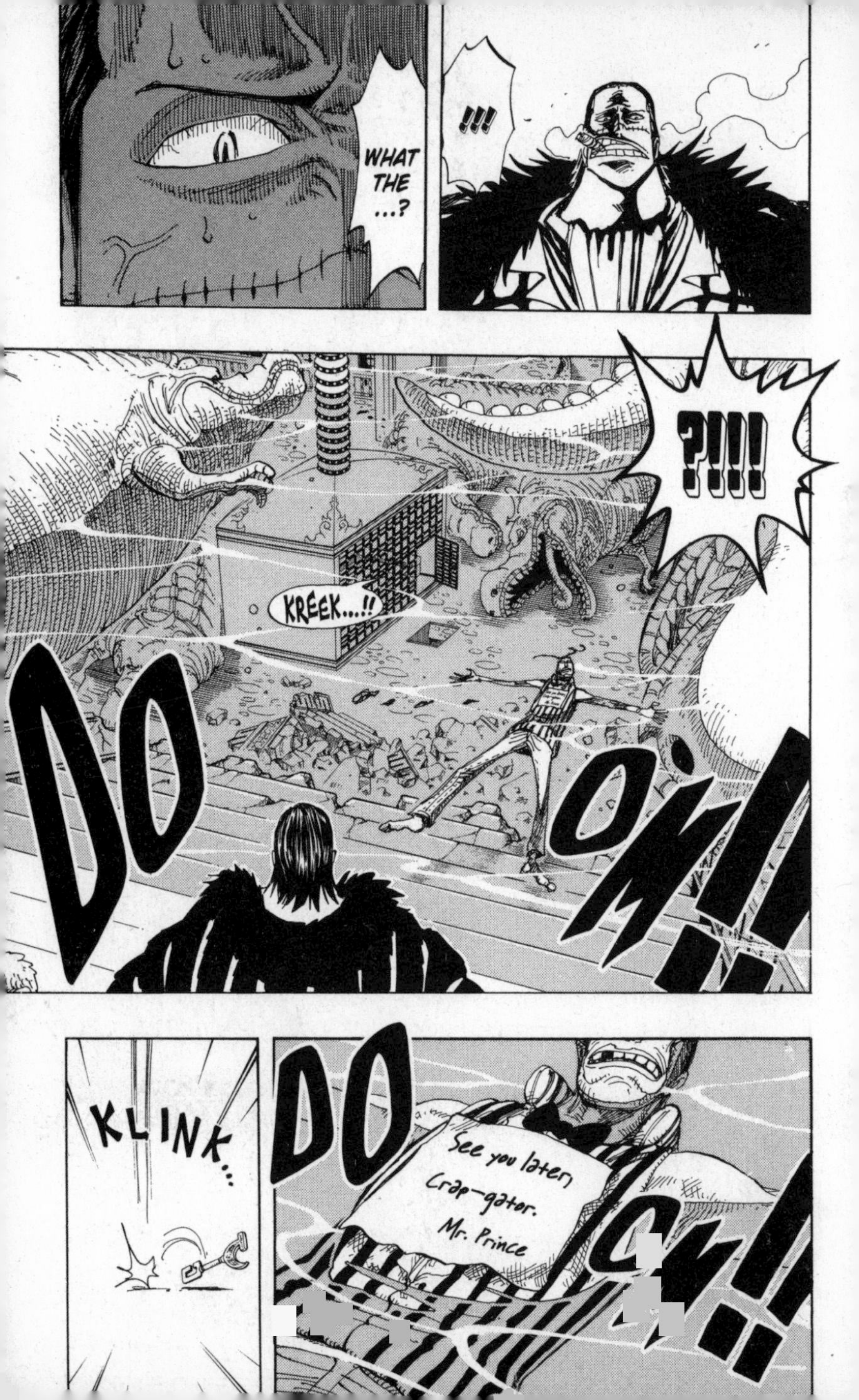
!!!
WHAT THE ...?
?!!!
KREEK...!!
DO
ON!!
DO
ON!!
See you later, Crap-gator. Mr. Prince
KLINK...

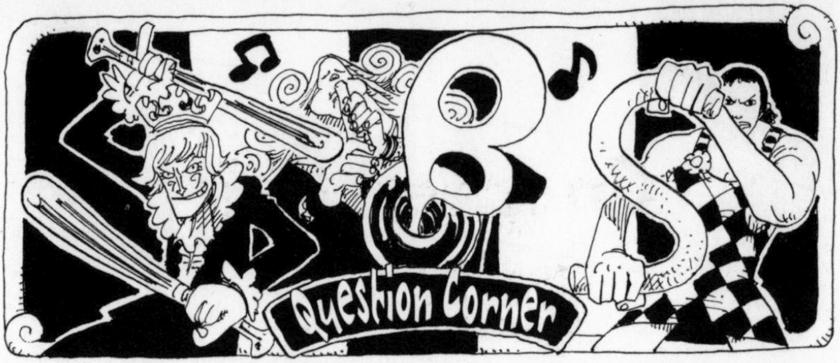
Question Corner

**Reader:** Howdy! Well, if it ain't that Eiichiro Oda kid! Thought I rec'nized y'all. Ya sure have grown! What? Ya think I'm cute? None of that now, ya hear?! But I'll leave you some onions and potatoes. Share 'em with yer friends.

--Belle of Kesennuma.

**Oda:** Y'all talk that Miyagi dialect. I cain't understand nothin' you said.

The General of Higo

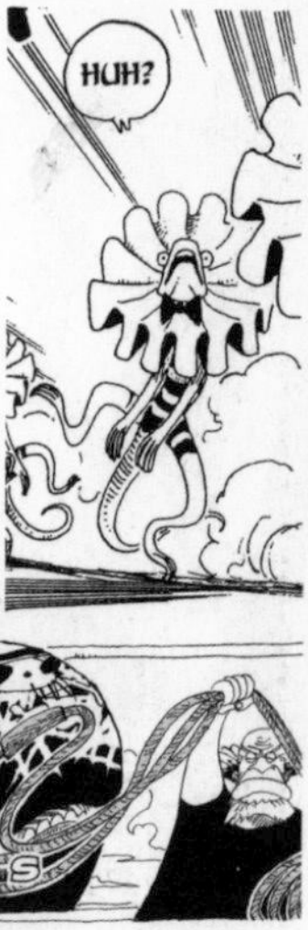
HUH?

**Reader:** Oda-san, one of the Lizard Runners from page 110 of Vol. 18 isn't wearing a tag on its neck. Why not? Bye now!

--Professor of Ancient Civilizations, Fourth Year

**Oda:** You're right. That one isn't carrying a message. Maybe that's why it's saying, "Huh?" as in "Huh? Why am I running?" Baroque Works will fire him, of course.

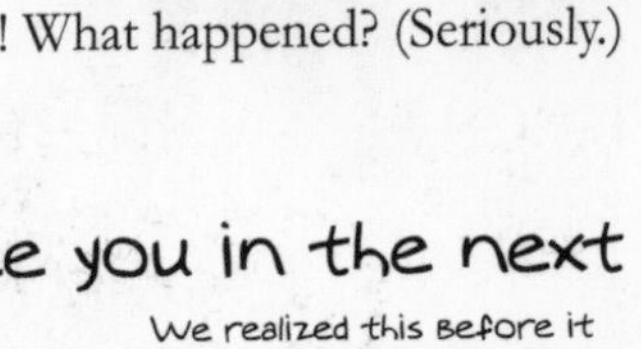
S B S

**Reader:** How do you do, Oda Sensei? Let me get right to the point. In Vol. 18, Crocus made a mistake. The two S's in SBS are written backwards!! Ha ha ha ha!! What happened? (Seriously.) Mr. Crocus? Well?

--Akiko

**Oda:** Uh-oh!! Um, well, see you in the next volume!! Sayonara!!

We realized this before it hit the store shelves, but it woulda been a pain to fix it.

# Chapter 176: RUSH!!

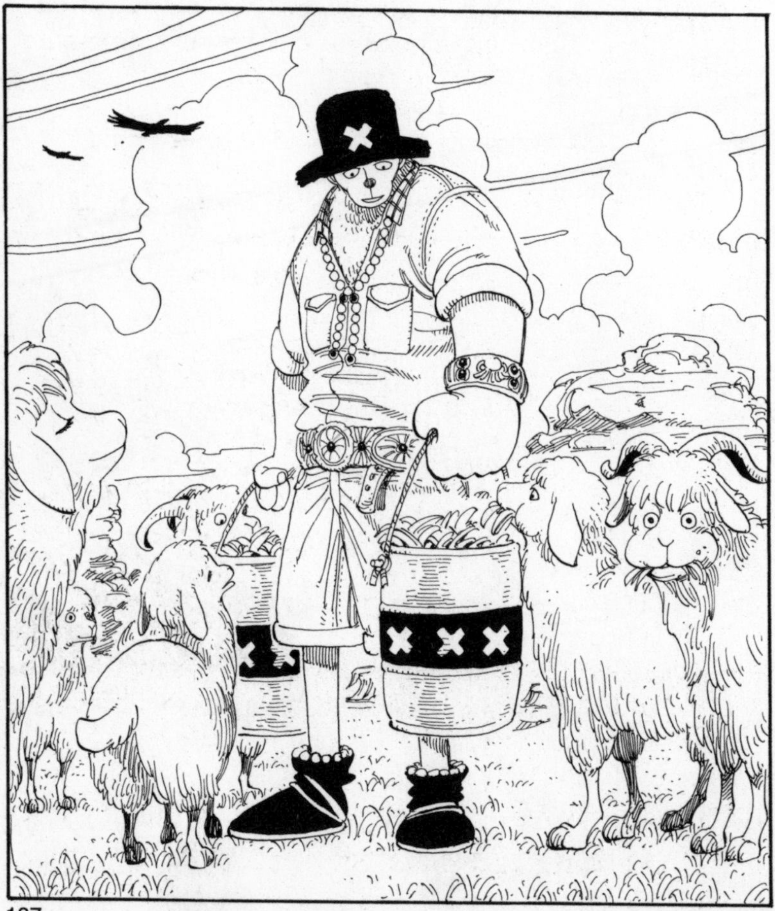

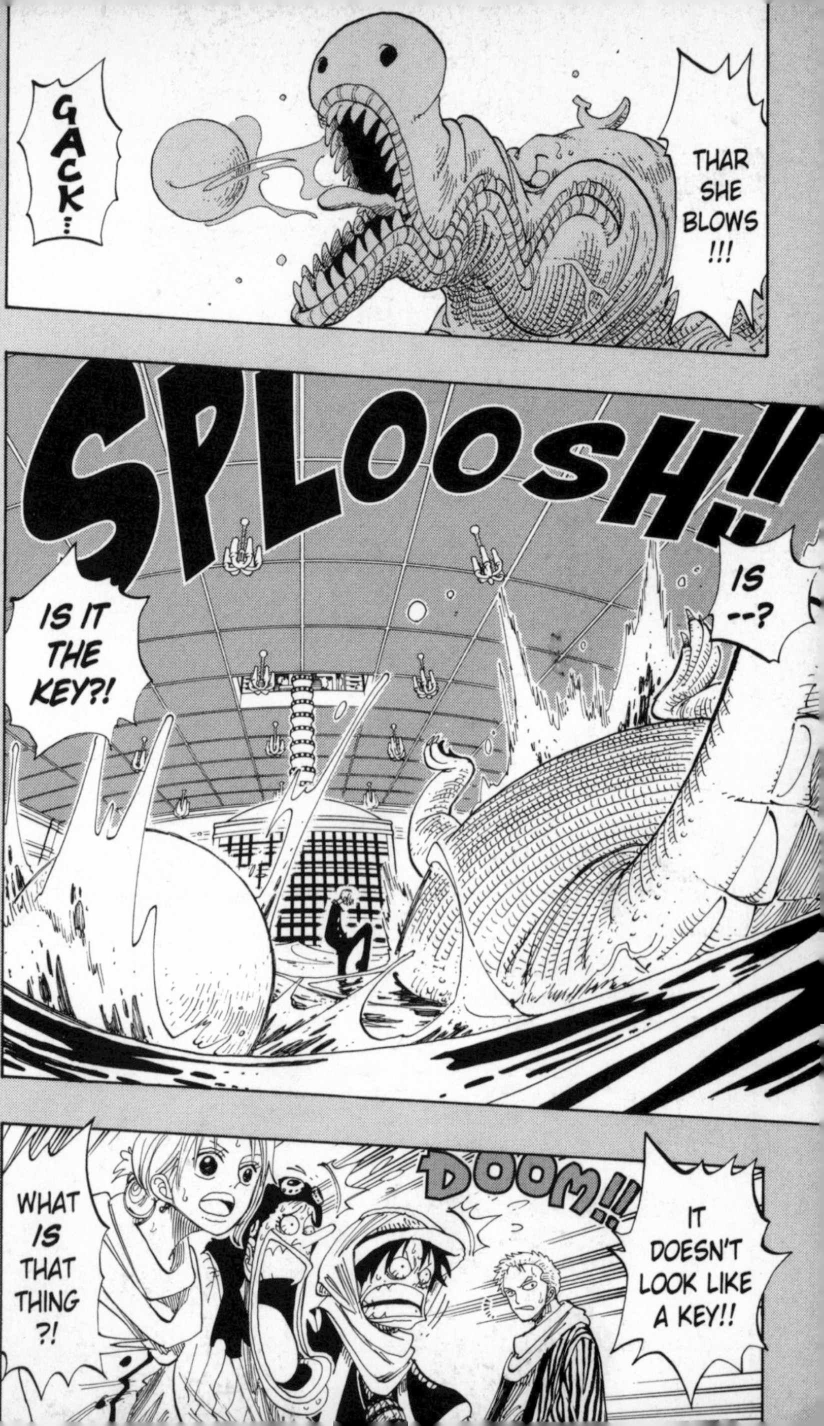
THAR SHE BLOWS!!!
GACK...
SPLOOSH!!
IS --?
IS IT THE KEY?!
DOOM!!
IT DOESN'T LOOK LIKE A KEY!!
WHAT IS THAT THING?!

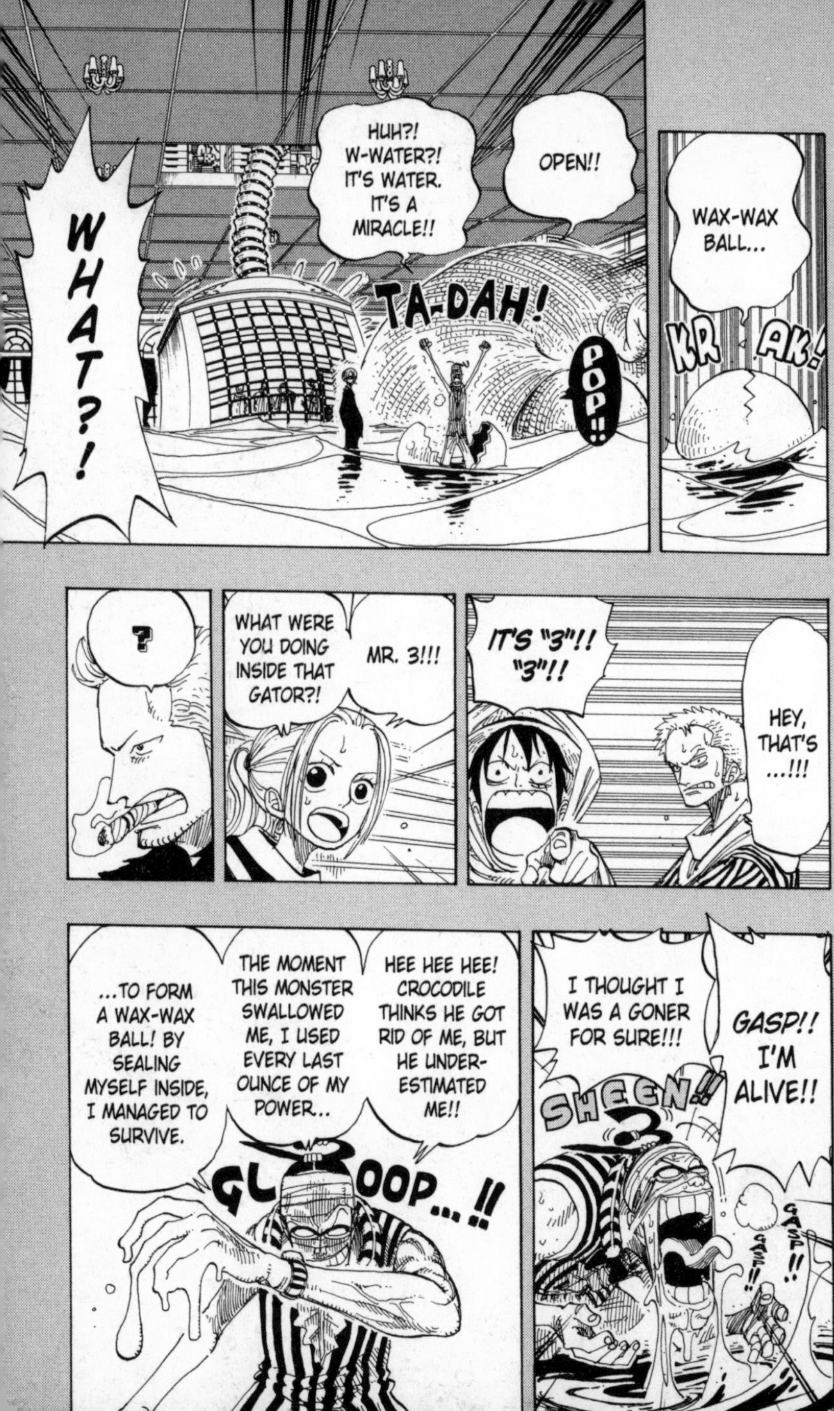
WAX-WAX BALL...
KR AK!
OPEN!!
HUH?! W-WATER?! IT'S WATER. IT'S A MIRACLE!!
TA-DAH!
POP!!
WHAT?!
HEY, THAT'S ...!!!
IT'S "3"!! "3"!!
MR. 3!!!
WHAT WERE YOU DOING INSIDE THAT GATOR?!
?
GASP!! I'M ALIVE!!
I THOUGHT I WAS A GONER FOR SURE!!!
SHEEN!!
GASP!!
GASP!!
HEE HEE HEE! CROCODILE THINKS HE GOT RID OF ME, BUT HE UNDER-ESTIMATED ME!!
THE MOMENT THIS MONSTER SWALLOWED ME, I USED EVERY LAST OUNCE OF MY POWER...
...TO FORM A WAX-WAX BALL! BY SEALING MYSELF INSIDE, I MANAGED TO SURVIVE.
GLOOP...!!

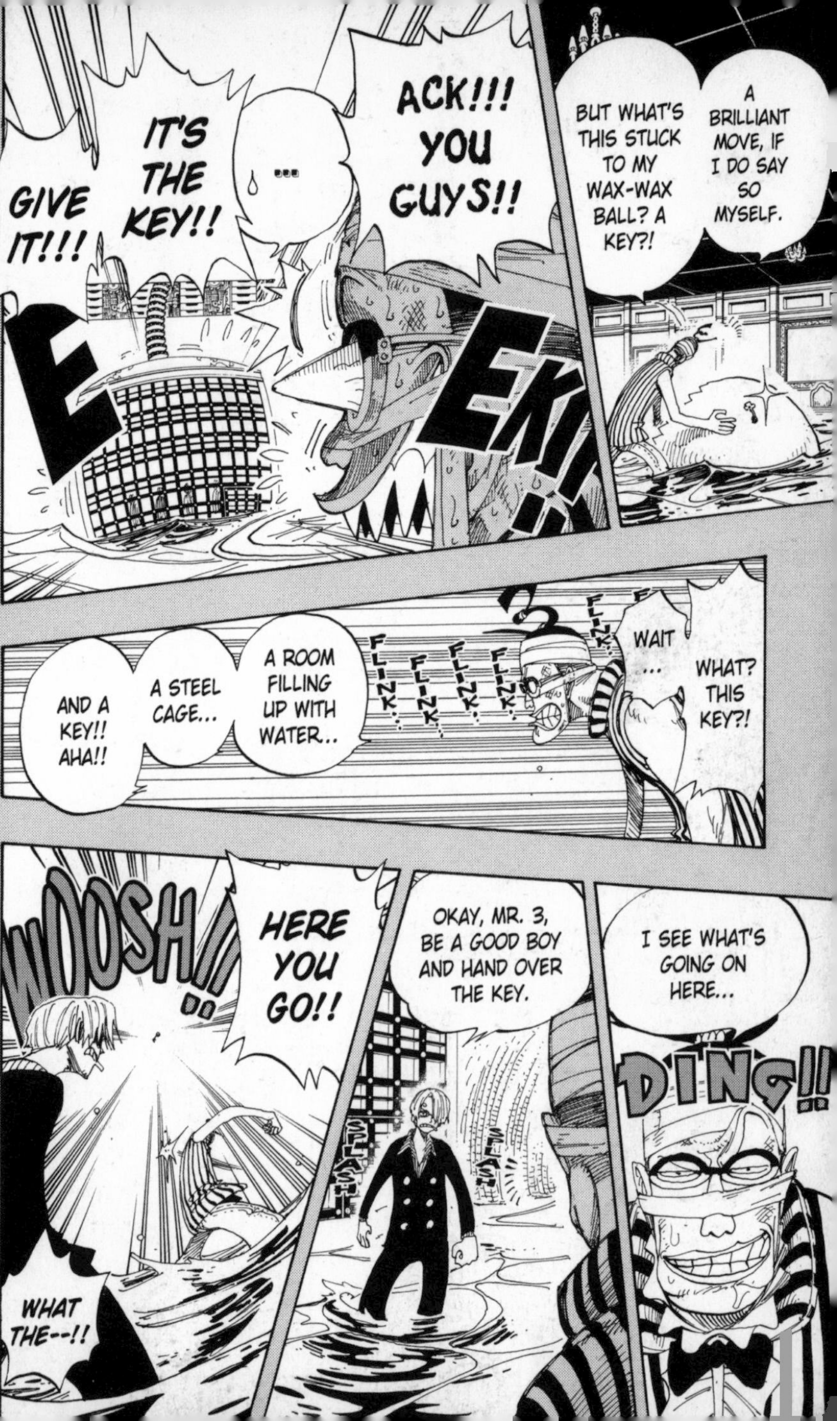
A BRILLIANT MOVE, IF I DO SAY SO MYSELF.
BUT WHAT'S THIS STUCK TO MY WAX-WAX BALL? A KEY?!
ACK!!! YOU GUYS!!
EEK!!
...
IT'S THE KEY!!
GIVE IT!!!
WAIT...
WHAT? THIS KEY?!
FLINK
FLINK...
FLINK...
FLINK...
FLINK...
A ROOM FILLING UP WITH WATER...
A STEEL CAGE...
AND A KEY!! AHA!!
I SEE WHAT'S GOING ON HERE...
DING!!
OKAY, MR. 3, BE A GOOD BOY AND HAND OVER THE KEY.
SPLASH!!
SPLASH!!
HERE YOU GO!!
WOOSH!!
WHAT THE--!!

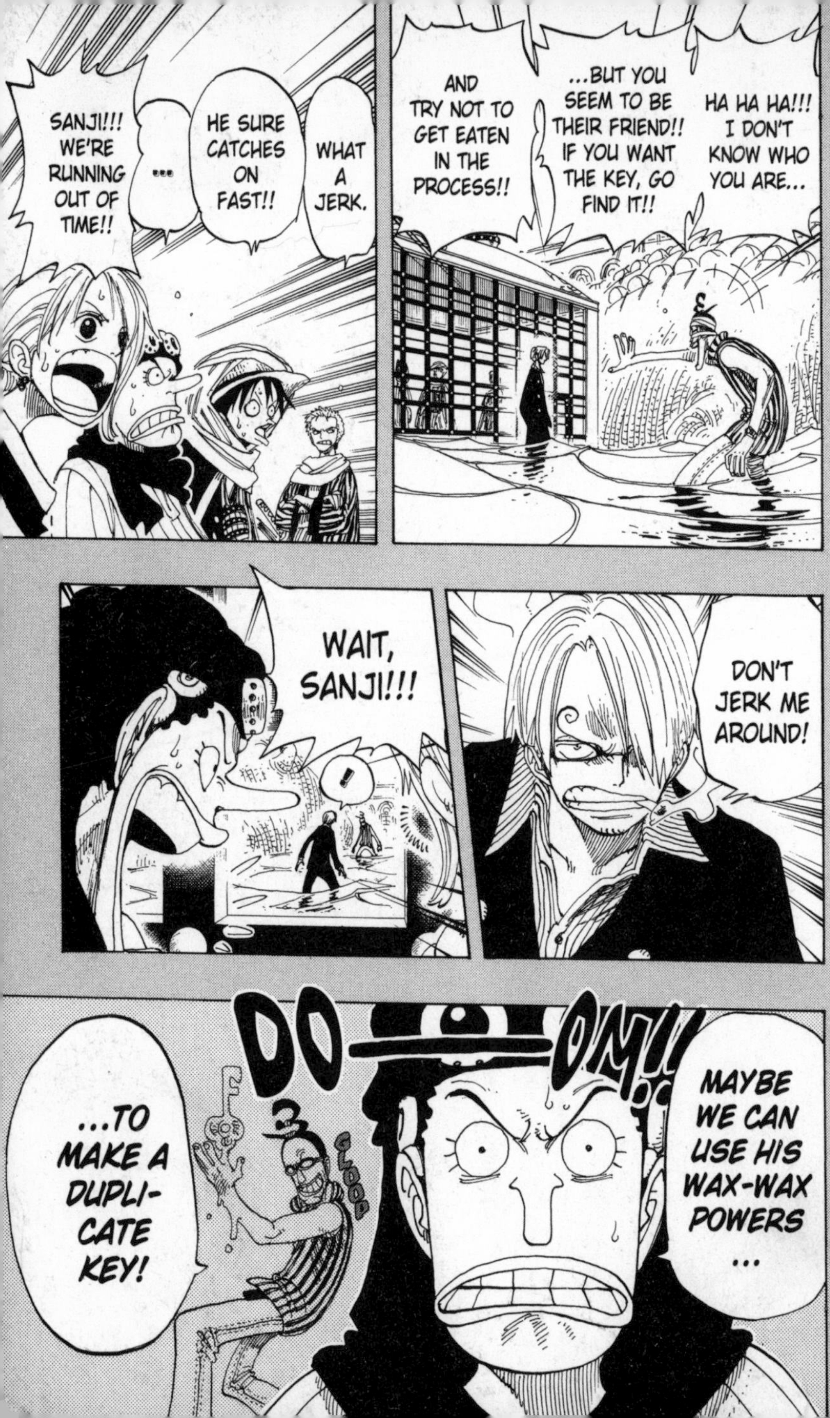
HA HA HA!!! I DON'T KNOW WHO YOU ARE...
...BUT YOU SEEM TO BE THEIR FRIEND!! IF YOU WANT THE KEY, GO FIND IT!!
AND TRY NOT TO GET EATEN IN THE PROCESS!!
WHAT A JERK.
HE SURE CATCHES ON FAST!!
...
SANJI!!! WE'RE RUNNING OUT OF TIME!!
DON'T JERK ME AROUND!
WAIT, SANJI!!!
!
DO—OM!!
MAYBE WE CAN USE HIS WAX-WAX POWERS ...
GLOOP
...TO MAKE A DUPLI-CATE KEY!

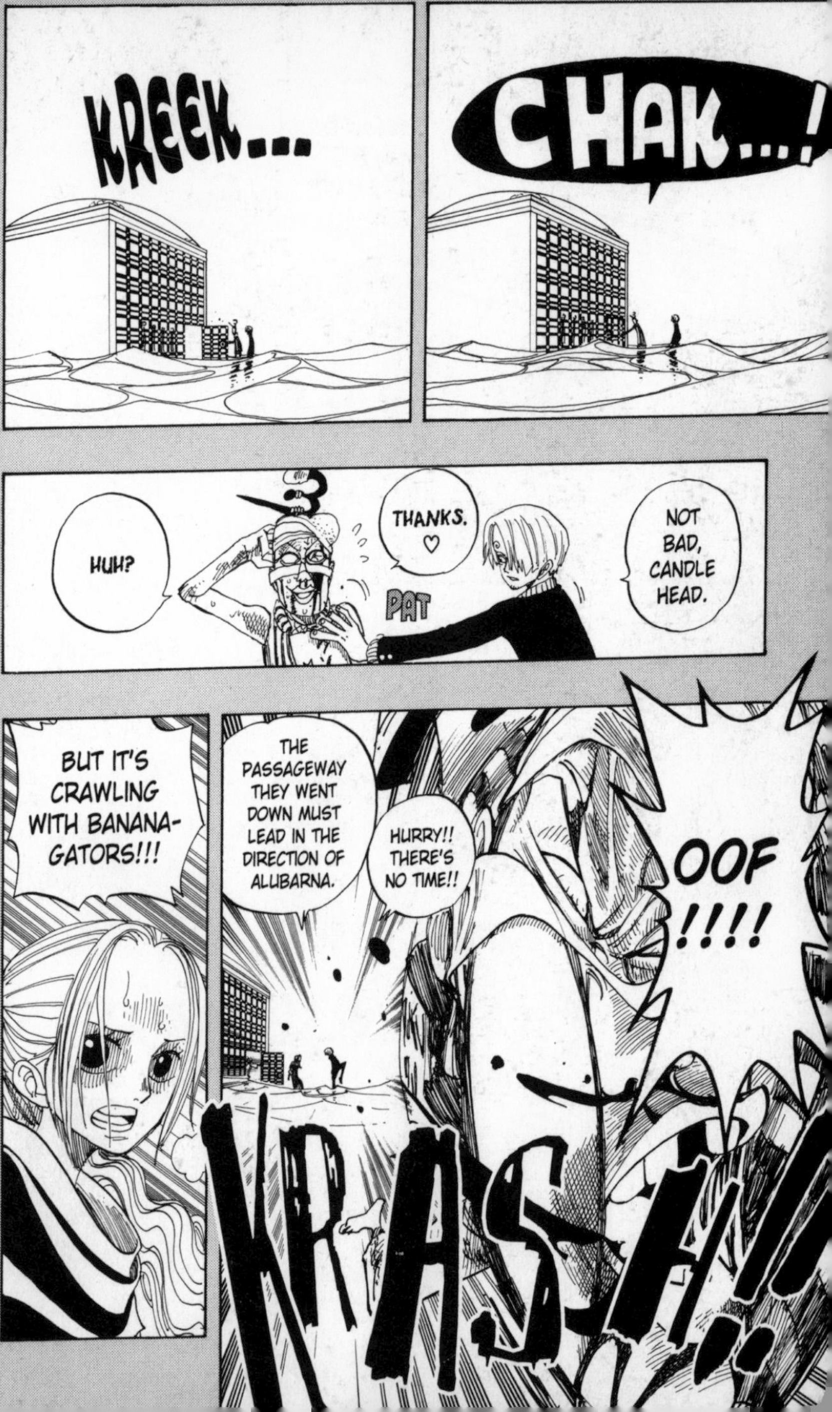
CHAK...!
KREEK...
NOT BAD, CANDLE HEAD.
PAT
THANKS. ♡
HUH?
OOF!!!!
HURRY!! THERE'S NO TIME!!
THE PASSAGEWAY THEY WENT DOWN MUST LEAD IN THE DIRECTION OF ALUBARNA.
KRASH!!
BUT IT'S CRAWLING WITH BANANA-GATORS!!!

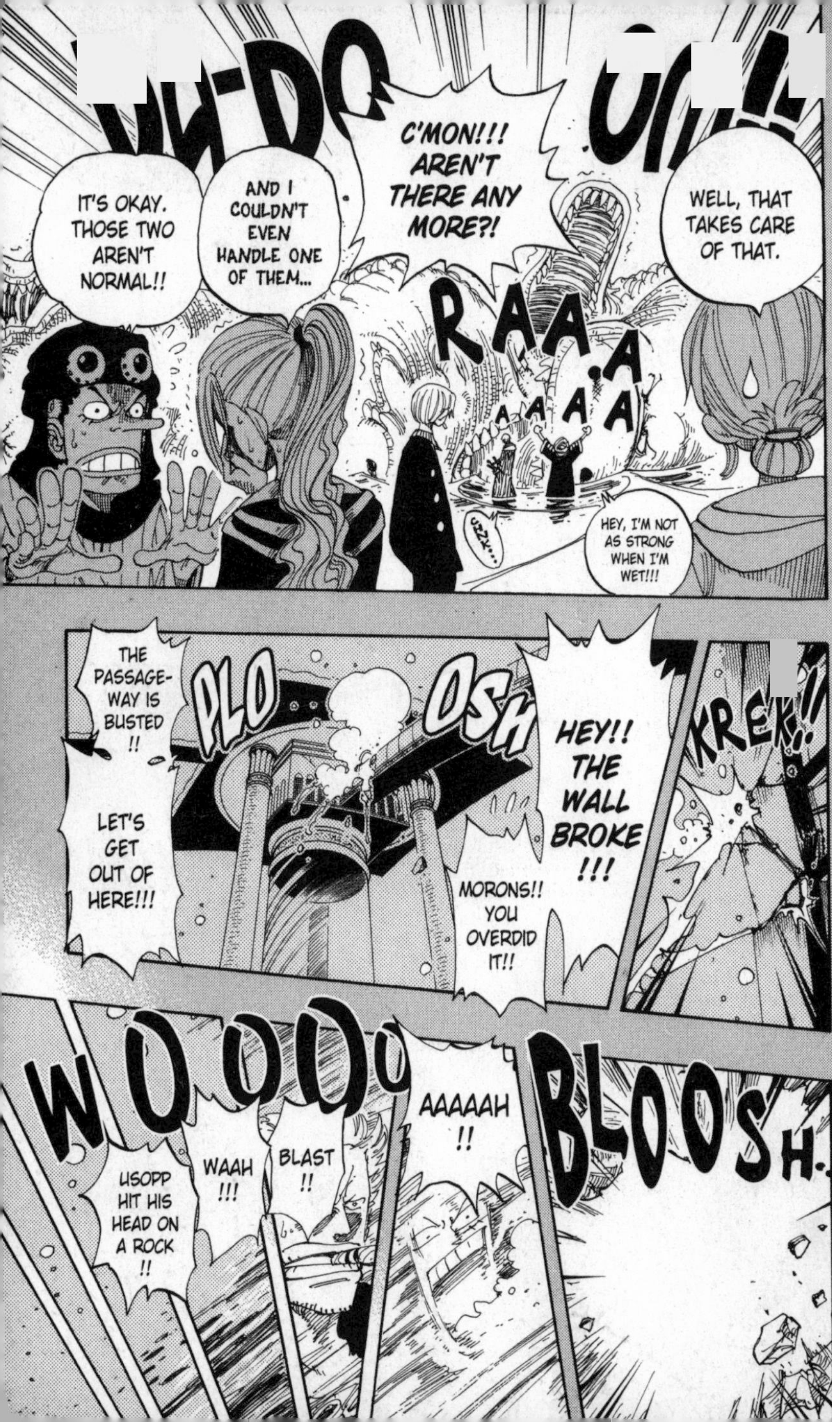
WELL, THAT TAKES CARE OF THAT.
HEY, I'M NOT AS STRONG WHEN I'M WET!!!
RAAAAAAA
C'MON!!! AREN'T THERE ANY MORE?!
AND I COULDN'T EVEN HANDLE ONE OF THEM...
IT'S OKAY. THOSE TWO AREN'T NORMAL!!
HEY!! THE WALL BROKE!!!
MORONS!! YOU OVERDID IT!!
PLOOSH
THE PASSAGE-WAY IS BUSTED!!
LET'S GET OUT OF HERE!!!
BLOOSH.
AAAAAH!!
BLAST!!
WAAH!!!
USOPP HIT HIS HEAD ON A ROCK!!
WOOOO

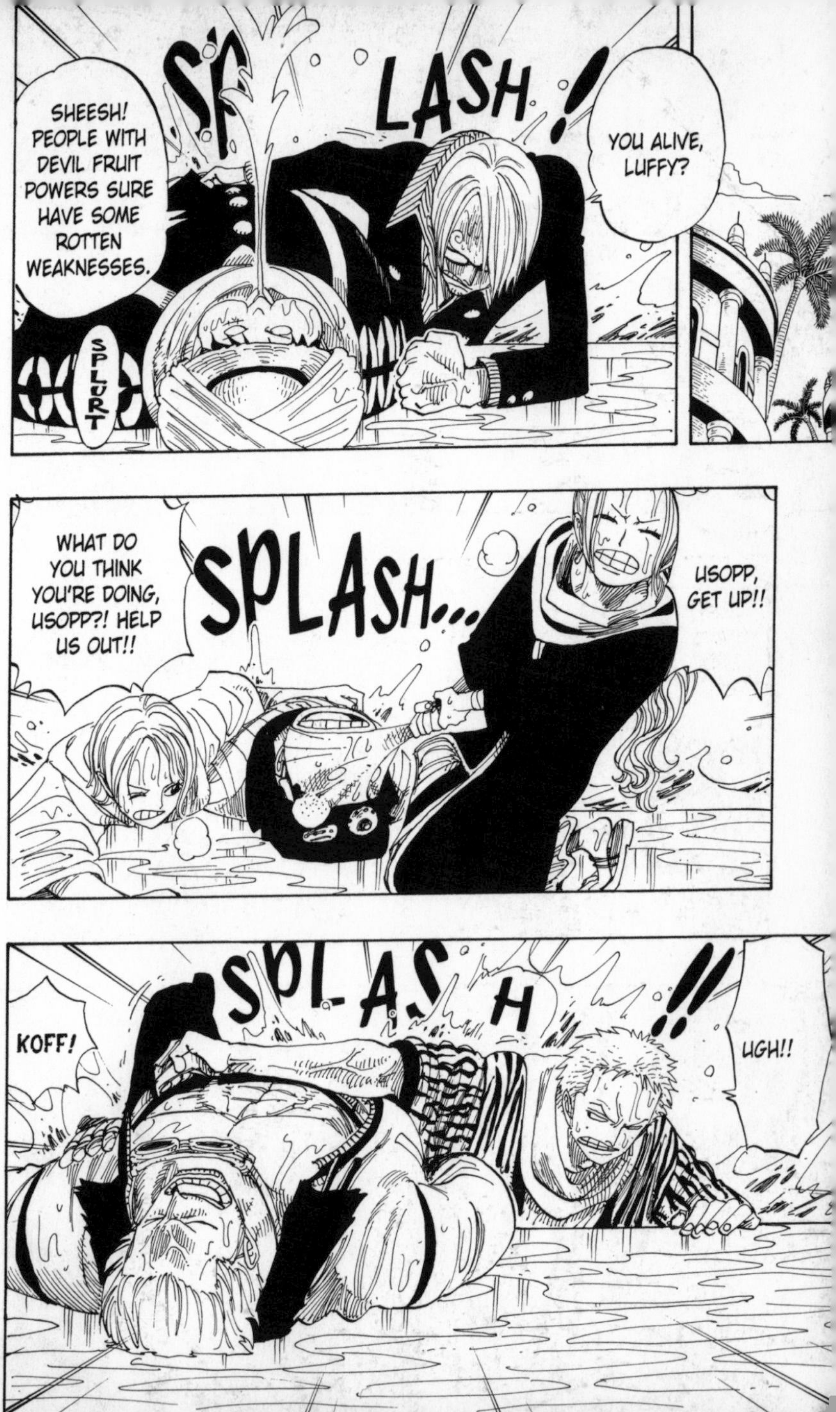
YOU ALIVE, LUFFY?
SPLASH!
SHEESH! PEOPLE WITH DEVIL FRUIT POWERS SURE HAVE SOME ROTTEN WEAKNESSES.
SPLURT
USOPP, GET UP!!
SPLASH...
WHAT DO YOU THINK YOU'RE DOING, USOPP?! HELP US OUT!!
UGH!!
SPLASH!!
KOFF!

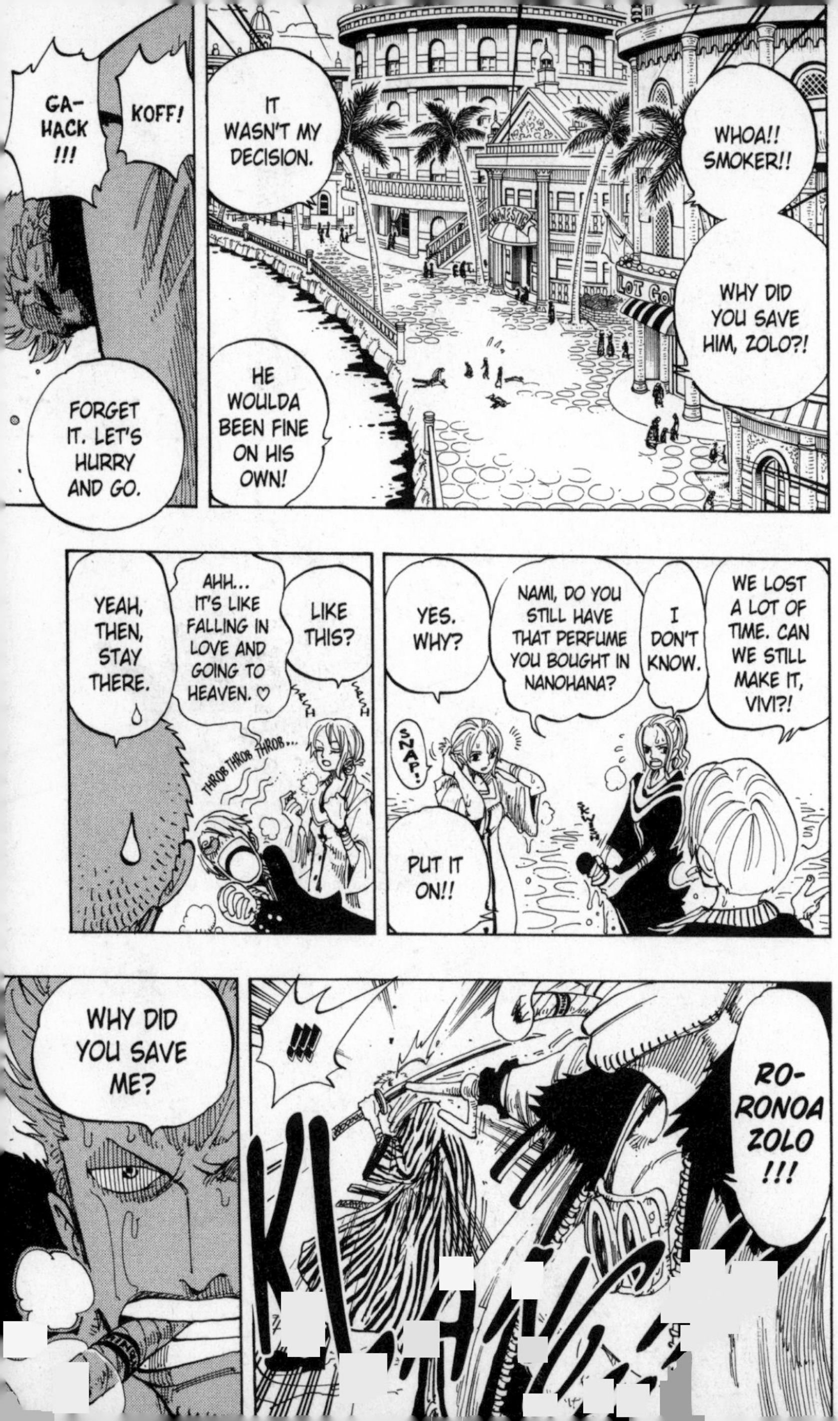
WHOA!! SMOKER!!
WHY DID YOU SAVE HIM, ZOLO?!
IT WASN'T MY DECISION.
HE WOULDA BEEN FINE ON HIS OWN!
KOFF!
GA-HACK!!!
FORGET IT. LET'S HURRY AND GO.
WE LOST A LOT OF TIME. CAN WE STILL MAKE IT, VIVI?!
I DON'T KNOW.
NAMI, DO YOU STILL HAVE THAT PERFUME YOU BOUGHT IN NANOHANA?
YES. WHY?
SNAP!
PUT IT ON!!
LIKE THIS?
AHH... IT'S LIKE FALLING IN LOVE AND GOING TO HEAVEN. ♡
THROB THROB THROB...
YEAH, THEN, STAY THERE.
RO-RONOA ZOLO!!!
!!!
WHY DID YOU SAVE ME?

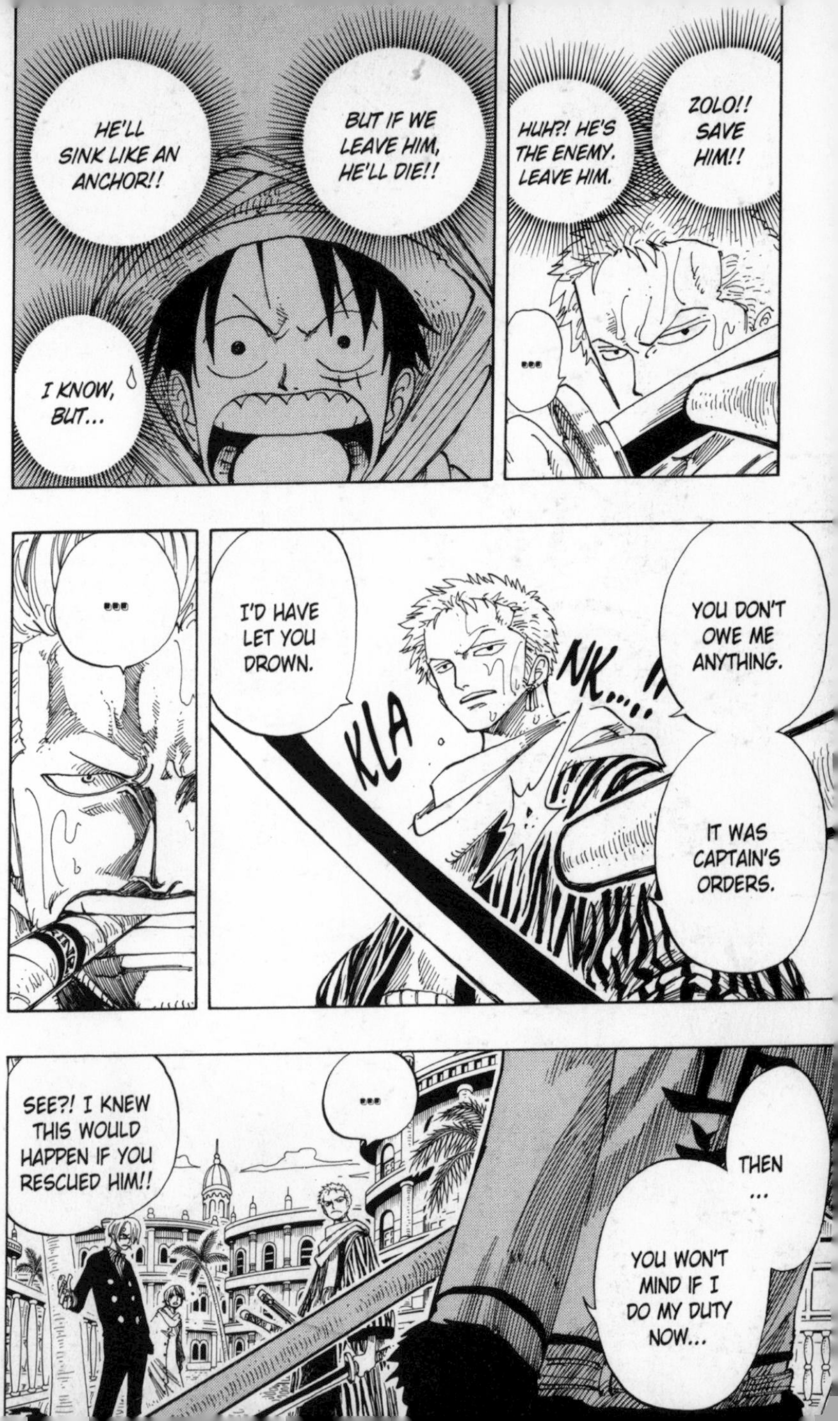
ZOLO!! SAVE HIM!!
HUH?! HE'S THE ENEMY. LEAVE HIM.
...
BUT IF WE LEAVE HIM, HE'LL DIE!!
HE'LL SINK LIKE AN ANCHOR!!
I KNOW, BUT...
YOU DON'T OWE ME ANYTHING.
IT WAS CAPTAIN'S ORDERS.
KLANK...!!
I'D HAVE LET YOU DROWN.
...
THEN...
YOU WON'T MIND IF I DO MY DUTY NOW...
...
SEE?! I KNEW THIS WOULD HAPPEN IF YOU RESCUED HIM!!

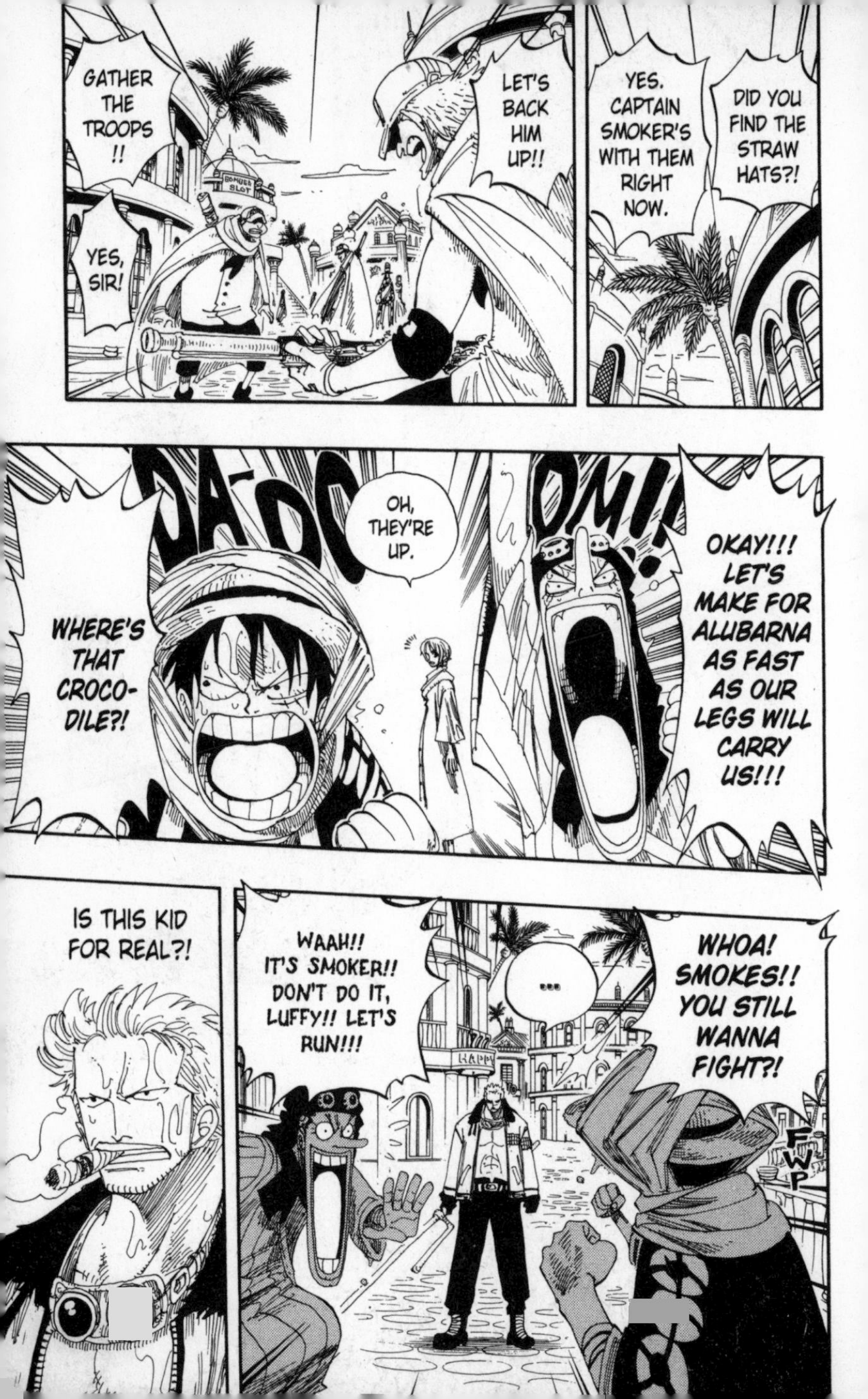

DID YOU FIND THE STRAW HATS?!
YES. CAPTAIN SMOKER'S WITH THEM RIGHT NOW.
LET'S BACK HIM UP!!
GATHER THE TROOPS !!
YES, SIR!
DA-DO
OM!!
OKAY!!! LET'S MAKE FOR ALUBARNA AS FAST AS OUR LEGS WILL CARRY US!!!
OH, THEY'RE UP.
WHERE'S THAT CROCODILE?!
WHOA! SMOKES!! YOU STILL WANNA FIGHT?!
FWP
...
WAAH!! IT'S SMOKER!! DON'T DO IT, LUFFY!! LET'S RUN!!!
IS THIS KID FOR REAL?!

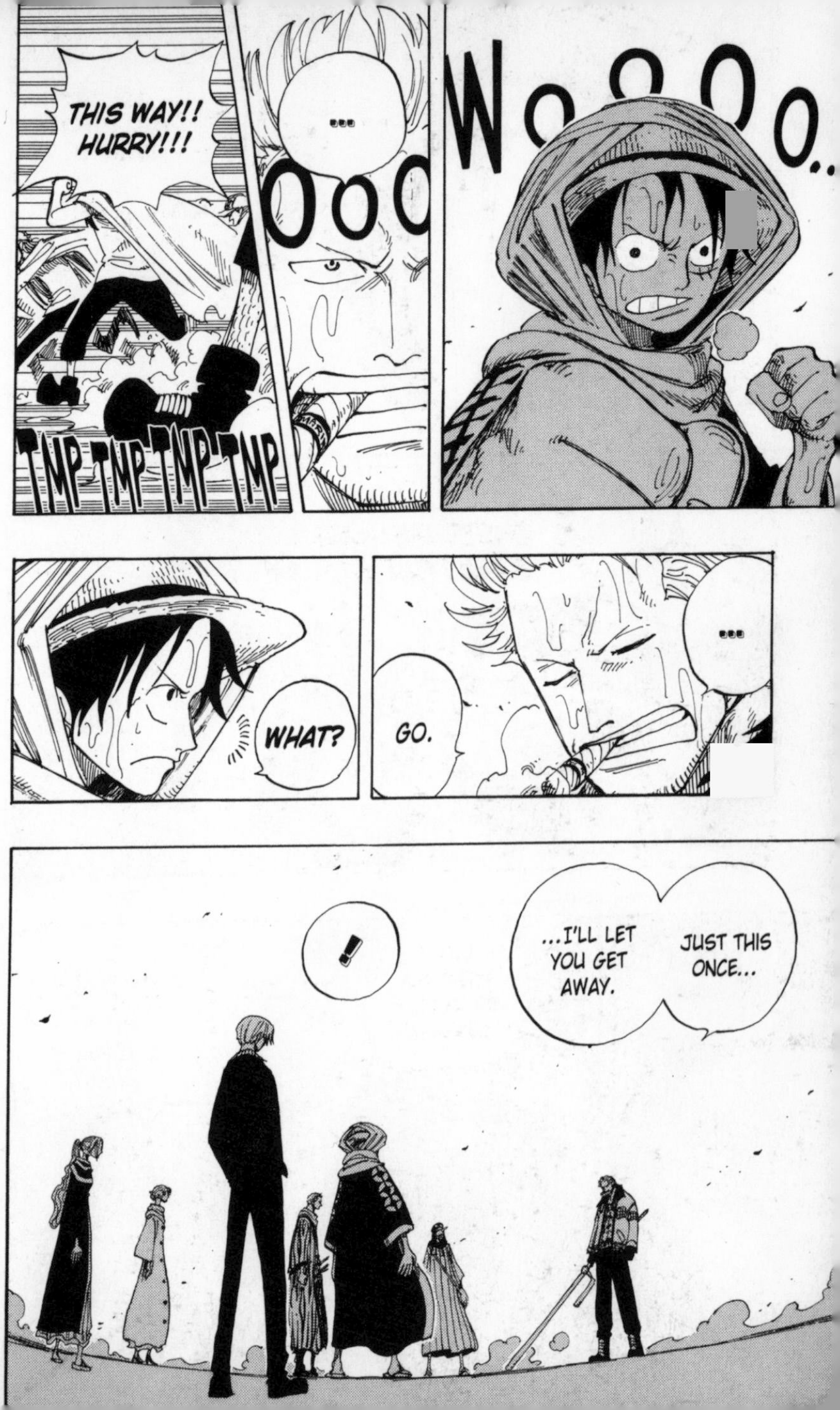
WOOOO..
...
OOO
THIS WAY!! HURRY!!!
TMP TMP TMP TMP
...
GO.
WHAT?
JUST THIS ONCE...
...I'LL LET YOU GET AWAY.
!

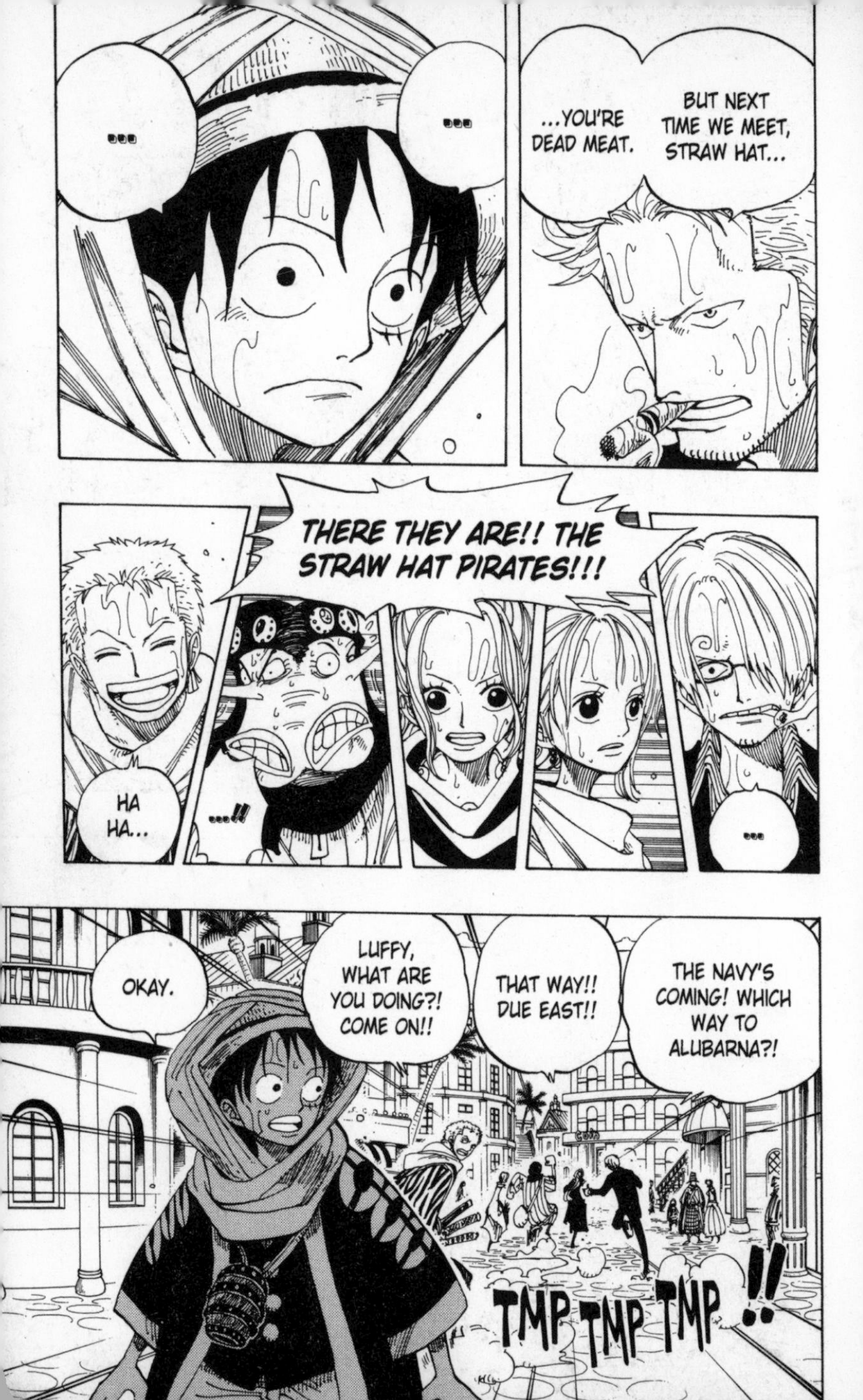
BUT NEXT TIME WE MEET, STRAW HAT...
...YOU'RE DEAD MEAT.
...
...
THERE THEY ARE!! THE STRAW HAT PIRATES!!!
...
...!!
HA HA...
THE NAVY'S COMING! WHICH WAY TO ALUBARNA?!
THAT WAY!! DUE EAST!!
LUFFY, WHAT ARE YOU DOING?! COME ON!!
OKAY.
TMP TMP TMP!!

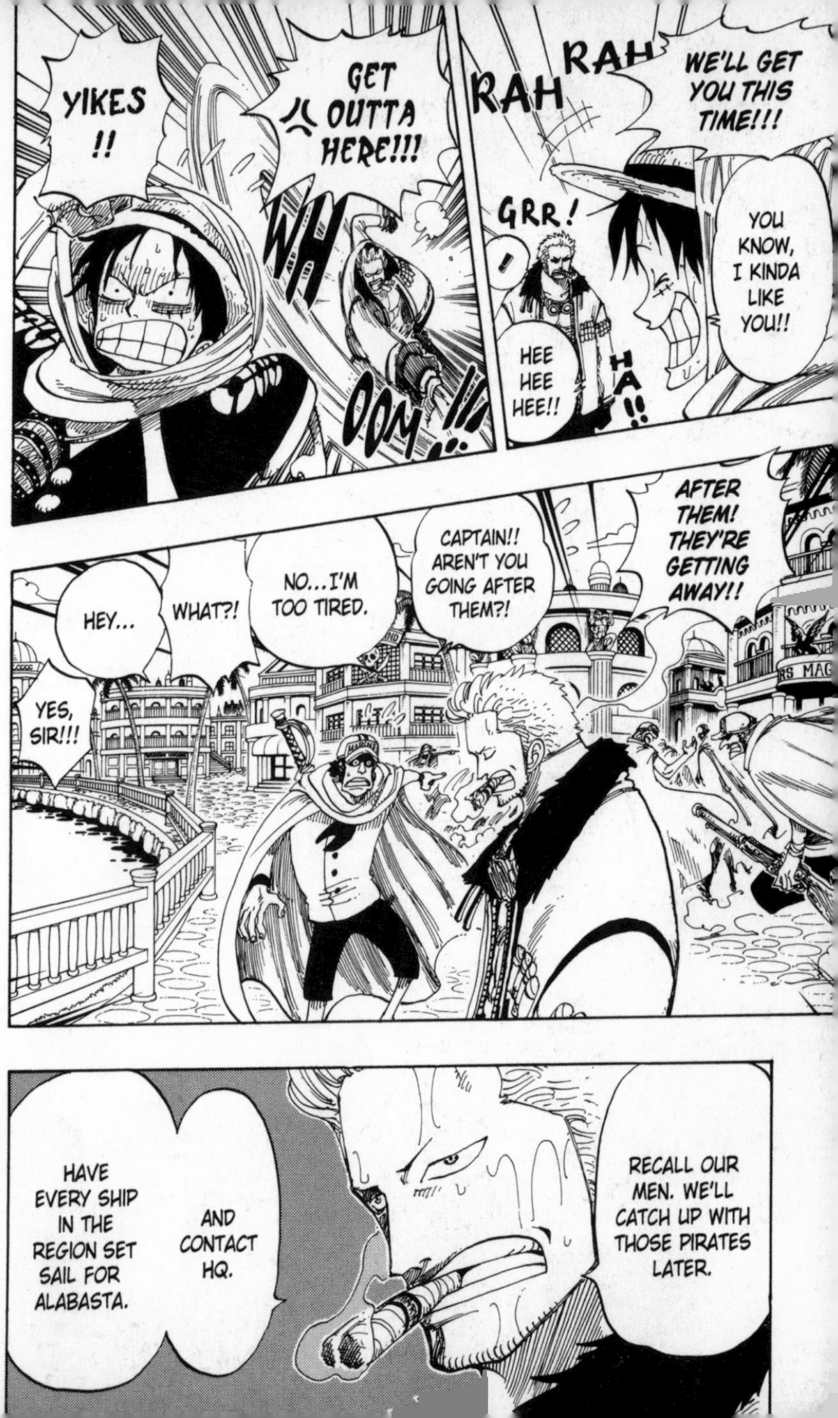
RAH
RAH
WE'LL GET YOU THIS TIME!!!
GRR!
!
YOU KNOW, I KINDA LIKE YOU!!
HA!!
HEE HEE HEE!!
GET OUTTA HERE!!!
WHOOM!!
YIKES!!
AFTER THEM! THEY'RE GETTING AWAY!!
CAPTAIN!! AREN'T YOU GOING AFTER THEM?!
NO...I'M TOO TIRED.
WHAT?!
HEY...
YES, SIR!!!
RECALL OUR MEN. WE'LL CATCH UP WITH THOSE PIRATES LATER.
AND CONTACT HQ.
HAVE EVERY SHIP IN THE REGION SET SAIL FOR ALABASTA.

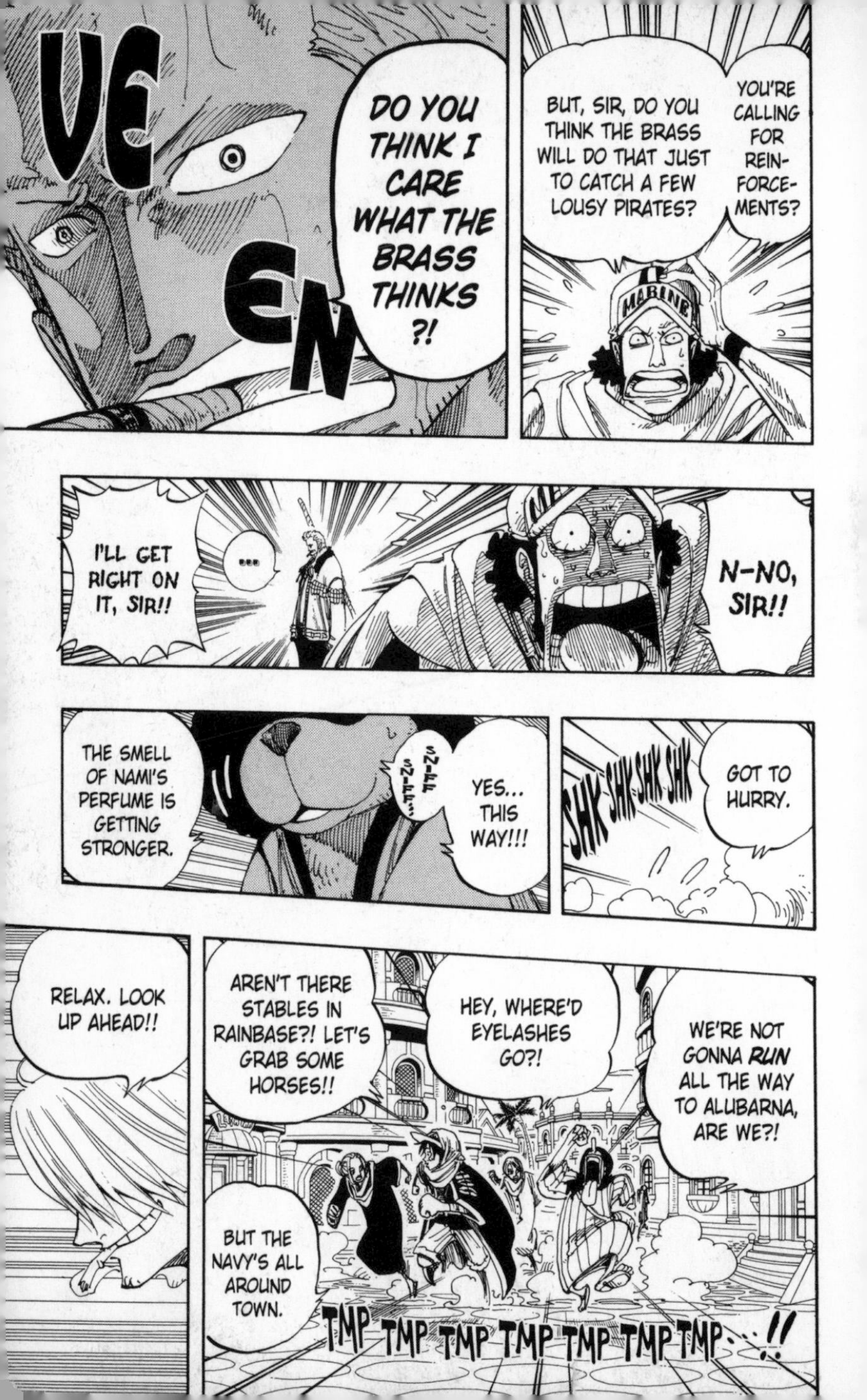
YOU'RE CALLING FOR REIN-FORCE-MENTS?
BUT, SIR, DO YOU THINK THE BRASS WILL DO THAT JUST TO CATCH A FEW LOUSY PIRATES?
DO YOU THINK I CARE WHAT THE BRASS THINKS ?!
VE
EN
N-NO, SIR!!
...
I'LL GET RIGHT ON IT, SIR!!
GOT TO HURRY.
SHK SHK SHK SHK
YES... THIS WAY!!!
SNIFF SNIFF...
THE SMELL OF NAMI'S PERFUME IS GETTING STRONGER.
WE'RE NOT GONNA RUN ALL THE WAY TO ALUBARNA, ARE WE?!
HEY, WHERE'D EYELASHES GO?!
AREN'T THERE STABLES IN RAINBASE?! LET'S GRAB SOME HORSES!!
BUT THE NAVY'S ALL AROUND TOWN.
TMP TMP TMP TMP TMP TMP TMP...!!
RELAX. LOOK UP AHEAD!!

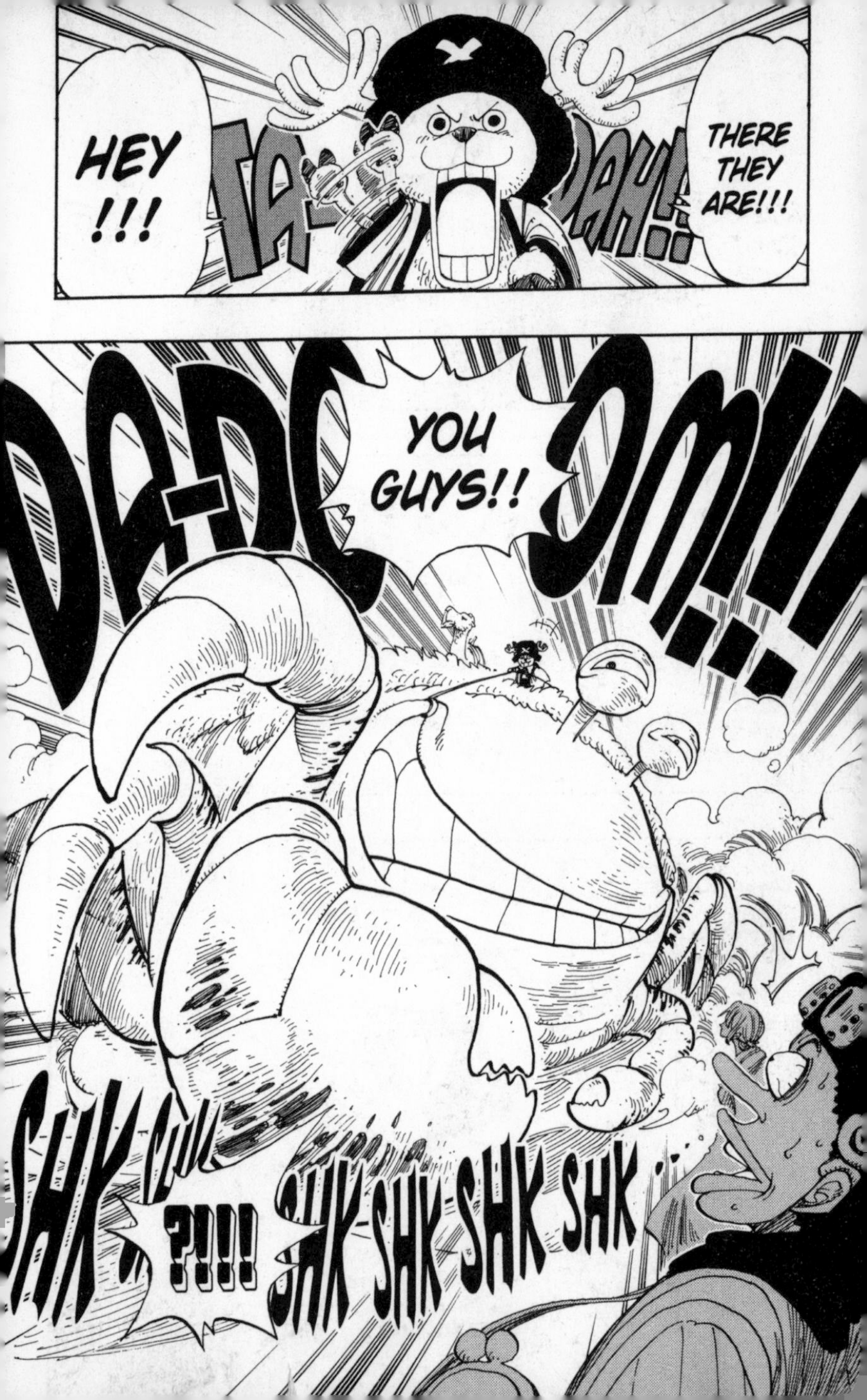
THERE THEY ARE!!!
TA-DAH!!
HEY!!!
YOU GUYS!!
SHK-SHK-SHK SHK
?!!!
SHK

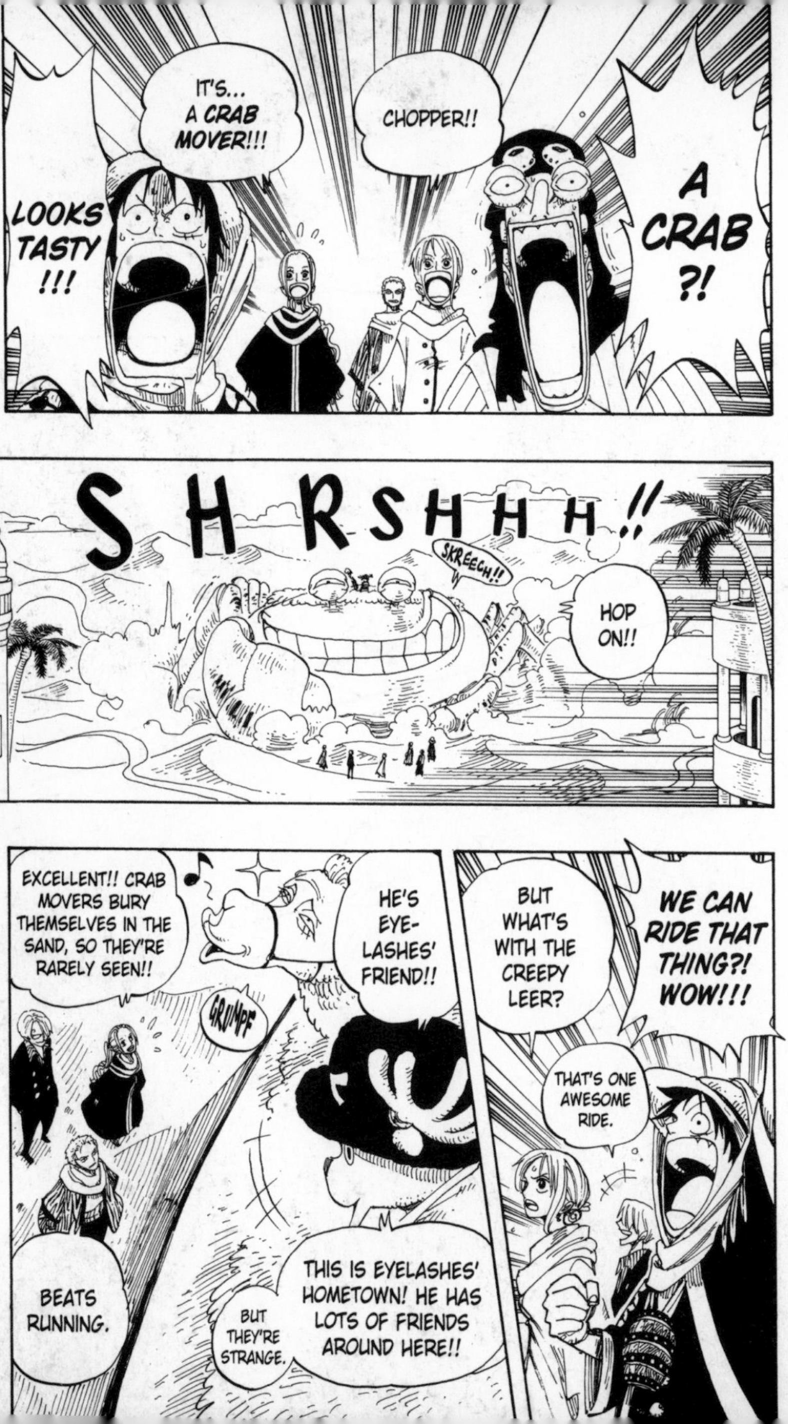
A CRAB ?!
CHOPPER!!
IT'S... A CRAB MOVER!!!
LOOKS TASTY !!!
SHRSHHHH!!
SKREECH!!
HOP ON!!
WE CAN RIDE THAT THING?! WOW!!!
BUT WHAT'S WITH THE CREEPY LEER?
THAT'S ONE AWESOME RIDE.
HE'S EYE-LASHES' FRIEND!!
EXCELLENT!! CRAB MOVERS BURY THEMSELVES IN THE SAND, SO THEY'RE RARELY SEEN!!
GRUMPF
THIS IS EYELASHES' HOMETOWN! HE HAS LOTS OF FRIENDS AROUND HERE!!
BUT THEY'RE STRANGE.
BEATS RUNNING.

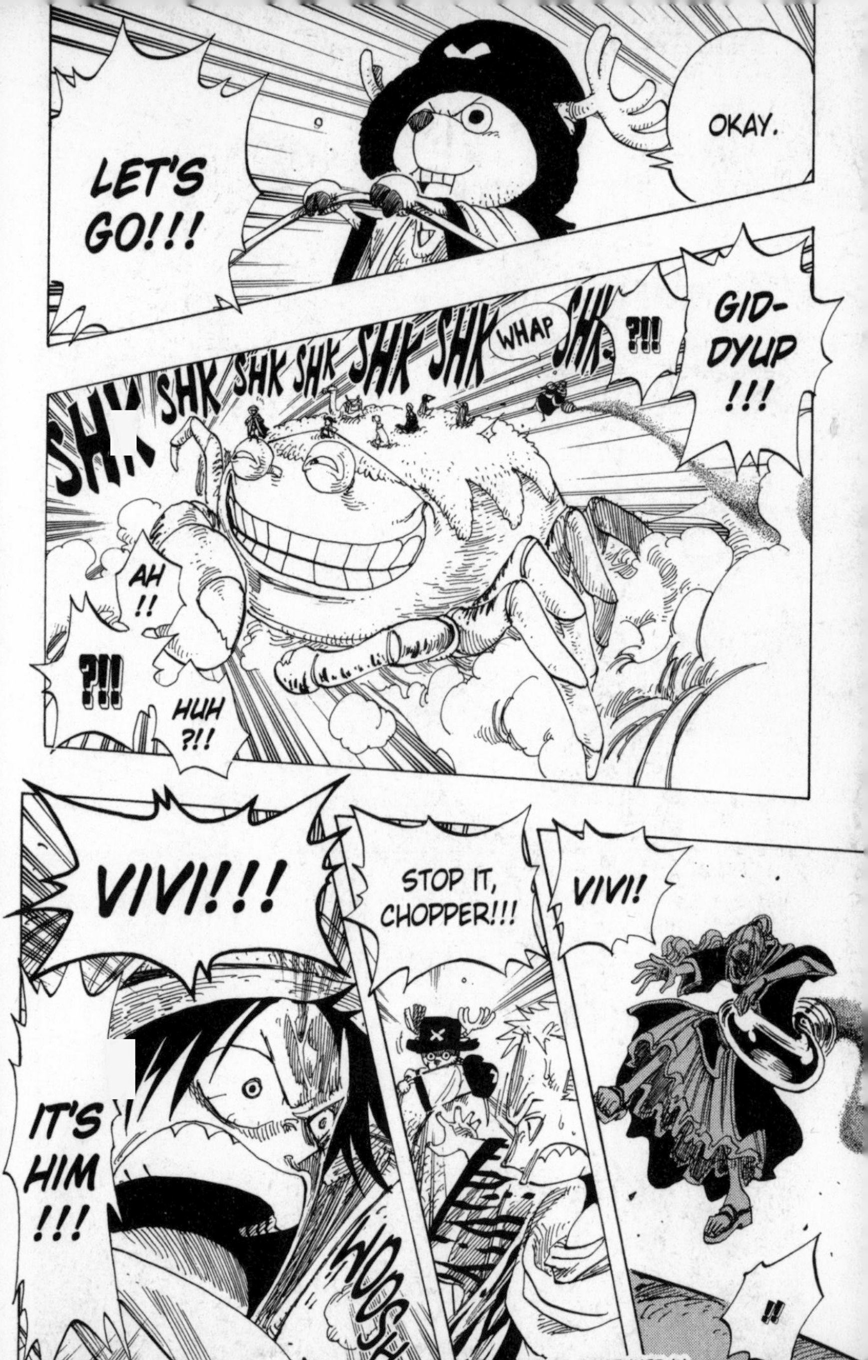
OKAY.
LET'S GO!!!
GID-DYUP!!!
?!!
SHK
WHAP
SHK SHK SHK SHK SHK
SHK
AH!!
?!!
HUH?!!
VIVI!
!!
STOP IT, CHOPPER!!!
VIVI!!!
IT'S HIM!!!
WOOSH
TO BE CONTINUED IN ONE PIECE, VOL. 20!

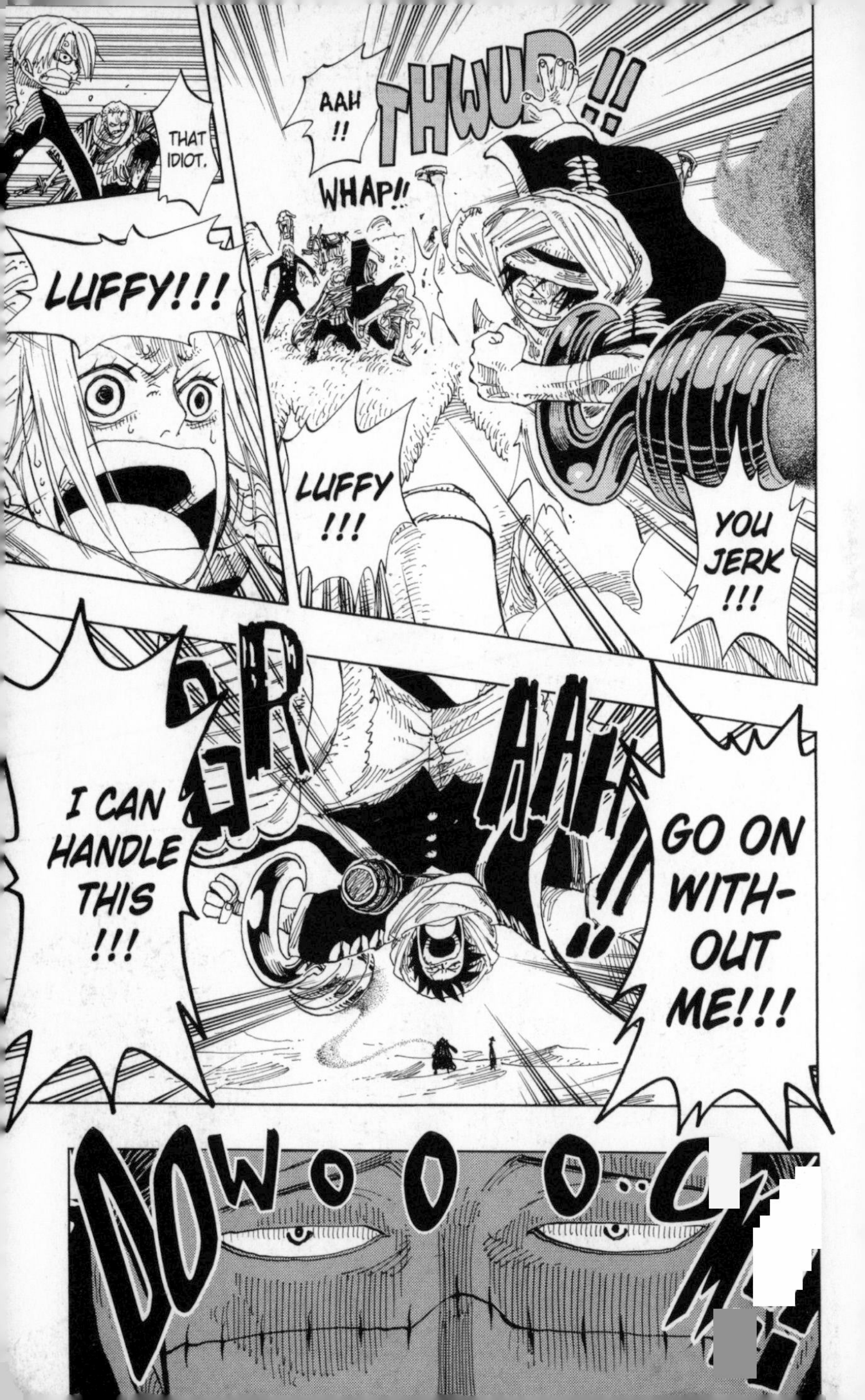

THWUD!!
AAH !!
WHAP!!
YOU JERK !!!
LUFFY !!!
THAT IDIOT.
LUFFY!!!
GO ON WITH-OUT ME!!!
GRAAAH!!
I CAN HANDLE THIS !!!
DOWOOOO

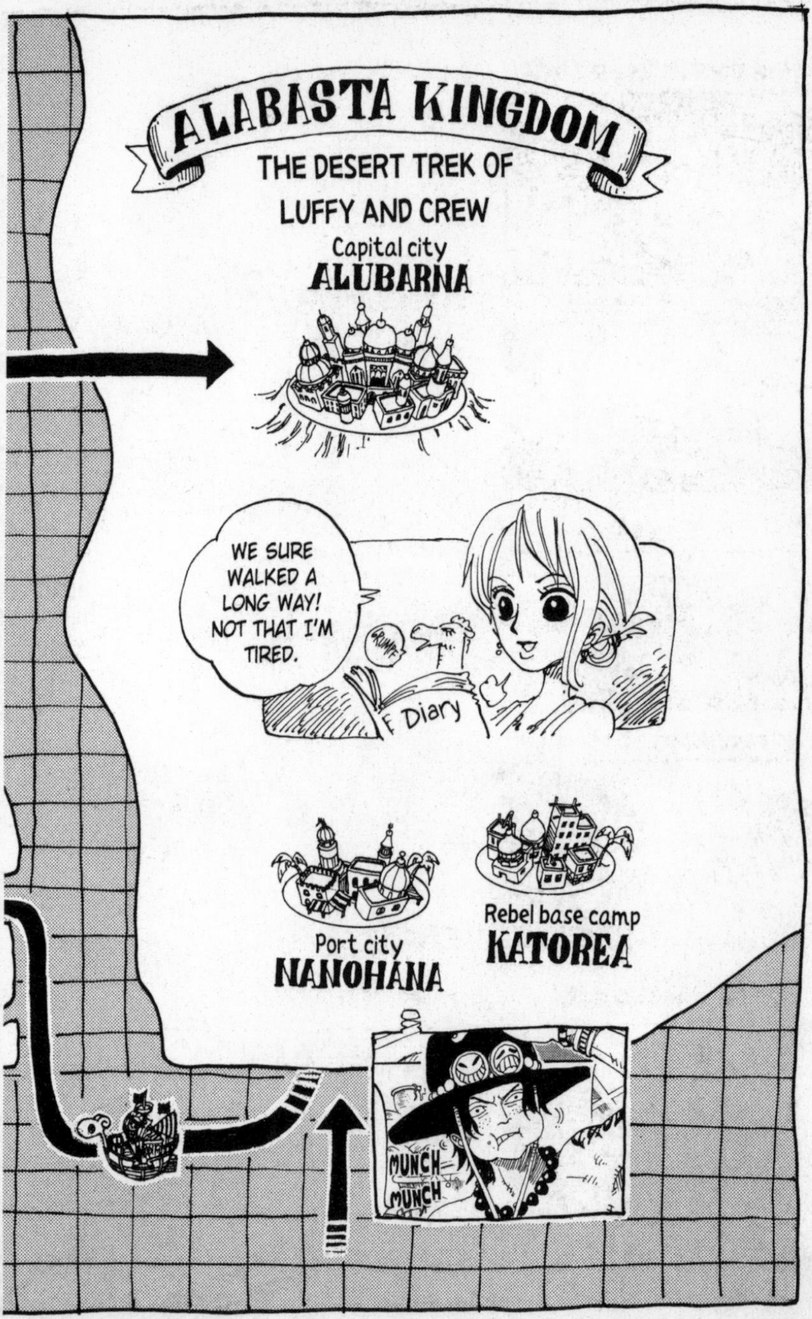
ALABASTA KINGDOM
THE DESERT TREK OF LUFFY AND CREW
Capital city
ALUBARNA
WE SURE WALKED A LONG WAY! NOT THAT I'M TIRED.
Diary
Rebel base camp
KATOREA
Port city
NANOHANA
MUNCH MUNCH

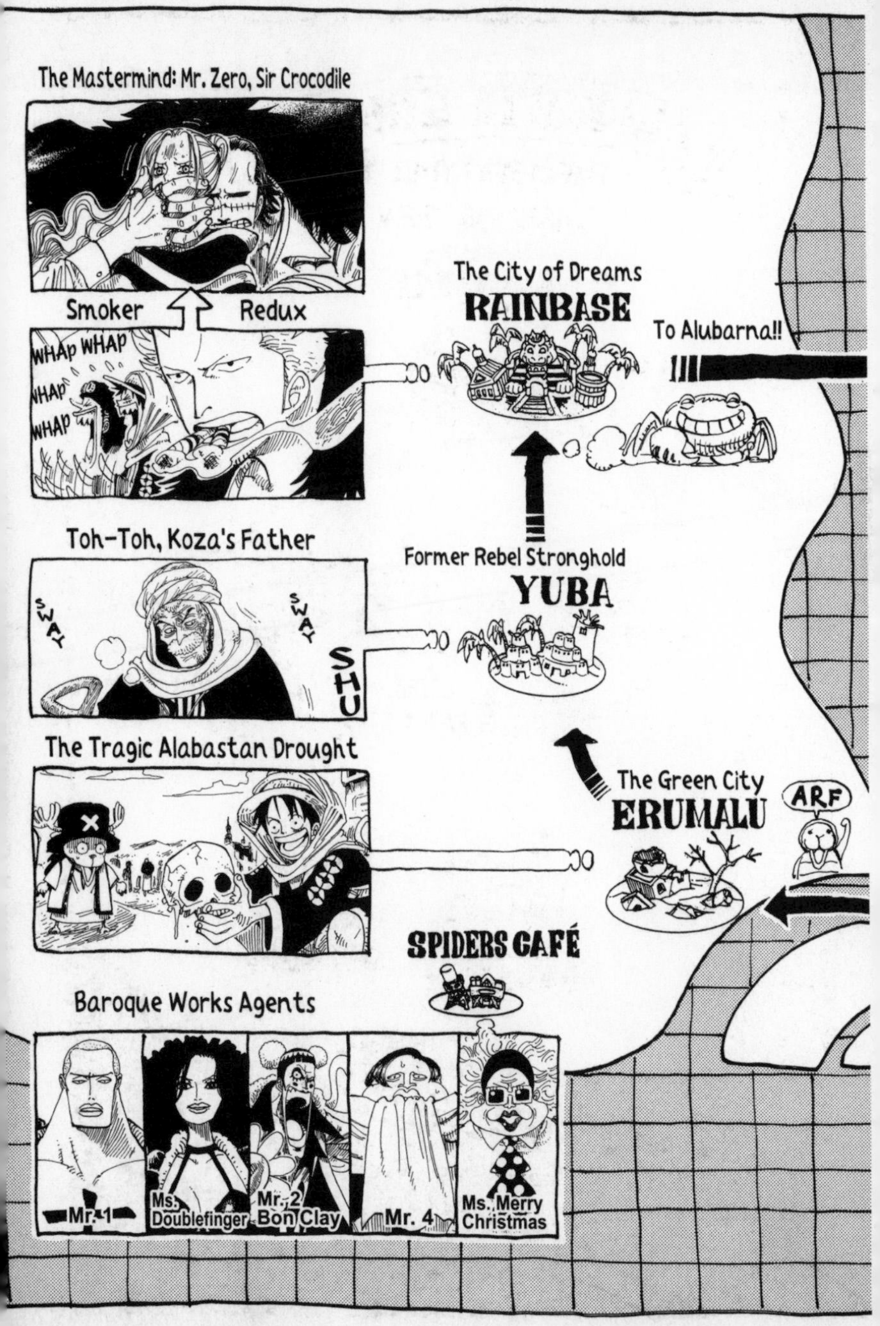

The Mastermind: Mr. Zero, Sir Crocodile
Smoker
Redux
WHAp WHAP
WHAP
WHAP
The City of Dreams
RAINBASE
To Alubarna!!
Toh-Toh, Koza's Father
SWAY
SWAY
SHU
Former Rebel Stronghold
YUBA
The Tragic Alabastan Drought
The Green City
ERUMALU
ARF
SPIDERS CAFÉ
Baroque Works Agents
Mr. 1
Ms. Doublefinger
Mr. 2 Bon Clay
Mr. 4
Ms. Merry Christmas

# COMING NEXT VOLUME:

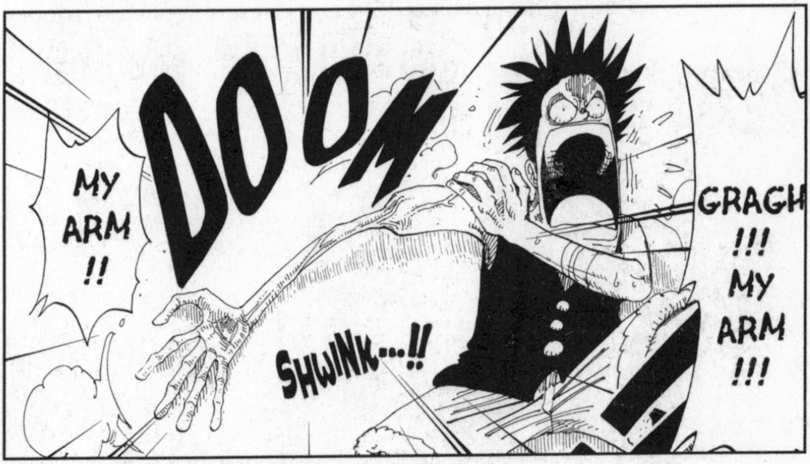
MY ARM !!
DOOOM
SHWINK...!!
GRAGH !!! MY ARM !!!

Wanting a little one-on-one time with Luffy, Crocodile pulls him aside for a private showdown. Faced with battling on the sand pirate's own turf, does Luffy even stand a chance?! Meanwhile, the rest of the gang soldiers on to Alubarna where the Officer Agents have been lying in wait for them outside the city gates. Before Vivi can stop the rebellion that will destroy her country, she and the Straw Hats will have to get past the gatekeepers first!

**ON SALE NOW!**

# ONE PIECE

Gorgeous color images from Eiichiro Oda's ONE PIECE!

**On Sale Now!**

ONE PIECE
by EIICHIRO ODA
COLOR WALK 1

- One Piece World Map pinup!
- Original drawings never before seen in America!
- DRAGON BALL creator Akira Toriyama and ONE PIECE creator Eiichiro Oda exclusive interview!

**viz media**

**ART OF ST**

**SHONEN JUMP**

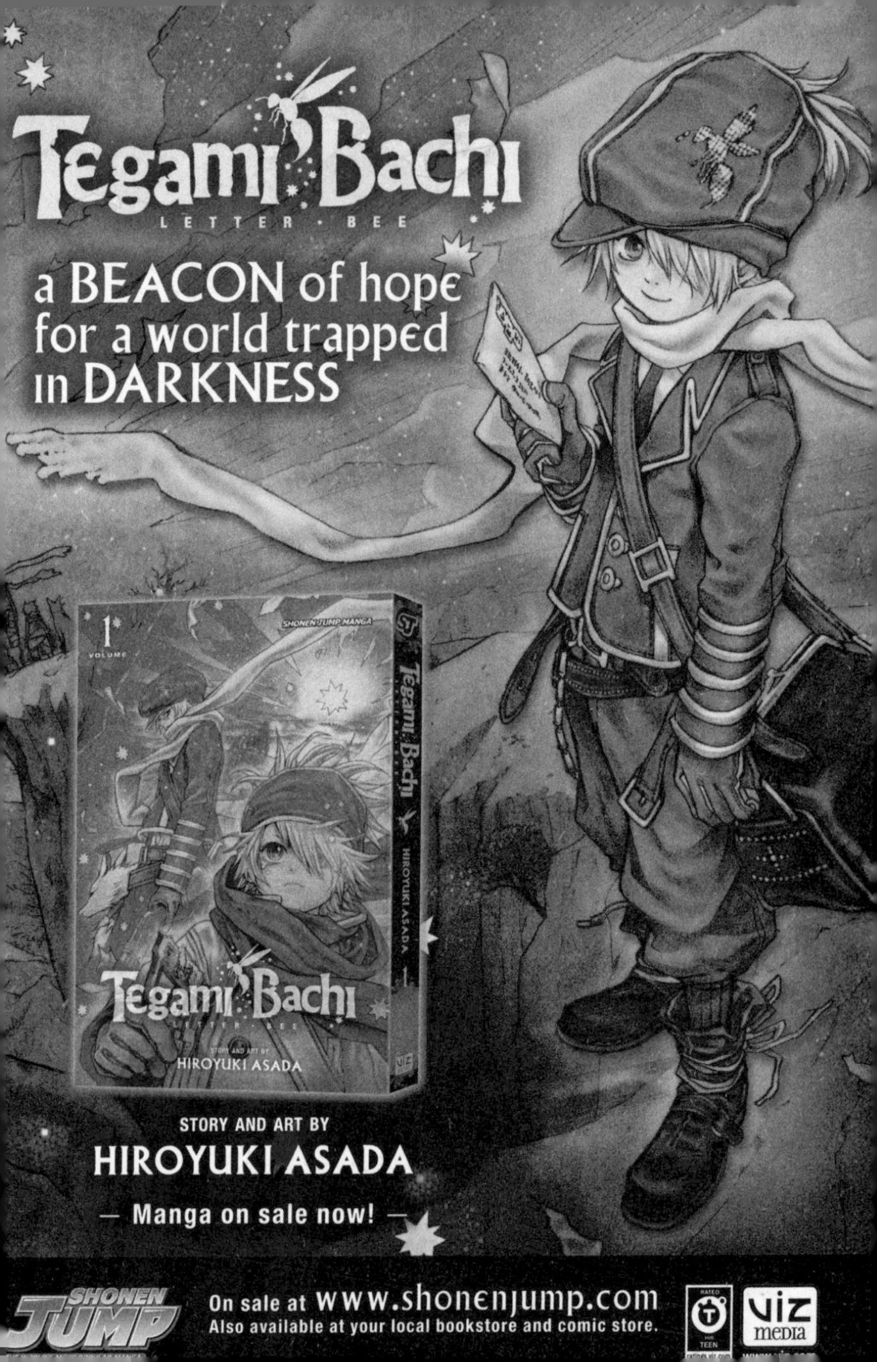

Tegami Bachi
LETTER · BEE
a BEACON of hope for a world trapped in DARKNESS
SHONEN JUMP MANGA
1 VOLUME
Tegami Bachi
LETTER BEE
STORY AND ART BY
HIROYUKI ASADA
STORY AND ART BY
HIROYUKI ASADA
— Manga on sale now! —
SHONEN JUMP
On sale at www.shonenjump.com
Also available at your local bookstore and comic store.
RATED T TEEN
VIZ media

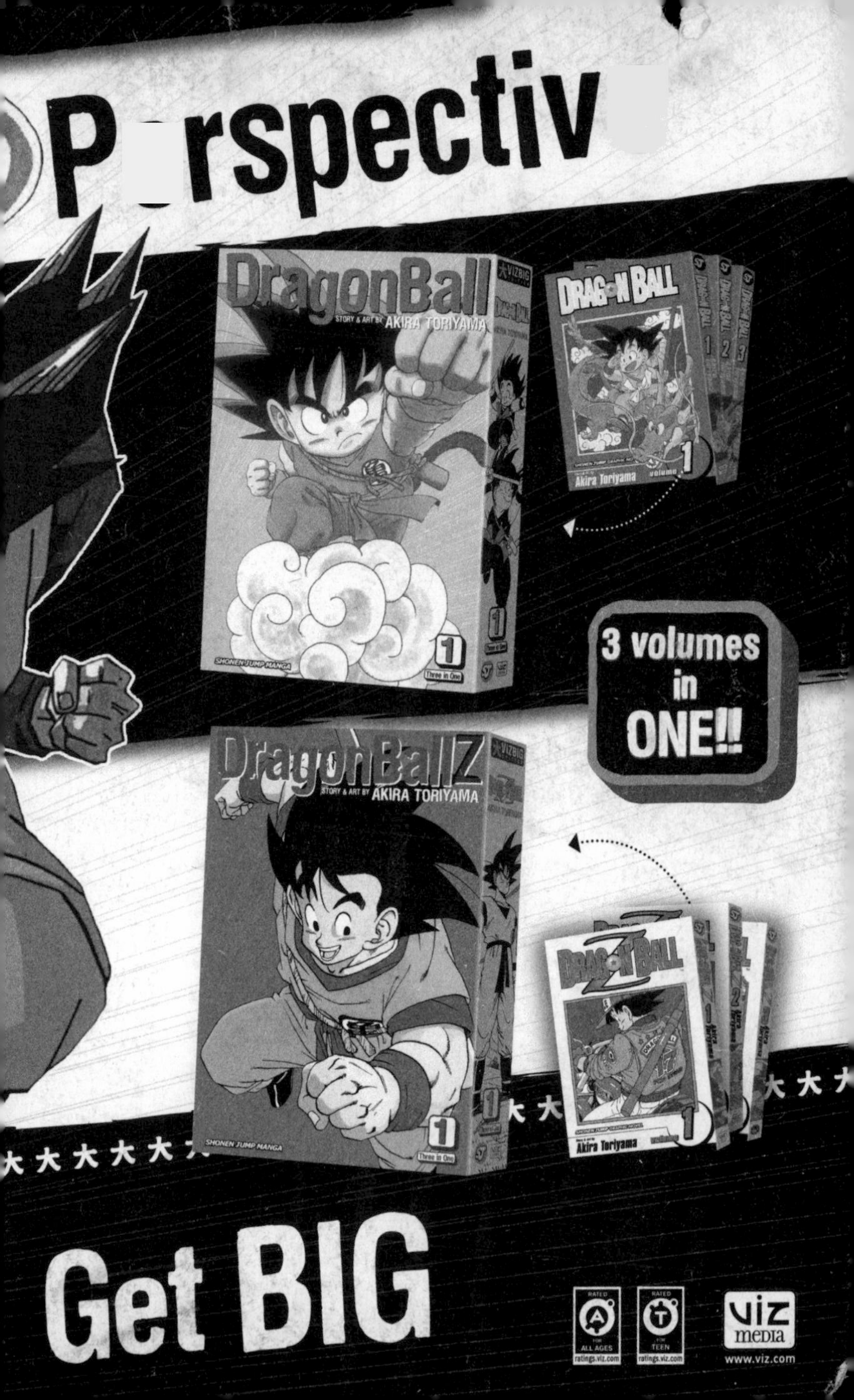

P rspectiv
DragonBall
STORY & ART BY AKIRA TORIYAMA
1
Three in One
SHONEN JUMP MANGA
DRAGON BALL
Akira Toriyama
volume 1
3 volumes in ONE!!
DragonBall Z
STORY & ART BY AKIRA TORIYAMA
1
Three in One
SHONEN JUMP MANGA
DRAGON BALL Z
Akira Toriyama
1
Get BIG
RATED A FOR ALL AGES ratings.viz.com
RATED T FOR TEEN ratings.viz.com
viz media
www.viz.com

# Tell us what you think about SHONEN JUMP manga!

Our survey is now available online.
Go to: www.SHONENJUMP.com/mangasurvey

# Help us make our product offering better!